ONE WEEK LOAN

Edition

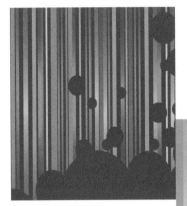

Marketing
Planning

A Global Perspective

Second Edition

Svend Hollensen

McGraw-Hill
Higher Education

London Boston Burr Ridge, IL Dubuque, IA Madison, WI New York San Francisco
St. Louis Bangkok Bogotá Caracas Kuala Lumpur Lisbon Madrid Mexico City
Milan Montreal New Delhi Santiago Seoul Singapore Sydney Taipei Toronto

Marketing Planning: A Global Perspective, Second edition
Svend Hollensen
ISBN-13 978-0-07-712713-8
ISBN-10 0-07-712713-7

McGraw-Hill
Higher Education

Published by McGraw-Hill Education
Shoppenhangers Road
Maidenhead
Berkshire
SL6 2QL
Telephone: 44 (0) 1628 502 500
Fax: 44 (0) 1628 770 224
Website: **www.mcgraw-hill.co.uk**

British Library Cataloguing in Publication Data
A catalogue record for this book is available from the British Library

Library of Congress Cataloguing in Publication Data
The Library of Congress data for this book has been applied for from the Library of Congress

Acquisitions Editor: Mark Kavanagh
Development Editor: Tom Hill
Marketing Manager: Alice Duijser
Production Editor: Louise Caswell

Text design by Hardlines
Cover design by Adam Renvoize
Printed and bound in the UK by Bell and Bain Ltd, Glasgow

ISBN-13 978-0-07-712713-8
ISBN-10 0-07-712713-7

The **McGraw·Hill** Companies

Brief Table of Contents

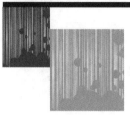

Detailed Table of Contents

Preface

The main purpose of this book is to take the reader through the process of marketing planning, while also providing a detailed explanation of all the concepts and methodologies used in that process.

In addition, a primary aim of this book is to introduce a *modern* and *well-structured* introduction to marketing planning from an academic/student viewpoint. The book's subtitle, 'A Global Perspective', is one example of this more 'modern' approach. All companies (even the smallest) are feeling the influence of the increasing globalization of the industries in which they are operating: their customers are getting bigger (via consolidation in the industry) and more globally oriented. These customers increasingly want to deal with suppliers that can work with customers on a global basis (global account management). At the same time, however, customers also want their suppliers to adapt their marketing plans to the different markets (countries) in which they operate.

Audience for this book

This book aims to target the academic market.

Primary audience

Undergraduate students: second and third year. Such groups could use this book as:

● the main textbook in short specialized courses like 'marketing', 'marketing planning', 'international marketing planning' and 'developing global marketing plans'
● supplementary text in general marketing/marketing management/international marketing courses.

Secondary audience

This audience is likely to comprise:

● marketing practitioners
● others who wish to learn 'how to prepare a marketing plan'.

Key features of this book

Focus on a 'global perspective'

'International/global marketing planning' is treated more extensively in this book than in competitor books. Many of the students using it are likely to go on to have marketing jobs in small and medium-sized enterprises (SMEs), which previously were not concerned with internationalization. However, these SMEs are now facing competition in their home markets from multinational companies, so they are not only competing locally and nationally, but globally as well. This 'global perspective' is also likely to result in cases where a company's product is sold to several markets at the same time.

Case studies from real companies

Unlike some other marketing planning books, this one contains case studies of real companies. This book (and its accompanying website) also includes references to web resources (market information in certain industries), which students can use as the basis for developing marketing plans. Furthermore, it deals with the development of the marketing plan in co-operation with other actors (e.g. customers).

Implementing a resource perspective

This book analyses internal competences as the basis for developing a marketing plan. The resource perspective (inside-out view) is gaining popularity in the marketing literature, but is overlooked by some competitor textbooks (although they all include details of strengths, weaknesses, opportunities, threats (SWOT) analysis). The input for the 'SW' part of this analysis, however, comes from this resource perspective. In students' later jobs as marketing planners and co-ordinators it would be a disaster for their companies to consider only external opportunities, without taking any internal restraints into consideration.

Financial consequences

This book offers extensive coverage of the marketing plan's financial consequences in the form of budgets, financial metrics, and so on.

Academic market

In other books, developing a marketing plan is based on a sort of 'recipe', with few references to other books and articles. This book differs in that it makes many references to books, journal articles, websites, web databases, and so on.

Outline of the book

The three parts into which this book is divided follow the three main steps involved in the marketing planning process:

1   analysis of the internal and external situation
2   developing the marketing strategy
3   implementing and managing the marketing plan.

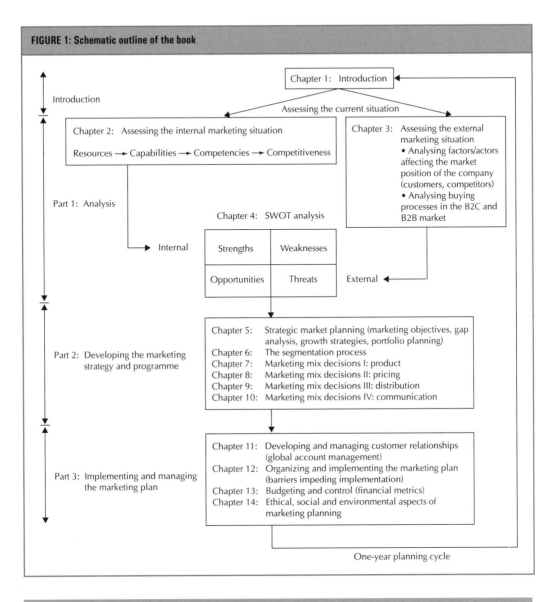

FIGURE 1: Schematic outline of the book

What is new in the second edition?

- First, there are 14 completely new case studies (one for each chapter) with global-oriented companies: Derby Bicycles, AG Barr (Irn-Bru), Suzlon wind turbines, Ducati motorbikes, Weetabix breakfast cereal, TAG Heuer watches, Dyson Airblade, Bang & Olufsen, H&M fashion retailer, Suntory whisky, Embraer business jets, Victoria's Secret's lingerie, Music World Entertainment (Beyoncé), (RED) AIDS organization.
- Chapter 3 – the section about the European Union (EU) and the Euro has been updated with new member countries and Euro zone members.
- Chapter 4 – the 'value net' perspective has been expanded.
- Chapter 6 – the 'good-enough-market' principle is introduced.

- Chapter 7 – co-branding and ingredient branding are introduced.
- Chapter 8 – the 'price bundling' strategy is introduced.
- Chapter 10 – the section about viral marketing has been expanded. A section about social media/social networking is introduced.
- Chapter 11 – more extensive coverage of 'global account management'.
- Chapter 14 – introducing a section about corporate social responsibility (CSR).

As well as all the above, references and data have been thoroughly updated and revised where necessary.

Additional features on companion website

Visit www.mcgraw-hill.com/textbooks/hollensen to access the following valuable supplementary material.

- **For students**: students can link to any of the online resources listed in the text, and there are also further opportunities to 'click' on to market information from different parts of the world.
- **For lecturers**: lecturers can access the 'Instructor's Manual' and PowerPoint slides on the password-protected section of the website.

Case studies

A relevant case study appears at the end of each chapter. Table 1 lists these.

Chapter	Case titles/subtitles	Headquarters in following country/area	Geographical target area in the case/Target market (B2B, B2C or both)
1 Introduction	**Derby Cycles** How should Derby create a marketing plan for penetrating the e-bicycle market?	USA	Europe B2C
2 Assessing the internal marketing situation	**AG Barr** Irn-Bru – Scotland's 'other national drink' – is looking for further market shares in the carbonated soft drinks market	UK	UK/World B2C
3 Assessing the external marketing situation	**Suzlon Energy** The Indian wind turbine manufacturer seeks new business opportunities in the world market	India	World B2B
4 SWOT analysis	**Ducati** The Italian motorbike icon is searching for new markets	Italy	World B2C and B2B
5 Strategic market planning	**Weetabix** Attacking Kellogg's in the breakfast cereal market	UK	World B2C
6 The segmentation process	**TAG Heuer** The Swiss watchmaker is segmenting and penetrating the Indian market	Switzerland	India B2C
7 Marketing mix decisions I: product	**Dyson Airblade** Penetrating the US hand dryer market with a new technology	UK	USA B2B
8 Marketing mix decisions II: pricing	**Bang & Olufsen** Is the image justifying the price level in a time of recession?	Denmark	World B2C and B2B

Chapter	Case titles/subtitles	Headquarters in following country/area	Geographical target area in the case/Target market (B2B, B2C or both)
9 Marketing mix decisions III: distribution	**Hennes & Mauritz (H&M)** Successful fashion retailer with one brand store concept	Sweden	World B2C
10 Marketing mix decisions IV: communication	**Suntory** 'For relaxing time, make it Suntory time'	Japan	Europe B2C
11 Developing and managing customer relationships	**Embraer** Are B2B buyer–seller relationships relevant in the business jet industry?	Brazil	World B2B
12 Organizing and implementing the marketing plan	**Victoria's Secret** Looking for new business opportunities in the European lingerie market	Germany	Europe/World B2C and B2B
13 Budgeting and control	**Music World Entertainment (MWE)** New worldwide organizational structure and the marketing planning and budgeting of Beyoncé's new album **(RED)**	USA	UK/Europe B2C
14 Ethical, social and environmental aspects of marketing planning	Fighting AIDS in Africa through alliances	USA	Europe/World B2C and B2B

TABLE 1 Overview of case studies

Guided Tour

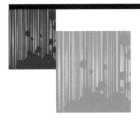

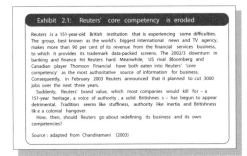

Learning Objectives

Each chapter opens with a set of learning objectives, summarizing what readers should learn from each chapter.

Figures and Tables

Each chapter provides figures and tables to help you to visualize the various marketing models, and to illusrate and summarize important concepts.

Exhibit Boxes

Exhibit boxes, distributed throughout the chapters, contain real-life examples designed to put the material covered into a question on how you might tackle a particular issue as a practising manager, or how you could apply the theory explained in the chapter. This can be used in a classroom setting or as an exercise for reflection.

Chapter Summary

This briefly reviews and reinforces the main topics you will have covered in each chapter to ensure you have acquired a solid understanding of the key themes.

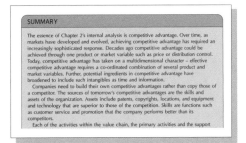

Questions for Discussion

These questions are designed to provoke interesting debates and discussions on the theories and concepts covered in each chapter. They are designed to promote understanding and conceptualization.

References

At the end of each chapter is a references section, which offers sources of alternative and more in-depth information on the topics covered.

Case Studies

Each chapter includes its own case study to highlight and clarify the material covered. Each case is accompanied by a set of questions to test understanding.

Technology to enhance learning and teaching

Visit **www.mcgraw-hill.co.uk/textbooks/hollensen** today

Online Learning Centre (OLC)

After completing each chapter, log on to the supporting Online Learning Centre website. Take advantage of the study tools offered to reinforce the material you have read in the text, and to develop your knowledge of marketing in a fun and effective way.

Resources for students include:
- Weblinks
- Marketing Planning Template
- Financial Planning Template
- MCQ Self-test Questions
- Additional Case Studies
- Suggested Answers to Discussion Questions

Resources available for lecturers:
- PowerPoint presentations
- Image Library
- Suggested Answers to Case Study Questions
- Guidance on Teaching using Case Studies

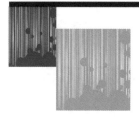

Custom Publishing Solutions: Let us help make our content your solution

At McGraw-Hill Education our aim is to help lecturers to find the most suitable content for their needs delivered to their students in the most appropriate way. Our custom publishing solutions offer the ideal combination of content delivered in the way which best suits lecturer and students.

Our custom publishing programme offers lecturers the opportunity to select just the chapters or sections of material they wish to deliver to their students from a database called CREATE™ at www.mcgrawhillcreate.com.

CREATE™ contains over two million pages of content from:

- textbooks
- professional books
- case books – Harvard Articles, Insead, Ivey, Darden, Thunderbird and BusinessWeek
- Taking Sides – debate materials

across the following imprints:

- McGraw-Hill Education
- Open University Press
- Harvard Business School Press
- US and European material

There is also the option to include additional material authored by lecturers in the custom product – this does not necessarily have to be in English.

We will take care of everything from start to finish in the process of developing and delivering a custom product to ensure that lecturers and students receive exactly the material needed in the most suitable way.

With a Custom Publishing Solution, students enjoy the best selection of material deemed to be the most suitable for learning everything they need for their courses – something of real value to support their learning. Teachers are able to use exactly the material they want, in the way they want, to support their teaching on the course.

Please contact your local McGraw-Hill representative with any questions or alternatively contact Warren Eels e: warren_eels@mcgraw-hill.com.

Acknowledgements

Author's acknowledgements

Writing any book is a long-term commitment and involves time-consuming effort. Its successful completion depends on the support and generosity of many people. The realization of this book is certainly no exception.

I wish to thank the many scholars whose articles, books and other materials I have cited or quoted. It is not, I'm afraid, possible to acknowledge everyone by name.

I also wish to acknowledge the help I have received from the companies highlighted in the case studies, whose managers provided the valuable material that enabled me to write up the cases. I have been in direct personal contact with some of the companies and I thank the managers involved for their very useful comments.

A number of reviewers have been involved in the development of this text, and I would like to thank them for their important and valuable contribution.

I am grateful to my publisher, McGraw-Hill. Throughout the revision of this text, I had the pleasure of working with the editors who have seen this project through to its completion. I would therefore like to thank Development Editor Thomas Hill and Acquisitions Editor Mark Kavanagh, and the team behind them, for their encouragement and professionalism in transforming my manuscript into the final book.

I also extend my greatest gratitude to my colleagues at the University of Southern Denmark for their constant help and inspiration.

Finally, I thank my family for their support throughout the writing process. I am pleased to dedicate this edition to Jonna, Nanna and Julie.

Svend Hollensen
July 2010

Publisher's acknowledgement

Our thanks go to the following reviewers for their comments at various stages in the text's development: Beejal Shah from the University of Hertfordshire, Chris Preston from Queen Margaret University, Magnus Hultman from Leeds University and John Staunton from University College Dublin.

Every effort has been made to trace and acknowledge ownership of copyright and to clear permission for material reproduced in this book. The publisher will be pleased to make suitable arrangements to clear permission with any copyright holders whom it has not been possible to contact.

About the Author

Svend Hollensen
(svend@sam.sdu.dk) is an Associate
Professor in Marketing at the
University of Southern Denmark. He
gained practical experience during
his job as a marketing co-ordinator
in a large Danish multinational
enterprise, as well as in his capacity
as international marketing manager
in a company producing agricultural
machinery. In both jobs, he was
involved in the development of
international marketing plans.
Having spent this time in industry
he received his Ph.D. from
Copenhagen Business School.

Svend has also worked as a
business consultant for several
multinational companies, as well as
global organizations such as the
World Bank.

Furthermore, he is the owner and
chief executive officer (CEO) of the
company Hollensen ApS, which
performs consulting activities for
companies and organizations.

PART 01

Analysis

CHAPTER 01

Introduction

Chapter contents

❖ *LEARNING OBJECTIVES*

After studying this chapter you should be able to do the following:

❖ Understand why marketing planning is so important.

❖ Explain the difference between marketing planning and a marketing plan.

❖ Explain the difference between goals and objectives.

❖ Explore and explain the different stages in developing a marketing plan.

1.1   Why prepare a marketing plan?

The purpose of this book is to provide an overview of the structured marketing planning process that contributes to the development of a viable marketing plan. There are some key reasons why marketing planning has become so important. Recent years have witnessed an intensifying of competition in many markets. Many factors have contributed to this, but among some of the more significant are (Mullins and Walker, 2010):

● a growth in global competition, as barriers to trade have been lowered and global communications improved

● linked to the above, the role of the multinational conglomerate has expanded; this now disregards geographical and other boundaries and seeks profit opportunities on a global scale

- in some economies, prevailing legislation and political ideologies have served to foster entrepreneurial and 'free market' values
- continual technological innovation, giving rise to new sources of competition for established products and markets.

The importance of competition, and hence competitor analysis, in contemporary strategic marketing cannot be overemphasized. For this reason we shall be looking at this aspect in more depth in later chapters. This importance is now widely accepted among both marketing academics and practitioners. Successful marketing in a competitive economy is about competitive success and that, in addition to a customer focus (a true marketing orientation), also includes competitive positioning.

The marketing concept holds that the key to achieving organizational goals lies in determining the needs and wants of target markets, and delivering the desired 'satisfaction' more effectively and efficiently than competitors (here again the competition aspect comes in).

Marketing planning is an approach adopted by many successful, market-focused businesses. While it is by no means a new tool, the degree of objectivity and thoroughness with which it is applied varies considerably. This book presents a straightforward format for conducting comprehensive marketing analyses, making the most of the resulting marketing intelligence to determine marketing strategies, and for ensuring detailed, actionable marketing programmes are put in place that implement the recommended strategies and achieve the desired marketing results: the ultimate objective of a marketing planning initiative.

Marketing planning can be defined as the structured process of researching and analysing marketing situations, developing and documenting marketing objectives, strategies and programmes, and implementing, evaluating and controlling activities to achieve the objectives. This systematic process enables companies to identify and evaluate any number of marketing opportunities that can serve as paths to the organization's goals, as well as potential threats that might block these paths. In practice, the marketing environment is so changeable that paths to new opportunities can open in an instant, even as others become obscured or completely blocked. Thus, marketing planning must be approached as an adaptable, ongoing process rather than a rigid, annual event designed only to produce a written report.

The outcome of this structured process is the marketing plan, a document that summarizes what the marketer has learned about the marketplace and indicates how the company plans to achieve its marketing objectives. The marketing plan not only documents the organization's marketing strategies and lists the activities employees will need to implement in order to achieve the marketing objectives, but also shows the mechanisms that will measure progress towards the objectives and allows for adjustment if actual results take the organization off course.

A marketing plan is one of several official planning documents created by a company. These include the business plan, which outlines the organization's overall financial and operational objectives and strategies, and the strategic plan, which discusses the organization's general long-term strategic direction.

Marketing plans generally cover a one-year period, although some (especially those dealing with new products or markets) may project activities and financial performance further into the future. Marketers must start the marketing planning process at least several months before the marketing plan is scheduled to go into operation; this allows sufficient time for thorough research and analysis, management review and revision, and co-ordination of resources among departments and business units.

Like all types of planning, marketing planning concerns the future. It is the approach to the future that is important. The future involves a time dimension, which needs to be clearly specified, and depends on a clear understanding of organizational and market needs.

The avoidance strategy of 'do nothing' achieves little; therefore, a planned approach to the future depends on the ability to predict, anticipate, prepare and adapt. Marketing planning means change. It is a process that involves deciding *now* what to do in the *future*, with a full appreciation of the resource position, the need to set clear, communicable, measurable objectives, the development of alternative courses of action, and a means of assessing the best route towards the achievement of specified objectives. Marketing planning is designed to assist the process of marketing decision-making under prevailing conditions of risk and uncertainty. Above all, the process of marketing planning has a number of benefits, as detailed below.

- *Consistency*: the individual marketing action plan will be consistent with the overall corporate plan and with other departmental or functional plans. It should also be consistent with those of previous years, minimizing the risk of management 'firefighting'; that is, incoherent, case-by-case action plans. In this way marketing planning prevents the short-sighted tendency to concentrate all effort on the 'here and now'.
- *Responsibility*: those who have responsibility for implementing the individual parts of the marketing plan will know what their responsibilities are and should have their performance monitored against the plan. Marketing planning requires management staff, collectively, to make clear judgemental statements about assumptions, and it enables a control system to be designed and established whereby performance can be assessed against predetermined criteria.
- *Communication*: those implementing the marketing plan will also know what the overall objectives are, the assumptions that lie behind them and the context for each of the detailed activities.
- *Commitment*: assuming that the plan is agreed upon by those involved in its implementation, as well as by those who will provide the resources, it should stimulate a group commitment to its implementation and ultimately lead to better decision-making.

Plans must be specific to an organization and its current situation. There is not one system of planning but many systems, not one style but many styles, and a planning process must be tailor-made for a particular company in a specific set of circumstances.

Marketing planning as a functional activity can only work within a corporate planning framework. The marketing planner must not lose sight of the need to achieve corporate-level objectives by means of exploiting product and market combinations. There is an underlying requirement for any organization adopting marketing planning systems to set a clearly defined business mission as the basis from which the organizational direction can develop.

Without marketing planning, it is more difficult to guide research and development (R&D) and new product development (NPD), set required standards for suppliers, guide the sales force in terms of what to emphasize, to whom and what/whom to avoid, set realistic, achievable sales targets, and avoid competitor actions or changes in the marketplace. Above all, businesses that fail to incorporate marketing planning in their marketing activities may not be in a position to develop a sustainable competitive edge in their markets.

1.2 The main stages in developing a marketing plan

Marketing planning is a systematic process involving the assessment of marketing opportunities and resources, the determination of marketing objectives, and the development of a plan for implementation and control.

Marketing planning is an ongoing analysis/planning/control process, or cycle (see Fig. 1.1). Many organizations update their marketing plans annually as new information becomes available. Some organizations operate three- or five-yearly planning cycles, some six-monthly. Most common perhaps is an annual revision with a three-year focus. In this way, the marketing plan can include detailed recommendations for the next two years, with extrapolations for the third.

Once incorporated, the key recommendations can then be presented to senior managers within the organization. Companies that are developing marketing plans for the first time are usually relieved to find that the workload reduces year on year, as updating requires less input. Much of the hard work comes in the initiation of marketing planning.

The final task of marketing planning is to summarize the salient findings from the marketing analyses, the strategic recommendations and the required marketing programmes in a short report: the written marketing plan. This document needs to be concise yet complete in terms of presenting a summary of the marketplace and the business's position, explaining thoroughly the recommended strategy and containing the detail of the required marketing mix actions. For many managers, the written plan will be all they glean from the marketing planning activity. It must therefore be informative and to the point, while mapping out a clear set of marketing activities designed to satisfactorily implement the desired target market strategy.

Figure 1.1 illustrates the several stages that have to be proceeded through in order to arrive at a finished marketing plan. Each of the stages illustrated is discussed in more detail later in this chapter.

As illustrated in Fig. 1.1, the development of a marketing plan is a process, and each step in that process has a structure that enables the marketing plan to evolve from abstract information and ideas into a tangible document that can easily be understood, evaluated and implemented. The following section is devoted to an in-depth discussion of each step in this process (Gilmore et al., 2001; Day, 2002; Lehmann and Winer, 2008).

1.2.1 Step 1: mission, corporate goals and objectives

An organization's mission is an expression of its purpose; it states what the organization hopes to accomplish and how it plans to achieve this goal. This expression of purpose provides management with a clear sense of direction.

The corporate mission statement requires detailed consideration by top management to establish the business the company is really in and to relate this to future business intentions. It is a general statement that provides an integrating function for the business, from which a clear sense of business definition and direction can be achieved. This stage is often overlooked in marketing planning and yet, without it, the plan will lack a sense of contribution to the development of the total business. By deriving a clear mission statement, boundaries for the 'corporate entity' can be conceived in the context of the environmental trends that influence the business.

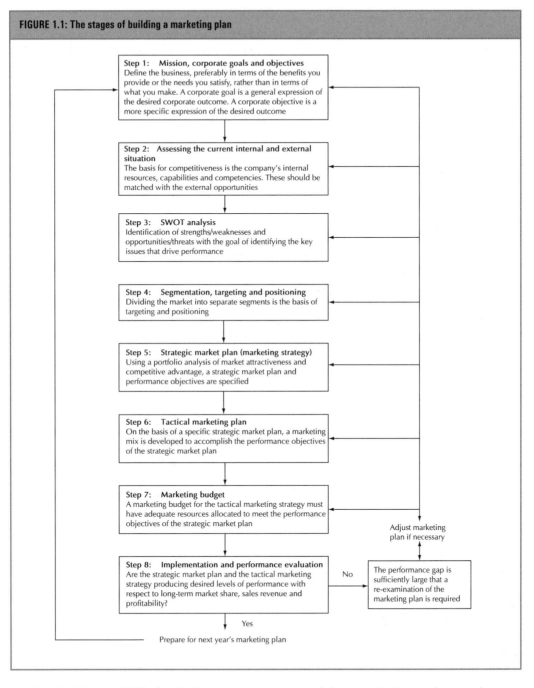

FIGURE 1.1: The stages of building a marketing plan

Step 1:   Mission, corporate goals and objectives
Define the business, preferably in terms of the benefits you provide or the needs you satisfy, rather than in terms of what you make. A corporate goal is a general expression of the desired corporate outcome. A corporate objective is a more specific expression of the desired outcome

Step 2:   Assessing the current internal and external situation
The basis for competitiveness is the company's internal resources, capabilities and competencies. These should be matched with the external opportunities

Step 3:   SWOT analysis
Identification of strengths/weaknesses and opportunities/threats with the goal of identifying the key issues that drive performance

Step 4:   Segmentation, targeting and positioning
Dividing the market into separate segments is the basis of targeting and positioning

Step 5:   Strategic market plan (marketing strategy)
Using a portfolio analysis of market attractiveness and competitive advantage, a strategic market plan and performance objectives are specified

Step 6:   Tactical marketing plan
On the basis of a specific strategic market plan, a marketing mix is developed to accomplish the performance objectives of the strategic market plan

Step 7:   Marketing budget
A marketing budget for the tactical marketing strategy must have adequate resources allocated to meet the performance objectives of the strategic market plan

Adjust marketing plan if necessary

Step 8:   Implementation and performance evaluation
Are the strategic market plan and the tactical marketing strategy producing desired levels of performance with respect to long-term market share, sales revenue and profitability?

No

The performance gap is sufficiently large that a re-examination of the marketing plan is required

Yes

Prepare for next year's marketing plan

It is helpful to establish the distinctive competencies of the organization and, in so doing, to focus on what customers are buying rather than on what the organization is selling. This will assist in the development of a more marketing-oriented mission statement. A clear mission statement should include the customer groups to be served, the customer needs to be served, and the technologies to be utilized (Abell, 1980).

The general purpose expressed in the organization's mission statement must be translated into more specific guidelines as to how these universal intentions will operate. Organizations and the people who manage them tend to be more productive when they have established standards to motivate them, specific directions to guide them, and stated achievement levels against which to compare their performance. The terms 'goals' and 'objectives' are defined and used in a variety of ways and often treated as interchangeable concepts. For our purposes, however, these terms have different meanings and uses.

A *goal* is a general and qualitative expression of a desired outcome that provides general guidelines by which management can direct its actions. Goals help identify, clarify and prioritize intended accomplishments, and help bridge the gap between the organization's mission and its objectives by focusing the efforts of the strategic business unit (SBU) management team. By refining and illuminating the mission statement, goals provide more specific direction as to which business opportunities the organization intends to pursue. Marketing goals are the general result the organization hopes to achieve through its marketing efforts. These goals also identify the general focus through which marketing resources will be directed and allocated. Marketing goals, then, are the benchmarks that establish direction for a strategic marketing plan.

In contrast, an *objective* is a specific and quantitative expression of a desired outcome. The corporate objectives of the organization are time-dependent and determined to achieve shareholder expectations. These should be derived from the mission statement to ensure integration within a corporate and marketing planning system. Strategy is the means by which objectives are achieved. If objectives specify *what* is to be done, then strategy lays down *how* it is to be done.

In step 5 (see below) we specify and explain the marketing objectives used in the strategic market plan.

1.2.2 Step 2: assessing the current internal and external situation

This situation analysis attempts to address the question 'Where is the organization now?' It encompasses external and internal forces that shape market attractiveness, competitive position and current performance. At the lower level of the planning process, the annual marketing planner has the advantage of the availability of the vast amount of information generated by previous strategic marketing plans. For the marketing planner, the issue often becomes one of determining which previously generated information is relevant and applicable to the particular business unit or product line and what new information is needed.

The basis for competitiveness is the organization's internal resources, capabilities and competencies (see Chapter 2); these should be matched with the external opportunities (see Chapter 3). All together, this adds up to step 3: SWOT analysis.

1.2.3 Step 3: SWOT analysis

SWOT analysis is critical in summarizing key strengths (S) and weaknesses (W), as well as opportunities (O) and threats (T). The steps that follow will be only as good as the situation analysis and key performance issues that are uncovered in the situation and SWOT analyses.

Perhaps the most difficult and elusive part of a marketing plan is the identification of key performance issues. A key performance issue is a problem or unaddressed opportunity that is an underlying cause, and that limits market or profit performance, or both.

In assessing current situations, SWOT analysis attempts to identify one or more strategic relationships or match-ups between the SBU's current strengths or weaknesses and its present or future opportunities and threats. Organizations must seek out 'strategic windows' in which the key requirements of a market and the particular competencies of the organization best fit together. Identifying these limited time periods is one reason to use SWOT analysis.

Strengths are the bases for building organization competencies and, ultimately, competitiveness. An internal organizational scan attempts to ascertain the type and degree of each SBU's strengths and weaknesses. By recognizing their special capabilities and serious limitations, organizations are better able to adjust to the external environmental conditions of the marketplace.

'Know yourself and your competency' is the basic tenet that guides this assessment of the abilities and deficiencies of an organization's internal operations. It is also the basic tenet in the so-called resource-based view (RBV), which is discussed in Chapter 2.

All businesses have *weaknesses*. Successful businesses try to minimize or conquer their shortcomings. A weakness can be any business function or operation that is not able to resist external forces or withstand attack. A weak business function or operation is one that is deficient or inferior in its ability to reap the benefits presented by an external opportunity. Weaknesses are mostly viewed in comparative terms: an organization has a weakness when it is unable to perform a business function or conduct a business operation as effectively and efficiently as its competitors.

The internal factors that may be viewed as strengths or weaknesses, depending on their impact on the organization's position (they may represent a strength for one organization but a weakness, in relative terms, for another), may include all of the 4Ps (product, price, place (distribution), promotion), as well as personnel, finance, and so on.

The second part of a SWOT analysis involves the organization's external environments. This environmental scanning process represents the opportunities and threats that are part of a SWOT analysis. The external factors, which again may be threats to one organization while offering opportunities to another, may include such matters as technological change, legislation and socio-cultural change, as well as changes in the marketplace or competitive position.

Opportunities are unsatisfied customer needs that the organization has a good chance of meeting successfully. For an environmental occurrence to be considered an opportunity by a particular business, a favourable combination of circumstances must exist. A unique business strength must fit an attractive environmental need in order to create a high probability of a successful match, as when a low-cost producer identifies an unserved market of low-income consumers. Good opportunities are needs that the organization can satisfy in a more complete fashion than can existing competitors. A sustainable competitive advantage is a key determinant in establishing what is and what is not a good opportunity for a particular business.

Threats are hostile aspects of the external environment that could potentially injure the organization.

The following actions suggested by the SWOT matrix are those that might be expected, and provide the strategic marketing manager with some options:

- match strengths and opportunities
- convert weaknesses to strengths
- convert threats to opportunities
- minimize, if not avoid, weaknesses and threats.

SWOT analysis is just one aid to assessing the current situation – it is not the only technique available. It has its weaknesses in that it tends to persuade organizations to compile lists rather than to think about what is really important to their business. It also presents the resulting lists uncritically, without clear prioritization, so that, for example, weak opportunities may appear to balance strong threats.

The aim of any SWOT analysis should be to isolate what will be important to the future of the organization and what subsequent marketing planning needs to address.

1.2.4 Step 4: segmentation, targeting and positioning

In addition to analysing the overall environment, marketers need to analyse their markets and their customers, whether consumers or businesses. This means looking closely at market share trends, changing customer demographics, product demand and future projections, buying habits, needs and wants, customer attitudes and customer satisfaction. Marketers have to apply their knowledge of the market and customers – acquired through research – to determine which parts of the market, known as segments, should be targeted for marketing activities. This means dividing the overall market into separate groupings of customers, based on characteristics such as age, gender, geography, needs, behaviour or other variables. With today's technology, some companies even build segments that consist of only one customer (at a time). The purpose of segmentation is to group customers with similar needs, wants, behaviour, or other characteristics that affect their demand for or usage of the good or service being marketed.

Once the market has been segmented, the next set of decisions centres on targeting, including whether to market to one segment, to several segments, or to the entire market, and how to cover these segments. The company also needs to formulate a suitable positioning, which means using marketing to create a competitively distinctive place (position) for the brand or product in the mind of targeted customers. This positioning must effectively set the product apart from competing products in a way that is meaningful to customers.

1.2.5 Step 5: strategic market plan (marketing strategy)

At this point in the marketing planning process, the company has examined its current situation, looked at markets and customers, set objectives, and identified targeted segments and an appropriate positioning. Now management can create the marketing strategies and tactics that will take the company down the path towards its customers, working with the basic marketing mix tools of product, place (or distribution), price and promotion, enhanced by service strategies to build stronger customer relationships.

Marketing strategies and programmes must be consistent with the company's overall corporate goals and objectives. Marketing objectives are essentially about the match between products and markets – what products and services will be in what position in what markets – so they must be based on realistic customer behaviour in those markets. Objectives for pricing, distribution, advertising, and so on, are at a lower level and should not be confused with marketing objectives, although they are part of the marketing strategy needed to achieve marketing objectives.

To be most effective, objectives should be measurable. This measurement may be in terms of sales volume, money volume, money value, market share or percentage penetration of distribution outlets. As it is measured, it can, within limits, be monitored and corrective action taken if necessary. Usually marketing objectives must be based, above all, on the company's financial objectives; financial measurements are converted into the related marketing measurements. An example of a measurable marketing objective might be 'to enter market X with product Y and capture 15 per cent of the market by value within the first three years'.

In principle, the strategic market plan describes how the company's marketing objectives will be achieved. It is essentially a pattern or plan that integrates a company's major goals, policies and action sequences into a cohesive whole. Marketing strategies are generally concerned with the 4Ps:

1   Product strategies
    ● developing new products, repositioning or relaunching existing ones and phasing out old ones
    ● adding new features and benefits
    ● balancing product portfolios
    ● changing the design or packaging.

2   Pricing strategies
    ● setting the price to skim or to penetrate
    ● pricing for different products and market segments
    ● deciding how to match competitive pricing.

3   Promotional strategies
    ● specifying the communication platform and media
    ● deciding the public relations brief
    ● organizing the sales force to cover new products and services or markets.

4   Placement (distribution) strategies
    ● choosing the channels
    ● deciding levels of customer service.

One aspect of the marketing strategy that is often overlooked is timing. Choosing the best time for each element of the strategy to come into play is often critical. Sometimes, taking the right action at the wrong time can be almost as bad as taking the wrong action at the right time. Timing is, therefore, an essential part of any plan and should normally appear as a schedule of planned activities.

Exhibit 1.1: *Global marketing of Masterfoods' M&M's*

It all started with Frank Mars back in 1911 when he and his wife Ethel started making and selling a variety of buttercream candies from the kitchen of their home in Tacoma, Washington. Working in Europe during the 1930s, it occurred to

Forrest Mars (son of Frank) to give chocolate a protective candy coating to stop it from melting. This idea gave birth to M&M's candies, and their success was assured when they were adopted as a staple ration for US forces. Today, Mars is a US$14 bn business operating in over 100 countries. Mars, Inc. now operates its three core businesses – snackfood, petcare and main meal food – under the Masterfoods name in most parts of the world. It is one of the world's largest fmcg businesses. Among its brands are M&M's, Mars, Snickers, Bounty, Starburst, Milky Way and Twix.

Forrest Mars Senior had developed his recipe for M&M's chocolate candies having seen soldiers eating pellets of chocolate encased in a sugary coating during the Spanish Civil War. M&M's became widely available to the US public during the 1940s. In 1948, the brown pouch we are familiar with today replaced the original cardboard tube.

As the USA entered the 1950s, M&M's Chocolate was becoming a household name, particularly with the growth of TV. In 1954, M&M's Peanut was introduced to the brand's portfolio, and the sales of both varieties continued to grow. That same year, the universally loved M&M's brand characters and the famous slogan, 'The milk chocolate melts in your mouth, not in your hand', debuted in the brand's initial TV advertising.

In 1960, M&M's Peanut added three new colours to the mix: red, green and yellow joined the original brown. In 1972, the first appearance of the M&M's brand characters on packaging reinforced brand awareness, as they became increasingly well known through print and TV advertising. In 1976, the colour orange was added to the M&M's Peanut mix.

The global characters

As a front runner, Red feels distinctly superior to Yellow and is proud to be a 'Spokescandy' for M&M's. He feels the need to continually remind consumers why he is so special and in his relationship with the other M&M's characters has a tendency to be scheming, attention-seeking and cunning. Red is the undoubted 'leader of the M&M's pack'. The slightly more hapless Yellow feels that, as a peanut, it is his right to be loved for being just what he is. Yellow relies on Red to tell him exactly what to do, and trusts him implicitly. This allows Red to take advantage of Yellow unmercifully, a situation that has existed since Yellow was introduced in late 1954. Despite his hard shell and peanut and chocolate centre, Yellow is at heart a softie.

The characters became a hit with consumers, surpassing the popularity of Mickey Mouse and Bart Simpson (*Source*: Marketing Evaluation, Inc.). In 1995, over half a century after the candies were introduced, consumers in the USA helped write a new chapter in the history of the brand with a huge marketing drive. They were asked to vote for a new colour to appear in the M&M's pack. The options available to them included blue, pink, purple or no change – 'no change' won by 54 per cent with over 10 million votes cast.

In 1996, the brand introduced M&M's MINIs in re-closable plastic tubes in six different colours. The historic moment of 1997 was the debut of Green, the first female M&M's character. This multifaceted 1990s woman and author starred in a number of popular commercials. Green toured the USA promoting her autobiography, *I Melt For No One*, and quickly matched the celebrity status of her male colleagues – Red, Yellow and Blue.

M&M's globalization strategy

Today M&M's is a US$3 bn global brand that has secured and retained its dominant market position as number one confectionery brand, through extensive use of global marketing strategies. This strategy has been underpinned with new product developments and strong advertising 'personalities' introduced to the M&M's family.

A global business identifies world markets for its products. Global companies plan and co-ordinate activities on a global basis. By operating in more than one country, benefits from savings or economies on activities such as R&D, marketing, operations and finance are achieved, which may not be available to purely domestic operators. M&M's is an example of a successful global business endeavour.

M&M's global branding has hinged on the deliberate development of distinct personalities or characters for each M&M's colour. Globally recognizable packaging, the 'melts in your mouth, not in your hand' slogan and the distinctive 'M' on each candy all play an important role in the global branding process.

Localization of M&M's global strategy

Localizing the product: it is important to conduct research on the customer's reaction to a new product. R&D is essential in order to adapt to changing market situations and customer needs. Masterfoods Ltd addressed this by refining the M&M's recipe, revamping packaging and introducing a new 'character' for the Irish market. Masterfoods Ltd found that Europeans preferred milk chocolate and this was a factor in the 1998 relaunch of M&M's in Ireland.

Localizing the packaging design: the strategy at relaunch included conducting local research to establish how best to build the M&M's brand to suit the Irish temperament. Packaging was revamped to include the characters of Red and Yellow on the packs. This was a key tool in increasing brand awareness. Using the M&M's characters in everyday situations allowed Irish consumers to relate to both Red and Yellow.

Localizing advertising and promotions: advertising is essential to inform customers that a product is available, to persuade or remind the customer to purchase the product by constantly bringing the product to their attention. To work effectively, a global brand must communicate a cohesive image and message about core brand values to all its consumers. It must stand on an easily recognizable transnational platform but also operate efficiently in a distinctly local environment. M&M's started out as a uniquely US phenomenon; its expansion on to a global stage and into different national markets has been characterized by impactful marketing and advertising, innovative product expansion and highly interactive promotions.

Sources: adapted from www.mars.com, www.masterfoods.com, www.business2000.ie

1.2.6 Step 6: tactical marketing plan

The next step in the marketing planning process is the development of a tactical marketing plan to put the strategic market plan into effect. Although the overall marketing strategy to protect, grow, reduce focus, harvest, enter or exit a market position is set by the strategic market plan, more specific tactical marketing strategies need to be developed for each of the key performance issues. Each element of a tactical marketing strategy is a specific response to a key performance issue that exists within the context of the market situation. Therefore, the company's overall marketing strategies need to be developed into detailed plans and programmes. Although these detailed plans may cover each of the 4Ps, the focus will vary, depending on the company's specific strategies. A product-oriented company will focus its plans for the 4Ps around each of its products. A market or geographically oriented company will concentrate on each market or geographical area. Each will base its plans on the detailed needs of its customers and on the strategies chosen to satisfy these needs.

The most important element is the detailed plans, which explain exactly what programmes and individual activities will take place over the period of the plan (usually over the next year). Without these specified – and preferably quantified – activities the plan cannot be monitored, even in terms of success in meeting its objectives.

1.2.7 Step 7: marketing budget

The classic quantification of a marketing plan appears in the form of budgets. The purpose of a marketing budget is to pull all the revenues and costs involved in marketing together into one comprehensive document. It is a managerial tool that balances what needs to be spent against what can be afforded, and helps in making choices about priorities; it is then used in monitoring the performance in practice. The marketing budget is usually the most powerful tool with which the relationship between desired results and available means can be 'thought through'.

Resources need to be allocated in a marketing budget based on the strategic and tactical market plans. Without adequate resources, the tactical marketing strategies cannot succeed and, as a consequence, performance objectives cannot be achieved.

Specifying a marketing budget is perhaps the most difficult part of the market planning process. Although specifying the budget is not a precise process, there must be a logical connection between the strategy and performance objectives and the marketing budget. Each area of marketing activity should be allocated to centres of responsibility. Indeed, as a key functional area of business the marketing budget is one of the key budgets used to manage the total budgetary control system of the organization. In many companies, budgeting is the transitional step between planning and implementation, because the budget, and allocated centres within it, will project the cost of each activity over a specified period of time, and also act as a guide for implementation and control.

1.2.8 Step 8: implementation and performance evaluation

The best marketing plan is useless without effective implementation. Once strategies and plans are implemented, the company needs to formulate ways to determine effectiveness by identifying mechanisms and metrics that can be used to measure progress towards objectives. Most companies use sales forecasts, budgets, schedules and other tools to set and record standards against which progress can be measured. By comparing actual results against daily, weekly, monthly, quarterly and yearly projections, management can see where the company is ahead, where it is behind and where it needs to make adjustments to get back on the right path. In the course of reviewing progress, marketers also should look at what competitors are doing, as well as what the markets are doing, so that they can put their own results into context.

To control implementation, marketers should start with the objectives they have set, establish standards for measuring progress towards those targets, measure the performance of the marketing programmes, diagnose the results, and then take corrective action if results fail to measure up. This is the marketing control process. This process is iterative: managers should expect to retrace their steps as they systematically implement strategies, assess results and take action to bring performance in line with expectations. Companies use this control process to analyse their marketing implementation on the basis of measures such as market share, sales, profitability and productivity.

There are three main marketing planning approaches in terms of involvement of the organization as a whole.

1 *Top-down planning*: here top management sets both the goals and the plan for lower-level management. While decision-making may be quick at the top level, implementation of the plans may not be as speedy because it takes time for various units (divisions, groups, departments) to learn about the plans and to reorganize their tasks accordingly to accomplish the new goals.
2 *Bottom-up planning*: in this approach, the various organizational units create their own goals and plans, which are then approved (or not) by higher-level management. This can lead to more creative approaches, but it can also pose problems for co-ordination. More pragmatically, strategy all too frequently emerges from a consolidation of tactics.
3 *Goals-down-plans-up planning*: this is the most common approach, at least among the companies that invest in such sophisticated planning processes. Top management set the goals, but the various units create their own plans to meet these goals. These plans are then typically approved as part of the annual planning and budgetary process.

Summary

Marketing planning is the structured process companies use to research and analyse their marketing situation, develop and document marketing objectives, strategies and programmes, and then implement, evaluate and control marketing activities to achieve their marketing objectives. The marketing plan, which documents the results of the marketing planning process, serves an important co-ordination function by helping to develop internal consensus, providing internal direction, encouraging internal collaboration, co-ordinating resource allocation, and outlining the tasks, timetable and responsibilities needed to achieve the marketing objectives.

There are many benefits to a good marketing plan. The process of market planning can lead a business to the discovery of new market opportunities, to better utilization of assets and capabilities, to a well-defined market focus, to improved marketing productivity and to a baseline from which to evaluate progress towards goals.

The eight broad steps in developing a marketing plan are:

1   mission, corporate goals and objectives
2   assessing the current internal and external situation
3   SWOT analysis
4   segmentation, targeting and positioning
5   strategic market plan (marketing strategy)
6   tactical marketing plan
7   marketing budget
8   implementation and performance evaluation.

The development of a marketing plan involves process and structure, creativity and form. The process begins with a broad view of market opportunities that encourages a wider consideration of many market opportunities. For each market opportunity, a strategic market objective is set, based on market attractiveness and competitive advantage attained or attainable in the market. For each market to be pursued, a separate situation analysis and marketing plan is required. The situation analysis enables the business to uncover key issues that limit performance. These key performance issues are the basic guidelines from which marketing strategies are developed.

With the marketing strategy and budget set, an estimate of market and financial performance metrics must be projected over a specified time frame. If the marketing plan fails to produce desired levels of performance, the marketing strategy needs to be re-examined.

Questions for discussion

1   How could businesses engaged in no market planning or in highly formalized market planning both miss meaningful market insights?
2   What are the differences between marketing objectives and marketing strategies? What should marketing strategies cover?
3   What is the relationship between the mission statement and SWOT analysis? What is the relationship between the mission statement and the company's objectives?
4   What is the role of SWOT analysis in the marketing planning process? What is the role of key issues in SWOT analysis?
5   Why is the development of a marketing budget so important to the success of the marketing plan?

6   What is the purpose of the performance evaluation? What role should it play in the successful implementation of a marketing plan?

7   In which ways may the whole company be involved in marketing planning?

References

Abell, D.F. (1980) *Defining the Business: The Starting Point of Strategic Planning.* Englewood Cliffs, NJ: Prentice-Hall.

Day, G.S. (2002) Managing the market learning process, *Journal of Business & Industrial Marketing,* 17(4): 240–52.

Gilmore, A., Carson, D. and Grant, K. (2001) SME marketing in practice, *Marketing Intelligence & Planning,* 19(1); 6–11.

Lehmann, D.R. and Winer, R.S. (2008) *Analysis for Marketing Planning.* New York: McGraw-Hill/Irwin.

Mullins, J.W. and Walker, O.C. (2010) *Marketing Management: A Strategic Decision-Making Approach,* New York: McGraw-Hill/Irwin.

CASE STUDY 1: DERBY CYCLES

How should Derby create a marketing plan for penetrating the e-bicycle market?

Derby Cycle Werke GmbH (abbreviated Derby) was founded in 1919, originally as the 'Firma Kalkhoff'. Derby (www.derby-cycle.de) is the biggest bike manufacturer in Germany and one of the three biggest manufacturers in Europe. The brand portfolio contains the complete band width of sportive mountain bikes and race machines for the ambitious leisure time biker and racers as well as trekking, city, off-road and kids' bikes for every day and for pleasure tours.

In the company's final assembly in Cloppenburg (Germany), all branded bikes are pre-assembled for 98 per cent. This reduces the assembly effort for the specialized trade and extends the margin. Thus, Derby's operations are highly dependent on components manufactured by non-US suppliers located primarily in Taiwan, Japan and China. As is common in the bicycle industry, a substantial majority of Derby's multi-speed bicycles contain components supplied by Shimano Inc., the world's largest bicycle component manufacturer and supplier, and a brand with a strong reputation among bicycle consumers. Shimano's headquarters are in Japan.

	2008 (€m)	2007 (€m)	2006 (€m)	2005 (€m)	2004 (€m)
Turnover	94.0	95.0	92.4	84.0	80.0
Number of employees	375	375	370	370	370

TABLE 1.1 Derby's financial results

Derby's most well-known brands are Focus, Kalkhoff and ZEG.

Focus: the sportive, international premium brand for race bikes and mountain bikes. Focus is counted among the top bike brands in the sportive sector. Focus supplies top professional and amateur cyclists as well as complete teams. Former champions as well as active professional cyclists take part in the bike development. This way a lot of practical race experience is involved. According to the requirements of these professionals, the bikes get improved as long as excellent results can be achieved under authentic competition conditions. Of course, Focus bikes can be simply used by 'normal' users for recreational activities or for relaxing tours to work.

Kalkhoff: the premium brand for comfort bikes with a tradition of more than 80 years. Kalkhoff is a leading brand for leisure, trekking and city bikes. This includes sportive fitness and trekking bikes, comfortable city and all-round bikes as well as trendy youth and kids' bikes. The strength of Kalkhoff is based on its outstanding technology, superior and trendy optical characteristics as well as technological leading, innovative equipment components. Kalkhoff relies on tradition as well as on consequent production in Germany.

ZEG: the exclusive city and trekking bike for the ZEG ('Zweirad-Experten-Gruppe'). Rixe assembles bikes in best quality and well equipped for decades. Rixe is one of the leading suppliers of trekking, city, sportive and youth bikes in Germany. Rixe bikes are especially featured by innovative, smart devised concepts, top components as well as by a good price–performance ratio. Rixe finds acceptance consistently due to its excellent quality and its brilliant design. Rixe is a brand of the specialized trade association ZEG. Rixe bikes can only be purchased by and from specialized trade dealers of the ZEG.

Currently, Derby has no electric bicycles (e-bikes) in their product range.

The bicycle world market

Currently, only 18 per cent of the world population sometimes uses a bicycle. This means that there is still a huge potential number of customers out there of 82 per cent of the world population.

According to Table 1.2 the global bicycle market, including bicycles, parts and accessories, is estimated to have total retail sales of about €36 bn. In 2008, worldwide demand of bicycles is approximately 90 million units, of which approximately 60 per cent are produced (but not bought) in China (with Taiwan as the core bicycle production centre). In comparison approximately 40 million cars were produced worldwide.

During the 1980s Taiwan took over Japan's role as the world's leading supply nation. The world bicycle market is highly fragmented. The world's biggest bicycle producer, Giant (Taiwan), produces almost two million bicycles, securing them a market share of 2.2 per cent. Taiwanese companies have opened their own overseas production centres. Meanwhile, Japan retains its prime role in the supply of cycle components, again drawing on cheap labour in other parts of the Far East. Japanese Shimano is one example of a huge component supplier.

The world electric bicycle (e-bike) market

The modern electric bicycle (e-bike) is true to the concept of a pedal bicycle with assisting propulsion, being rideable without power. Batteries have finite capacity, which means that the hybrid human/electric power mix is much more likely to be emphasized than is the case with a combustion engine. Electric bicycles are gaining acceptance, especially in Europe and Asia, in response to increasing traffic congestion, an ageing population and concern about the environment.

Electric motorized bicycles can be *power-on-demand*, where the motor is activated by a handlebar-mounted throttle, and/or a *pedelec* (from **ped**al **elec**tric), also known as 'electric assist', where the electric motor is regulated by pedalling. These have a sensor to detect the pedalling speed, the pedalling force, or both. An electronic controller provides assistance as a function of the sensor inputs, the vehicle speed and the required force. Most controllers also provide for manual adjustment.

Range is a key consideration with electric bikes, and is affected by factors such as motor efficiency, battery capacity, efficiency of the driving electronics, aerodynamics, hills and weight of the bike and rider. The range of an electric bike is usually stated as somewhere between 7 km (uphill on electric power only) to 70 km (minimum assistance) and is highly dependent on whether or not the bike is tested on flat roads or hills.

There have been some interesting advances in materials science and battery technology that now make electric bicycles more practical than in previous years. Much of this has come from the computer industry. For example, battery technology has advanced a great deal. The battery systems to choose from include lead-acid, *NiCd*, *NiMH* and Li-ion batteries.

Three factors are important when choosing the right battery: weight, how long the battery lasts, and how long it takes to recharge.

Lithium-ion batteries are very common in consumer electronic devices, especially the portable type. The qualities that make them ideal in consumer electronics also make them ideal for bicycles. For example, they have one of the best energy-to-weight ratios of any battery type and recharging them is straightforward. Additionally, they do not suffer from 'memory effect', which is when a battery that is only partially discharged is subsequently recharged but never regains its full capacity again. Furthermore, the charge lost over time when not in use is negligible.

But lithium-ion batteries do have certain drawbacks. For one, the shelf life is limited in comparison to nickel cadmium batteries. From time of manufacturing, regardless of the number of charge and discharge cycles, the battery's capacity will decline. This means that the battery has to be exchanged every second or third year.

Worldwide, the total e-bike market (which in Table 1.2 is regarded as a part of the total world bicycle market) is estimated to be 18 million units, which represents a value of approximately €9 bn. Most of the worldwide demand for e-bikes is found in China, where consumers buy 54 per cent of all worldwide e-bikes.

The share of e-bikes (of the total bicycle market) varies a lot from market to market. In Europe (except the Netherlands) the percentage is still relatively low, whereas in Asia, the percentage is as high as 50 per cent (e.g. in China).

In April 2009 the EN 15194 standard for 'Electronically Power Assisted Cycles' (EPAC) was officially announced by the National Standards Boards (NSBs) of 30 countries (27 EU member states and Iceland, Norway and Switzerland of the European Free Trade Association).

Current Derby international marketing strategy

Currently Derby produces approximately 2,500 bikes per day and sells approximately 500 000 units per year. Seventy per cent of these units are sold in Germany, the rest (30 per cent) are sold outside Germany, mainly in the UK and the Netherlands.

These sales figures result in a 14 per cent market share in the German market, and 1–2 per cent market share in other European countries. In Germany its biggest competitor is the Mifa (with headquarters in Germany), which has a market share of around 12 per cent of the German market, but with a broader distribution, also through mass merchandisers like Metro Cash & Carry Deutschland, Kaufland Warenhandel GmbH, Neckermann Versand AG and Aldi GmbH.

The international market for bicycles, parts and accessories is highly competitive. Competition in the bicycle industry is based upon price, quality, brand name and service. In all its product categories, Derby competes with other manufacturers and distributors, some of which have well-recognized brand names and substantial financial, technological, distribution, advertising and marketing resources.

Additional competitors could enter the European bicycle market, as the barriers to entering the bicycle designing and manufacturing businesses are low. However, it would be difficult for a new competitor to build a distribution network as effective as, for example, Derby's distribution network in Germany.

Market volume (1,000 units of bicycles – consumption)	Germany	France	UK	Italy	NL	Rest of EU	Total EU	Japan	China	USA	Total world (incl ROW, etc. Taiwan)
Total market (1000)	4,500	3,500	3,400	2,000	1,400	13,200	28,000	10,000	28,000	18,000	90,000
Most important manufacturers/ brands	● MIFA ● Derby Cycle Werke	● Eddy Merckx ● Peugeot	● Raleigh	● Bianchi ● Alan ● Cinelli	??	??	??	??	● Giant Co Tianjin ● Xinri Shandong	● Cannon-dale ● Merlin	● Giant Man Ltd (Taiwan)
Derby brand market shares (%)	14%	<1%	1–2%	<1%	1–2%	<1%	1–2%	0%	0%	??	??
% volume – e-bikes	2.6	1.5	2.1	1.5	7.0	1.0	1.8	3.0	54.0	1.7	20.0
Total e-bikes market (1,000)	117	52	71	30	98	132	500	300	15,000	300	18,000
Market value (€m)											
Total value (€m) – all bicycles (average price: €400 per unit – except for China)	1,800	1,400	1,360	800	560	5,280	11,200	4,000	5,600 (average price: €200 per unit)	7,200	36,000
Total value – e-bikes (€m) (average price: €1,500 per unit – except for China)	175	78	96	45	147	198	750	450	4,500 (average price: €300 per unit)	450	9,000
% value – e-bikes	9.7	5.5	7.1	5.6	26.0	3.8	6.7	11.3	80.4	6.3	25.0

TABLE 1.2 Total European and world bicycle market plus e-bikes (2008)

Source: www.bike-eu.com (market reports), China Sourcing Reports (Bicycles)

Currently, Derby mainly distributes its branded bicycles through local market networks of independent bicycle dealers, as well as through national retailers. However, most of its distribution of bicycles goes through specialty bicycle stores.

Questions

1 What are Derby's most important steps in marketing planning?
2 Should Derby enter the international e-bikes market?
3 If Derby enters the international e-bikes market, what are the key success factors in this market?

Sources: adapted from www.bike-eu.com market reports; Global Bicycle Stats www.quickrelease.tv/?p=279; www.bikebiz.com/news/29247/Guardian-profiles-Gouldthorp; www.guardian.co.uk/business/2007/nov/23/cycling; www.tectrends.com/tectrends/article/00169044.html

CHAPTER

02

Assessing the internal marketing situation

❖ LEARNING OBJECTIVES

After studying this chapter you should be able to do the following:

- ❖ Describe the difference between the market orientation view (MOV) and the resource-based view (RBV).
- ❖ Discuss the connection between MOV/RBV and market driven/market driving.

- ❖ Explain the 'competitive triangle'.
- ❖ Describe and discuss the drivers for customers' 'perceived value' and 'relative costs'.

2.1 Introduction

The foundation of any marketing plan is the company's mission and vision statement, which answers the question, 'What business are we in and where should we go?' Business mission definition profoundly affects the company's long-run resource allocation, profitability and survival. The mission statement is based on a careful analysis of benefits sought by present and potential customers, and analysis of existing and anticipated environmental conditions.

When examining internal *strengths* and *weaknesses*, the marketing manager should focus on organizational resources, company or brand image, employee capabilities and available technology.

When examining external *opportunities* and *threats*, the marketing manager must analyse aspects of the marketing environment. This process is called environmental scanning – the collection and interpretation of information about forces, events and relationships in the external environment that may affect the future of the organization or the implementation of the marketing plan. Environmental scanning helps identify market opportunities and threats, and provides guidelines for the design of marketing strategy. The six macro-environmental forces studied most often are social, demographic, economic, technological, political and legal, and competitive. These forces are examined in Chapter 3.

The matching of internal strengths and weaknesses with external opportunities and threats automatically leads us to the two important views that we discuss in this chapter:

1   the Market Orientation View (MOV) – outside-in perspective (see Sec. 2.2)
2   the Resource-Based View (RBV) – inside-out perspective (see Sec. 2.3).

2.2 Market orientation view (MOV)

The term market (or marketing) orientation generally refers to the implementation of the marketing concept. Kohli and Jaworski (1990: 130) define market orientation in the following terms:

> 66 A market orientation entails (1) one or more departments engaging in activities geared toward developing an understanding of customers' current and future needs and the factors affecting them, (2) sharing of this understanding across departments, and (3) the various departments engaging in activities designed to meet select customer needs. In other words, a market orientation refers to the organization-wide generation, dissemination, and responsiveness to market intelligence. 99

One key is achieving an understanding of the market and the customer throughout the company, and building the capability for responsiveness to market changes. The real customer focus and responsiveness of the company is the context in which marketing strategy is built and implemented.

Another issue is that the marketing process should be seen as interfunctional and cross-disciplinary, and not simply the responsibility of the marketing department. This is the real value of adopting the process perspective on marketing, which is becoming more widely adopted by large organizations.

In MOV, it is also clear that a deep understanding of the competition in the market from the customer's perspective is critical. Viewing the product or service from the customer's viewpoint is often difficult, but without such a perspective a marketing strategy is highly vulnerable to attack from unsuspected sources of competition.

In essence, market orientation refers to the way an organization implements the marketing concept. In principle, this three-component view of market orientation (generation of, dissemination of and responsiveness to market intelligence) makes it possible to diagnose a company's level of market orientation, pinpoint specific deficiencies and design interventions tailored to the particular needs of an organization. It should be emphasized that a market orientation is not the exclusive responsibility of a marketing department but, rather, is a company-wide mode of operation.

Research suggests that market orientation is related positively to business performance (Narver and Slater, 1990). Further, it is likely to be strongly related to performance under conditions of high market turbulence, technological stability, strong competition and a weak economic environment. A market orientation yields higher customer satisfaction and repeat business, and appears to increase employees' commitment to their companies. In seeking to implement a market orientation, these authors suggest that the commitment of top management to the idea is key, particularly in reminding employees that it is critical for them to be sensitive and responsive to market developments. In addition, market orientation seems to require a certain level of risk tolerance on the part of senior managers and a willingness to accept an occasional failure as a normal part of transacting business. The nature of interdepartmental dynamics also plays a very important role: interdepartmental conflict reduces market orientation, while interdepartmental connectedness facilitates it. Moreover, the role of market-based reward systems and decentralized decision-making in engendering market orientation is strong, suggesting that reward systems should take into account an individual's ability to sense and respond to market needs. A market orientation flourishes in corporate environments in which continuous learning and improvement are encouraged. Thus, the concept of market orientation is likely come to full fruition only when it is enveloped in the learning organization (O'Driscoll et al., 2001).

2.3 Resource-based view (RBV)

The traditional market orientation literature emphasizes the superior performance of companies with high-quality, organization-wide generation and sharing of market intelligence leading to responsiveness to market needs; the RBV suggests that high performance strategy is dependent primarily on historically developed resource endowments.

Resource-based marketing essentially seeks a long-term fit between the requirements of the market and the abilities of the organization to compete in it. This does not mean that the resources of the organization are seen as fixed and static. Far from it: market requirements evolve over time and the resource profile of the organization must be continuously developed to enable it to continue to compete, and indeed to enable it to take advantage of new opportunities. The essential factor, however, is that opportunities are seized where the organization has an existing or potential advantage through its resource base, rather than just pursued *ad hoc.*

Why do organizations exist? The simple answer for commercial organizations may be 'to earn returns on their investments for the shareholders and owners of those organizations'. For non-commercial organizations, such as charities, faith-based organizations, public services, and so on, the answer may lie in the desire to serve specific communities. However, organizations, both commercial and non-profit, are rarely driven by such simple goals. Often there are many demands, sometimes complementary, sometimes competing, that drive decisions.

In the context of commercial organizations, a number of primary stakeholders can be identified. These include shareholders and owners, managers, employees, customers and suppliers. While the MOV discussed above serves to place customers high in the priority ranking, the reality for most organizations will be a complex blend of considerations of all relevant stakeholders.

The RBV of the organization discussed above implies that the first stage in assessing strengths and weaknesses should be to conduct an audit of the resources available to the company, including both the tangible and intangible (see Fig. 2.1). The types of resources and capabilities listed earlier can be simplified as follows (Collis and Montgomery, 2008).

- *Technical resources*: a key resource in many organizations, and one becoming increasingly important in a world of rapidly changing technology, is technical skill. This involves the ability of the organization to develop new processes and products, through research and development, which can be utilized in the marketplace.
- *Financial standing*: a second important resource is the organization's financial standing. This will dictate, to a large extent, its scope for action and ability to put its strategies into operation. An organization of sound financial standing can raise capital from outside to finance ventures. In deciding marketing strategy a major consideration is often what financial resources can or cannot be put into the programme.
- *Managerial skills*: managerial skills in the widest possible sense are a further resource of the organization. The experience of managers and the way in which they discharge their duties and motivate their staff have a major impact on corporate performance.
- *Organization*: the very structure of the organization can be a valuable asset or resource. Some structures, such as the matrix organization, are designed to facilitate wide use of skills throughout the organization. This system has proved useful in focusing control at the brand level, encouraging a co-ordinated marketing mix and facilitating a flexible, rapid response to changing circumstances. It is not without its drawbacks, however. The product management system can lead to responsibility without authority, conflicts between product managers within the same organization, and the syndrome where managers move on to their next product management job having maximized short-term returns at the expense of longer-term market position.
- *Information systems*: the information and planning systems in operation also provide a valuable resource. For example, those organizations such as banks dealing in foreign currency speculation rely heavily on up-to-the-minute and accurate information systems. New technological developments, such as electronic point-of-sale scanning, allow data to be collected and processed in a much shorter time than was the case a few years ago. Those organizations with the systems in place to cope with the massive increases in data that such newer collection procedures are creating will be in a stronger position to take advantage of the opportunities afforded.

A resource-based model for sustainable competitive advantage in a global environment is presented in Fig. 2.1. It adopts the basic logic of earlier models that link resources, competitive advantage and performance (Day and Wensley, 1988) but extends this earlier work by demonstrating the richness of the resource pool that is potentially available to an organization operating in a global environment. In the literature generally, resources have

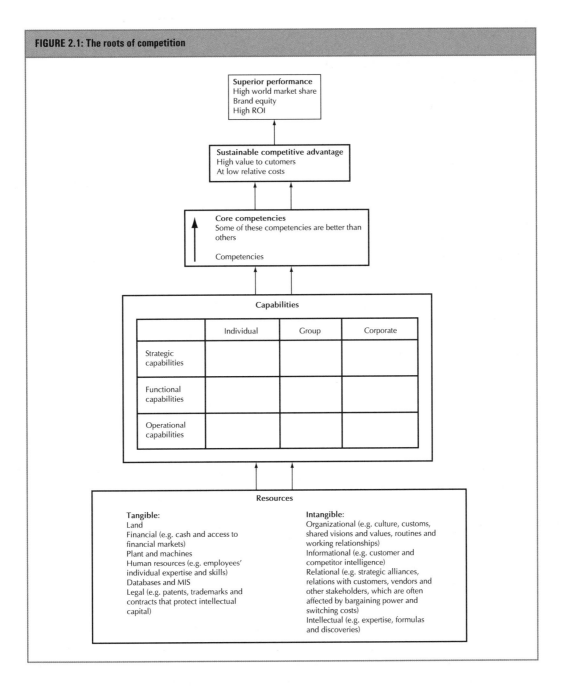

FIGURE 2.1: The roots of competition

Superior performance
High world market share
Brand equity
High ROI

Sustainable competitive advantage
High value to cutomers
At low relative costs

Core competencies
Some of these competencies are better than others

Competencies

Capabilities

	Individual	Group	Corporate
Strategic capabilities			
Functional capabilities			
Operational capabilities			

Resources

Tangible:
Land
Financial (e.g. cash and access to financial markets)
Plant and machines
Human resources (e.g. employees' individual expertise and skills)
Databases and MIS
Legal (e.g. patents, trademarks and contracts that protect intellectual capital)

Intangible:
Organizational (e.g. culture, customs, shared visions and values, routines and working relationships)
Informational (e.g. customer and competitor intelligence)
Relational (e.g. strategic alliances, relations with customers, vendors and other stakeholders, which are often affected by bargaining power and switching costs)
Intellectual (e.g. expertise, formulas and discoveries)

been categorized on the basis of barriers to duplication, and a broad distinction is made between assets and capabilities. Assets, in turn, can be thought of as being either tangible or intangible. Tangible assets refer to the fixed or current assets of an organization, which have a relatively long fixed-run capacity and include plant, equipment, land, other capital goods and stocks, debtors, and bank deposits. Intangible assets include an organization's intellectual property, its corporate reputation and its brand equity; these have relatively unlimited capacity and can be used in-house, rented or sold. Capabilities have been described using a variety of terms, including skills, invisible assets and intermediate goods.

Resources are broken down into two fundamental categories:

1 tangible resources
2 intangible resources.

Tangible resources include those factors containing financial or physical value as measured by the organization's balance sheet. Intangible resources, on the other hand, include those factors that are non-physical (or non-financial) in nature and are rarely, if at all, included in the organization's balance sheet.

Intangible resources essentially fall into two categories: assets and skills (or capabilities). If the intangible resource is something that the organization 'has', it is an asset. If the intangible resource is something that the organization 'does', it is a skill and it is being turned into a capability. However, the distinction between assets and capabilities may not be so easy to make.

Intangible assets such as copyrights, patents, registered designs and trademarks are all afforded legal protection through property rights. Such legal protection can create barriers to competitive duplication. Other forms of intellectual property include held-in-secret technology. Held-in-secret technology – technology developed specifically to fit the organization's unique strategy and particular business model – can lead to unique, socially complex and context-specific assets that may be difficult for competitors to understand let alone duplicate. Given their legally enforceable protection or held-in-secret standing, intellectual property assets are argued to be more difficult to duplicate than tangible resources.

According to Fig. 2.1 capabilities can be seen as strategic, functional or operational.

- *Strategic capabilities* underpin the definition of direction for the organization. They include issues such as the dominant logic or orientation guiding management (which will strongly influence strategic direction), the ability of the organization to learn (to acquire, assimilate and act on information), and the ability of senior managers to manage the implementation of strategy.
- *Functional capabilities* lie in the execution of functional tasks. These include marketing capabilities, financial management capabilities and operations management capabilities.
- *Operational capabilities* are concerned with undertaking individual line tasks, such as operating machinery, the application of information systems and completion of order processing.

Second, capabilities may lie with individuals, with groups or at the corporate level.

- *Individual competencies* are the skills and abilities of individuals within the organization. They include the ability of the individual to analyse critically and assess a given situation (whether this is a chief executive officer (CEO) assessing a strategic problem or the shop floor worker assessing the impact of a machine failure).
- *Group competencies* are where individual abilities come together in teams or *ad hoc*, informal, task-related teams. While the abilities of individuals are important, so too is their ability to work together constructively.

- *Corporate-level competencies* relate to the abilities of the organization as a whole to undertake strategic, functional or operational tasks. This could include the ability of the organization to internalize learning, so that critical information is held not just by individuals but is shared throughout the organization.

There is always a risk that such lists are arbitrary and simplistic when we come to study a real organization, but perhaps the most fundamental importance of the RBV of the organization is that it underlines the fact that many important resources and capabilities are created through its history; they are the result of enduring accumulation and learning processes. Often they cannot be changed easily or rapidly. This approach should enrich our understanding of an organization's potential in the marketplace, and can be linked to the issue of market orientation through the competitive positioning of the organization (i.e. choice of market targets and pursuit of competitive advantage).

The RBV can also be linked to the core competencies issue considered below. They are different approaches to a similar issue – understanding what a company is capable of achieving by exploiting its capabilities in the marketplace. In recent years much attention has been devoted to identifying and understanding the 'core competencies' of organizations. The need to identify the 'distinctive competency' of an organization is underlined by a very influential analysis of successful international businesses by Prahalad and Hamel (1990), who argue that a company is likely to be genuinely world class at perhaps five or six activities, and superior performance will come from focusing on those to the exclusion of others. The late 1990s saw much effort to refocus major organizations on to their core activities.

Prahalad and Hamel (1990) define core competencies as the underlying skills, technologies and competencies that can be combined in different ways to create the next generation of products and services:

- at 3M a core competency in sticky tape has led the organization into markets as diverse as Post-it notes, magnetic tape, photographic film, pressure-sensitive tapes and coated abrasives
- Black & Decker's competency is in small electrical motors, which can be used to power many tools and appliances
- for Canon the core competencies are its skills and technologies in optics, imaging and microprocessor controls, which have enabled it to survive and thrive in markets as diverse as copiers, laser printers, cameras and image scanners.

Three tests are suggested by Prahalad and Hamel (1990) for identifying core competencies.

1 A core competency should be *difficult for competitors to copy*. Clearly, a competency that can be defended against competitors has greater value than a competency that other organizations can share.
2 A core competency provides *potential access* to a wide variety of markets. Competencies in display systems are needed, for example, to enable a company to compete in a number of different markets, including flat-screen TVs, calculators, laptop or notebook computers, mobile phones, and so on.
3 A core competency should make a *significant contribution* to the benefits the customer derives from using the ultimate product or service. In other words, the competency is important where it is a significant determinant of customer satisfaction and benefit.

Note that these requirements are essentially the same as those emerging from the earlier RBV literature to define resources capable of creating sustainable competitive advantage. Added to these three characteristics a further useful test is whether the competency can be combined with other skills and capabilities to create unique value for customers – the grouping of competencies discussed earlier. It could be, for example, that a competency does not fulfil the above criteria, but when combined with other competencies, it is an essential ingredient in defining the organization's uniqueness. Put another way: what would happen if we did not have that competency?

Prahalad and Hamel (1990) argue that the critical management ability for the future will be to identify, cultivate and exploit the core competencies that make growth possible. The argument about core competencies is compelling, and (according to Prahalad and Hamel) it is certainly driving major corporate changes, such as:

- the emergence of a network of strategic alliances, where each partner brings its core competency into play to build a market offering
- the demerger and sale of non-core activities and brands
- organizational changes away from SBUs and towards a new 'strategic architecture'.

However, we should bear in mind that strategy is about more than simply choosing to focus on a few core competencies (Porter, 1985).

It is very easy to be impressed with excellence in the way a company performs an activity or produces a product or service, and to believe this to be a core competency. This must be tested against the market before we accept it as a foundation for our competitive positioning. It may be helpful to identify core competencies but then to see which of them are 'differentiating capabilities' (i.e. which produce competitive advantage).

Activities are not the same as competencies: 'quality products' and 'marketing strength' are not competencies; they are attributes emerging from core competencies. In the 1980s General Electric focused on marketing to build a strong brand image but lost out to Panasonic (Matsushita), which understood that excellence in components and assembly had a greater impact on value added for the customer. Honda's core competency is in small engine manufacture. It has moved from an initial position in motorbikes and transferred its small engine expertise into small cars, pumps, lawnmowers and other products where engines are the significant value-added element.

Avoid lists: by definition, core competencies should be no more than a handful of activities. Most successful organizations have targeted one or two key activities – their identification is a major management issue.

Achieve management consensus: if competencies are to be nurtured and shared widely in the organization as the basis for strategy, then management must agree what they are and act accordingly. It was noted earlier that this might not be straightforward.

Leverage core competencies: it is not enough to identify core competencies and agree what they are. This is pointless unless they underpin all strategic decision-making (Trott et al., 2009).

Share core competencies outside the organization: focusing on core competencies may well favour the use of collaboration to link to the value-adding competencies of other organizations. Indeed, it may be logical for organizations to share their specialist expertise with others, a good example being the automotive sector. A similar approach is seen in the intra-organization transfer of best practices.

As shown in the upper part of Fig. 2.1, sustainable competitive advantage is one thing that cannot be copied by the competition. Dell Computer is a good example of a company that has a sustainable competitive advantage. Others include Rolex (high-quality watches), Nordstrom department stores (service) and Ryanair (low price).

2.4 Market driven versus market driving

The market-driven approach is derived from the construct and principles of 'market orientation' that are in many ways synonymous with 'market driven'. However, instead of *following* the requests of the customer and adapting offerings, organizations sometimes need to undertake a more proactive approach in order to reshape, educate and lead the customer or, more generally, the market. Academicians define this kind of orientation as 'driving market' or 'market driving'.

The primary differences between a market-driving philosophy and the existing paradigms of market-driven behaviour, customer leading and product pioneering are summarized in Table 2.1.

	Market driven	Market driving
General	Company responds to act within the framework and constraints of existing market structure and characteristics	Company can and will act to induce changes in the market structure and changes in the behaviour of the players (customers and competitors)
Customer orientation	Adaptation	Be at the cutting edge of new customer needs
Identifying, analysing and answering to the customer	● Predict which technologies are likely to be successful given consumer needs and preferences ● Respond to market structure	● Shape customers' behaviour proactively ● Pioneer ● Predict how customer needs and market boundaries evolve with various technological futures
Competitor orientation	● Continuous benchmarking ● Imitating	● Shape the market structure proactively ● Identify and develop difficult-to-imitate internal and external competencies ● Discontinuous disruption

TABLE 2.1 Market-driven versus market-driving perspectives

As previously suggested, market-driven behaviour relies heavily on exploitative learning, which occurs within *existing* market boundaries, and hence is primarily regarded as a reactive rather than a proactive stance. The customer-leading philosophy, also known as proactive market orientation, is essentially an extension of market-driven activity. Customer leading makes use of the untapped market space uncovered by exploratory learning. Organizations utilizing this approach are more likely to introduce innovations that radically change customer behaviours and preferences.

Two contributions have recently been put forward that focus on internal and external market-driving issues. First, Jaworski et al. (2000) discuss how market driving may be achieved through influencing the fundamental structure of a market and/or the behaviours of key players. Second, Kumar et al. (2000) advance an analysis of intra-organization behaviours that facilitate market driving. These two contributions require further discussion.

Jaworski et al. (2000) were among the first to initiate the market-driving approach based on the consideration that the current literature has an unbalanced focus on preserving the status quo (i.e. on existing customer attribute preferences and current market structure). Jaworski et al. (2000) focus their analysis on the strategic business unit (SBU) level and construct a conceptual framework through plotting the market orientation approach against two dimensions of market structure and market behaviour.

A market-driven approach occurs where market behaviour and structure are 'given' (i.e. where existing market structures and behaviours are accepted by the organization). However, market driving is possible when organizations 'shape' market structure through altering the composition of market players and/or when they 'shape' market behaviour through varying the behaviour of market players; for example, shaping customer behaviour by identifying, advancing and exploiting customer-valued product attributes previously overlooked by other players (see Fig. 2.2).

FIGURE 2.2: Market driven versus market driving strategy

Market driven Market structure and market behaviour are given		Market driving Market structure and market behaviour can be shaped

Market orientation view (MOV) ←——————————————→ Resource-based view (RBV)

A market-driven approach is defined as 'the activities of learning, understanding, and responding to stakeholder perceptions and behaviours within a given market structure', while a market-driving approach is defined as 'changing the composition and/or roles of players in a market and/or the behaviour(s) of players in the market' (Jaworski et al., 2000: 45). Market driving is argued to be a 'multiplicative function', with those organizations that influence more players or affect market structure more significantly being viewed as *more* market driven. In this respect, market-driving approaches are similar to market-driven approaches in that they are presented as a continuous variable.

Exhibit 2.1: *Reuters' core competency is eroded*

Reuters is a 151-year-old British institution that is experiencing some difficulties. The group, best known as the world's biggest international news and TV agency, makes more than 90 per cent of its revenue from the financial services business, to which it provides its trademark data-packed screens. The 2002/3 downturn in banking and finance hit Reuters hard. Meanwhile, US rival Bloomberg and Canadian player Thomson Financial have both eaten into Reuters' 'core competency' as the most authoritative source of information for business. Consequently, in February 2003 Reuters announced that it planned to cut 3000 jobs over the next three years.

Suddenly, Reuters' brand value, which most companies would kill for – a 151-year heritage, a voice of authority, a solid Britishness – has begun to appear detrimental. Tradition seems like stuffiness, authority like inertia and Britishness like a colonial hangover.

How, then, should Reuters go about redefining its business and its own competencies?

Source: adapted from Chandiramani (2003)

2.5 Major sources of competitive advantage: value and costs

Companies producing offerings with a higher perceived value and/or lower relative costs (compared to competitors) are said to have a competitive advantage and thus win the competitive game. The 'high perceived value' advantage can be considered as differentiation, but the elements of this must be evaluated from a comparative customer perspective. The word 'perceived' is used to emphasize the fact that value is a subjective evaluation rather than a direct measure of utility. This involves an element of judgement and is sometimes seen as irrational: it is how customers themselves rate the offering in relation to other competitive products or services that is critical in a purchase decision.

The prime consideration of the value of any resource to an organization lies in the answer to the question 'Does this resource contribute to creating value for customers?' Value creation may be direct, such as through the benefits conveyed by superior technology, better service, meaningful brand differentiation and ready availability. The resources that contribute to these benefits (technology deployed, skilled and motivated personnel, brand name and reputation, and distribution coverage) create value for customers as soon as they are employed. Other resources may, however, have an indirect impact on value for customers. Effective cost control systems, for example, are not valuable to customers in and of themselves. They add value for customers only when they translate into lower prices charged, or via the ability of the company to offer additional customer benefits through the cost savings achieved.

The value of a resource in creating customer value must be assessed relative to the resources of competitors. For example, a strong brand name such as Nike on sportswear may convey more value than a less well-known brand. In other words, for the resource to contribute to sustainable competitive advantage, it must serve to distinguish the company's offerings from those of competitors (Hooley et al., 2004). The 'value' of a product or service should be seen in relation to the customer's cost of obtaining the product/service and the cost of ownership.

These costs will include such issues as the buying price of an offering compared to the price of a competitive offering. These elements might be modified by the perceived cost of obtaining and cost of ownership. The way components are assessed and compared could vary from one customer to another. It is possible to 'delight' customers by exceeding their expectations.

The 'perceived value' (compared to price), together with the relative cost, is illustrated in Fig. 2.3. The underlying drivers for 'perceived value' (value drivers) are also listed in this figure. These drivers are discussed in more detail below.

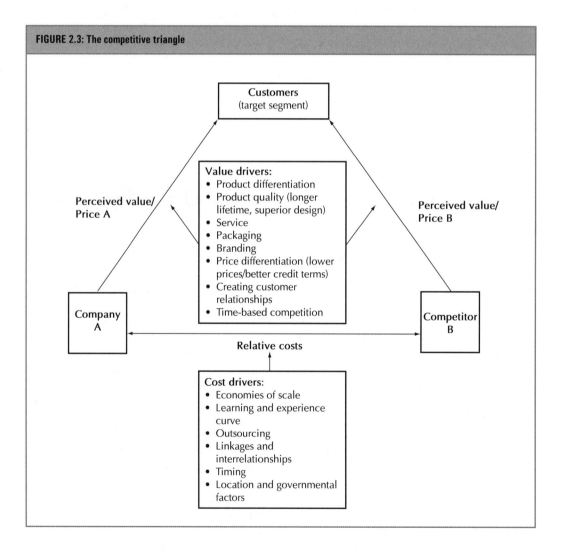

FIGURE 2.3: The competitive triangle

2.5.1 Cost drivers

Economies of scale

Economies of scale are perhaps the single most effective cost driver in many industries. Scale economies stem from doing things more efficiently or differently in volume. In addition, sheer size can help in creating purchasing leverage to secure cheaper and/or better-quality (i.e. less waste) raw materials and securing them in times of limited availability.

There are, however, limits to scale economies. Size can bring with it an added complexity that can lead to diseconomies. For most operations there is an optimum size above and below which inefficiencies occur.

The effects of economies of scale are often more pronounced in the manufacturing sector than in services. While manufacturing operations such as assembly lines can benefit through scale, the advantages to service organizations such as advertising agencies are less obvious.

Capacity utilization has been shown to have a major impact on unit costs. The profit impacts of marketing strategies (PIMS) study has demonstrated a clear positive association between utilization and return on investment.

Learning and experience curves

Further cost reductions may be achieved through learning and experience effects. *Learning* refers to increases in efficiency that are possible at a given level of scale through an employee having performed the necessary tasks many times before.

Experience curves tell us that costs decline at a predictable rate as experience with a product increases. The experience curve effect encompasses a broad range of manufacturing, marketing and administrative costs. Experience curves reflect learning by doing, technological advances and economies of scale. Organizations such as Airbus and Texas Instruments use historical experience curves as a basis for prediction and setting prices. Experience curves allow management to forecast costs and set prices based on anticipated costs as opposed to current costs.

The Boston Consulting Group (BCG) extended the experience curve beyond manufacturing and looked at the increased efficiency that was possible in all aspects of the business (e.g. in marketing, advertising and selling) through experience. BCG estimated empirically that, in many industries, costs reduced by approximately 15–20 per cent each time cumulative production (a measure of experience) doubled. This finding suggests that companies with larger market share will, by definition, have a cost advantage through experience, assuming that all companies are operating on the same experience curve. This is, incidentally, why relative market share is used as a proxy for cash generation in the BCG matrix.

Experience can be brought into the company by hiring experienced staff, and be enhanced through training. Conversely, competitors may poach experience by luring away skilled staff.

Outsourcing

Labour cost can be an important component of total costs in low-skill, labour-intensive industries such as product assembly and apparel manufacturing. Many US and European manufacturers outsource production activities to Mexico, eastern Europe and China in order to achieve cheaper manufacturing costs. Increasing numbers of companies are also outsourcing activities such as software programming and other labour-intensive jobs to India.

Linkages and interrelationships

External linkages with suppliers of factor inputs or distributors of the firm's final products can also result in lower costs. Recent developments in just-in-time (JIT) manufacturing and delivery can have a significant impact on stockholding costs and work in progress. Beyond the cost equation, however, the establishment of closer working links has far wider marketing implications. For JIT to work effectively requires a very close working relationship between buyer and supplier. This often means an interchange of information, a meshing of forecasting and scheduling, and the building of a long-term relationship. This in turn helps to create high switching costs (the costs of seeking supply elsewhere) and hence barriers to competitive entry.

Interrelationships with other SBUs in the overall corporate portfolio can help to share experience and gain economies of scale in functional activities (such as marketing research, research and technology (R&D), quality control, ordering and purchasing).

Timing

Timing, though not always controllable, can lead to cost advantages. Often the first mover in an industry can gain cost advantages by securing prime locations, cheap or good-quality raw materials and/or technological leadership. Second movers can often benefit from exploiting newer technology to leapfrog first-mover positions.

Location and governmental factors

The final cost drivers are location (geographic location to take advantage of lower distribution, assembly, raw materials or energy costs) and institutional factors such as government regulations (e.g. larger lorries on the roads can reduce distribution costs but at other environmental and social costs). The sensitivity of governments to lobbyists and pressure groups will dictate the ability of the company to exercise institutional cost drivers.

Sometimes, governments may provide assistance to target industries with grants and interest-free loans. Government assistance enabled Japanese semiconductor manufacturers to become global leaders.

2.5.2 Value drivers

Product differentiation

Product differentiation seeks to increase the value of the product or service to the customer. Levitt (1986) suggested four levels of a product: core offer, expected offer, augmented offer and potential offer. Differentiation is possible at all four levels.

1 *Core offer* (*basic offering*): a different way of satisfying the same basic want or need. It is typically created by a change in the technology, the application of innovation.
2 *Expected offer*: additional benefits normally provided with the core offer. This often involves improvements on expected features such as warranties, packaging quality or service (e.g. it could mean offering a lifetime guarantee on audiotape, as Scotch did).
3 *Augmented offer*: additional benefits not normally provided, but serving to differentiate from competitors' offers. These could be credit facilities, additional features, branding, delivery, and so on.

4   *Potential offer*: anything else that could (in future) be used to differentiate from existing competitors' offerings. These features can, potentially, attract and hold customers.

In most highly competitive markets, any breakthrough or development is soon spotted and often copied quickly, and many skill-based augmentations are easy for competitors to imitate. For this reason, many advantages last for only a very short period of time. If an advantage is offset by a competitor, what was once an augmentation by one supplier can become an expected feature demanded from all suppliers. This illustrates one aspect of migration between the levels of a total product. Thus, a continuing migration might take place, with features moving in from the outer to the inner ring of Fig. 2.4.

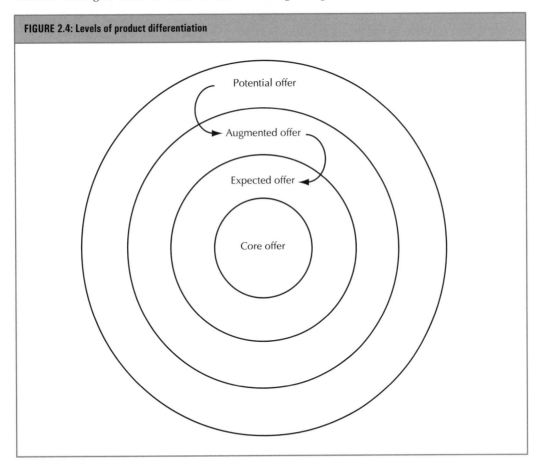

FIGURE 2.4: Levels of product differentiation

2.5.3 Product quality and service

For manufactured products, quality can include durability, product features and superior design. For services it often comes down to the tangible elements of the service, the reliability and responsiveness of the service provider, promptness, assurance provided, and the empathy and caring attention (willingness to help) demonstrated.

For a marketer it will be obvious that quality (satisfying customer needs) is a *necessary* objective, but it may not be *sufficient* to gain a sale or ensure repeat business. There will be certain levels of quality that are expected as 'order qualifying'. These have to be met in order to be considered in the marketplace, but this is the minimum acceptable level and does nothing to contribute towards achieving a competitive advantage. As discussed in previous chapters, customers will assess the comparative value of competitive offerings and will decide based on their own perceptions and personal frames of reference.

Quality programmes that lead towards the delivery of 'superior' customer value are the only ones that really count. These could be the result of including real tangible and intangible features that enhance the benefits of the offering. The ultimate test, however, is the perception by a customer that an offering not only meets their needs, but also does so in a way that offers the greatest *added* value to them.

It is important, too, to remember that a quality programme of service delivery cannot save a poor product. While the activities that surround the promotion of an offering can sometimes dominate at the point of sale, the true test is whether the product/service meets the customer's basic needs, both current and over the life of the product. This will be the ultimate test and will be remembered long after the clever advertising or the low price is forgotten (Adcock, 2000).

2.5.4 Packaging

Packaging can also be used to differentiate a product. Packaging has five main functions, each of which can be used as a basis for differentiation (Adcock, 2000).

1   Packaging *protects* the product during transit and prior to consumption to ensure consistent quality (e.g. the use of foil packs for potato crisps to ensure freshness).
2   Packaging *stores* the product, and hence can be used to extend shelf life or facilitate physical storage (e.g. Tetra Paks for fruit juice and other beverages).
3   Packaging *facilitates use* of the product (e.g. applicator packs for floor cleaners, wine boxes, domestic liquid soap dispensers).
4   Packaging helps *create an image* for the product through its visual impact, quality of design, illustration of uses, and so on.
5   Packaging helps *promote* the product through eye-catching, unusual colours and shapes, and so on.

2.5.5 Branding

A brand name is an indication of what to expect from a product – a quality statement of a value-for-money signal. It is often the feeling among managers that the ability of most companies to copy the tangible aspects of competitors' actions, such as production method or application of technology, and to replicate service levels, will mean that these offer little in the way of sustainable competitive advantage.

A brand, however, is an intangible, which develops out of exchanges with customers, and is impossible for competitors to copy. Therefore, it is able to distinguish a specific offer, separating it from others in the same product class. If branding is considered from the perspective of a potential customer, it can be seen as a way of helping buyers to choose between different offerings and to determine those that best meet given needs. The ability to identify a particular brand thus makes the purchase decision quicker and easier, and offers some reassurance by reducing the risk of unfamiliar selection.

A sustainable competitive advantage is a function of the speed with which competitors can imitate a leading company's strategy and plans.

The rate of technological and market change is now so fast and products so transient that customers find security and continuity in the least tangible of the company's assets: the reputation of its brands and company name.

2.5.6 Price differentiation

Lower price as a means of differentiation can be a successful basis for strategy only when the company enjoys a cost advantage or where there are barriers to competing companies with a lower cost structure competing at a lower price. Without a cost advantage a price war can be a disastrous course to follow. Premium pricing is generally only possible where the product or service has actual or perceived advantages to the customer and therefore is often used in conjunction with or to reinforce a differentiated product. In general, the greater the degree of product or service differentiation the more scope there is for premium pricing. Where there is little other ground for differentiation, price competition becomes stronger and cost advantages assume greater importance.

2.5.7 Creating customer relationships

Creating closer bonds with customers through enhanced service can help establish a position in the market that is easier to defend. As suggested above, a major advantage of JIT manufacturing systems is that they require closer links between supplier and buyer. As buyers and suppliers become more enmeshed so it becomes more difficult for newcomers to enter.

Creating switching costs (the costs associated with moving from one supplier to another) is a further way in which customer linkages can be enhanced. This enhancement of linkages with customers makes it less likely they will shop around for other sources of supply.

2.5.8 Time-based competition

Competitive advantage and how one gains it have changed much over the years. In less-developed markets advantage can be gained through simple market mechanisms such as achieving distribution where none existed before. As markets mature, competitive advantage becomes increasingly difficult to attain. Many factors contribute to this, including increases in the sophistication of competitors and consumers, consumer mobility, distribution intensity, and flow of product and market information. At a macro level, such things as the structural nature of industries, networking, alliances and governmental interventions contribute to difficulties in achieving competitive advantage in a mature market.

In essence, time-based competition focuses on gaining advantage by being faster than competitors – faster in responding to market changes, faster with new product development and introductions, faster in integrating new technology into products, and faster in distribution and customer service. Success stories of time-based competitors are numerous; for example, the Japanese used time-based competition as a fundamental component of their automobile manufacturing strategy, which caught US companies off guard. Japanese car manufacturers reduced new car design time to two and a half to three years as compared to Detroit's four to over six years. Being twice as fast resulted in the Japanese having fresher designs that embodied more current and sophisticated technology.

The fundamental ingredients of time-based competition are low-cost variety and fast response time. Companies using this strategy concentrate on compressing the time required to manufacture and distribute their products and cutting the time required to develop and introduce new products. By doing this companies can offer a broader product line, cover more market segments and rapidly increase the technological sophistication of their products. The benefits of these practices can be generically expressed as gains in faster *response time*.

In essence, time-based competition is a customer-focused strategy. Speed and variety are the means by which a company can do more for its clients. However, succeeding at this requires a co-ordinated company effort. A time-based competitor develops the high degree of internal responsiveness and co-ordination among different parts of the company that allows it to discern differences among key customers and customize the products and services delivered to each. Thus, the ultimate purpose of the time-based competitor is not maximizing speed and variety, but owning the customer (Stalk and Hout, 1990; Johnson et al., 2000).

SUMMARY

The essence of Chapter 2's internal analysis is competitive advantage. Over time, as markets have developed and evolved, achieving competitive advantage has required an increasingly sophisticated response. Decades ago competitive advantage could be achieved through one product or market variable such as price or distribution control. Today, competitive advantage has taken on a multidimensional character – effective competitive advantage requires a co-ordinated combination of several product and market variables. Further, potential ingredients in competitive advantage have broadened to include such intangibles as time and information.

Companies need to build their own competitive advantages rather than copy those of a competitor. The sources of tomorrow's competitive advantages are the skills and assets of the organization. Assets include patents, copyrights, locations, and equipment and technology that are superior to those of the competition. Skills are functions such as customer service and promotion that the company performs better than its competitors.

Each of the activities within the value chain, the primary activities and the support functions, can be used to add value to the ultimate product or service.

The traditional MOV, or the outside-in perspective, emphasizes the customers and places their needs and wants high in the priority ranking.

Termed the RBV, or the inside-out perspective, of the company or the focus on 'core competencies', this new approach suggests that performance is essentially driven by the resource profile of the company and that the source of superior performance lies in the possession and deployment of distinctive, hard-to-imitate or protected resources.

Compared to its competitors, the company that is producing offerings with a higher perceived value (compared to the price) and/or lower relative costs is said to win the 'competitive game'.

The drivers for a better relative cost position are:

- economies of scale (high volume)
- learning and experience curve
- outsourcing

- linkages and interrelationships
- timing
- location and governmental factors.

The drivers for a better 'perceived value' position are:

- product differentiation (more features)
- product quality (longer lifetime, superior design)
- service
- packaging
- branding
- price differentiation (lower prices/better credit terms)
- creating customer relationships
- time-based competition.

Questions for discussion

1 Explain the difference between the RBV and the MOV.
2 What does it mean to be 'market driven' or 'market driving'?
3 List the major sources for creating organizational competitiveness.
4 Explain the idea behind the 'competitive triangle'.
5 Which are the main value and cost drivers in the 'competitive triangle'?

References

Adcock, A. (2000) *Marketing Strategies for Competitive Advantage*. Chichester: Wiley.

Chandiramani, R. (2003) What must Reuters do to battle leaner rivals? *Marketing*, 27 February: 13.

Collis, D.J. and Montgomery C.A. (2008) Competing on resources, *Harvard Business Review*, July–August: 140–50.

Day, G. and Wensley, R. (1988) Assessing advantage: a framework for diagnosing competitive superiority, *Journal of Marketing*, 52: 1–20.

Hooley, G., Saunders, J. and Piercy, N. (2004) *Marketing Strategy and Competitive Positioning*, 3rd edn. London: Financial Times/Prentice Hall.

Jaworski, B., Kohli, A. and Sahay, A. (2000) Market-driven versus driving markets, *Journal of Academy of Marketing Science*, 28(1): 45–54.

Johnson, J., Busbin, J. and Bertsch, T. (2000) Uses and repercussions of the Internet on global market entry strategies, *Journal of Global Competitiveness*, American Society for Competitiveness, Spring: 5–15.

Kohli, A.K. and Jaworski, B.J. (1990) Market orientation: the construct, research propositions, and managerial implications, *Journal of Marketing* 54: 1–18.

Kumar, N., Scheer, S. and Kotler, P. (2000) From market driven to market driving, *European Management Journal,* 18(2): 129–41.

Levitt, T. (1986) *The Marketing Imagination.* New York: The Free Press.

Narver, J.C. and Slater, S.F. (1990) The effect of market orientation on business profitability, *Journal of Marketing,* 54: 20–35.

O'Driscoll, A., Carson, D. and Gilmore, A. (2001) The competence trap: exploring issues in winning and sustaining core competence, *Irish Journal of Management,* 22(1): 73–90.

Porter, M.E. (1985) *Competitive Advantage.* New York: The Free Press.

Prahalad, C.K. and Hamel, G. (1990) The core competence of the corporation, *Harvard Business Review,* May–June: 79–91.

Stalk, G. Jr and Hout, T.M. (1990) *Competing Against Time: How Time-based Competition is Reshaping Global Markets.* New York: The Free Press.

Trott, P., Maddocks, T. and Wheeler, C. (2009) Core competencies for diversifying: case study of a small business, *Strategic Change,* 18: 27–43.

CASE STUDY 2: AG BARR

Irn-Bru – Scotland's 'other national drink' – is looking for further market shares in the carbonated soft drinks (CSD) market

The company dates back to 1830, with the foundation of Robert Barr's cork-cutting business in Falkirk. In 1875, the company diversified into aerated water production, and in 1887 operations were extended to Glasgow. The Glasgow-based company was renamed AG Barr in 1904. The two companies in Falkirk and Glasgow were run separately until 1959, when AG Barr bought out the other company.

AG Barr makes the renowned Irn-Bru soft drink, introduced in 1901, which, in 2008 had about 5 per cent of the UK CSD market. Despite tough domestic competition, Irn-Bru is Scotland's largest selling single-flavoured CSD and is the third best-selling soft drink in the UK, after Coca-Cola and Pepsi. Besides whisky, Irn-Bru is known as Scotland's 'other national drink'.

From the 1950s, the company expanded with a series of acquisitions of regional soft drinks companies in Scotland and Northern England, including Tizer Ltd, in 1972. The company was floated on the London Stock Exchange in 1965. However, despite being a public company, the Barr family retained tight control, with Robin Barr serving as executive chairman, until he finally stepped down from the company's chief executive spot, naming Roger White, the first time someone from outside of the Barr family, to lead the company in 2004. White has promised to expand the group's range of products, in particular by adding juice-based products and other bottled water products, while retaining and expanding its traditional carbonated beverage core. The first step in that expansion came with the launch of a new range of fruit-flavoured Tizer-branded soft drinks.

AG Barr is also the franchise partner of Schweppes International Ltd in the UK, where it manufactures and sells Orangina under licence and has a partnership with Rockstar Inc in the US to sell and distribute their Rockstar energy drink brand in the UK and Ireland.

AG Barr markets a wide product portfolio, including Irn-Bru, the mother brand, and other brands including Tizer, D'N'B, KA, Barr, Strathmore Spring Water, St Clements and Simply. The company also manufactures and sells Orangina under licence and partnership of Schweppes International Ltd and has a partnership with Rockstar Inc that enables it to sell and distribute the energy drink. Recent acquisitions include the Vitsmart enhanced water, TAUT sports drink and Rubicon juice drinks brands.

AG Barr is usually up to date with current market dynamics and positioned in mature areas of the market, except for fruit juices, smoothies and diet products that are still undergoing much growth. The company typically follows the market with the exception of Irn Bru that was innovative at the time. Today, the company attempts to develop new fruit flavours that has been recently seen with its Tizer drinks.

The company's main strength lies in its Irn-Bru brand, which showed no sign of a sales decline in 2008 and seemed unaffected by the general switch to fruit/vegetable juice among consumers or the poor summer weather of the year. It is possible, however, that Irn-Bru drinkers are not as concerned with health issues as consumers of non-carbonate brands. In any case, the company has extended the brand with a low-calorie version to appeal to those drinkers who look for a healthier option.

In 2008 the AG Barr turnover was £170 m (2008) with an operating profit of £23.4 m – see Table 2.2 regarding the financial development in AG Barr during the last five years.

	2008 (£m)	2007 (£m)	2006 (£m)	2005 (£m)	2004 (£m)
Turnover	170	148	142	129	127
Profit (before tax)	23	21	16	17	16

TABLE 2.2 AG Barr's five-year financial development
Source: adapted from www.agbarr.com

Despite AG Barr's international expansion plans, only 1 per cent of the total turnover was generated outside UK in 2008.

Irn-Bru

The Barr family has been making fizzy drinks in Scotland since 1880, but it was in 1901 they launched their mixed flavour drink called Iron-Brew. At the time it was just one of many mixed flavour drinks called Iron Brew, each manufacturer compiling his own recipe for the beverage.

During World War II, the soft drinks industry was rationalized, which meant that Barr could no longer produce under its pre-war trade name. Iron-Brew was not recognized as a 'standard necessary drink' by the government, so disappeared from the shelves of shops for the duration of the war.

But when the war ended, as unavailable products started to be reintroduced to shops, the government brought in new food labelling regulations, and Iron-Brew, which was not actually brewed, had to change its name. It was the company chairman that came up with the idea of using the phonetic spelling, which was duly registered as Barr's own trade name.

So in 1946 Barr's Irn-Bru went on to the shelves of shops all over Scotland. Irn-Bru was quick to recapture the market. From the beginning Irn-Bru was heavily advertised.

In 1993, a new design for Irn-Bru was introduced across the entire product range, giving Irn-Bru a more contemporary look, as well as making it more visible in the stores. For example, the increased amount of blue on the cans contrasts with the orange to give it a vibrant and eye-catching look.

Irn-Bru unleashed its website in 1996. The site is not only an online advert, but strives to be a multidimensional and interactive web experience. Consumer communication continues to develop within the FMCG sector and Irn-Bru has increased its digital presence with new websites and a number of digital campaigns aimed at reaching the growing audience of, especially younger, consumers who spend increasing time online. However, it has also continued to utilize the more traditional mainstream advertising activity with, for example, a TV advertising campaign going out across the summer months.

Irn-Bru is also involved with a programme of sponsoring the Scottish football leagues. In addition to its Scottish Football League sponsorship Irn-Bru has started up a new sponsorship deal with the Rugby League. Irn-Bru is now the official soft drink of Superleague – a three-year deal. In addition, it secured full broadcast sponsorship of Sky Sports Rugby League coverage for the 2009 season. This coverage reached over 10 million consumers over the course of the season and was designed to reinforce Irn-Bru's position over the whole of the UK.

Although other companies have tried to copy Barr's Irn-Bru, the formula for Irn-Bru is a closely guarded secret, known only by two of Barr's board members. Irn-Bru is most famous for its eccentric bright orange colour, making it easily recognizable even when not in its packaging.

Irn-Bru holds the *Guinness World Records* title for the largest Can Can. This was achieved in Glasgow Green on Sunday 13 September 2009 when 10 000 people attended the 'IRN-BRU Can Clan' event as part of the brands support of 'Home Coming Scotland'.

Carbonated soft drinks in the UK

Unlike fruit juices and bottled waters, there is no formal legal definition or compositional standard of a carbonated drink but they can include sparkling juices, colas, mixers, tonic and bitter drinks, shandy and flavoured waters to name but a few.

Carbonated drinks have been in existence since the late eighteenth century, when Dr Joseph Priestley discovered a means of artificially carbonating water. Once this initial discovery was made, it was not long before further scientific development enabled artificially carbonated water and other soft drinks to be produced and packed in commercial quantities.

The carbonated drink sector is still the largest category of soft drinks, comprising a 42 per cent market share. Colas are the most popular flavours for carbonated drinks, with fruit flavours such as lemon and orange following. *In the other flavoured carbonates category, Irn-Bru is the biggest selling single-flavour brand.* The biggest change in the carbonated sector has been in the growth of low and zero sugar variants, as manufacturers continue to meet the demands of health conscious consumers.

Indeed, consumption of diet, low calorie and no added sugar drinks, including bottled water and fruit juice, has reached 61 per cent of the overall soft drinks market.

Key distribution channels in the UK

Key channels of distribution for soft drinks in the UK can be divided into two broad categories:

1 *Off-trade*: take home (multiple grocers) + impulse (corner shops, newsagents, off licences, etc.)
2 *On-trade*: on premise (pubs, clubs, hotels, cafés, restaurants, etc.).

Until now the strength of Irn-Bru has mainly been in the off-trade sector. The on-trade channel has traditionally been a weakness in Irn-Bru's route to the market. Barr has tried to tacle this with investment in sales resources and the portfolio development of the energy drink, Irn-Bru 32.

Top 10 Brand	Company	% off-trade volume			
		2005	2006	2007	2008
Diet Coke	Coca-Cola Enterprises Ltd	16.8	17.0	16.5	15.9
Coca-Cola	Coca-Cola Enterprises Ltd	14.3	13.9	14.3	14.6
Tesco	Tesco Plc	5.8	5.7	6.4	6.5
Pepsi	Britvic Soft Drinks Ltd	4.7	4.5	4.8	5.7
Sainsbury	J Sainsbury Plc	5.2	5.4	5.6	5.6
Fanta	Coca-Cola Enterprises Ltd	5.5	5.4	5.3	5.0
Pepsi Max	Britvic Soft Drinks Ltd	4.9	4.6	4.3	4.3
Diet Pepsi	Britvic Soft Drinks Ltd	3.2	2.9	3.0	3.2
Irn-Bru	Barr (AG) Plc	2.7	2.9	2.9	3.1
Schweppes	Coca-Cola Enterprises Ltd	2.5	2.7	2.8	2.9
Rest	Various	34.4	35.0	34.1	33.2
Total		100	100	100	100

TABLE 2.3 UK brand shares of carbonates by off-trade volume (2005–8)
Source: adapted from www.euromonitor.com

Irn-Bru's international expansion

In the late 1980s, Barr actively began to look at expansion through international markets. It considered France, Germany and Benelux countries among others but found that Coca-Cola and Pepsi dominated these mature markets. Competition was fierce and margins tight. Consequently, it examined other emerging markets and was attracted to Russia. In the years following the break-up of the Soviet Union, Russia showed much potential with a large population, growing prosperity and standard of living, and a rising demand for consumer goods. Moreover, the Russians, like the Scots, have a 'sweet tooth' leading to high soft drinks consumption. As part of the international expansion strategy, in 1994, Barr began direct exports of its trademark Irn-Bru to Russia.

In 2002, Barr arranged a new manufacturing franchise contract with the Pepsi Bottling Group (PBG) of Russia to manufacture, distribute and sell Irn-Bru. PBG (Russia) has over 2,000 employees and distributes the Pepsico brands throughout Russia. Since February 2002, the distribution network has been greatly enlarged especially by using the PBG retail space and coolers in the retail outlets improving brand availability to the trade, retailers, wholesalers and clubs. The brand is produced in 250 ml glass bottles, 330 ml cans, 600 ml, 1.25 l and 2 l plastic bottles.

Value of the Russian distribution alliance for both partners:

Irn-Bru:

● Irn-Bru in Russia has been a part of AG Barr's international expansion plan.
● Irn-Bru has provided extra turnover and profit for AG Barr.

PBG:

- In many Russian retail stores (with a broader PBG product range) Irn-Bru has blocked the available shelf space for Pepsi's main competitor, Coca-Cola.
- Irn-Bru has provided extra turnover and profit for PBG.

Irn-Bru is now established as one of the leading soft drink brands in Russia.

Besides Russia, the biggest international Irn-Bru markets are Poland, Spain, Norway, Australia and the Middle East.

Questions

1 How has AG Barr used the two concepts of 'market driven' and 'market driving' regarding expansion of the sales?
2 What are the key competencies of AG Barr (Irn-Bru) compared with its competitors?
3 What are the biggest challenges for AG Barr (Irn-Bru) in trying to get further market shares on the CSD world market?

Sources: www.irn-bru.co.uk/; www.agbarr.co.uk

CHAPTER

03

Assessing the external marketing situation

Chapter contents

❖ LEARNING OBJECTIVES

After studying this chapter you should be able to do the following:

❖ Explain the elements in the PEST analysis.

❖ Discuss the focal company's relationships to the different actors in the value net.

❖ Understand how the company can establish relationships to competitors.

❖ Discuss how B2B customers make purchase decisions.

3.1 Introduction

Of central importance in developing a robust marketing plan is awareness of how the environment in which the marketing takes place is changing. At its simplest, the whole marketing system can be divided into three levels as follows (see Fig. 3.1).

1 *The focal company*: understanding and analysing the internal situation, dealt with in Chapter 2.

2 *Industry level/value net*: the focal company's most important actors/stakeholders at this level are suppliers, partners/complementors, competitors and, of course, the customers.

3 *Macro level*: the most important changes taking place in the macro environment can be summarized in the so-called PEST analysis:

P Political and legal factors

E Economic factors

S Socio-cultural factors

T Technological factors.

The following section examines each of the four elements of the PEST analysis.

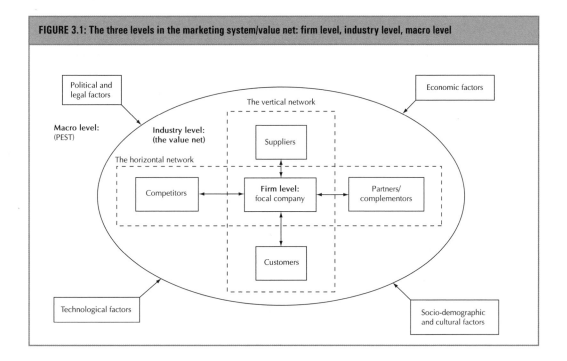

FIGURE 3.1: The three levels in the marketing system/value net: firm level, industry level, macro level

3.2 PEST analysis

3.2.1 Political, legal and economic factors

During the past 20 years, a new and fundamentally different form of international commercial activity has developed, greatly increasing worldwide economic and political interdependence. Very few countries remain isolated in the world of business; rather than merely buying resources from and selling goods to foreign nations, multinational companies (MNCs) now make direct investment in fully integrated operations that cover the spectrum of goods and services. Today, MNC networks control a large and growing share of the world's technology, marketing and productive resources.

Rates of economic growth fluctuate over time and across the globe. While growth is undoubtedly cyclical, the indications are that the developed economies are unlikely to see again the rate of growth experienced in the first decades after World War II.

The state of national and international economies affects businesses directly in a number of ways; for example, it affects interest rates and hence the cost of borrowing. In times of slow economic growth governments, or their central banks, tend to reduce interest rates to make borrowing cheaper and hence stimulate spending. When economic growth is rapid, concerns for growing inflation, or economic 'overheating', lead to increased interest rates to dampen demand.

Interest rates have a number of effects in addition to directly raising or lowering the cost of borrowing. In particular, they have a psychological effect on the confidence of consumers and businesses, affecting purchasing decisions beyond purely rational, or economic, judgement.

Company investment decisions are often delayed in times of relatively high interest rates and that can then have an obvious knock-on effect on suppliers further down the supply chain. Consumers too may delay purchases, especially where they are to be made using loans that are increasingly expensive. The housing market, for example, is particularly vulnerable to interest rate changes.

Perhaps one of the most obvious ways in which the political and economic environment affects demand is through the fiscal, or taxation, policy of the regime that is in power. Where taxation rates are high, they result in low disposable incomes, which can depress demand. Low taxation tends to be a spur to growth. But there are two main types of tax and their effects may be different. Direct taxation taxes income and hence affects the overall disposable income available for purchases. Indirect taxation, on the other hand, taxes purchases and may, through its selective application, shift demand from one area to another.

Employment and unemployment rates also follow economic and business cycles. In times of economic slowdown, firms may find their order books less full and hence be forced to pursue efficiency gains through 'downsizing'.

National governments, through their economic and fiscal policies, set the economic climate in which companies operate. The political hue, or leaning, of a government can affect the policies it pursues in a number of ways. Crudely, the position of a government on the political spectrum from left to right, from centrally planned (as in the communist era in the Soviet Union) to market-led free-for-all (as most exemplified in the USA), indicates the broad manner in which decisions are likely to be made.

The extent to which fiscal policy will have a direct effect on the strategy pursued by an individual organization will clearly vary significantly. What is important here is to recognize the impact and, as importantly, predict how this may change with changes in government or changes in local or international legislation.

3.2.2 The EU: the Euro and the enlargement

January 1992 saw the realization of the dream of many Europeans with the creation of the European single market. This single market of over 320 million consumers was created to allow the free flow of products and services, people and capital between the member states. By January 2002 a single European currency, the Euro (€), had been introduced into all but a handful of the European Union (EU) member states, further facilitating trade and exchange across the old political borders.

As at 1 January 2010 the EU is composed of 27 sovereign member states: Austria, Belgium, Bulgaria, Cyprus, Czech Republic, Denmark, Estonia, Finland, France, Germany,

Greece, Hungary, Ireland, Italy, Latvia, Lithuania, Luxembourg, Malta, Netherlands, Poland, Portugal, Romania, Slovakia, Slovenia, Spain, Sweden and the UK.

Only 16 of the 27 members of the EU are part of the Eurozone (the name for the collection of EU countries that utilize the Euro). Notably, the UK, Denmark and Sweden have thus far decided not to convert to the Euro.

However, Andorra, Kosovo, Montenegro, Monaco, San Marino and the Vatican City are not EU members but do officially use the Euro as their currencies. This means that as at 1 January 2010 these 22 countries use the Euro: Andorra, Austria, Belgium, Cyprus, Finland, France, Germany, Greece, Ireland, Italy, Kosovo, Luxembourg, Malta, Monaco, Montenegro, Netherlands, Portugal, San Marino, Slovakia, Slovenia, Spain and the Vatican City.

3.2.3 Socio-demographic and cultural environment

Demographic factors

The western 'demographic time bomb' has started to have an impact on diverse businesses. With generally better standards of living, life expectancy has increased. In the developed West the over-60s age group currently makes up around 20 per cent of the population, and this figure is predicted to rise to nearer one-third by 2050. These 'grey' consumers are relatively rich. The over-50s own around three-quarters of the world's financial assets and control half of the discretionary budget. Perhaps surprisingly, however, around 95 per cent of consumer advertising is aimed at the under-50s. It is likely that marketers will increasingly come to recognize the potential value of this market and target more offerings and promotions towards it. At the other end of the spectrum, the youth market has also become more affluent and poses new opportunities for marketers. The fashion and music industries have been quick to recognize this new-found affluence. Related to this youth market has been the emergence of the enigmatic 'Generation X' consumer, who is hostile to business values and traditional advertising and branding, and rejects many conventional product offers. The pay-off in understanding the values and preferences of this type of consumer has been substantial for companies such as Nike in clothing.

Many western societies are becoming increasingly multi-ethnic. In the UK, for example, by the late 1990s ethnic minorities comprised 5.5 per cent of the population and forecasts predicted the number would double in the next 50 years.

Social factors

A number of significant pressures on companies can be identified. First and foremost, customers are becoming increasingly demanding of the products and services they buy. Customers demand, and expect, reliable products with quick, efficient service at reasonable prices. Furthermore, there is little long-term stability in customer demand.

A further social change has been in attitudes to, and concern for, the physical environment. Environmental pressure groups impact on businesses, so much so that major oil multinationals and others spend large amounts of money on corporate advertising each year to demonstrate their concern and care for the environment. The activities of Greenpeace have begun to have a major impact on public opinion and now affect policy-making at national and international levels. It is to be expected that concern for the environment will increase and hence will be a major factor in managing that prime marketing asset – company reputation.

Cultural factors

Before an American can be a successful leader among different cultures, they must clearly understand their own culture and be aware of imposing that culture or traditions on those of other cultures; Edward T. Hall (1976) has suggested the concept of high and low-context communication as a way of understanding different cultural orientations. The American communicates in a low-context nature, which means that messages are explicit. Words carry most of the information in communication. In a low-context culture one gets down to business quickly. In a high-context culture it takes considerably longer to conduct business because of the need to know more about a business person before a relationship develops. In Asia, if you are not willing to take the time to sit down and have a cup of green tea with people, you have a problem. In a high-context culture, such as France, Japan and most of the Middle East, less information is contained in the verbal part of the message. Much more information resides in the context of communication, including the background, associations and basic values of the communicators (Hall, 1976).

In the 1970s, Geert Hofstede developed methods to detect and measure elements of national cultural systems that affect behaviour in work situations. Hofstede's 'research' was extracted from an existing bank of paper-and-pencil survey results collected within subsidiaries of one large multinational business organization in 40 countries and covering, among others, many questions about values. The survey was held twice, around 1968 and around 1972, producing a total of over 116 000 questionnaires. Theoretical reasoning and statistical analysis revealed the four main dimensions on which country cultures differ. These were labelled 'Power Distance', 'Uncertainty Avoidance', 'Individualism' and 'Masculinity'. Each of the 40 countries could be given a score on these four dimensions (Hofstede, 1980). Later research, which dealt with Asians as the subject, added the dimension 'Long-term Orientation'. By learning how each country scored on these dimensions, a human resource (HR) professional can understand the culture of a country and then implement practices that are appropriate for that culture. Descriptions of Hofstede's five dimensions follow.

Power distance

Power distance is the extent to which the less powerful members of society accept that power is, and should be, distributed *unequally*. Inequality can occur in areas such as prestige, wealth and power, or in teacher–student and parent–child relationships. Different societies place different weights on status. In corporations, inequality in power is inevitable because it serves an important function and is usually formalized in hierarchical boss–subordinate relationships.

Uncertainty avoidance

This is the extent to which people try to avoid situations where expectations and outcomes are not clear. These are situations where people feel threatened by poorly defined or ambiguous conditions, and vary considerably among people in different countries. Employees with high uncertainty avoidance would tend not to break company rules even when they think it is in the company's best interest to do so, and tend to remain within the same company for long periods of time. They prefer to work with long-term acquaintances and friends rather than with strangers (Gannon, 2001).

Individualism

Individualism describes the relationship between an individual and the groups to which they belong. Individualism is described by Griffin and Pustay (1998) as a cultural belief that the person comes first. People with high individualism put their own interests and those of their immediate families ahead of those of others.

Masculinity (*goal orientation*)

This is aggressive and materialistic behaviour. Hofstede described this dimension as masculinity versus femininity; however, authors referring to Hofstede's study tend to call this dimension goal orientation, due to the misunderstandings that using the word 'masculinity' can give rise to.

Long-term orientation

The time horizon of long-term orientation is the extent to which people within a culture have a long-term versus a short-term outlook on work, life and other aspects of society. Asian cultures have long-term future orientations that value hard work, perseverance and dedication. Other cultures tend to focus on the past and present, with respect for tradition and the fulfilment of social obligations.

  Last but not least, religions and religious institutions affect markets in a variety of ways. Religion is one of the foundations of moral teaching in most civilizations, and as such it defines and informs the kinds of problem faced in the market by buyers (consumers) and sellers (marketers). Marketers need to understand the effects of religion on the kinds of issue they face in business and, more important, how these issues are defined, informed and regulated by religion. Understanding the relationships between religions and markets should be important to macro marketing since religions affect the foundations of people's understanding of the world, and thus their understanding and acceptance of markets and marketing institutions. Religion affects perceptions of development, quality of life, appropriate standards of exchange and competition.

Exhibit 3.1: *McDonald's France: a faster penetration of the French market than expected*

At first glance McDonald's fast food and French gastronomy do not go together very well. Indeed, from the beginning, McDonald's was afraid of entering the French market. The French traditionally have a very complex relationship with the USA because they like the US people, but not US politics. When McDonald's launched its first restaurant in Paris in 1979, it tried to combat these perceptions by positioning itself as a family restaurant brand, rather than a burger bar or a US-themed restaurant. McDonald's recognized the increasing importance of kids influencing family decisions. Furthermore, the company has tried hard to adapt to French habits. It has put regional specialities and recipes on its menu, including well-known French brands such as Danone yoghurt and Kronenbourg beer.

> ### The result
>
> Surprisingly, McDonald's France grew from zero restaurants to over 1,000 in 24 years. The same progress took more than 30 years in the UK and German markets.
>
> *Source*: adapted from Jones (2004)

3.2.4 Technological factors

The latter part of the twentieth century saw technological change and development impact on virtually every industry. The microprocessor, for instance, has been attributed with heralding the post-industrial age and it is probably this invention above all others that has had the most profound effect on our lives today. Microprocessors have revolutionized data collection, processing and dissemination. They have caused major changes in production technology and have served to increase the rate of technological change. This shortening of commercialization times has, in turn, led to a shortening of product life cycles, with products becoming obsolete much more quickly than before. Computer integration of manufacturing and design is helping to shorten product development times.

Newer technology has had a major impact on particular aspects of marketing. Computers, and their wide availability to management, have led to increased interest in sophisticated market modelling and decision support systems. Increased amounts of information can now be stored, analysed and retrieved much more quickly than in the past. In 1965 Gordon Moore of Intel predicted exponential growth in the numbers of transistors that would be possible on integrated circuits. Moore's Law, as it became known, holds that 'the processing power of the silicon chip will double every 18 months'. This prediction has proved remarkably accurate. Of course, the Internet – the global electronic communications network – is also fast emerging, not only as a new marketing communications vehicle, but as potentially a whole new way of going to market, which may significantly change the competitive structure of industries.

Time and distance are shrinking rapidly as firms use the Internet to aim their offerings at truly global markets. One result is that cross-national segments are now emerging for products and services from fast foods, through books and toys, to computers and automobiles.

3.3 Relations to actors in the industry value net

This task environment refers to the immediate external market where interactions that have a direct effect on our company take place. Since the company has relationships with different types of interdependency, with different objectives for the development of the relationship, and so on, it is important organizationally to differentiate between how different relationships are handled. In particular, relationships and interactions are typically established with the following actors (see Fig. 3.1):

- suppliers
- customers
- complementors/partners
- competitors.

The value net reveals two fundamental symmetries. Vertically, customers and suppliers are equal partners in creating value. The other symmetry is on the horizontal for competitors and complementors. The mirror image of competitors is complementors. A complement to one product or service is any other product or service that makes the first one more attractive; that is, computer hardware and software, hot dogs and mustard. The value net helps you understand your competitors and complementors 'outside in'. Who are the players and what are their roles and the interdependencies between them? Re-examine the conventional wisdom of 'Who are your friends and who are your enemies?' The suggestion is to know your business inside out and create extra value to the customer through a co-operation with the other players. These relationships are discussed in more detail below.

3.3.1 Relationships with suppliers

There seem to be three major strategic issues related to purchasing management:

1   the decision of whether to make an item in-house or to buy from external suppliers
2   the development of appropriate relationships with suppliers
3   the managing of the supplier base in terms of size and relationships between suppliers.

The first strategic issue is to decide what items to procure. This is defined by the scope of the operations that are undertaken in-house by the buying company. This determines the degree of vertical integration, which in purchasing terms has been addressed as the 'make-or-buy issue'.

What to produce internally and what to buy from external suppliers has been an issue in manufacturing firms for a very long time, despite the fact that it was apparently not identified as a matter of strategic importance until the 1980s. It is evident that buying firms over time have come to rely more on 'buy' than 'make'. Consequently, outsourcing to external suppliers has increased dramatically over time.

Having suppliers that compete with one another is one way of increasing efficiency in purchasing operations. A buying company can switch from one supplier to another and thus encourage the vendors to improve their efforts. The opportunity to play off suppliers against each other in terms of price conditions has, in particular, been a recommended purchasing strategy. The secret of this strategy is to avoid becoming too integrated with suppliers, because integration leads to dependency. Customer relationships based on this logic are characterized by low involvement from both parties.

The tendency in the overall industrial system towards increasing specialization has called for more co-ordination between individual companies. This, in turn, leads to more adaptation between buyer and seller in terms of activities and resources. These adaptations are made because they improve efficiency and effectiveness. They also create interdependencies between customer and supplier. Such relationships are characterized by a high-involvement approach.

High-involvement relationships typically provide different types of benefit from low-involvement ones, since it is not the individual transaction that is optimized. On the contrary, customers are eager to improve long-term efficiency and effectiveness. Instead of focusing on price in each transaction, efforts are concentrated on affecting long-term total costs. The purchasing behaviour of buying companies affects a number of costs, of which price is sometimes only a minor consideration in comparison with other costs. For example, product development has become increasingly common. Integrating resources with suppliers can reduce lead times in product development and decrease total research and development (R&D) spending (Hughes, 2008). Furthermore, the revenues of the buying company might increase owing to enhanced product quality.

The widely recognized lean and agile supply practices in such relationships have demonstrated that buyers and suppliers can work together to improve supply relationship, or even supply network, performance and consequently allow the supply chain to deliver better value to the ultimate customer. Lean supply techniques aim to eliminate waste in all areas of the business, from the shop floor to manufacturing processes, and from new product development to supply chain management. Agile supply techniques, on the other hand, are directed towards reducing the time it takes for a supply chain to deliver a good or service to the end customer, and are aimed at supply chains that have to respond to volatile demand patterns. Both the 'lean' and 'agile' supply schools have provided a great deal of case evidence that demonstrates that collaboration, in the cause of lean or agile goals, can be effective in bringing down costs and/or increasing product functionality. For example, the lean school has often referred to the Japanese automobile industry, especially the Toyota Motor Corporation, as a good example of lean practice. The agile school, in turn, has pointed to the production of the Smart Car, a car that offers total customization, backed up by a service that offers responsiveness to customer demands.

However, the idea that collaboration constitutes 'best practice' ignores two key factors. First, not all transactions will justify the resources required for a collaborative relationship. Entering a collaborative relationship will only make economic sense if the expected financial and strategic rewards are deemed to be higher than the costs associated with the establishment of such a relationship. Second, not all the suppliers that buyers deal with will wish to allocate the resources required for a collaborative relationship to be developed. A buyer may have both the resources and the inclination to develop a collaborative relationship in a given situation. However, the supplier in question may have other priorities. The supplier may prefer to allocate its resources to other customers – those that it deems more relevant to the achievement of its business goals.

Furthermore, even where collaborative relationships are developed, there is by no means just one form of collaboration. For example, in some power situations getting suppliers to collaborate will not be possible. In particular, such relationships will differ in both their conduct and outcome depending on the power–dependency relationships concerned. As has long been argued in the social science literature, there are four generic buyer–supplier power structures: buyer dominance, interdependence, independence and supplier dominance (Hollensen, 2003: 229).

There are two generic ways of working in the context of supplier relationship management: *arm's length* and *collaborative*. An arm's length way of working involves a low level of contact between buyer and supplier. Low contact means the absence of initiatives that are aimed at cost reduction or functionality enhancement. In arm's length exchanges, the buyer and supplier simply exchange the contractual information that is required for the transaction to take place; for example, information about the placing of the order, the recording of the fulfilment and the payment of the invoice.

A collaborative way of working is much more proactive. It involves high contact and close communication, and is aimed at the creation of surplus value in a relationship. With this approach, buyers work jointly with suppliers either to reduce suppliers' costs or to increase the functionality of the product. The buyer will often closely monitor and measure the performance of suppliers, but will also take on board suggestions about performance improvement that come from suppliers. The buyer will also often get involved in developing suppliers' skills and capabilities through joint development activities.

The bond between buyers and suppliers can also increase through investing in relationship-specific adaptations to processes, products or procedures. Relationship-specific adaptations are those adaptations that are non-transferable to relationships with other buyers or suppliers. These could be adaptations of the following kind: product specification, product design, manufacturing process, delivery procedures, stockholding, planning procedures, administrative procedures and financial procedures.

To understand the power relationship, the power resources of both sides need to be looked at together: when the buyer has high power resources and the supplier has low power resources, the buyer will be dominant; when the buyer has low power resources and the supplier has high power resources, the supplier will be dominant; when the power resources are high for both buyer and supplier, then they will be interdependent; when both parties have low power resources, they will be independent from each other (Freytag and Mikkelsen, 2007).

Exhibit 3.2: *Dell faces different buying behaviour in different countries*

Dell's experience shows that different nationalities do indeed have different preferences when it comes to buying computers. Customers in France and Germany tend to use their credit cards less than others; therefore, they may be less likely to buy online. People in the Nordic countries are very willing to buy online. A German customer is more likely to be interested in all the technical and pricing details. On the other hand, a Swedish customer likes to make a more spontaneous decision when talking to the sales person. Customers in the UK and France are very sensitive to price.

These cultural differences are important because all advertisements and other promotional material must be designed to suit each country. Dell has an advertising manager in each country who is consulted about the details of any local campaign. National differences also influence the type of media used for an advertisement. For example, in the UK and Spain, there are TV channels with very large audiences. Accordingly, TV advertising is used more frequently in these countries.

Source: adapted from www.dell.com, www.business2000.ie

3.3.2 Relationships with customers

In the relationship approach a specific transaction between the focal company and a customer is not an isolated event but takes place within an exchange relationship characterized by mutual dependency and interaction over time between the two parties. An analysis could stop at the individual relationship. However, in the network approach such relationships are seen as interconnected. Thus, the various actors in a market are connected to each other, directly or indirectly. A specific market can then be described and analysed as one or more networks.

An exchange relationship implies that there is an individual specific dependency between the seller and the customer. The relationship develops through interaction over time and signifies a mutual orientation of the two parties towards each other. In the interaction the buyer is equally as active as the seller. The interaction consists of social, business and information exchange, and an adaptation of products, processes and routines to better achieve the economic objectives of the parties involved.

Suppose we regard the environment of the individual relationship as consisting of other relationships. Suppose, further, that the relationships are connected, directly or indirectly, to each other. Then we can envision the market as a network. Following a sociological definition, networks are sets of interconnected exchange relationships between actors. Exchange in one relationship is conditioned by exchange in other relationships. Instead of the concept 'markets-as-networks', the ideas of 'industrial networks' and 'business networks' are used, signifying a somewhat different emphasis of the analyses. A relationship between two actors is 'embedded' in a network.

Marketing planning should start at the relationship level. Interaction with the buyers and potential buyers is an important aspect of the planning process. The planning should include objectives and activities concerning the development of the relationships. The objectives should not only be formulated for the business exchange, such as sales volume and type of product, but also for social and information exchange, and for adaptation processes for products, processes and routines. The development of individual relationships should not be restricted to aggregated data on sales, market shares, customer satisfaction, and so on.

3.3.3 Relationships with partners/complementors

This kind of relationship is based on collaboration between manufacturers of complementary functions and/or products/services. In such a collaboration, each partner has a strategic resource that the other needs and, in this way, each partner is motivated to develop some kind of exchange process between supplier and customer.

For example, partners divide value chain activities between themselves. One partner develops and manufactures a product while letting the other partner market it. The focal company (see Fig. 3.1), A, may want to enter a foreign market, but lacks local market knowledge and does not know how to get access to foreign distribution channels for its products. Therefore, A seeks and finds a partner, B, which has its core competencies in the downstream functions, but is weak in the upstream function. In this way A and B can form a coalition whereby B can help A with distribution and selling in a foreign market, and A can help B with R&D or production. Another example is a joint marketing agreement where the complementary product lines of two firms are sold together through existing or new distribution channels, thus broadening the market coverage of both firms.

3.3.4 Relationships with competitors

Before entering any relationship with competitors, it is important to analyse the competition insofar as it will affect ease of market entry and potential profitability. The domination of a market by a few large companies may suggest difficulties in market entry and subsequent distribution. A more fragmented structure may pose fewer problems. In analysing the competition, a number of factors need to be considered. These range from the number and size of competitors, their capabilities (strengths and weaknesses), their international marketing strategies, and their sales volume and relative market share, to the type of competitor (i.e. multinational versus local and their relative resources). The major multinational competitors, such as Microsoft and Unilever, have access to extensive financial and other resources, but local competitors should not be ignored as they have fewer administrative overheads, lower operating costs and greater flexibility.

Generally, the relationships between competitors (horizontal network) have not been analysed to the same extent as vertical relationships. Co-operative relationships in the vertical network (see Fig. 3.1) are easier to grasp as they are built on a distribution of activities and resources among players in a supply chain. Horizontal networks, on the other hand, are more informal and invisible, and based more on social exchanges.

When competitors are involved in resource exchange alliances, competition introduces some problems. The dilemma is that in creating an alliance with a competitor, a company is, in fact, making them more competitive.

For collaboration to succeed, each competitor must contribute something distinctive: basic research, product development skills, manufacturing capacity and access to distribution. In the network approach, the market includes both complementarities and substitutes, both co-operating and competing firms. Competitors also strive to develop their own networks. Such competitive activity is a major force for change in these networks. Competitors are predominantly negatively connected to each other; they might compete for customers, suppliers or other partners. Competing firms also often have customers, distributors or suppliers in common. Sometimes this implies a negative connection, but sometimes competing firms do not have conflicting objectives *vis-à-vis* a common counterpart.

Interaction among competitors has traditionally been treated within economic theory, and has been explained in terms of the structure of an industry within which it operates. It is further argued that intensity in competition is dependent on the degree of symmetry between companies, while the degree of concentration determines whether competitors act in collusion or competition with each other. Variations in patterns of interaction are also viewed via a relational approach to competitive interaction.

Based on the motives for interaction and the intensity of the relationship concerned, five types of interaction are distinguished: conflict, competition, coexistence, cooperation and collusion. Conflict and competition are described as active *vis-à-vis* competitors, although they differ in terms of the motives for specific interaction. Conflict represents object-oriented competition, geared to destroying the opposing counterpart. Competition is goal-oriented, directed towards achieving one's own goals even though this may have a negative effect on other competitors. Coexistent competition occurs when actors do not see one another as competitors, and therefore act independently of each other. Tacit collusion arises from implicit agreements among the actors to avoid active competition. Finally, in co-operation, the companies involved strive towards the same goals; for example, by working together in strategic alliances or projects. The interaction between competitors is variable and can involve both co-operative and competitive interaction.

Exhibit 3.3: *The nature of fashion markets*

Fashion is a broad term that typically encompasses any product or market where there is an element of style that is likely to be short-lived. Fashion markets typically exhibit the following characteristics.

- *Short life cycles*: the product is often ephemeral, designed to capture the mood of the moment; consequently the period in which it will be saleable is likely to be very short and seasonal, measured in months or even weeks.
- *High volatility*: demand for these products is rarely stable or linear. It may be influenced by the vagaries of the weather, films, or even by pop stars and footballers.
- *Low predictability*: because of the volatility of demand it is extremely difficult to forecast with any accuracy even total demand within a period, let alone week-by-week or item-by-item demand.
- *High-impulse purchasing*: many buying decisions by consumers for these products are made at the point of purchase. In other words, the shopper when confronted with the product is stimulated to buy it, hence the critical need for 'availability'.

Today's fashion marketplace is highly competitive and the constant need to 'refresh' product ranges means that there has been an inevitable move by many retailers to extend the number of 'seasons' (i.e. the frequency with which the entire merchandise within a store is changed). In extreme cases, typified by the successful fashion retailer Zara, there might be 20 seasons in a year.

Sources: adapted from www.fashion.com; Christopher, M., Lowson, R. and Peck, H. (2004) Creating agile supply chains in the fashion industry, *International Journal of Retail & Distribution Management*, 32(8): 367–76.

3.4 Analysing buying processes in the B2B market

It could be relevant to look at buying processes in both the B2B and B2C markets. However, in this book's context the focus is on the B2B buying process as this reflects the views of the direct business customer. Organizational purchasing decisions are made to meet the objectives of an organization rather than the needs of an individual buyer.

Consumer behaviour relates to the buying behaviour of individuals (or families) when purchasing products for their own use. Organizations buy to enable them to provide goods and services to the final customer. This has implications for marketing management, as we shall see later. Organizational buying behaviour has many similarities to consumer behaviour; both encompass the behaviour of human beings, whether individually or in groups. Organizational buyers do not necessarily, though, act in a more rational manner than individual consumers. Organizational buyers are affected by environmental and individual factors, as outlined in the previous section. One of the main differences from consumer buying is that organizational buying usually involves group decision-making (known as the 'decision-making unit' (DMU) and sometimes referred to as the buying centre). In such a group individuals may have different roles in the purchase process. These can be categorized as follows (Bonoma, 2006):

- *Initiator*: the person who first suggests making a purchase.
- *Influencers/evaluators*: people who influence the buying decision. They often help define specifications and provide information for evaluating options. Technical personnel are especially important as influencers.
- *Gatekeepers*: group members who regulate the flow of information. Frequently, the purchasing agent views the gatekeeping role as a source of his or her power. A secretary may also act as a gatekeeper by determining which vendors get an appointment with a buyer.
- *Decider*: the person who has the formal or informal power to choose or approve the selection of the supplier or brand. In complex situations, it is often difficult to determine who makes the final decision.
- *Purchaser*: the person who actually negotiates the purchase. This could be anyone from the president of the company to a purchasing agent, depending on the importance of the decision.
- *Users*: members of the organization who will actually use the product. Users often initiate the buying process and help define product specifications.

One person may play all the above roles in the purchase decision or each role may be represented by a number of personnel. The sales person trying to sell to an organization should be aware of the roles people assume in the buying centre.

Another difference in organizational buying is that some products are more complex than others and it requires specialist knowledge to purchase them. As many products are changed according to the specifications of the buyer, there is more communication and negotiation between buyer and seller. After-sales service is also very important in organizational buying, and suppliers are often evaluated quite rigorously after purchase. In general, organizational markets have fewer, larger, buyers who are geographically concentrated. Another aspect of organizational buying is the nature of derived demand; that is, demand for organizational (especially industrial) goods is derived from consumer markets. If demand for the end-product consumer good falls then this has an effect along the production line to all the inputs. So, in organizational marketing the end consumers should not be ignored and trends should be monitored.

Organizational buying decisions can be categorized into 'buy classes' in terms of how complex they are (similar to the low-/high-involvement decision-making in consumer markets). These classes are described below.

1 *Straight re-buys*: these occur often, are relatively cheap and are usually a matter of routine. If the supplier is an 'in supplier' – that is, they are on the company's approved list of suppliers – then they have to perform in a way that ensures they do not get taken off the list. If they are 'out suppliers' they have to try to get on to the approved list.

2   *Modified re-buy*: this situation requires some additional information about, or evaluation of, suppliers. It is usually the case that specifications and so on have been modified since the last purchase.

3   *New task*: a new task, or new buy, situation (i.e. when the company has not bought the product before) is the most complex purchase decision. Search and evaluation procedures are extensive.

Summary

In this chapter, the influences of the environment are divided into three levels, as follows.

1   *Macro level*: the most important changes taking place in the macro environment can be summarized using the so-called PEST analysis:

   P   Political and legal factors

   E   Economic factors

   S   Socio-cultural factors

   T   Technological factors.

2   *Industry level/value net*: the focal company's most important actors/stakeholders at this level are suppliers, partners/complementors, competitors and, of course, the customers.

3   *The focal company*: understanding and analysing the internal situation, dealt with in Chapter 2.

This chapter states that it is not enough to discuss the activities that a single company performs: it is essential to *understand* how these activities are linked to the activities in the company's value net (i.e. to the company's customers, suppliers, partners/complementors and competitors). Hence, companies are dependent for their success on their relationships with others. Many of the strategic choices a company makes will be in response to the actions of these other companies. In this way, a company's strategy may be thought of as a kind of game, because there is nothing predetermined about the various choices it might make.

   Relationships in the value net perspective enable firms to develop competitive advantage by leveraging the skills and capabilities of their partners to improve the performance of the total value chain. Firms not only compete as individual companies, they also compete as groups of companies that co-operate to bring value to the ultimate customer.

   The last part of the chapter focused on the buying decision process of the most important and direct customer: the B2B customer. In B2B decision-making, two additional influences are included. These are group influences and organizational factors. The actual decision-making process will depend on whether the purchase is a new task, a modified re-buy or a straight re-buy for the organization. The process involved is similar to the consumer decision-making process.

Questions for discussion

1 Explain the importance of a common European currency (the Euro) to firms selling goods to the European market.
2 Why is the international marketer interested in the age distribution of the population in a market?
3 Why is political stability so important for international marketers? Find some recent examples from the press to underline your points.
4 How can the change of major political goals in a country have an impact on the potential for success of an international marketer?
5 Explain why a country's balance of trade may be of interest to an international marketer.
6 Do you think that cultural differences between nations are more or less important than cultural variations within nations? Under what circumstances is each important?
7 What layers of culture have the strongest influence on business people's behaviour?
8 Identify some constraints in marketing to a traditional Muslim society.
9 What are the major differences in buying behaviour in the two main markets, B2C and B2B?
10 What is the buying centre in a company? Describe its functions and the implications for the selling organization.
11 Explain the idea behind the value net model.
12 Why is it sometimes necessary to establish relationships with competitors?

References

Bonoma, V. (2006) Major sales – who really does the buying?, *Harvard Business Review,* July–August: 172–81.

Freytag, P.V. and Mikkelsen, O.S. (2007) Sourcing from outside – six managerial challenges, *Journal of Business & Industrial Marketing,* 22: 187–95.

Gannon, M. (2001) *Understanding Global Cultures: Metaphorical Journeys through 23 Nations,* 2nd edn. Thousand Oaks, CA: Sage Publications, Inc.

Griffin, R.W. and Pustay, M.W. (1998) *International Business: A Management Perspective.* Harlow: Addison Wesley.

Hall, E.T. (1976) *Beyond Culture.* Garden City, NY: Anchor.

Hofstede, G. (1980) *Culture's Consequences: International Differences in Work-related Values.* Beverly Hills, CA, and London: Sage Publications.

Hollensen, S. (2003) *Marketing Management.* London: Financial Times/Prentice Hall.

Hughes, J. (2008) From vendor to partner: why and how leading companies collaborate with suppliers for competitive advantage, *Global Business and Organizational Excellence,* 27(3): 21–37.

Jones, M.C. (2004) Special size French fries, *Brand Strategy*, April: 28–9.

CASE STUDY 3: SUZLON ENERGY

The Indian wind turbine manufacturer seeks new business opportunities in the world market

Wind energy, as a power generation technology, greatly aids in offsetting carbon (CO) emissions from burning of two fossil fuels for electricity generation. The 120.8 gigawatt (GW) of global wind capacity, installed by the end of 2008, will produce 260 terawatt hours (TWh) of electricity and save 158 million tonnes of CO every year (*Source*: Global 2 Wind 2008 Report: GWEC).

Wind energy has become increasingly cost-competitive when compared with conventional modes of power generation, with improvements in efficiency and increased scale of both turbine sizes and project capacities. It also is one of the most promising sources of energy, critical in terms of the global resource availability versus installed base, availability of capital equipment and manpower, and employment generation potential.

Suzlon Energy

Suzlon Energy is a wind power company in India. In terms of market share, the company is the largest wind turbine manufacturer in Asia (and the fifth largest worldwide).

With headquarters in Pune, it has several manufacturing sites in India including Pondicherry, Daman, Bhuj and Gandhidham as well as in mainland China, Germany and Belgium. The company is listed on the National Stock Exchange of India and on the Bombay Stock Exchange.

Suzlon was founded by Tulsi Tanti in 1995, when he was working in a family-owned textile company. In that year, India's shaky power grid and the rising cost of electricity offset any profits the company would make. With the help of some of his friends of Rajkot, he moved into wind energy production as a way to secure the textile company's energy needs, and founded Suzlon Energy. In 2001, Tanti sold off the textile business, so he could focus on the development of his wind energy business. In 2009, Suzlon is still actively run by Tulsi Tanti, now in the role of chairman and managing director.

Suzlon is a vertically integrated wind power company. The company manufactures blades, generators, panels and towers in-house, as well as gearboxes through its partial ownership of Hansen Transmissions and state-of-the-art large or offshore turbines through its partial ownership of German REpower. The company is integrated downstream and delivers turnkey projects through its project management and installation consultancy, and operations and maintenance services. Suzlon is a multinational company with offices, R&D and technology centres, manufacturing facilities and service support centres spread across the globe.

Suzlon has design and R&D teams and facilities in Germany, India and the Netherlands to retrofit blades for clients. The international sales business of Suzlon is managed out of Aarhus, Denmark, while its global management office is in Amsterdam.

	2008–9	2007–8	2006–7	2005–6	2004–5
Installed MW	2,790	2,311	1,456	963	506
Turnover (Rs Crore)	26,082	13,679	7,986	3,841	1,942
Net profit	236	1,030	864	760	365

TABLE 3.1 Financial development of Suzlon Energy over the last five years
Source: www.suzlon.com

In 2008, investors and media reported doubts on the quality of Suzlon's technology, after Suzlon recalled 1,251 blades, the majority of the blades sold to date in the USA. And in 2009, while Suzlon was working on fixing blade cracks in the USA, Brazil and Europe, subsidiary REpower rejected Suzlon's blades for a joint project in China and obtained them from other suppliers.

The global wind turbine market

The year 2008 was another record year for the industry, with global annual installations growing by 36 per cent to over 28 500 megawatts (MW) (see Table 3.2). The global installed wind power capacity grew by 28 per cent to reach 122 000 GW, making wind power one of the fastest growing sources of utility-scale electricity generation. This reflects a huge and growing global demand for emissions-free, sustainable and local sources of power generation.

Manufacturer	Country	Market share (%) – 2008
Vestas	Denmark	19
GE Wind	USA	18
Gamesa	Spain	12
Enercon	Germany	10
Suzlon	India	9
Siemens	Germany/Denmark	6
Sionvel	China	5
Acciona	Spain	4
Goldwind	China	4
Nordex	Germany	3
Repower	Germany	3
Others	–	7
Total		100
Total installed MW		28,500 MW
Accumulated total installed MW		122,000 MW

TABLE 3.2 Market shares of major world turbine manufacturers
Source: www.suzlon.com

Together with German Repower (where Suzlon is a majority shareholder), Suzlon ranked third in the world in 2008 in terms of annual installations with market share of 12 per cent (9 + 3 per cent – see Table 3.2).

Suzlon has consistently held its number one position in India for almost a decade now (over 50 per cent market share) and has also been the industry leader in Australia over the last couple of years.

Top world wind turbine markets	Installations of MW % distribution (2008)	Accumulated MW installations % distribution (2008)
USA	31	26
China	23	15
India	7	6
Germany	6	15
Spain	6	8
Italy	4	4
France	3	3
UK	3	4
Portugal	3	2
Canada	2	2
Rest of the world	12	15
Total	100	100
Total MW	28,500 MW	122,000 MW

TABLE 3.3 Top world wind turbine markets and accumulated installations

Most noticeably, during 2008, the USA surpassed Germany to become the number one wind power market in terms of annual installations, with 8.5 GW installed during the year. China continued to grow with its total capacity doubling for the fourth year in a row, with 12.2 GW installed against 5.9 GW installed until the end of 2007.

Europe, North America and Asia are continuing to drive global wind development, with new installations in 2008 majorly distributed between them.

By 2012 it is expected that annual new installations will grow from today's level of 28 500 to 51 000 MW. In the next four years, the USA is likely to overtake most European nations, to become the leading country in terms of annual installations. In Asia, strong growth is expected in China and India; new capacity additions are expected to be around 2,000 MW every year. Cumulative annual growth rate for new installations up to 2012 is expected to be 16 per cent.

The Chinese wind turbine market

Seeking to rein in its emissions of greenhouse gases, China is on an ambitious spending spree in wind power. The government is working on plans to shell out 1 trillion yuan

(US$146 bn) to build seven massive wind farms with a combined capacity of more than 120 000 MW, roughly equal to the world's total installed wind power plants in 2008.

The world's largest producer of carbon emissions has been doubling its wind power capacity every year since 2006; it was the world's second largest buyer of wind turbines in 2008. Yet, about 30 per cent of its wind power assets are not in use – much of that not even connected to the transmission grid – a result of Chinese power companies turning to wind as the cheapest, easiest way to satisfy on paper government requirements to boost renewable energy capacity. Whether the massive new building push will be any more efficient is an open question, given that much of it is slated for out of the way places, mainly in the north, making it uneconomical to build the lengthy extensions to China's grid that would be required to transmit the power to distant population centres.

China has been actively developing wind energy over the past three years. The country added 6,300 MW of capacity in 2008, doubling its total wind power capacity to 12 200 MW, in the process becoming the world's second biggest wind turbine buyer behind the USA and the world's fourth biggest producer of wind power after the USA, Germany and Spain, according to the annual report of the World Wind Energy Association.

Citigroup estimates China's wind power capacity could easily grow to 130 000 MW by 2020.

Development of wind turbine sizes

In many geographic areas even 2 MW turbines are considered big turbines, and it causes problems, but we have never seen a company downsizing and optimizing their old 750 kW and 1 MW turbines to produce cheap and efficient turbines. The average turbine installed in China last year was 1 MW, which was largely due to the fact that the majority of the Chinese manufacturers are making 750 kW turbines. Nevertheless, they are progressing very fast in China and within a few years the average size will be 1.5 MW.

There will be a market for huge 5 MW to 10 MW turbines dedicated to offshore. Offshore is still a niche market which in 2007 represented 1 per cent of the world market and in 2008 will perhaps reach 1.5 per cent. Our five-year forecast at a world level states that offshore wind will represent 4.5–5 per cent of the market. This means that the number of turbines produced for offshore in the future will never be huge, and therefore will not benefit from the economies of scale enjoyed by smaller turbines. At the same time there will be a market for wind farms utilizing 2–3 MW turbines, and there will be a market for 1 MW turbines, which will be a big market in the future. So there will be two or three different levels, and there will be manufacturers that focus on one or several of the segments.

Questions

1   What are the long-term key drivers for the world wind power industry?
2   Which screening criteria should Suzlon use for selecting new markets to focus on?

Sources: www.suzlon.com, www.vestas.com, www.btm.dk, www.gwec.net

CHAPTER 04

SWOT analysis

Chapter contents

❖ LEARNING OBJECTIVES

After studying this chapter you should be able to do the following:

❖ Explain how a SWOT analysis can capitalize on a company's internal and external issues.

❖ Understand the reasons for matching strengths and opportunities, and converting weaknesses and threats.

❖ Discuss the importance of doing some research as the basis for SWOT analysis.

❖ Discuss the barriers to and benefits of conducting SWOT analyses.

❖ Explain the reasons for preparing multilevel SWOT analyses.

4.1 Introduction

Successful SWOT (strengths, weaknesses, opportunities and threats) analysis is fundamentally a process of finding the optimum fit between the company's controllable strengths and weaknesses and the uncontrollable opportunities and threats posed by the environment in which it operates (not just the current environment, but also that of the foreseeable future). This explains why drawing up a SWOT profile is by far the most popular of all marketing planning approaches. It provides a means by which all the key internal (company-related) and external (environment-related) issues can be summarized at a glance. A good SWOT profile facilitates the development of a strategy that capitalizes on a company's strengths, minimizes any weaknesses, exploits emerging opportunities and avoids, as far as possible, any threats.

By carefully matching environmental trends to the company's own distinctive competencies, the strategic market planner is able to devise strategies that build on its strengths, while at the same time minimizing its weaknesses. By doing this, the marketer aims to achieve what is termed a 'strategic fit' between the competencies of the company (strengths) and the needs of the potential customers (opportunities) (Vignali and Curland, 2008).

Among the many fads and fashions in strategic management, the SWOT framework has enjoyed consistent popularity among both researchers and practitioners during the past few decades. SWOT analysis originated from efforts at Harvard Business School (HBS) to analyse case studies (Panagiotou, 2003). In the early 1950s, two Harvard business policy professors, George Albert Smith Jr and C. Roland Christensen, started to investigate organizational strategies in relation to their environment. In the late 1950s, another HBS business policy professor, Kenneth Andrews, expanded on this thinking by stating that all companies must have clearly defined objectives and keep abreast of them. In the early 1960s, classroom discussions in business schools were focusing on organizational strengths and weaknesses in relation to the opportunities and threats (or risks) in their business environments. In 1963, a business policy conference was held at Harvard, where SWOT analysis was widely discussed and seen as a major advance in strategic thinking.

The SWOT framework became popular during the 1970s because of its inherent assumption that managers can plan the alignment of a company's resources with its environment. Subsequently, during the 1980s, Porter's (1980) introduction of the industrial organization paradigm, with his five forces/diamond models, gave primacy to a company's external environment, overshadowing the popularity of SWOT analysis. In the 1990s, Barney reinvented SWOT as the foundation framework linking the company's resources to sustained competitive advantage (Barney, 1991).

Looking back to Chapters 2 and 3, Fig. 4.1 illustrates the 'roots' of the marketing planning approach. In Chapter 2, in particular, there was comprehensive discussion of the roots of the resource-based view (RBV, inside out), based on the company's strengths and weaknesses, and the market orientation view (MOV, outside in), based on opportunities and threats in the environment.

The roots discussed in Chapters 2 and 3 lead to the processes described in this chapter, where we will see how SWOT analysis can help these roots grow into a flourishing marketing plan.

4.2 Elements of the SWOT analysis

When implementing a SWOT analysis to devise a set of strategies, the following guidelines should be used.

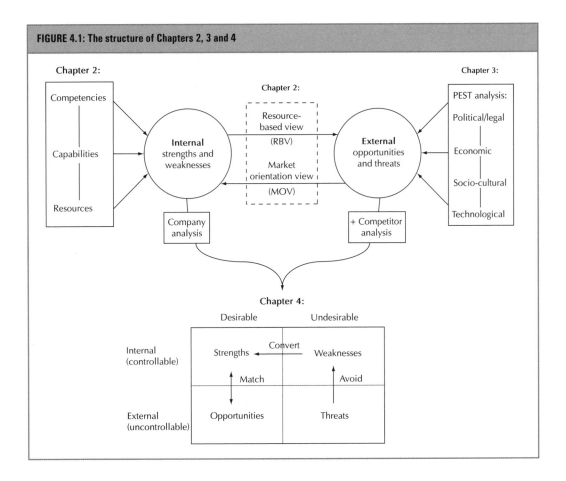

FIGURE 4.1: The structure of Chapters 2, 3 and 4

4.2.1 Strengths

Determine your organization's strong points, from an internal perspective as well as from the perspective of external customers. Do not be humble; be as pragmatic as possible. Are there any unique or distinct advantages that make your organization stand out from the crowd? What makes customers choose your organization over the competition? Are there any products or services your competition cannot imitate (both currently and in the future)?

4.2.2 Weaknesses

Determine your organization's weaknesses, again not only from an internal point of view, but also, and more importantly, from that of your customers. Although it may be difficult for an organization to acknowledge its weaknesses, it is best to handle the bitter reality without procrastination. Are there any operations or procedures that can be streamlined? How and why do competitors operate better than your organization? Is there any way that your organization could avoid its weaknesses? Does the competition have a certain market segment conquered?

4.2.3 Opportunities

Another major factor is to determine how your organization can continue to grow within the marketplace. After all, opportunities are everywhere, such as changes in technology, government policy, social patterns, and so on. Where and what are the attractive opportunities within your marketplace? Are there any new emerging trends within the market? What does your organization predict in the future that may offer new opportunities?

4.2.4 Threats

No one likes to think about threats, but they still have to be faced, despite the fact that they are external factors that are out of the organization's control (e.g. the major worldwide economic slump after 11 September 2001). It is vital to be prepared and to face up to threats, even during turbulent times. What is your competition doing that is suppressing your own organizational development? Are there any changes in consumer demand that make new demands on your products or services? Is changing technology damaging your organization's position within the marketplace?

4.3 Matching and converting in the SWOT matrix

SWOT analysis should not just be an academic exercise used to classify information correctly. Rather, it should serve as a catalyst to facilitate and guide the creation of marketing strategies that will produce the desired results. The process of organizing information within the SWOT analysis can help the organization see the difference between where it thinks it is, where others see it as being and where it hopes to be.

To address these issues properly, the marketing manager should appraise every strength, weakness, opportunity and threat in order to determine its total impact on the organization's marketing efforts. This assessment will also give the manager an idea of the basic strategic options they have (see also Fig. 4.1). The following actions are those suggested by the SWOT matrix:

1 make a match between strengths and opportunities
2 convert weaknesses to strengths
3 convert threats to opportunities
4 minimize, if not avoid, weaknesses and threats.

4.4 The application of the SWOT analysis

The application of SWOT analysis is the matching of specific internal and external factors, which creates a strategic matrix that makes sense. It is essential to note that the internal factors are within the control of your organization (these include operations, finance, marketing and other areas). The external factors are outside your organization's control (these include political and economic factors, technology, competition and other areas). The four combinations that could result from SWOT analysis are called the Maxi-Maxi (strengths/opportunities), Maxi-Mini (strengths/threats), Mini-Maxi (weaknesses/opportunities) and Mini-Mini (weaknesses/threats), as illustrated in Table 4.1.

	Strengths (S)	Weaknesses (W)
Opportunities (O)	Maxi-Maxi (S/O)	Maxi-Mini (S/T)
Threats (T)	Mini-Maxi (W/O)	Mini-Mini (W/T)

TABLE 4.1 The application of the SWOT matrix

- *Maxi-Maxi* (*S/O*): this combination shows the organization's strengths and opportunities. In essence, an organization should strive to maximize its strengths to capitalize on new opportunities.
- *Maxi-Mini* (*S/T*): this combination shows the organization's strengths in consideration of threats (e.g. from competitors). In essence, an organization should strive to use its strengths to parry or minimize threats.
- *Mini-Maxi* (*W/O*): this combination shows the organization's weaknesses in tandem with opportunities. It encourages the organization to conquer its weaknesses by making the most of any new opportunities.
- *Mini-Mini* (*W/T*): this combination shows the organization's weaknesses in comparison with current external threats. This is most definitely a defensive strategy: to minimize an organization's internal weaknesses and avoid external threats.

As mentioned above, the SWOT analysis is the matching of specific internal and external factors. However, what about matching items within internal factors and items within external factors? The primary reason this is not done is that matching these factors will create strategies that do not make sense. Let's take the example of a combination of strength and weakness (both internal factors): let's say one of your organization's strengths is 'plenty of financial resources' and one of its weaknesses is 'lack of sales training'. Mixing these two factors together, your management team might simply decide to plan more training for the sales force. The obvious riposte to this purposeless strategy is 'So what!' This is because there is no point in sales training just for the sake of it. A successful sales training programme must have a specific target in response to external changes; the specific needs of the sales force for training must be determined in line with external and internal factors. In other words, the strategy must have an external factor as a trigger in order for it to be feasible (this could, for example, be the customer's need for advice and service from the sales people before buying any products (Lee et al., 2000)).

4.5 Necessary analyses

A well-conceived SWOT analysis depends on an extensive analysis of the company itself, its competitors and its environment (market and industry). An internal (company) analysis involves a comprehensive appraisal of company strengths and weaknesses, and every aspect of the business should be assessed. For example, coverage should include financial capabilities, technical abilities, location, plant and equipment, personnel, distributor relationships, customer relationships, and so on. In particular, the company should try to identify its core competencies (Hamel and Prahalad, 1994). This concept is useful because it emphasizes the need to consider market opportunities in the light of a company's particular skills relative to its actual or potential competitors. When analysing actual or potential competitors, not only should their numbers be taken into consideration but also key competitors should be examined individually (see Fig. 4.1) in an effort to identify the company's potential for creating a sustainable competitive advantage in the market. The main questions to ask about competitors are as follows.

● What is their (marketing mix) offer?
● What is their competitive advantage?
● How well are they performing?
● What does their SWOT profile look like?
● How are they likely to compete in future?

In conducting a market analysis, there are two types of 'market' that should be considered: the 'immediate market' and the 'wider world'. The immediate market refers to the specific market(s) in which the company actually/potentially operates, with customers and other, more general, market characteristics comprising the most important aspects of this analysis. A customer analysis revolves around asking questions such as why customers buy and what benefits they seek, when and where they buy, and who is involved in the purchase decision. Central to a customer analysis is the concept of *market segmentation.* This is the process of subdividing a market into smaller groups of customers with similar needs and wants/responsiveness to market offerings, which are, or may become, significant for planning a separate target marketing strategy. Having defined candidate market segments, a more general market analysis then involves the assessment of the relative 'attractiveness' of each segment. This necessitates estimating their size, growth rates, competitive structure and potential for profitability. Ideally, a profile of each market should gradually be built up so that each segment can be evaluated in light of the company's particular strengths and weaknesses, and its ability to compete. Finally, the 'wider world' comprises all those factors relating to the political, economic, social and technological environments surrounding a company that, albeit over the longer term, continually act to reshape both buyer and competitor behaviour. It is therefore important to analyse these factors so that any new opportunities or threats emanating from the wider world can be anticipated and acted upon (Brooksbank, 1996).

4.6 Benefits of and barriers to conducting a SWOT analysis

To its credit, SWOT analysis is supremely simple; possibly its greatest advantage is that its use allows management to focus its attention on key issues that affect business development and growth. The benefits of the SWOT analysis are not only seen in its outputs (which may be used in the development of sound strategic business plans) but also in the very *process* of carrying it out. SWOT is not only a static analytical tool that helps generate an understanding of business activity, but also a dynamic part of the management process, which can actually facilitate management development and can be harnessed to the advantage of all involved. It can be seen as a valuable management tool, which may easily be absorbed to good effect into the realities and practicalities of a company's existing planning and strategy formulation processes.

On the other hand, the reasons why so many companies take the 'ask the manager' approach and not a more analytical path in the form of a SWOT analysis are numerous. They include the following (Jenster and Hussey, 2001; Hussey, 2002):

- *Lack of guidance on how to do it*: there are very few books that attempt to explain how to undertake an integrated company analysis. It is also true to say that many MBA programmes spend very little time on this. Being told that something is important but not the detail of how to do it certainly makes it harder to do the job well.
- *Better management information systems*: managers today have access to better, more comprehensive and more up-to-date management information systems than was the case in the past. This can greatly facilitate the corporate appraisal, provided the right information has been collected in the first place, which does not always happen. Regular access to information can mean that managers really are informed about every important aspect of their business and therefore do not need special exercises. It can also lead to complacency and a situation where critical factors are not related to each other or thoroughly understood, and the view taken of the company is fragmented and purely functional.
- *Pressure on managers*: the pressure on managers for immediate results has always been high but is currently greater than ever. It is certainly much quicker to ask them to define corporate strengths and weaknesses than to spend precious time on special analyses; therefore, managers have to be convinced that this extra time is justified. The pressure for a quick fix means that managers will often be tempted to reach for a faddy technique instead of going back to basic principles, and this is rarely the most effective way to deal with a strategic problem.
- *The complexity of many companies*: many companies are very large and complex, which can make the task of carrying out a comprehensive appraisal seem rather daunting, and with the decline of large strategic staff departments the task of organizing such a study is devolved to busy line managers. However, it is a task that lies within the competence of most managers and if approached in a sensible way need not be overwhelming.

Those who still doubt that an analytical approach can yield additional and important strategic information should ponder the following three points.

1 Why is it that a change of chief executive so often leads to a more careful company analysis and a completely different insight into the appropriate vision and strategy for the organization?
2 Similarly, why are management consultants so often able to give a company clarity of thinking about itself after they have been called in to undertake a general review of it?
3 Why does it sometimes take the implementation turmoil after a major acquisition to reveal things about both the buying and the acquired company that were not known before?

Exhibit 4.1: *SWOT analysis of Honda Motor Company corporate level*[1]

Honda Motor Company, based in Tokyo, Japan, is the world's largest motorbike manufacturer and also the third largest car manufacturer in Japan. The company produces and develops a broad spectrum of products, such as passenger cars, motorbikes and general-purpose engines for speciality sports cars. Besides being the manufacturer of the end product (cars, motorbikes, etc.), Honda is also a major original equipment manufacturer (OEM) supplier of small engines to manufacturers of, for example, motorbikes, pleasure boats, snowmobiles and golf cars (Table 4.2).

Strengths	Weaknesses
Globalization strategy: Honda meets the requirements of local markets by not only establishing regional sales networks, but also developing and manufacturing products locally. As a result, it has over 120 manufacturing facilities in 29 countries that pool resources to serve local needs. *Asian operations*: rapid economic growth in the region has expanded the market for motorbikes and cars significantly. However, the low ratio of vehicle ownership also creates a latent demand. Between 1998 and 2004, overall demand for motorcyles in India, Indonesia, Thailand, China, Malaysia, the Philippines and Vietnam expanded by about 75 per cent. Honda has successfully tapped into this opportunity by launching new products at affordable prices, which are a result of cost-setting efforts.	*Weakening financials*: a key worrying factor for the company is its mounting debt levels. *Poor presence in pick-ups*: in the North American market, which provides Honda with more than half of its global sales and profits, the company has kept away from the lucrative full-size pick-ups segment. The company has been so focused on passenger cars that it has not built the necessary infrastructure for the pick-ups segment. *Mixing OEM and end-product market*: in the motorbike market, in particular, Honda is both a supplier of small engines (OEM supplier) and, at the same time, offers the end product itself: the motorcycle. Consequently, Honda can be in a situation where it is competing with its own customers.
Opportunities	**Threats**
Expanding Asian market: the company stands to benefit from the expanding motorbike market in Asia. Honda has been making aggressive sales and marketing efforts in the region, which resulted in significant sales increases in Asia during fiscal 2004, with unit sales up 18 per cent. *Environment-friendly products*: Honda has always maintained a focus on safety and environmental aspects. It has actively explored alternative fuels and developed hybrid vehicles with gasoline-electric engines. Also helping the company are electric vehicles and others powered by compressed natural gas and fuel cells.	*Exposure to currency risks*: the high degree of foreign sales exposes the company to a high degree of currency risk, especially in the dollar–yen relationship, as over 50 per cent of Honda's sales are in the USA. *Volatile pricing environment*: prices for cars, motorbikes and power products in certain markets have, at times, experienced sharp changes over short periods of time. *Counterfeit products*: though China offers the company the largest potential, the market there is flooded with counterfeit products. *Competitive price pressure*: overcapacity within the industry has increased and will probably continue to increase if the economic downturn continues in Honda's major markets or worldwide, leading, potentially, to further increased price pressure.

TABLE 4.2 Honda Motor Company's SWOT analysis

Note:
1 It does not claim to be complete.

4.7 Multilevel SWOT analyses

SWOT analysis may be undertaken on different organizational levels. When we talk about SWOT analysis, we actually mean a *series of analyses*, each focusing on a specific organizational level or product/market combination. Of course, we can talk about a corporate SWOT analysis (as described in Exhibit 4.1 or strategic business unit (SBU) SWOT analysis), but in Fig. 4.2 we can also see that the following four combinations are possible on a product/market level:

1 Product 1 and Market 1
2 Product 1 and Market 2
3 Product 2 and Market 1
4 Product 2 and Market 2.

FIGURE 4.2: Multilevel SWOT analysis

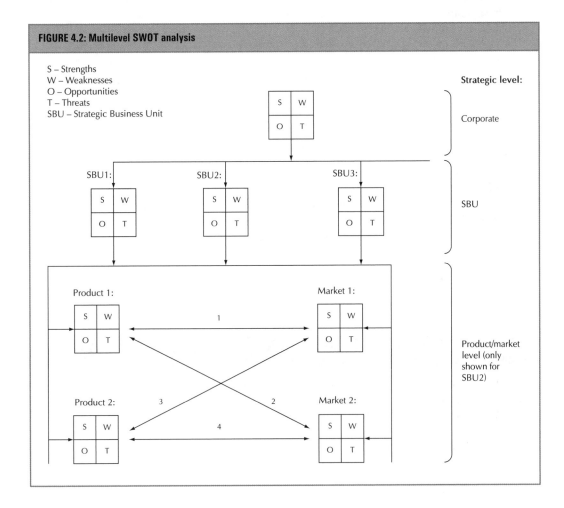

In Fig. 4.2 the different combinations are shown only for SBU2. There would be similar combinations for the other SBUs.

4.7.1 The result of a SWOT analysis

No matter how subjective or objective SWOT analysis becomes, it may be significantly enhanced by considering it as a management process in which the very activity of carrying out the analysis is as important as the final result.

Summary

The SWOT profile is by far the most popular of all marketing planning tools. It provides a means by which all the key internal (company-related) and external (environment-related) issues can be summarized at a glance. A good SWOT profile facilitates the development of a strategy that capitalizes on a company's strengths, minimizes any weaknesses, exploits emerging opportunities and avoids, as far as possible, any threats.

The *internal* (company) analysis involves a comprehensive appraisal of company *strengths* and *weaknesses*, and every aspect of the business should be assessed. For example, coverage should include financial capabilities, technical abilities, location, plant and equipment, personnel, distributor relationships, customer relationships, and so on.

The *external* analysis helps identify market *opportunities* and *threats*, and provides guidelines for the design of the marketing strategy.

Those macro-environmental forces most studied are the so-called PEST (political/legal, economic, socio-cultural and technological) factors. Furthermore, there is, of course, 'competition', which is often a threat, but as we saw in Chapter 3's value net, it can also be an opportunity where those involved can supplement each other's competencies. The company, then, should try to identify its core competencies. This concept is useful because it emphasizes the need to consider market opportunities in the light of a company's particular skills relative to its actual or potential competitors.

Questions for discussion

1   What are the purposes of carrying out a SWOT analysis?
2   What are the major steps in a SWOT analysis?
3   What is the idea of matching a company's strengths with opportunities in the market?
4   Why is the final result less important than the process involved in the SWOT analysis?

References

Barney, J.B. (1991) Firm resources and sustained competitive advantage, *Journal of Management,* 17(1): 99–120.

Brooksbank, R. (1996) The BASIC marketing planning process: a practical framework for the smaller business, *Marketing Intelligence & Planning,* 14(4): 16–23.

Hamel, G. and Prahalad, C.K. (1994) *Competing for the Future.* Boston, MA: Harvard Business School Press.

Hussey, D. (2002) Determining strategic capability, *Strategic Change,* 11: 43–52.

Jenster P. and Hussey D. (2001) *Company Analysis: Assessing Strategic Capability.* Chichester: Wiley.

Lee, S.F., Lo, K.K., Leung, R.F. and Ko, A.S.O. (2000) Strategy formulation framework for vocational education: integrating SWOT analysis, balanced scorecard, QFD methodology and MBNQA education criteria, *Managerial Auditing Journal,* 15(8): 407–23.

Panagiotou, G. (2003) Bringing SWOT into focus, *Business Strategy Review,* 14(2): 8–10.

Porter, M. (1980) *Competitive Strategy.* New York: The Free Press.

Vignali, C. and Curland, S. (2008) Liquid applepie: market entry strategy for a new lifestyle drink, *Journal of Foods Products Marketing,* 14: 3–5

CASE STUDY 4: DUCATI

The Italian motorbike icon is searching for new markets

Ducati Motor Holding, whose red racing machines are known as 'Dukes', builds monster high-performance motorcycles; it also makes sports bikes (Multistrada and SportClassic), as well as a branded line of clothing. Although many 'Ducatists' prefer performance over comfort, Ducati has attempted to expand into new markets with products such as touring bikes and a supermoto model.

History

Bologna's Ducati family founded Ducati Motor Holding in 1926 as the Societa Radio Brevetti Ducati, a builder of radio equipment. During World War II, the company's plant in Bologna was destroyed. In 1946 the Ducati brothers began producing a small motor to be attached to bicycles. The company soon put the motor on a special frame of its own and produced its first motorcycle, the miniature Cucciolo.

The Cucciolo, and later full-sized models, established the Ducati name in the world of motorcycles. During the 1960s Ducati bewitched fans with its 450 Mark 3D, capable of speeds in excess of 100 m.p.h. Claudio and Gianfranco Castiglioni bought Ducati in 1983 and moved the company into the Cagiva Group.

Cagiva planned to rebadge Ducati motorcycles with the lesser-known Cagiva name (at least outside of Italy). By the time the purchase was completed, Cagiva kept the 'Ducati' name on its motorcycles. In 1996, Texas Pacific Group bought a 51 per cent stake in the company for US$325 m; then, in 1998, it bought most of the remaining 49 per cent to become the sole owner of Ducati.

While the company excelled at racing during the 1990s, it didn't fare well financially under Cagiva Group's leadership. In 1996 investment company Texas Pacific Group (TPG) became Ducati's largest shareholder and turned the company around.

Ducati is riding a strategy that combines the characteristics of its traditional high-performance/racing motorcycle with those of a touring machine. With its affiliate, Gio.Ca.Moto, Ducati has entered the market for high-performance motorcycle accessories. After having been a privately owned company since 1926, Ducati went public in 1999. TPG issued an IPO of Ducati stock and renamed the company *Ducati Motor Holding SpA*. TPG sold over 65 per cent of its shares in Ducati, leaving TPG the majority shareholder. In December 2005, Ducati returned to Italian ownership with the sale of Texas Pacific's stake (minus one share) to Investindustrial Holdings, the investment fund of Carlo and Andrea Bonomi.

The last surviving founder of the company, Bruno Cavalieri Ducati, died in 2001 at the age of 96.

Ducati today

The company operates over 150 Ducati stores in major Italian cities, as well as in New York, Frankfurt, London, Cape Town, Tokyo and Sydney, and sells its motorcycles worldwide. Italy and the USA are the company's largest single markets.

Additionally, Ducati offers ultra bikes such as the Streetfighter, which is the symbol for the company's 'big naked concept' of race technology. The track-designed superbike, with its Testastretta Evoluzione engine, will be premiering an 848 Nicky Hayden Edition in 2010. Hayden (2006 MotoGP World Champion) has signed a one-year extension to his contract with Ducati for the 2010 MotoGP (Grand Prix) season.

And rounding the curve of Ducati's portfolio comes the Hypermotard – a hybrid motorcycle with combined elements of motocross bikes and street racers. The bikes are used in supermoto, a relatively new form of racing that combines dirt and street racing into one event. The new model managed to jumpstart lagging sales after it was introduced in 2007, and was the primary contributor to an 18 per cent increase in unit sales.

Ducati's attempts to tap into new markets have been mixed. Its touring bikes were deviations from the company's normal sports bikes, but their sales lagged and several of the models were discontinued.

The overall market for luxury bikes decreased by 30 per cent in the first half of 2009. While Ducati has reduced production and salaries to match the decrease, it has enhanced its customer service by offering zero per cent financing and introducing a factory-backed service agreement that provides a free one-year maintenance service for newly purchased street bikes. It has partnered with Tata Consultancy Services in a three-year, multi-million-dollar deal to help improve its business efficiency through supply chain management. To expand its geographic tyre print, the company is tapping additional markets by launching its superbikes in India in 2008, as well as expanding its product offerings in Japan.

The company underwent an ownership change in late 2008 when Performance Motorcycles acquired Ducati and privatized it. Performance Motorcycles was created by three of Ducati's largest shareholders – Investindustrial, BS Investimenti, and Hospitals of Ontario Pension Plan. The new owners are not planning any radical changes to Ducati's operation other than ensuring the company has the financial strength to meet its goal of introducing 10 new models by 2010. Today *Performance Motorcycles SpA* controls 85 per cent of Ducati.

Currently, there are four Ducati companies: Ducati Motor Holding (the subject of this article), Ducati Corse (which runs the Ducati racing programme and is wholly owned by Ducati Motor Holding), Ducati Energia, a designer and manufacturer of electrical and electronic components and systems, and Ducati Sistemi, a subsidiary of Ducati Energia. All are located in Bologna, Italy.

Ducati Motor Holding often uses electrical components and subsystems from Ducati Energia.

Products

Among the motorcycles the *Monster* (informally called *Il Mostro* in Italian) is a motorcycle designed by Miguel Angel Galluzzi and has been produced by Ducati Motor Holding in Bologna, Italy since 1993. It is of the *naked bike* style, which is characterized by a sport bike with a fully exposed engine and frame. In 2008, Monster sales accounted for half of Ducati's worldwide sales.

Ducati Meccanica (as the company was previously known) has its marque on non-motorcycle products as well. In the 1930s and 1940s, Ducati manufactured radios, cameras and electrical products such as a razor. The Ducati Sogno was a half-frame Leica-like camera, which is now a collector's item.

Ducati has a wide range of accessories, lifestyle products and co-branded merchandise bearing its logos and designs. The company has a licensing agreement with Tumi Inc. which launched a collection of eight co-branded luggage pieces in 2006, selling them through both brands' retail outlets.

Ducati enters the bicycle market

In 2007 Ducati began the sales of its new bicycles (www.bianchiducati.com) that are a result of close collaboration between Ducati and Bianchi, two prestigious Italian brands famous throughout the world for their success in sport and racing competition in particular. The two companies have designed a range of bicycles and technical clothing and accessories, such as helmets and water bottles. The bicycles are produced by Bianchi and cost between €1000 and €5000 each, with models for all tastes, from those for the city to mountain bikes and road bikes. The colour will mainly be the colour of Ducati – red.

This exclusive range of bicycles was distributed throughout the world in specialized shops from 1 January 2007. The co-operation has been the result of the combination of a captivating young design and meticulous materials research.

In September 2009 Ducati even got its own electrical bicycle brand. Ducati Motor Holding and the Italwin Group signed a three-year licensing agreement, which sees the two Italian companies, both leaders in their own sectors, working in close collaboration. Italwin is an Italian company in the sector of electric bicycles. The company was founded in 1997 by the idea of Mauro Tomasoni as an additional activity for the family company. From 2003 he invested in electric vehicles characterized by exclusive design, lightness and quality.

The first product to come out of this new partnership was the new Ducati electric bicycle by Italwin. It was unveiled at a worldwide launch at Eurobike, the top bicycle exhibition held in Friedrichshafen (Germany) from 2 to 5 September 2009.

The bike has been named City Pearl, describing its intended area of use and perceived value for customers. City Pearl combines design with technology, eco sustainability and innovation, making it ideal for those who want to enjoy a stylish, speedy, stress-free form of transport, even in zones with restricted vehicle access.

Table 4.3 shows the financial results of Ducati from 2004 to 2008.

Ducati's financial results

	2008 (€ m)	2007 (€ m)	2006 (€ m)	2005 (€ m)	2004 (€ m)
Turnover	495	398	305	309	388
Net profit/loss before tax	35	18	(2)	(41)	5

TABLE 4.3 Ducati – financial results over five years
Source: adapted from www.ducati.com/company/

In 2008 approximately *44,000 motorbikes* were sold, which means that the average ex-factory price is about *€11,250,* the average number of employees was approximately 1200 and the turnover and number of motorbikes was distributed as follows.

Ducati's marketing strategy and geographic markets

A key part of Ducati's marketing strategy since the 1990s has been fostering a distinct community identity in connection with branding efforts, including online communities, and local, regional and national Ducati enthusiast clubs. There are more than 400 Ducati clubs worldwide, 20 000 registered users of the Ducati Owners Club website and 17 000 subscribers to the racing website.

In North America there are several Ducati enthusiasts' organizations, with varying degrees of factory sponsorship. The Ducati Enthusiast Sport Motorcycle Organization (DESMO) is a North American group affiliated with the factory Desmo Owners Club. Some groups are focused on vintage Ducatis, while several are based primarily or entirely on email discussion lists or web forums, such as Ducati.net.

Ducati's geographic markets

Ducati's biggest market is the home market, Italy, but still 74 per cent of the motorbikes are sold outside Italy (Table 4.4).

	2008 (€m)
Turnover	€495 m
Number of motorbikes sold	44,000
	%
Italy	26
USA	20
France	9
UK	5
Germany	8
Japan	5
Benelux	6
Other countries	21
Total	100

TABLE 4.4 Ducati's sales of motorbikes in different countries
Source: adapted from www.ducati.com/company/

The competition on the world motorbike market – the up- and downturn of the Japanese manufacturers' market shares

In 1981 Japan's motorbike industry was in a state of blissful ignorance. Its manufacturers had managed to dominate the world in not much over a decade and annual production had hit 7.4 million units. Although they did not know it, this was to be their best year.

Two decades later and Japanese manufacturers are nowhere near as dominant. While they still loom large on the global motorbike market, 1981's record domestic production has declined to just 2.4 million. This serves as a stark reminder of a painful trend for all types of Japanese manufacturer as their domestic costs have risen, their markets have matured and their rivals have sharpened their game.

In 2001 two Japanese manufacturers – Suzuki and Kawasaki – joined forces to jointly produce and develop new bikes, marking the end of the 'big four' in Japan, where they ruled alongside much bigger rivals Honda and Yamaha.

The 'hollowing out' shift to overseas production through joint ventures and wholly owned plants has also cut into domestic production in Japan.

The Suzuki–Kawasaki tie-up also serves as a symbol for what has happened to Japan's motorbike industry in the last two decades. Once lazy and inefficient rivals such as Ducati, BMW and Harley-Davidson have found a way of replying to the competitive threat from Japan and are clawing back market share. In Europe, for example, Japan's market share has fallen from 80 per cent to 50 per cent over five years, although numbers have risen. And in the vital US market its share has fallen by 10 per cent over the past decade.

The rise and rise of the Japanese motorbike manufacturers owed as much to luck as to design. Manufacturers were servicing a huge domestic market for many years, which generated the profits that financed the export drive. It also gave the Japanese a finely honed design and production machine that churned out faster, more reliable and better-looking bikes – and did so every year. The weak yen also made Japanese exports intensely competitive.

In addition, they were up against severely weakened domestic manufacturers in the West. Triumph, BSA and Norton in the UK, for example, were spent forces, and the country was in the middle of labour disputes that generated a lazy attitude towards design and technology, producing machines that looked old-fashioned in comparison to their Japanese rivals.

But the Japanese manufacturers, perhaps complacent in their success, failed to spot a key change in the motorbike buying world. They were too obsessed with technology and assembly quality and did not recognize that motorbikes had become consumer goods, which had a brand value. Harley-Davidson led the way here with branded goods ranging from desk clocks to women's thongs, feeding hugely into profits.

Japanese manufacturers based their bikes on racing models. Undoubtedly, Japanese bikes are lighter and faster, but it takes a lot of skill to ride them. Western manufacturers have been designing for people who like to ride normal bikes in a normal environment. As Japan's rivals have caught up with the technology, they have also managed to inject something extra.

Ducati conveys on two wheels the kind of image its Italian counterpart, Ferrari, has on four. Triumph has capitalized on its Britishness and the appeal of the marque's previous incarnation with such models as the Bonneville. Harley-Davidson has built up an appeal for weekend rebels with US $70 000-plus salaries. BMW has combined engineering excellence with design flair.

But to talk of the demise of the Japanese motorbike industry would be unwise. Honda remains the largest manufacturer of motorbikes in the world. However, the Japanese are removing themselves from the big bike category. Honda, Yamaha and Suzuki are concentrating on 100–500 cc bikes for mass production in the developing countries of Asia. The bulk of Japanese-made bikes are small and service the growing economies of Asia, where having a 50 cc or 100 cc bike is the first step on a transportation ladder that eventually leads to a Toyota Corolla. India and China are huge and growing markets for the Japanese and Suzuki says it hopes its new link with its smaller rival will help its efforts in China.

The alliance between Suzuki and Kawasaki has more to do with these markets than the competition in the superbike league. It allows them to pare costs considerably by jointly procuring parts and joining forces on product design, development and production.

It also matches similar moves by Honda, which has reduced the number of its Japanese motorbike production lines from five to two in recent years. While Japanese manufacturers may be facing competition at the top end of the market, motorbikes are a high-volume game – and in this game the Japanese are still the winners.

The global competitive situation today

The competitive market situation in the three main regions of the world is shown in Table 4.5.

	North America	Europe	Asia/Pacific
Total industry (1,000s)	**480**	**397**	**80**
Market share	%	%	%
Harley-Davidson/Buell	48	9	25
Honda	14	12	17
Yamaha	9	13	12
Kawasaki	7	11	13
Suzuki	12	16	10
BMW	2	15	5
Ducati	2	8	5
Triumph	2	7	4
Others	4	9	9
Total	100	100	100.0

TABLE 4.5 The three main market areas for heavyweight motorbikes (more than 650cc) number of registrations (2008)
Source: adapted from Harley-Davidson Financial Report 2008, and other public sources

Market trends

In industrialized wealthy economies such as Japan, the USA and Europe motorbikes were often purchased for recreation in addition to basic transport. In developing economies and others with low-income per capita, motorbikes or smaller two-wheelers were purchased primarily for basic transport, and the market was distinctly different. Historically, large touring bikes, cruisers and racers sold almost exclusively in the wealthy economies while motorcycles with small engine displacement and mopeds made up the vast majority of sales in the developing nations. Decreasing trends in the overall market in some nations were due in large part to replacement of two-wheeled vehicles by cars as the countries became more affluent.

Questions

1 What are the core competencies of Ducati?

2 Please perform a multilevel SWOT analysis, based on Ducati: on corporate level and on the two SBU levels: motorbikes and bicycles.

Sources: www.ducati.com; www.harley-davidson.com

PART 02

Developing the Marketing Strategy and Programme

Strategic market planning

Chapter contents

❖ LEARNING OBJECTIVES

After studying this chapter you should be able to do the following:

- ❖ Understand the importance of strategic marketing planning.
- ❖ Identify the main steps in strategic marketing planning.
- ❖ Develop an appropriate business mission statement.

- ❖ Describe the criteria for stating good strategic marketing objectives.
- ❖ Understand how portfolio models are used to select alternatives.
- ❖ Explain the advantages and disadvantages of using strategic models like Ansoff's growth matrix, and the Boston Consulting Group (BCG) and General Electric (GE) models.

5.1   Introduction

The word 'strategy' is derived from a Greek term, translated roughly as the 'art of the general (or commander-in-chief)'. It should be borne in mind, though, that military strategy, and relatively traditional perspectives at that, is only one source of insight into the nature of marketing strategy. Useful analogies can also be found in both sports and evolutionary ecology, as well as in more formal game theory. Strategy, then, originally referred to the *skills and decision-making processes* of the general (executive), while 'stratagem', translated as 'an operation or act of generalship', referred to a *specific decision* made by the executive.

To complicate matters even further, some writers suggest that a 'strategy' implies a formal and explicitly stated logic, while others have argued that a strategy can emerge from a set of decisions and need not be stated explicitly. Mintzberg and Walters (1985) even distinguished specifically between 'deliberate' and 'emergent' strategies.

Planning is a complex process and in explaining it to anyone, there must be consideration of communication. Presenting a model of a number of stages is a common way to attempt to effect communication. All the stages are interrelated, but this approach, like the final plan itself at a particular point in time, is like a freeze-frame photograph. With time there is change, hence planning is a continuous process where each stage needs to be considered and reconsidered for relevancy and in relation to the other stages. The plan is the stages 'frozen' in time; the process is a continuous assessment of the relevancy of each of these stages with changes in time.

In planning we look ahead to decide what to do. The planning process itself is a systematic way of approaching the following questions, and they will be used as a framework for the rest of this chapter.

- What business are we in (vision and mission statement – Section 5.2)?
- Where are we today (situation analysis – Chapter 4)?
- Where do we want to go (strategic objectives – Section 5.3)?
- How do we get there?
  - estimation of the planning gap, and problem diagnosis (Section 5.4)
  - the search for strategic alternatives (Ansoff's growth matrix, Porter's three generic strategies, the BCG and GE models – Section 5.5)
  - strategy evaluation and selection (Section 5.6)
  - estimating financial consequences/How can progress be measured (marketing metrics – Section 5.7)?

Although there is never any certainty about the future, every business or organization will sensibly lean towards a proactive rather than a reactive stance. A proactive stance is one where the organization tries to forecast the future in order to influence it; that is, plan to adapt to it rather than just surrender to it. This contrasts with a more reactive stance, where action mainly takes place in response to events with no plan to anticipate them or seek to influence them. This is similar to the two concepts explained in Chapter 2: market driving (resource-based view) versus market driven (market orientation view).

5.2 Vision and mission statement

The vision and mission concepts are often interlinked, but generally there is a difference:

- A business *mission* statement describes 'who we are and what is the overall purpose of our business'.

- A business *vision* statement describes 'where we wish to go', 'what we wish to become'; it provides a mental image of the successful accomplishment of the mission; it is typically:
  - short
  - idealistic and imaginative
  - enthusiasm-inspiring
  - ambitious.

The rest of this section will primarily be about the mission: the mission reflects the unique qualities of the programme.

Whether the organization is a large corporation or a small non-profit agency, its mission statement articulates its strategic scope clearly. The mission statement should answer fundamental questions such as 'What is our business?', 'Who are our constituencies?', 'What value do we provide to customers, employees, suppliers and other constituent groups?' and 'What should our business be in the future?' Senior management staff in all businesses need to answer such questions. The responsibility for developing and articulating a mission statement is at the corporate level. Mission statements should be driven by three factors: heritage, resources and environment.

The organization's *heritage* is its history – where it has been, what it has done well and what it has done poorly. A good mission statement cannot ignore previous events and how they have shaped the organization. It also must be sensitive to the organization's image in the minds of its constituencies. Past successes should be extended, past failures avoided, and the organization's current image must be addressed realistically. For example, for a food company to adopt a mission statement such as 'to be a world leader in information technology in five years' will be perceived as unrealistic by customers, employees and shareholders. Such a mission statement is likely to elicit more scepticism than support.

Resources refers to everything the organization can manage, such as cash reserves, recognized brands, unique technologies and talented employees. Resources can also include borrowing power, existing relationships with distributors and excess plant capacity. A good mission statement notes the organization's resources and sets paths that are compatible with what the organization has at its disposal. As in the case of heritage, mission statements that are out of touch with the organization's resources elicit scepticism and can do more harm than good. If a minor regional brand were to include 'penetrating Asian markets' in its mission statement, this would be met with substantial scepticism.

The *environment* is everything happening currently that affects the organization's ability to achieve objectives or implement strategies, both inside and outside it. Some environmental factors are temporary, such as a hurricane. Most temporary factors are too short-lived to be considered in a mission statement. Other factors, however, such as changes in the political system of the Russian Republic, the rise of Islamic fundamentalism, terrorist acts, and the rise or fall of oil prices, may have a longer life and should be considered in the mission statement *if* they affect the organization's ability to survive and prosper.

At the corporate level, the mission statement defines the organization's business and reflects fundamental beliefs about its strengths and weaknesses, as well as its environment. Corporate mission statements can vary in length, but should always communicate a clear sense of the organization's purpose, and be specific enough to be useful in developing goals and objectives. Typically, mission statements focus on meeting customer needs and providing value to shareholders. In addition, they often include judgements about the most promising directions for organizations, implying that those directions not listed are not as promising and should be given lower priority or ignored altogether.

Not all organizations have mission statements, and not all mission statements meet the ideal standards described here. Developing a company mission statement that provides long-term vision and guidance in developing goals and objectives can be difficult. Writing an effective mission statement requires senior managers to struggle with the questions listed earlier – questions that sound simple but can be tough issues for an organization to address. The increasing visibility and importance of marketing as a philosophy for doing business, however, forces many organizations to tackle the task of defining their corporate mission. At the same time, an emphasis on marketing also helps organizations ensure that meeting customer needs profitably lies at the centre of any mission statement.

5.3 Strategic objectives

Strategic management also requires that organizations set *strategic objectives*: specific and measurable performance standards for strategically important areas. Whereas a mission statement may set broad goals, such as 'being the best company in the world', strategic objectives must specify what it means to be 'best'. Management must define the criteria it will use to assess performance and then specify a desired level of achievement for each criterion.

An organization cannot set realistic, realizable objectives until it has the requisite information but, on the basis of experience, marketing management will none the less have tentative views on sales volume, market share or whatever indicators represent progress towards accomplishing its vision. What exactly these tentative views are will be influenced by subjective estimates of what is considered reasonable at the time in relation to what resources are likely to be available.

For a manager to be able to direct an activity towards the achievement of some objectives, it must be possible to imagine the goal in a way that is meaningful for guiding the activity. This is why objectives purely concerned with profit are inadequate: they offer too little guidance.

Strategic objectives can be stated in terms of different criteria, such as euro sales, market share or return on investment, or they can be stated in absolute or relative terms. To be effective, objectives must be specific in terms of:

- the performance dimension being measured
- the measures most appropriate for the performance dimension
- the target value for each measure
- the time by which the target should be achieved.

The emphasis given to each component of the organization's objectives, and the level at which measures and the time horizon are set, can vary according to position in the organizational hierarchy. At the corporate level, profit and growth objectives might be most important and the time horizon might be set in five-year increments. At a business-unit level, however, cash flow and cost reductions may be most important in declining markets, and market share gains in emerging markets. Likewise, the time horizon might be shorter than five years for business units because a new technology will render current operations obsolete, or it might be longer because market acceptance is slow. The characteristics of business units and their immediate environment should primarily determine strategic objectives, provided that the objectives do not violate the organization's mission. The objectives should also be compatible with the culture unless the business unit is soon to be divested.

Strategic objectives at different organizational levels can sometimes conflict. Conflict can also arise between the different levels of organizational thinking. An organization might set objectives pertaining to a desired culture that conflict with its more specific objectives for staff development. Consider, for example, a mission statement that lists as a goal 'providing opportunities for employees' personal development' at the same time as the company claims to value teamwork. Maximizing individual employee development can undermine teamwork if the primary means of development is to promote high performers quickly. Such a company has conflicting objectives, even if they are implicit and not easily recognized.

Managers must establish strategic objectives with great care. These must be articulated at every level of the organization at which it makes sense to have objectives. They must be expressed in terms that are easily understood by the people who are required to achieve them, they must be measurable and specific, and they must be set at achievable levels. Setting objectives at attainable, yet challenging, levels is important.

It should be clear that strategic objectives must be compatible with the organization's mission; at the same time, they may conflict over what are relevant evaluation criteria, performance measures and time horizons. Conflict between strategic objectives must be resolved through compromise, and it is senior management's job to reconcile these differences within the broad framework of having a market-oriented philosophy of doing business.

5.4 Estimation of the planning gap, and problem diagnosis

What do the 'facts' suggest will be the future if the organization takes no action to change current strategies? Such a prediction is known as a 'reference projection'. A reference projection is the future that can be expected in the absence of planned change. The reference projection is compared with 'target projection', or the setting of tentative goals, which the organization sets for itself. The planning (performance) gap is the difference between the target and the reference projections (see Fig. 5.1).

The gap may stem from the difference between future desired profit objectives and a forecast of projected profit based on past performance and following existing strategy.

In the face of such a planning gap, a number of options are available; the intention, however, is to close the gap. This could be achieved by revising objectives in a downward direction; such a step might be taken where the initial objectives are unrealistic. Alternatively, or in addition, the gap could be closed by actions designed to move the company off the projection curve and towards the desired curve.

The planning gaps identified will depend on which performances are of interest. At the highest level, this could be cash flow projections, economic value added, cash flow return on investment, earnings per share, sales and market share or various financial indices like return on investment (ROI). At the marketing level, this could be in terms of sales, market share, costs, market penetration or various behavioural indices like buyer attitudes.

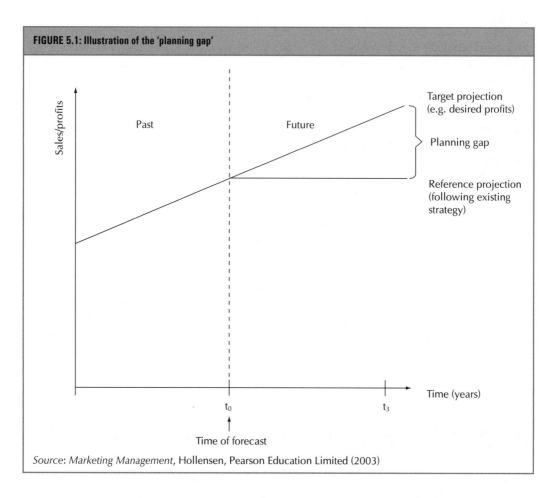

FIGURE 5.1: Illustration of the 'planning gap'

Source: *Marketing Management*, Hollensen, Pearson Education Limited (2003)

5.4.1 Problem diagnosis

If an organization has a large planning gap, we would be likely to pinpoint this as a problem; or, more accurately, to state that the planning gap itself is not the problem but the symptom of one. The recognition of a problem situation is not in itself the identification of the actual problem. We do not discover a problem, we diagnose one. Problem diagnosis aims to identify the *type* of solution that applies, which is the first step on the road to developing an actual solution, just as diagnosing a failure to start the car as being due to some electrical fault is the first step towards getting the car started again. Unfortunately, different people will make different diagnoses, depending on their experience, professional expertise and their concerns. Of course, some companies may evade responsibility and define the problem as a problem of persuading the government to increase tariffs on their foreign competitors' products. Here the solution is viewed as increasing the organization's political muscle.

We cannot understand a problem without understanding what would count as a solution, just as we cannot understand an objective without understanding what would count as the achievement of it. The actual problem that is addressed depends to some extent on which individual or group can make the problem, as they see it, count. But all management groups in a company are influenced by credible arguments and so true technical expertise usually wins the day. Hopefully it must, for if the wrong problem is addressed, the wrong decisions are made and this can be more wasteful of resources than solving the right problem in an inefficient way. Although we hesitate to acknowledge it, the fact is that once we move away from some pure deductive system like mathematics, we are in the realm of persuasion, where persuasive rhetoric is crucial so that a dramatic description of what is considered to be the problem can emotionally compel attention and, often, our assent.

Exhibit 5.1: *Starbucks considers India as a new market*

Today, Starbucks operates 8000 cafés worldwide, including in over 100 locations in China. Its long-term expansion goal is to have 30 000 cafés worldwide.

India, on target to become the most populous country in the world after China, produces and consumes the most tea in the world. Strangely enough, though, it could be next on Starbucks' list of hot new markets for gourmet coffee outside of the USA.

Both India and China are still small players in terms of domestic coffee consumption. China has one of the world's smallest coffee markets, whereas India ranks 36 out of 53 nations with the biggest sales of packaged coffee, according to market research company ACNielsen. The USA tops the list, followed by Germany, France, Japan and Italy.

India is a tea-based culture. Starbucks and other coffee bars are substitutes, but these cafés offer an opportunity for younger people to socialize outside of the home. 'With the liberalization of the economy, there are a large number of young Indians with good jobs and attractive incomes,' says Brotin Banerjee, vice president of marketing at New Delhi-based Barista Coffee Company. 'Many still live with their parents. So their income is largely disposable and they need to spend it on something. Why not on gourmet coffee?'

Competition

Industry reports suggest that India's nascent gourmet coffee market holds the potential for 5000 cafés over the next five years.

Barista opened its first 'coffee bar' in India four years ago. Today it operates 130 cafés around the country, which bear a resemblance to Starbucks. Barista already has a brand identity and customer loyalty. It also has prime locations in big metropolitan cities. Barista's menu features everything from latte to cappuccino, caramel caffé, caffé mocha, flavoured coffee and desserts like brownies and cakes.

Strategy opportunities for Starbucks

Starbucks is keen to tap in to India's burgeoning middle-class market of 200 million people. However, unlike its domestic US approach, where its stores are largely company-owned, government regulations in India will require it either to form joint ventures with local players or create franchise operations. Apparently that is not an issue, since the company faced a similar hurdle in China and opted for the joint venture route.

Source: adapted from Bhatnagar (2004)

5.5   The search for strategic alternatives for closing the 'planning gap'

The strategic options for closing the planning gap should not only fit the problematic situation and take account of trends and competition, but should also exploit the organization's core competencies and strengths. Where the solution is other than a crisis one, there is time for more reflective planning, guided by:

● the situation as revealed by the performance gap
● the perceived problem
● the strengths, weaknesses, opportunities and threats identified in the historical review/situation analysis
● current strategies and policies
● existing capabilities or competencies.

The strategy search process should always allow for the possibility of inspiration, which may beat anything arrived at by methodical analysis. It is not uncommon for someone to come up with an idea that is instantly recognizable as being the right answer: genius sometimes lies in what appears, once stated, as a truism. The inspired solution is thus accepted, not because it saves time (this would just be to accept a faster way of producing unsatisfactory end results) but because it is perceived to be superior and effective. This said, the identification of appropriate strategies rests on having the requisite experience, and the content of the strategy, not the procedure, is all important. Where the requisite experience is lacking, the search for strategies is likely to be hampered by obstacles.

The mental screening and evaluation of strategies can be demanding. In effect, we are mentally rehearsing hypotheses about the relationship between strategies and their likely benefits – but not *just* benefits, since strategies can have side effects that can constitute dysfunctional consequences.

5.5.1 Ansoff's generic strategies for growth

One aspect of strategic management is the development of specific strategies for achieving organization objectives. Strategies must respond to the environment and provide specific guidelines for decision-making. Because organizations face unique combinations of internal and external factors, the strategies developed by any one organization are unlikely to be entirely adaptable to any other organization. At a more general level, however, it is possible to discern recurring patterns in the strategies adopted by organizations. These recurring patterns are called *generic strategies*.

If we elaborate on the 'planning gap' depicted in Fig. 5.1, we get what is illustrated in Fig. 5.2, where the 'gap' is filled up with Ansoff 's expansion strategies (Ansoff, 1965).

Market penetration

Organizations seeking to grow by gaining a larger market share in their current industry or market follow a *penetration* strategy. The following alternatives are available:

● increase market share on current markets with current products
● increase product share (increase frequency of use, increase quantity used, new applications).

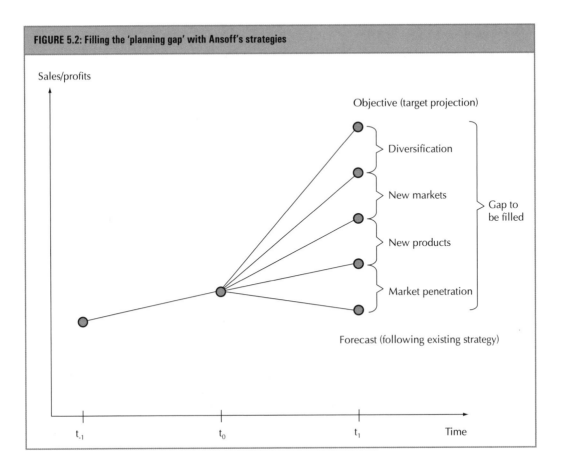

FIGURE 5.2: Filling the 'planning gap' with Ansoff's strategies

Sales/profits

Objective (target projection)

Diversification

New markets

Gap to be filled

New products

Market penetration

Forecast (following existing strategy)

t$_{-1}$ t$_0$ t$_1$ Time

Penetration strategies can be very successful when the company has a technological or production advantage that allows it to take market share away from competitors while still operating profitably. However, such strategies can also be very costly if they rely primarily on setting prices below those of competing products.

Product development strategies

Organizations can also remain within their established industries or markets and seek expansion by introducing new products or services in current markets. This is also called a *technology development* strategy. This strategy may take the following forms:

- product improvements
- product line extensions
- new products for same market.

Product development strategies are in peril if competitors can easily copy the new product being introduced by using lower manufacturing or delivery costs. They can also be at risk if the products are not different enough from existing products to inspire demand.

Market development strategies

When an organization retains the same products but seeks new markets, it is following a *market development* strategy. This strategy involves the following strategic possibilities:

- geographic expansion (new countries/regions)
- new segments/customer groups.

Diversification strategies

Pursuing a growth strategy by introducing new products or technologies in new markets or industries is called *diversification.* The following alternatives are available:

- vertical integration (forward integration or backward integration)
- diversification into related businesses (concentric diversification)
- diversification into unrelated businesses (conglomerate diversification).

This term 'diversification' is frequently associated with expansion into areas unrelated to the organization's current operations in order to offset cyclical downturns in one area with cyclical growth in other areas. Diversification was popular with many large organizations in the 1970s and gave rise to legendary conglomerates.

Another way of illustrating the 'planning gap' and moving the organizations towards the desired curve (or position in the market) is to look at existing sales and compare these with total served market and the market potential (Fig. 5.3). The single organization is mainly able to increase market share by filling the '4Ps gaps', by using one or more Ps in combination. However, unless the organization is a major player in the industry, it will not be able to influence the size of the unserved market or the degree of market penetration. (We look at the 4Ps in more detail in later chapters.)

Market potential

The most difficult estimate to make is probably that of 'market potential' in the whole market, including all segments. In the B2C market it is often achieved by determining the maximum potential individual usage and then extrapolating this by the maximum number of potential consumers (in the B2B market it would be the maximum number of organizations). The maximum potential individual usage, or at least the maximum attainable average usage, will usually be determined from market research figures. For guidance one can look at the numbers using similar products. Alternatively, a marketer can look at what has happened in other countries. It has often been suggested that Europe follows patterns set in the USA, but with a certain time lag.

5.5.2 Porter's three generic strategies

Strategies based on distinctive advantage and business scope

According to Porter (1985), forging successful strategy begins with an understanding of what is happening in one's industry and deciding which of the available competitive niches one should attempt to dominate. For example, an organization may discover that the largest competitor in an industry is aggressively pursuing cost leadership, that others are trying the differentiation route, and that no one is attempting to focus on some small speciality market.

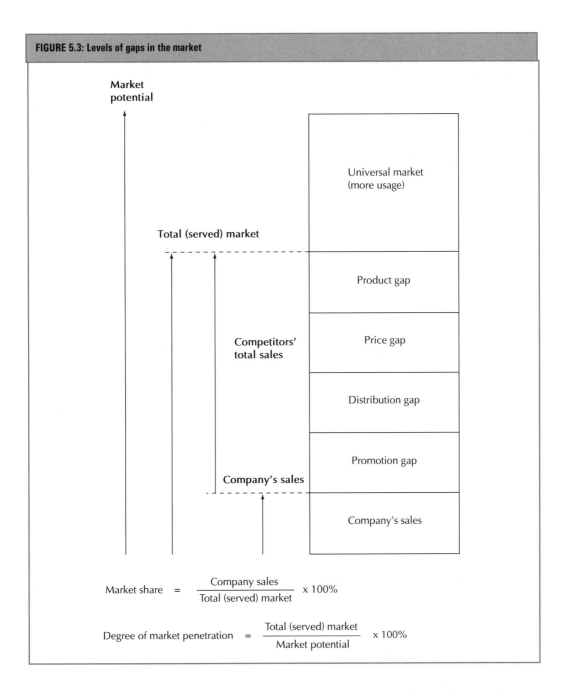

FIGURE 5.3: Levels of gaps in the market

On the basis of this information, the organization might sharpen its efforts to distinguish its product from others or switch to a focus game plan. As Porter (1985: 119) says, the idea is to position the organization 'so it won't be slugging it out with everybody else in the industry; if it does it right, it won't be directly toe-to-toe with anyone'. The objective is to mark out a defensible competitive position – defensible not just against rival companies, but also against the forces driving industry competition (Akan et al., 2006).

What it means is that the give-and-take between organizations already in the business represents only one such force. Others are the bargaining power of suppliers, the bargaining power of buyers, the threat of substitute products or services, and the threat of new entrants (Porter's 'five forces' model).

Combining the dimensions of distinctive advantage and business scope in a matrix results in the strategic orientation typology illustrated in Fig. 5.4. A cost leadership orientation suggests that the company will try to be the low-cost producer in the markets and industries in which it competes, as in the case of Texas Instruments.

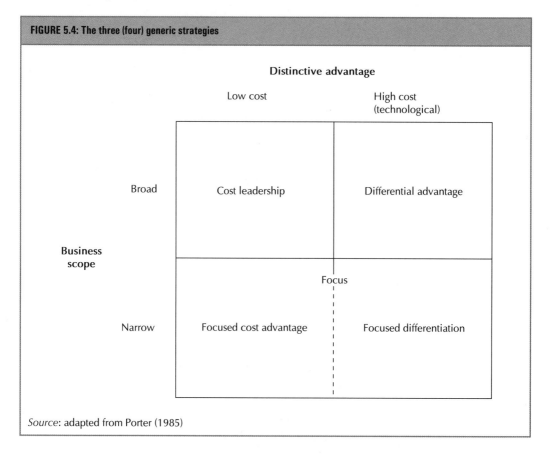

FIGURE 5.4: The three (four) generic strategies

Distinctive advantage

	Low cost	High cost (technological)
Broad	Cost leadership	Differential advantage
Narrow	Focused cost advantage	Focused differentiation

Business scope

Focus

Source: adapted from Porter (1985)

A *differential advantage* orientation occurs when the organization focuses on staying ahead of its competitors in the technological and performance stakes. Hewlett-Packard adopted this strategic orientation when the market for handheld calculators was in its early stages. Its calculators were more expensive than Texas Instruments' products, but HP's technology and performance were superior. In later years, Texas Instruments matched the performance and technological features of Hewlett-Packard calculators while retaining its cost leadership, forcing HP to reduce its prices.

Focused cost advantage and *focused differentiation* are similar to the broader strategies, but have limited target markets. An organization with a focused cost orientation seeks to be a low-cost producer in only one product line or in a limited geographic market. German company Lidl initially followed a focused cost strategy, seeking to be the low-cost retailer in small cities and towns that were overlooked by other discounters. Focused differentiation can also be seen in British Triumph Motor Cycles Ltd's decision to stay in the heavyweight motorbike segment, where it had distinctive features.

5.5.3 The Boston Consulting Group (BCG) portfolio matrix model

A good planning system must guide the development of strategic alternatives for each of the organization's current businesses and new business possibilities. It must also provide for management's review of these strategic alternatives and for corresponding resource-allocation decisions. The result is a set of approved business plans that, taken as a whole, represent the direction of the organization. This process starts with, and its success is largely determined by, the creation of sound strategic alternatives.

The top management of a multi-business organization cannot generate these strategic alternatives. It must rely on the managers of its business ventures and on its corporate development personnel. However, top management can and should establish a conceptual framework within which these alternatives can be developed. One such framework is the portfolio matrix associated with BCG. Briefly, the portfolio matrix is used to establish the best mix of businesses in order to maximize the long-term earnings growth of the organization. The portfolio matrix represents a real advance in strategic planning in several ways:

- It encourages top management to evaluate the prospects of each of the organization's businesses individually and to set tailored objectives for each business based on the contribution it can realistically make to corporate goals.
- It stimulates the use of externally focused empirical data to supplement managerial judgement in evaluating the potential of a particular business.
- It explicitly raises the issue of cash-flow balancing as management plans for expansion and growth.
- It gives managers a potent new tool for analysing competitors and for predicting competitive responses to strategic moves.
- It provides not just a financial but also a strategic context for evaluating acquisitions and divestitures.

The portfolio matrix approach has given top management the tools to evaluate each business in the context of both its environment and its unique contribution to the goals of the organization as a whole, and to weigh the entire array of business opportunities available to the organization against the financial resources required to support them.

The portfolio matrix concept addresses the issue of the potential value of a particular business for the organization. This value has two variables: first, the potential for generating attractive earnings levels now; second, the potential for growth or, in other words, for significantly increased earnings levels in the future. The portfolio matrix concept holds that these two variables can be quantified. Current earning potential is measured by comparing the market position of the business to that of its competitors. Empirical studies have shown that profitability is directly determined by relative market share.

Growth potential is measured by the growth rate of the market segment in which the business competes. Clearly, if the segment is in the decline stage of its life cycle, the only way the business can increase its market share is by taking volume away from competitors.

Although this is sometimes possible and economically desirable, it is usually expensive, leads to destructive pricing and the erosion of profitability for all competitors, and ultimately results in a market that is ill served.

Figure 5.5 shows a matrix with its two sides labelled 'Market growth rate' and 'Relative market share'. The area of each circle represents sales. The market share of each circle is determined by its horizontal position. Each circle's product sales growth rate (corrected for inflation) in the market in which it competes is shown by its vertical position.

FIGURE 5.5: The BCG model

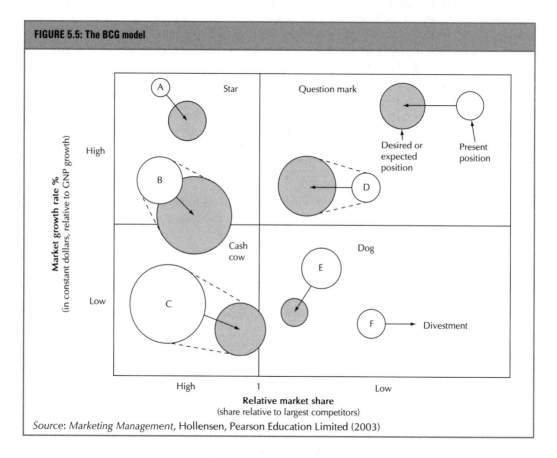

Source: *Marketing Management*, Hollensen, Pearson Education Limited (2003)

With regard to the two axes of the matrix, relative market share is plotted on a logarithmic scale in order to be consistent with the experience curve effect, which implies that profit margin or rate of cash generation differences between two competitors tends to be proportionate to the ratio of their competitive positions. A linear axis is used for growth, for which the most generally useful measure is volume growth of the business concerned; in general, rates of cash use should be directly proportional to growth.

Classification of the BCG boxes

Using the two dimensions illustrated in Fig. 5.5, one can classify businesses and products into four categories. Businesses in each category exhibit different financial characteristics and offer different strategic choices, as described below.

Stars

High-growth market leaders are called *stars*. They generate large amounts of cash, but the cash they generate from earnings and depreciation is more than offset by the cash that must be put back in the form of capital expenditure and increased working capital. Such heavy reinvestment is necessary to fund the capacity increases and inventory and receivable investment that go along with market share gains. Thus, star products represent probably the best profit opportunity available to a company, and their competitive position must be maintained. If a star's share is allowed to slip because the star has been used to provide large amounts of cash in the short run or because of cutbacks in investment and rising prices (creating an umbrella for competitors), the star will ultimately become a dog (see below).

The ultimate value of any product or service is reflected in the stream of cash it generates net of its own reinvestment. For a star, this stream of cash lies in the future – sometimes in the distant future. To obtain real value, the stream of cash must be discounted back to the present at a rate equal to the return on alternative opportunities. It is the future pay-off of the star that counts, not the present reported profit. For GE, the plastics business is a star in which it keeps investing. As a matter of fact, the company even acquired French company Thomson's plastics operations to further strengthen its position in the business.

Cash cows

Cash cows are characterized by low growth and high market share. They are net providers of cash. Their high earnings, coupled with their depreciation, represent high cash inflows and they need very little in the way of reinvestment. Thus, these businesses generate large cash surpluses that help to pay dividends and interest, provide debt capacity, supply funds for research and development, meet overheads, and also make cash available for investment in other products. Thus, cash cows are the foundation on which everything else depends. These products must be protected. Technically speaking, a cash cow has a return on assets that exceeds its growth rate. Only if this is true will the cash cow generate more cash than it uses.

Question marks

Products in a growth market with a low share are categorized as *question marks*. Because of growth, these products require more cash than they are able to generate on their own. If nothing is done to increase market share, a question mark will simply absorb large amounts of cash in the short run and later, as the growth slows down, become a dog (see below). Thus, unless something is done to change its perspective, a question mark remains a cash loser throughout its existence and ultimately becomes a cash trap.

What can be done to make a question mark more viable? One alternative is to gain share increases for it. Because the business is growing, it can be funded to dominance. It may then become a star and later, when growth slows down, a cash cow. This strategy is a costly one in the short run. An abundance of cash must be poured into a question mark in order for it to win a major share of the market, but in the long run this strategy is the only way to develop a sound business from the question mark stage. Another strategy is to divest the business. Outright sale is the most desirable alternative. But if this does not work out, a firm decision must be made not to invest further in the business. The business must simply be allowed to generate whatever cash it can while none is reinvested.

Dogs

Products with a low market share positioned in low-growth situations are called *dogs.* Their poor competitive position condemns them to poor profits. Because growth is low, dogs have little potential for gaining a sufficient share to achieve viable cost positions. Usually they are net users of cash. Their earnings are low, and the reinvestment required just to keep the business together eats cash inflow. The business, therefore, becomes a cash trap that is likely to regularly absorb cash unless further investment is rigorously avoided. An alternative is to convert dogs into cash, if there is an opportunity to do so. GE's consumer electronics business had been in the dog category, maintaining only a small percentage of the available market in a period of slow growth, when the company decided to unload the business (including the RCA brand acquired in late 1985) to Thomson, France's state-owned, leading electronics manufacturer.

Table 5.1 summarizes the investment, earning and cash flow characteristics of stars, cash cows, question marks and dogs. Also shown are viable strategy alternatives for products in each category.

Quadrant	Investment characteristics	Earning characteristics	Cash-flow characteristics	Strategy implication
Stars	Continual expenditures for capacity expansion	Low	Negative cash flow (net cash user)	Continue to increase market share, if necessary at the expense of short-term earnings
Cash cows	Capacity maintenance expenditures	High	Positive cash flow (net cash contributor)	Maintain share and leadership until further investment becomes marginal
Question marks	Heavy initial capacity expenditures; high research and development costs	Negative to low	Negative cash flow (net cash user)	Assess chances of dominating segment: if good, go after share; if bad, redefine business or withdraw
Dogs	Gradually deplete capacity	Medium	Positive cash flow (net cash contributor)	Plan an orderly withdrawal so as to maximize cash flow

TABLE 5.1 Characteristics and strategy implications of products in the strategy quadrants

Strategy implications

In a typical company, products could be scattered in all four quadrants of the portfolio matrix. The appropriate strategy for products in each cell is given briefly in Table 5.1. In summary, the portfolio matrix approach provides for the simultaneous comparison of different products. It also underlines the importance of cash flow as a strategic variable. Thus, when continuous long-term growth in earnings is the objective, it is necessary to identify high-growth product/market segments early, develop businesses and pre-empt the growth in these segments. If necessary, short-term profitability in these segments may be forgone to ensure achievement of the dominant share. Costs must be managed to meet scale-effect standards. The appropriate point at which to shift from an earnings focus to a cash-flow focus must be determined and a liquidation plan for cash-flow maximization established. A cash-balanced mix of businesses should be maintained.

The portfolio matrix approach is not, however, a panacea for strategy development. In reality, many difficulties limit the workability of this approach. Some potential mistakes associated with the portfolio matrix concept are:

- overinvesting in low-growth segments (lack of objectivity and 'hard' analysis)
- underinvesting in high-growth segments (lack of guts)
- misjudging the segment growth rate (poor market research).

The GE multifactor portfolio matrix

The BCG model discussed above provides a useful approach for reviewing the roles of different products in a company. However, the growth rate–relative market share matrix approach leads to many difficulties. At times, factors other than market share and growth rate bear heavily on cash flow, the mainstay of this approach. Some managers may consider return on investment a more suitable criterion than cash flow for making investment decisions. Further, the two-factor portfolio matrix approach does not address major investment decisions between dissimilar businesses. These difficulties can lead a company into too many traps and errors. For this reason, many companies (such as GE and the Shell Group) have developed the multifactor portfolio approach.

Unit of analysis

The framework discussed here may be applied to either a product/market or a strategic business unit (SBU). As a matter of fact, it may be equally applicable to a much higher level of aggregation in the organization, such as a division or a group.

For an individual business, there can be four strategy options: (1) investing to maintain or (2) investing to grow (the dark area of Fig. 5.6); (3) investing to maintain or regain; and (4) investing to exit (the light area of Fig. 5.6). The choice of a strategy depends on the current position of the business in the matrix (i.e. towards the high side, along the diagonal or towards the low side) and its future direction, assuming the current strategic perspective continues to be followed. If the future appears unpromising, a new strategy for the business is called for.

An analysis of the present position on the matrix may not pose any problem. At GE, for example, there was little disagreement on the position of the business. The mapping of future direction, however, may not be easy. A rigorous analysis must be performed, taking into account environmental shifts, competitors' perspectives, and internal strengths and weaknesses.

5.5.4 A new product portfolio approach

As discussed earlier, Porter identified three generic strategies: (1) overall cost leadership (i.e. making units of a fairly standardized product and underpricing everybody else); (2) differentiation (i.e. turning out something customers perceive as unique – an item whose quality, design, brand name or reputation for service commands higher-than-average prices);

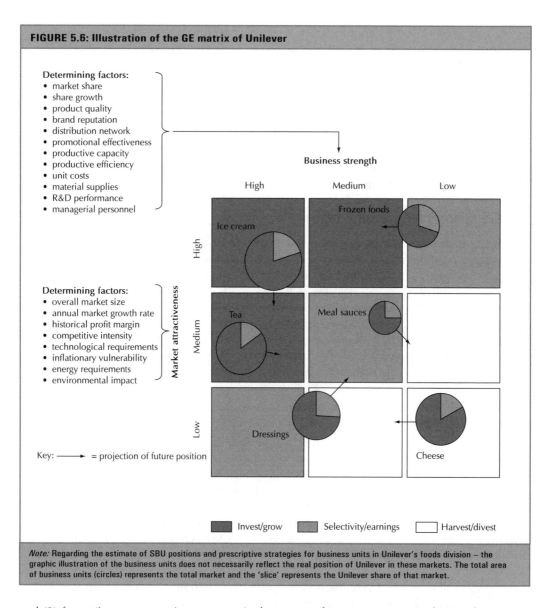

FIGURE 5.6: Illustration of the GE matrix of Unilever

Note: Regarding the estimate of SBU positions and prescriptive strategies for business units in Unilever's foods division – the graphic illustration of the business units does not necessarily reflect the real position of Unilever in these markets. The total area of business units (circles) represents the total market and the 'slice' represents the Unilever share of that market.

and (3) focus (i.e. concentrating on a particular group of customers, geographic market, channel of distribution or distinct segment of the product line).

Porter's choice of strategy is based on two factors: the strategic target at which the business aims and the strategic advantage the business has in aiming at that target.

In summary, Porter's framework emphasizes not only that certain characteristics of the industry must be considered in choosing a generic strategy, but that they in fact dictate the proper choice.

Portfolio approaches provide a useful tool for strategists. Granted, these approaches have limitations, but all these limitations can be overcome with a little imagination and foresight. The real concern about the portfolio approach is that its elegant simplicity often tempts managers to believe that it can solve all problems of corporate choice and resource allocation. The truth is that it addresses only half of the problem: the back half. The portfolio approach is a powerful tool for helping the strategist to select from a menu of available opportunities, but it does not put the menu into his or her hands. That is the front half of the problem. The other critical dimension in making strategic choices is the need to generate a rich array of business options from which to choose. No simple tool is available that can provide this option-generating capability. Here only creative thinking about one's environment, business, customers and competitors can help.

For a successful introduction of the portfolio framework, the strategist should heed the following advice:

1   Once introduced, move quickly to establish the legitimacy of portfolio analysis.
2   Educate line managers in its relevance and use.
3   Redefine SBUs explicitly because their definition is important for using the portfolio framework in an adequate way.
4   Use the portfolio framework to seek the strategic direction for different businesses without haggling over the fancy labels by which to call them.
5   Make top management acknowledge SBUs as portfolios to be managed.
6   Seek top management time for reviewing different businesses using the portfolio framework.
7   Rely on a flexible, informal management process to differentiate and influence patterns at the SBU level.
8   Tie resource allocation to the business plan.
9   Consider strategic expenses and human resources as explicitly as capital investment.
10 Plan explicitly for new business development.
11 Make a clear strategic commitment to a few selected technologies or markets early.

5.6   Strategy evaluation and selection

The time required to develop resources is so extended, and the timescale of opportunities so brief and fleeting, that a company that has not carefully delineated and appraised its strategy is in trouble. This underlines the importance of strategy evaluation. The adequacy of a strategy may be evaluated using the following criteria.

- *Suitability* – is there a sustainable advantage?
- *Validity* – are the assumptions about the external environment realistic?
- *Feasibility* – do we have the skills, resources and commitment?
- *Internal consistency* – does the strategy hang together?
- *Vulnerability* – what are the risks and contingencies?
- *Workability* – can we retain our flexibility?
- *Appropriate time horizon* – do we allow enough time for implementation?

We now look at each of these in turn.

Suitability

Strategy should offer some sort of competitive advantage. In other words, strategy should lead to a future advantage or an adaptation to forces eroding current competitive advantage. The following steps may be followed to judge the competitive advantage a strategy may provide:

(1) review the potential threats and opportunities to the business; (2) assess each option in light of the capabilities of the business; (3) anticipate the likely competitive response to each option; and (4) modify or eliminate unsuitable options.

Validity

Strategy should be consistent with the assumptions about the external product/market environment. At a time when more and more women are seeking jobs, say, a strategy assuming traditional roles for women (e.g. raising children and staying home) would be inconsistent with the environment.

Feasibility

Money, competency and physical facilities are the critical resources a manager should be aware of in finalizing strategy. A resource may be examined in two different ways: as a constraint limiting the achievement of goals and as an opportunity to be exploited as the basis for strategy. It is desirable for a strategist to make correct estimates of resources available without being excessively optimistic about them. Further, even if resources *are* available in the corporation, a particular product/market group may not be able to lay claim to them. Alternatively, resources currently available to a product/market group may be transferred to another group if the SBU strategy deems it necessary.

Internal consistency

Strategy should be in tune with the different policies of the corporation, the SBU and the product/market arena. For example, if the corporation decided to limit the top five customers' business of any unit to 40 per cent of total sales, a product/market strategy emphasizing greater than 40 per cent reliance on the top five customers would be internally inconsistent.

Vulnerability

The degree of risk may be determined on the basis of the perspectives of the strategy and available resources. A pertinent question here is 'Will the resources be available as planned in appropriate quantities and for as long as it is necessary to implement the strategy?' The overall proportion of resources committed to a venture becomes a factor to be reckoned with: the greater the quantities of resources, the greater the degree of risk.

Workability

The workability of a strategy should be realistically evaluated with quantitative data. Sometimes, however, it may be difficult to undertake such objective analysis. In such a case, other indications may be used to assess the contributions of a strategy. One such indication could be the degree of consensus among key executives about the viability of the strategy. Identifying ahead of time alternative strategies for achieving the goal is another indication of the workability of a strategy. Finally, establishing resource requirements in advance, which eliminates the need to institute crash programmes of cost reduction or to seek reduction in planned programmes, also substantiates the workability of the strategy.

Appropriate time horizon

A viable strategy has a time frame for its realization. The time horizon of a strategy should allow implementation without creating havoc in the organization or missing market availability. For example, in introducing a new product to the market, enough time should be allotted for market testing, training of sales people, and so on. However, the time frame should not be so long that a competitor could enter the market first and skim the cream off the top.

5.6.1 Strategy selection

After information on trade-offs between alternative strategies has been gathered as discussed above, a preferred strategy should be chosen for recommendation to management. Usually, there are three core marketing strategies that a company may use: (1) operational excellence; (2) product leadership; and (3) customer intimacy. Operational excellence strategy amounts to offering middle-of-the-market products at the best price with the least inconvenience. Under this strategy, the proposition to the customer is simple: low price or hassle-free service or both. Wal-Mart, Price/Costco and Dell Computer epitomize this kind of strategy. The product leadership strategy concentrates on offering products that push performance boundaries. In other words, the basic premise of this strategy is that customers receive the best product. Moreover, product leaders do not build their propositions with just one innovation: they continue to innovate year after year.

For product leaders, competition is not about price or customer service, it is about product performance. The customer intimacy strategy focuses not on what the market wants but on what specific customers want. Businesses following this strategy do not pursue one-time transactions, they cultivate relationships. They specialize in satisfying unique needs, which often only they recognize, through a close relationship with and intimate knowledge of the customer. The underlying proposition of this strategy is: we have the best solution for you, and provide all the support you need to achieve optimum results.

The core strategy combines one or more areas of the marketing mix. For example, the preferred strategy may be product leadership. Here the emphasis of the strategy is on product, the area of primary concern. However, in order to make an integrated marketing decision, appropriate changes may have to be made in price, promotion and distribution areas. The strategic perspectives in these areas may be called *supporting strategies.* Thus, once the core strategy has been selected, supporting strategies should be delineated. Core and supporting strategies should fit the needs of the marketplace, the skills of the company and the vagaries of the competition.

Reformulation of current strategy may range from making slight modifications in existing perspectives to coming out with an entirely different strategy. How much examination and review a product/market strategy requires depends on the nature of the strategy (in terms of the change it seeks from existing perspectives) and the resource commitment required. Another point to remember in developing a core strategy is that the emphasis should always be placed on searching for new ways to compete. The marketing strategist should develop strategy around those key factors in which the business has more freedom than its competitors.

Exhibit 5.2: *International service strategies*

Service businesses tend to be more diverse than manufacturing companies. The latter generally are less exposed to cultural differences overseas, whereas services more directly affect the behaviour of customers and service employees. Customers enter service outlets; they do not generally enter manufacturing plants. Service expectations often vary from country to country. Because the companies tend to be more deeply embedded in the culture of each country, differences in social customs, behaviour and manners must be built into the design and delivery of the service. Cultural norms governing time and the centrality of work in people's lives influence employee behaviour and commitment. In many emerging markets, public transport rarely runs on time, businesses rarely open on time and employees usually show up for work late.

Both service products and their delivery systems often require adaptation in international markets. Manufactured products may need to be modified overseas, but the process generally remains much the same. Service companies, in contrast, have to develop appropriate systems to serve the different needs of customers overseas. When they do not fit the needs of the local market, they will likely fail. In 1996, Wal-Mart began opening its superstores in Indonesia. The stores were large, clean and clearly laid out, but Indonesians rejected the layout: they preferred to shop at Matahari, a chain of small, shabby local stores that resembled traditional street vendors where customers could haggle over prices. After two years of rejection of its retail model, Wal-Mart closed its stores and withdrew completely from the Indonesian market.

Unlike most dotcoms, bricks-and-mortar service companies and stores need to achieve service density. They benefit from focusing sales in defined areas rather than spreading them broadly across a country or region. Most developing countries exhibit substantial differences in per capita income between rural and urban inhabitants. Most international consumer service businesses locate first in the major urban centres, seeking to take advantage of the purchasing power and critical mass of city dwellers. Urban centres help maximize the sales of each store or outlet. They create the potential for service density, which offers the fastest path to returns on invested capital. With the largest number of outlets of any chain store in the world, 7-Eleven is an example of an international retailer that has focused on building service density as it expands. Locating stores in Japan in clusters of 30 shops delayed the achievement of full national distribution but made 7-Eleven the most profitable chain in Japan during the 1990s.

Source: adapted from www.wal-mart.com; www.7-eleven.com; Davis, T.R.V. (2004) Different service companies, different international strategies, *Business Horizons*, 47(6): 51–9

5.7 Estimating financial consequences

Most forms of corporate strategic analysis have to include not only a financial evaluation of the current position but also an assessment of the financial impact of future strategic choices. Such a financial evaluation often relies on the management and financial accounting information systems within the company, but more recently a number of key conceptual issues have been raised. Most important has been the development of so-called ABC (activity-based costing) which, broadly, attempts to shift the focus of cost analysis towards individual elements in the various business activities or processes involved in the development and delivery of products and services. This follows on from earlier developments in management accounting, which looked at ways of constructing management accounts so that financial performance could be measured along various dimensions (such as product groups, sales territories and key customers) as a form of strategic diagnosis.

In interpreting financial data for strategic purposes, it is inevitable that two fundamental conceptual issues almost always occur at some stage: the nature of opportunity cost, and the distinction between fixed and variable costs. For financial accounting purposes, it is a well-established principle that the 'cost' of a particular activity should be based on adjusted, 'real', historic costs. It is also clear that for strategic management accounting purposes, the costs should be an 'opportunity' cost based on alternative possible uses of the assets concerned. This inevitably leads to the difficult position that the cost of any specified activity depends on the cost of other alternatives. Indeed strong advocates of developments in strategic management accounting would argue that even this cost should be compared with one's competitors' costs rather than treated as an absolute figure.

In terms of the variability of costs, the simple principle is that while in the short run almost all costs are fixed, strategic analysis with its focus on the longer term tends towards a situation in which, to paraphrase the famous Keynesian dictum, 'In the long run, all costs are variable'.

The task for much strategic financial analysis is therefore to ensure that the assumptions about what is fixed and what is variable, which are built into the financial analysis, are consistent with the actual resource choices that the company or organization faces.

Summary

In the process of selecting the right marketing strategies, we need to examine past errors and recognize that learning is impeded when the chief concern is to defend past decisions. Of course, nothing can guarantee that a decision, however well made, will turn out right. It is wrong to assume that a bad outcome implies the decision was badly made since it may have been the most rationally defensible answer at the time. In any case, past strategies are seldom absolutely wrong or right, but have different degrees of imperfection.

A diversified organization needs to examine its widely different businesses at the corporate level to see how each fits within the overall corporate purpose and to come to grips with the resource allocation problem. The portfolio approaches described in this chapter help management determine the role that each business plays in the corporation and allocate resources accordingly.

The various portfolio techniques, like BCG's growth market share matrix, GE's business screen and Porter's work, plus various quantitative techniques, all help to order and bring out the implications of the data collected. These techniques can be useful in offering frameworks, analogies and models that help to structure a problem situation and reduce mental overload, as well as protecting organizations from a complete degeneration into *ad hoc* analysis.

Various portfolio approaches were critically examined in this chapter. The criticisms relate mainly to operational definitions of dimensions used, weighting of variables and product/market boundary determination.

The Ansoff growth matrix suggests that if an organization lacks new products with which to generate growth in coming years, investments may be made in new products. If growth is hurt by the early maturity of promising products, the strategic effort may be directed towards extension of their life cycles.

The BCG model suggests locating products or businesses on a matrix with relative market share and growth rate as its dimensions. The four cells in the matrix, whose positions are based on whether growth is high or low and whether relative market share is high or low, are labelled stars, cash cows, question marks and dogs. The strategy for a product or business in each cell, which is primarily based on the business's cash flow implications, was outlined.

The third approach, the GE model, again uses two variables (industry attractiveness and business strengths), but these two variables are based on a variety of factors. Here, again, a desired strategy for a product/business in each cell was recommended. The focus of the multifactor matrix approach is on the return-on-investment implications of strategy alternatives rather than on cash flow, as in the growth rate–relative market share matrix approach.

Portfolio techniques also tend to ignore interaction or synergy between the different business opportunities being evaluated. Further, these techniques are limited because they rely on imperfect measures and estimates. Even with comparatively simple dimensions such as relative market share and market growth, the actual estimation of these factors for each alternative being evaluated must rely on incomplete, and sometimes incorrect, historical information, and on estimates by experts whose 'crystal balls' may be cloudy. Pessimistic projections can cause companies to ignore high-potential products, and overly optimistic projections can lead companies to make large investments in ventures that are doomed to fail.

However, portfolio techniques are attractive to managers for several reasons. First, they make it possible to compare widely diverse alternatives by using the same factors in a relatively consistent manner. They also allow managers to simplify very complex problems to more manageable levels by eliminating hundreds of details. Reducing the information-processing load of decision-makers enables them to understand problems better and to project into the future with more confidence and accuracy. In short, portfolio techniques make the evaluation of strategic alternatives simpler and more manageable, and for these reasons alone they are valuable.

Questions for discussion

1   What is the main difference between a vision and a mission?
2   How might corporate objectives be derived from the corporate mission?
3   What is the difference between the mission statement and the company objective?
4   What purpose might a product portfolio serve in the context of marketing strategy?
5   What are the advantages and disadvantages of using portfolio models in strategic market planning?
6   What is the meaning of relative market share in the BCG model?
7   What are the most important advantages and disadvantages of using the GE matrix compared to the BCG matrix?

References

Akan, O., Allen, R.S., Helms, M.M. and Spralls, S.A. (2006) Critical tactics for implementing Porter's generic strategies, *Journal of Business Strategy,* 27(1): 43–53.

Ansoff, H.I. (1965) *Corporate Strategy: An Analytical Approach to Business Policy for Growth and Expansion.* New York: McGraw-Hill.

Bhatnagar, P. (2004) *Starbucks: A Passage to India.* Available online at CNNMoney, money.cnn.com.

Hollensen, S. (2003) *Marketing Management.* London: Financial Times/Prentice Hall.

Mintzberg, H. and Walters, J.A. (1985) Of strategies, deliberate and emergent, *Strategic Management* Journal, 6: 257–72.

Porter, M. (1985) *Competitive Advantage: Creating and Sustaining Superior Performance.* New York: The Free Press.

CASE STUDY 5: WEETABIX

Attacking Kellogg's in the breakfast cereal market

The Weetabix Food Company has been creating breakfast cereals since 1932. Its headquarters are part of a 75-acre site in Kettering, Northamptonshire where it produces popular cereals including Weetabix, Oatibix, Alpen, Ready brek, Weetabix Minis and Weetos. The Weetabix brands fight it out on store shelves with cereals made by General Mills and Kellogg's. Its flagship cereal brand, Weetabix (a UK version of shredded wheat), is one of the UK's favourite breakfast brands, accounting for 8 per cent of the country's total cereal sales with annual sales worth over £95 m – in total, the Weetabix Ltd company has about 15 per cent of the UK breakfast cereal market. The company now sells its flakes and muesli in more than 80 countries, but without significant market shares outside UK.

But Weetabix faces other foes as well: private-label cereals, ever more popular cereal bars, and busy people skipping breakfast. In order to revive sales, the company began marketing snack-sized versions of its cereals; responding to niche marketing trends, it added a line of organic wheat biscuits (Oatibix).

HM Capital Partners (at the time known as Hicks, Muse, Tate & Furst) bought Weetabix in 2003 from the George family for about US$1 bn in cash. Sir Richard George remains with the company as its non-executive chairman. A year later, Hicks Muse's European unit split off, naming itself Lion Capital, and took Weetabix with it. Lion Capital acquired all of the issued share capital of Weetabix Ltd. Weetabix Ltd now forms part of the group of companies in the Lion portfolio.

The company also owns Barbara's Bakery in the USA, which, in addition to making its own cookies, crackers, breakfast cereals, instant mashed potatoes and salty snacks, produces and distributes Weetabix products for the North American market. As seen in Table 5.2, Weetabix has been able to increase the total sales, but without the resulting lift in net profits.

	2008 (£m)	2007 (£m)
Total sales	314	295
Net profit (before tax)	77	79

TABLE 5.2 Weetabix Ltd financial figures
Source: www.weetabix.co.uk

Since the beginning of 2009 Weetabix has the following subsidiaries around the world:

- Vibixa Ltd (UK)
- Ryecroft Foods Ltd (UK)
- The Weetabix Company Inc. (USA)
- Barbara's Bakery Inc. (USA)
- Weetabix GmbH (Germany)
- Weetabix Iberica SL (Spain)
- Melck Street Management (Proprietary) Ltd (South Africa).

At the end of 2008 Weetabix Ltd had a total of 1,300 employees.

History of breakfast cereals

Ready-to-eat cereals first appeared during the late 1800s. According to one account, John Kellogg, a doctor who belonged to a vegetarian group, developed wheat and corn flakes to extend the group's dietary choices. John's brother, Will Kellogg, saw potential in the innovative grain products and initiated commercial production and marketing. Patients at a Battle Creek, Michigan, sanitarium were among Kellogg's first customers.

Another cereal producer with roots in the nineteenth century was the Quaker Oats Company. In 1873, the North Star Oatmeal Mill built an oatmeal plant in Cedar Rapids, Iowa. North Star reorganized with other enterprises and together they formed Quaker Oats in 1901.

The Washburn Crosby Company, a predecessor to General Mills, entered the market during the 1920s. The company's first ready-to-eat cereal, Wheaties, was introduced to the US public in 1924. According to General Mills, Wheaties was developed when a Minneapolis clinician spilled a mixture of gruel that he was making for his patients on a hot stove.

The world market for breakfast cereals

In the early 2000s breakfast cereal makers were facing stagnant, if not declining, sales. Gone are the days of the family breakfast, of which a bowl of cereal was standard fare. The fast-paced US lifestyle has more and more consumers eating breakfast on the go. Quick-serve restaurants like McDonald's, ready-to-eat breakfast bars, bagels and muffins offer consumers less labour-intensive alternatives to cereal. Although the value of product shipped by cereal manufacturers has grown in absolute figures, increased revenues came primarily from price hikes rather than market growth.

English-speaking nations represented the largest cereal markets. Consumption in non-English markets was estimated at only one-quarter the amount consumed by English speakers (see Table 5.3), where the breakfast cereal consumption per capita is 6 kg in the UK, but only 1.5 kg in south-west Europe (France, Spain and Portugal). On the European continent, consumption per capita averaged 1.5 kg per year.

Growth in the cereal industry has been slow to non-existent in this century. The question at hand for the industry is how to remake cereal's image in light of the new culture. Tinkering with flavourings and offerings, such as the recent trend towards the addition of dried fresh fruit, proves some relief, but with over 150 different choices on store shelves and 20 new offerings added annually, variety has done more to overwhelm than excite consumers. In addition, cereal companies are committing fewer dollars to their marketing budgets.

Region	Per capita consumption per year (kg)
Sweden	9.0
Canada	7.0
UK	6.0
Australia	6.0
USA	5.0
South-west Europe (France, Spain)	1.5
South-east Asia	0.1
Russia	0.1

TABLE 5.3 Breakfast cereal consumption per capita per year (2008)

Region	US$ (bn)	%
North America	10	50
Europe	6	30
Rest of the world	4	20
Total	20	100

TABLE 5.4 World market for breakfast cereals by region (2008)

Development in geographical regions

As seen in Table 5.4, the USA is by far the largest breakfast cereals market in the world. In total, North America accounts for 50 per cent of the global sales of US$20 bn in 2008. The USA accounts for about 90 per cent of the North American market.

The European region accounts for 30 per cent of global sales, at US$6 bn in 2008. By far the largest market is the UK, contributing nearly 30 per cent of the regional total, with France and Germany other key, if notably smaller, players. Eastern Europe is a minor breakfast cereal market, reflecting the product's generally new status in the region. It contributed just 6 per cent of world sales in 2008. However, the market is vibrant as new lifestyles born from growing urbanization and westernization – key themes in emerging market development – have fuelled steady sales growth. Despite its low level of per capita spending, Russia is the largest market in eastern Europe, accounting for over 40 per cent of regional sales in 2008. The continued steady growth of this market underpinned overall regional development over the review period. Cereals remain a niche market in Russia, as they do across the region, with the product benefiting from a perception of novelty. A key target for manufacturers has been children and young women, at which advertising has been aimed.

The Australasian breakfast cereals sector, like western Europe and North America, dominated by a single nation, Australia, is becoming increasingly polarized. In common with the key US and UK markets, breakfast cereals in Australia are suffering from a high degree of maturity, with annual growth at a low single-digit level.

The Latin American breakfast cereals sector is the third largest in the world, but at US$2 bn in 2008 it is notably overshadowed by the vastly larger North American and western European markets. However, in common with these developed regions, one country plays a dominant role in the regional make-up, Mexico, accounting for nearly 60 per cent of the overall breakfast cereal markets in Latin America.

In common with eastern Europe, breakfast cereal sales, while small in Africa and the Middle East, have displayed marked growth in recent years as a direct result of greater urbanization and a growing trend (in some areas) towards westernization. Given the overriding influence of this factor on market development, sales are largely concentrated in the more developed regional markets, such as Israel and South Africa, where the investment by multinationals has been at its highest.

In Asia the concept of breakfast cereals is relatively new, with the growing influence of western culture fostering a notable increase in consumption in major urban cities. Market development has been rapid in China, reflecting the overall rate of industry expansion in the country, with breakfast cereals sales rising by 19 per cent in 2008. In the region's developed markets, in particular Japan, market performance is broadly similar, although the key growth driver is different, in that it is health. Overall, in both developed and developing markets, breakfast cereals are in their infancy.

So, although the Russian and Chinese markets are still relatively small in global terms (with $US263 m and $US71 m of sales in a $US20 bn global industry), they are growing rapidly. Moreover, per capita consumption rates are still very low (particularly in China), leaving considerable scope for future growth.

Health trend

With regard to health, breakfast cereals have been hurt by the rise of fad diets such as Atkins and South Beach, which have heaped much scorn on carbohydrate-based products. The influence of these diets is on the wane but their footprint remains highly visible on national eating trends. In addition, the high sugar content of children's cereals has come under intense scrutiny, which caused a downturn in this sector, although the industry is now coming back with a range of 'better for you' variants.

Regarding convenience, this trend, once a growth driver for breakfast cereals, has now become a threat, with an increasing number of consumers opting to skip breakfast. Portability has become a key facet of convenience, a development that has fed the emergence and expansion of breakfast bars at the expense of traditional foods, such as breakfast cereals. In an increasingly cash-rich, time-poor society, consumers are opting to abandon a formal breakfast meal and instead are relying on an 'on-the-go' solution, such as breakfast bars or pastries. These latter products, in particular breakfast bars, are taking share from cereals, a trend that looks set to gather pace in the short term.

Trends in product development

Consumer awareness of health and nutrition has also played a major part in shaping the industry in recent years. Cereal manufacturers began to tout the benefits of eating breakfast cereal right on the package – vitamin-fortified, low in fat, and a good source of fibre. Another trend, begun in the 1990s and picking up steam in the 2000s, is adding dehydrated whole fruits to cereal, which provides colour, flavour and nutritional value. Yet touting health benefits to adults and marketing film characters to children have not been sufficient to reinvigorate this mature industry.

Under the difficult market conditions, cereal packaging is receiving new attention. Packaging was a secondary consideration, other than throwing in special offers to tempt children. But these days, with meal occasions boiled down to their bare essentials, packaging and delivery have emerged as key weapons in the cereal marketer's arsenal. New ideas circulating in the industry usually include doing away with the traditional cereal box, which has undergone little change in its lifetime. Alternatives range from clear plastic containers to a return of the small variety six-packs.

Trends in distribution

Supermarkets tend to be the dominant distribution format for breakfast cereals. The discounter format is dominated by mass merchandisers, the most famous example of which is Wal-Mart in the USA. This discounter format tends to favour shelf-stable, packaged products and as a result they are increasingly viewed as direct competitors to supermarkets.

Independent food stores have suffered a decline during the past years. They have been at a competitive disadvantage compared to their larger and better resourced chained competitors.

Traditional channels

Traditional retailers such as supermarkets continue to play a major role in the distribution of General Mills's products, and the company has an extensive number of cereal, snack, meal and yoghurt brands to maintain shelf space in major retail outlets.

Private label competition intensifies

Across many categories, rising costs have led to price increases in branded products that have not been matched by any pricing actions taken in private labels. As a result, the price gaps between branded and private label products have increased dramatically and in some cases can be as much as 30 per cent.

This creates intense competitive environments for branded products, particularly in categories such as cereals, which is one of General Mills's biggest markets, as consumers have started to focus more on price than brand identity. This shift in focus is partly the result of private labels' increased quality as they compete for consumer loyalty and confidence in their label products.

Competitors

Kellogg's

The company that makes breakfast foods and snacks for millions began with only 25 employees in Battle Creek in 1906. Today, Kellogg's employs more than 25 000 people, manufactures in 17 countries and sells its products in more than 180 countries.

Kellogg's was the first US company to enter the foreign market for ready-to-eat breakfast cereals. Company founder, Will Keith (W.K.) Kellogg, was an early believer in the potential of international growth and began establishing Kellogg's as a global brand with the introduction of *Kellogg's Corn Flakes* in Canada in 1914. As success followed and demand grew, Kellogg's continued to build manufacturing facilities around the world, including Sydney, Australia (1924), Manchester, England (1938), Queretaro, Mexico (1951), Takasaki, Japan (1963), Bombay, India (1994) and Toluca, Mexico (2004).

Kellogg's Company is the leader among global breakfast cereal manufacturers with 2005 sales revenue of US$10.2 bn (net earnings were US$980 m). Wal-Mart Stores, Inc. and its affiliates, accounted for approximately 17 per cent of consolidated net sales during 2005.

Established in 1906, Kellogg's was the world's market leader in ready-to-eat cereals throughout most of the twentieth century. In 2005, Kellogg's had 30 per cent of the world market share for breakfast cereals (see Table 5.5). Canada, the UK and Australia represented Kellogg's three largest overseas markets.

A few well-known Kellogg's products are Corn Flakes, Frosted Mini-Wheats, Corn Pops and Fruit Loops.

Manufacturer	Germany % market share	UK % market share	USA % market share	World % market share
Kellogg Company	25	30	30	30
CPW (General Mills and Nestlé)	13	13	26[1]	20
PepsiCo (Quaker)	–	5	15	10
Weetabix	–	15	–	5
Private label	35	16	10	15
Others	27	21	19	20
Total	100	100	100	100

[1] In the USA General Mills and Nestlé market each of their breakfast cereal products independently, because CPW only covers international markets outside the USA.

TABLE 5.5 The world market for breakfast cereals, by company (2008)

Cereal Partners Worldwide (CPW)

CPW markets cereals in more than 130 countries, except for the USA and Canada, where the two companies market themselves separately. The joint venture was established in 1990 and the agreement also extends to the production of private-label cereals in the UK. Volume growth for CPW was 4 per cent in 2008. The company's cereals are sold under the Nestlé brand, although many originated from General Mills. Brand names manufactured (primarily by General Mills) under the Nestlé name under this agreement include Corn Flakes, Crunch, Fitness, Cheerios and Nesquik. Shredded Wheat and Shreddies were once made by Nabisco, but are now marketed by CPW.

Headquartered in Lausanne, Switzerland, CPW has 14 factories and employs over 3500 people around the world. CPW turnover in 2008 was a little less than $US2 bn. CPW is number 2 in most international markets, but it is also market leader in some of the smaller breakfast cereal markets like China (50 per cent market share), Poland (40 per cent market share), Turkey (50 per cent market share), east/central Europe (50 per cent market share) and Southeast Asia (50 per cent market share).

CPW has performed best in developing markets such as Russia and China, where market leader Kellogg's has not yet established a strong presence.

PepsiCo

In August 2001, PepsiCo merged with Quaker Foods, thereby expanding its existing portfolio. Quaker's family of brands includes Quaker Oatmeal, Cap'n Crunch and Life cereals, Rice-A-Roni and Near East side dishes, and Aunt Jemima pancake mixes and syrups.

Quaker Food's first puffed product, 'Puffed Rice', was introduced in 1905. In 1992, Quaker Oats held an 8.9 per cent share of the ready-to-eat cereal market, and its principal product was Cap'n Crunch. Within the smaller hot cereal segment, however, the company held approximately 60 per cent of the market. In addition to cereal products, Quaker Oats produced Aunt Jemima Pancake mix and Gatorade sports drinks.

The PepsiCo brands in the breakfast cereal sector include Cap'n Crunch, Puffed Wheat, Crunchy Bran, Frosted Mini Wheats and Quaker.

Despite recent moves to extend its presence into new markets, PepsiCo tends to focus on its North American operations.

Questions

1 What are Weetabix's key challenges for its strategic planning process?
2 Please prepare the BCG or the GE model for Weetabix's major geographical markets. If necessary, please state your assumptions for the development of the positions in the model.

Sources: www.weetabix.co.uk; www.euromonitor.com; www.datamonitor.com; www.marketwatch.com; Bowery, J. (2006) Kellogg broadens healthy cereals portfolio, *Marketing*, 8 February, p. 5; Sanders, T. (2006) Cereals spark debate, *Food Manufacture*, 81(8): 4; Reyes, S. (2006) Saving private label, *Brandweek*, 47(19): 30–4

06

The segmentation process

Chapter contents

❖ LEARNING OBJECTIVES

After studying this chapter you should be able to do the following:

- ❖ Understand the advantages of segmentation.
- ❖ Describe the steps involved in segmentation.
- ❖ Explain the STP process.

- ❖ Discuss criteria for successful segmentation in B2C and B2B markets.
- ❖ Discuss ways of segmenting global markets.
- ❖ Discuss possible barriers to implementing segmentation in the organization.

6.1 Introduction

Segmentation sounds like a process of breaking large markets into smaller ones. In the extreme, it involves designing a unique product and marketing programme for each buyer; examples would include designing office buildings and insurance plans to meet the needs of individual corporations. However, segmentation is really a process of aggregation. The idea is to pull together groups of customers who resemble each other on some meaningful dimensions.

Segmentation is the strategy of developing different marketing programmes for different customer groups or segments. It recognizes heterogeneity in the market. Each customer segment has its own unique demand function based on price, physical product characteristics, and non-physical attributes reflecting image and performance. You build volume by appealing to group preferences.

First, you need to identify the best ways to segment a market and then pin down the characteristics of each group (this second step is called *profiling*). Next, you must evaluate the attractiveness of the segments and select the most appropriate target markets. Finally, you need to position your product or service relative to competitive offerings within the chosen market segments.

6.2   The benefits and underlying premises of market segmentation

There are a number of important benefits that can be derived from segmenting a market, which can be summarized in the following terms:

- Segmentation is a particularly useful approach to marketing for the smaller company. It allows target markets to be matched to company competencies (see also Chapter 2) and makes it more likely that the smaller company can create a defensible niche in the market.
- It helps to identify gaps in the market; that is, unserved or underserved segments. These can act as targets for new product development or the extension of the existing product or service range.
- In mature or declining markets, it may be possible to identify specific segments that are still in growth. Concentrating on growth segments when the overall market is declining is a major strategy in the later stages of the product life cycle.
- Segmentation enables the marketer to match the product or service more closely to the needs of the target market. In this way a stronger competitive position can be built.
- The dangers of not segmenting the market when competitors do so should also be emphasized. The competitive advantages noted above can be lost to competitors if the company fails to take advantage of them. A company practising a mass marketing strategy in a clearly segmented market against competitors operating a focused strategy can find itself falling between many stools.

Let us first consider the underlying requirements for market segmentation and take an overview of segmentation issues (Hooley et al., 2004).

It is possible to describe three basic propositions that underpin market segmentation as a component of marketing strategy.

1   For segmentation to be useful customers must *differ from one another* in some important respect, and this can be used to divide the total market. If they were not different in some significant way, if they were totally homogeneous, then there would be no need or basis on which to segment the market. However, in reality, all customers differ in some respect. The key to whether a particular difference is useful for segmentation purposes

lies in the extent to which the differences are related to different behaviour patterns (e.g. different levels of demand for the product or service, or different use/benefit requirements) or susceptibility to different marketing mix combinations (e.g. different product/service offerings, different media, messages, prices or distribution channels); that is, whether the differences are important to how we develop a marketing strategy.

2   The operational use of segmentation usually requires that segment targets can be *identified by measurable characteristics* to enable their potential value as a target market to be estimated and for the segment to be identified. Crucial to utilizing a segmentation scheme to make better marketing decisions is the ability of the marketing strategist to evaluate segment attractiveness and the current or potential strengths the company has in serving a particular segment. Depending on the level of segmentation analysis, this may require internal company analysis or external market appraisal.

3   The effective application of segmentation strategy also requires that selected segments be *isolated* from the remainder of the market, enabling them to be targeted with a distinct market offering. Where segments are not distinct they do not form a clear target for the company's marketing efforts.

For any segmentation scheme to be useful it must possess those three characteristics.

6.3   The STP (segmentation, targeting and positioning) approach

Most marketers recognize the three stages of market segmentation: segmentation, targeting and positioning (STP). According to this model (illustrated in Fig. 6.1), the process begins with the aggregation of customers into groups, to maximize homogeneity within, and heterogeneity between, segments.

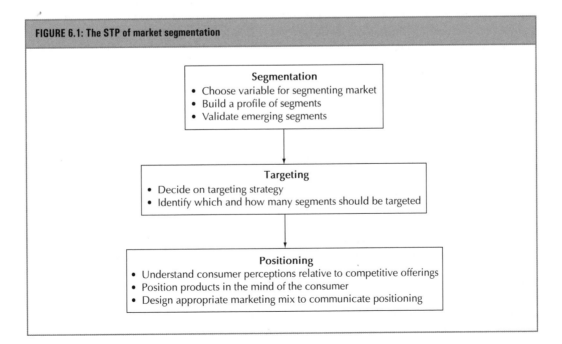

FIGURE 6.1: The STP of market segmentation

Segmentation
- Choose variable for segmenting market
- Build a profile of segments
- Validate emerging segments

Targeting
- Decide on targeting strategy
- Identify which and how many segments should be targeted

Positioning
- Understand consumer perceptions relative to competitive offerings
- Position products in the mind of the consumer
- Design appropriate marketing mix to communicate positioning

Managers attempt to *segment* the market; that is, to identify groups of consumers that are internally homogeneous, but distinct from each other. Very small groups of customers identified through the segmentation process are called *niche* markets. Managers then select one or more market segments and niches to *target* with their marketing programmes. For each target market, they need to make decisions on how to *position* their products in order to differentiate themselves from the competition and to create a unique spot in customers' minds. Figure 6.1 illustrates the process of STP.

The implicit goal of all STP is to improve marketing performance over what it would be without this process. Thus, an organization may aim to use STP to increase customer satisfaction, competitive differentiation and/or profitability. The STP process offers additional benefits when used properly. It greatly increases marketers' ability to develop a thorough understanding of the needs of their well-defined customer segments, and it improves their ability to respond to changing segment needs. Marketing efficiency is improved as resources are targeted at segments that offer the most potential for the organization. Because the marketing programme is better matched with segment requirements, its effectiveness is enhanced. Specifically, STP analyses help marketing managers design a product line to meet market demand, determine the advertising messages that will have most appeal, select media that will have maximum impact for each segment, and time product and advertising launches to capitalize on market responsiveness.

Prior to conducting STP analyses, managers should define the purpose and scope of segmentation, including their marketing objectives, whether the purpose is to explore new segments or better serve existing ones, whether existing data will be used or money invested in market research, and the level of detail they need from the STP exercise. These choices help to focus the segmentation effort on the most important issues for the organization. For example, when the purpose is to better serve current segments, researchers need to pay greater attention to profiling these segments. On the other hand, if the purpose is to identify new segments, researchers will pay greater attention to grouping customers, identifying the number of segments, and profiling new segments. Evidence of how this process works in practice raises two fundamental concerns:

1 Businesses that believe they are applying a market segmentation approach may not necessarily be doing so.
2 Marketers who are following the prescribed steps may not be achieving results that can be implemented.

The first problem arises in part from the imprecise use of segmentation language. The intrinsic attractiveness of the process and the pleasing nature of the benefits on offer have resulted in the label of 'segment' being applied to almost any grouping of customers. In many cases these groupings do not consist of customers with homogeneous needs and buying behaviour.

The second problem concerns the fact that marketers who follow the prescribed segmentation sometimes fail to generate a usable segmentation solution. In this respect the apparent simplicity of the three-stage STP process belies some of the underlying difficulties.

6.3.1 Bases for segmenting markets

Some of the major issues in market segmentation centre on the bases on which the segmentation should be conducted and the number of segments identifiable as targets in a particular market. The selection of the base for segmentation is crucial to gaining a clear picture of the nature of the market – the use of different bases can result in very different outcomes. In fact, the process of segmentation and the creative selection of different segmentation bases can often help the company to gain new insights into old market structures that, in turn, may offer new opportunities – this is not merely a mechanical piece of statistical analysis.

In addition to choosing the relevant bases for segmentation, to make the segments more accessible to marketing strategy, the segments are typically described further on common characteristics. Segments formed on the basis of brand preference, for example, may be further described in terms of customer demographic and attitudinal characteristics to enable relevant media to be selected for promotional purposes and a fuller picture of the chosen segments to be built up.

The next section examines the major bases used in B2C markets, and the section after that looks at B2B markets.

6.4   Segmenting consumer markets (B2C)

As previously mentioned, a market may be segmented using a number of different bases. At the end of the day, the bases selected – for, as we shall see later, they are often used in combination to segment markets – must fulfil the criteria outlined earlier for effective segmentation. However, there are a number of bases in consumer markets that, in the past, have been widely used in segmenting these markets. What this section does, then, is discuss some of the most frequently used bases. It starts with some of the more traditional and conventional bases of segmentation in consumer markets, such as geographic and demographic bases. It then looks at some of the more recent developments in segmentation, and in particular the use of geo-demographic, lifestyle and combination bases. Finally, this section on consumer market segmentation examines what are often referred to as *behavioural segmentation bases*, which use the behaviour of consumers themselves as the basis for identifying market segments.

Let's start with two of the more conventional, and still widely used, bases for segmenting consumer markets: geographic and demographic bases for segmentation.

6.4.1   Socio-demographic segmentation

This approach comprises a wide variety of bases for subdividing markets; some of the more common bases used include the following.

Geographic segmentation

This consists of dividing a market on the basis of different geographical units. In international marketing, different countries may be deemed to constitute different market segments. Similarly, within a country a market may be segmented regionally into, for example, northern versus southern segments.

Geographic segmentation is still widely used, at least as one element in a combination of segmentation bases. Clearly, geographic segmentation is potentially at its most powerful and useful when considering international markets, and therefore is considered in more detail in Section 6.6.

Gender

A basic approach to segmentation of the market for household consumables and for food purchases is to identify 'housewives' as a specific market segment. For marketing purposes, 'housewives' can include both females and males who have primary responsibility for grocery purchase and household clothes. This segmentation of the total potential market of, say, all adults will result in a smaller (around half the size) identified target. Many segmentation schemes use gender as a first step in the segmentation process, but then further refine their targets within the chosen gender category (e.g. by social class). In some markets the most relevant variable is gender preference (e.g. the 'gay' market for certain products and services).

Age

Age has been used as a basic segmentation variable in many markets. The market for holidays is a classic example, with holiday companies tailoring their products to specific age groups such as the 'under-30s' or 'senior citizens'. In these segmentation schemes it is reasoned that there are significant differences in behaviour and product/service requirements between the demographic segments identified.

Family life cycle

This basis for *life cycle/stage segmentation* centres on the idea that consumers pass through a series of quite distinct phases in their lives, with each phase being associated with different purchasing patterns and needs. The unmarried person living in their parents' home, say, may have very different purchasing patterns from a chronological counterpart who has left home and recently married. It is also recognized that the purchasing pattern of adults often changes as they approach and move into retirement.

Producers of baby products, for example, build mailing lists of households with newborn babies on the basis of free gifts given to mothers in maternity hospitals. These lists are dated and used to direct advertising messages for further baby, toddler and child products to the family at the appropriate time as the child grows.

The basic life cycle stages are presented in Table 6.1.

In some instances segmentation by life cycle can help directly with product design, as is the case with package holidays. In addition to using age as a segmentation variable, holiday companies target different stages of the life cycle very specifically, from the Club Med emphasis on young singles, to Centre Parcs family holidays, to coach operators' holidays for senior citizens.

Occupation/social class

These are linked together because, in many developed economies, official socio-economic group (social class) categorizations are based upon occupation. In the UK, this occupation is that of the 'head of the household', because this is what is regarded as being the criterion that determines the social class of the household. One way of doing it is shown in Table 6.2.

Stage	Financial circumstances and purchasing characteristics
Bachelor	
Young, single, not living at parental home	Few financial burdens, recreation-oriented; holidays, entertainments outside home
Newlywed	
Young couples, no children	Better off financially, two incomes; purchase home, some consumer durables
Full nest I	
Youngest child under 6	Home purchasing peak; increasing financial pressures, may have only one income earner; purchase of household 'necessities'
Full nest II	
Youngest child over 6	Financial position improving; some working spouses
Full nest III	
Older married couples with dependent children	Financial position better still; update household products and furnishings
Empty nest I	
Older married couple, no children at home	Home ownership peak; renewed interest in travel and leisure activities; buy luxuries
Empty nest II	
Older couples, no children at home, retired	Drastic cut in income; medical services bought
Solitary survivor	
Still in labour force	Income good, but likely to sell home
Solitary survivor	
Retired	Special needs for medical care, affection and security

TABLE 6.1   Stages of the family life cycle

Social class grading	Occupation
A	Higher managerial
B	Intermediate management
C1	Supervisory/lower management
C2	Skilled manual
D	Semi-skilled/unskilled
E	Lowest levels of subsistence, e.g. pensioners (with no supplementary income)

TABLE 6.2   Social class/occupation

As occupation is the only factor in this system that is used to ascribe social class, it is obviously important that the codes used to classify occupations into the different social categories – six in this case – are valid. Of greatest importance in this validity aspect is that the different occupations used to designate social class actually discriminate and distinguish between different customer groups, and their purchasing habits and needs.

Quite simply, although this long-established system of assigning social class is widely used in marketing, there is increasing doubt as to the extent to which social class is nowadays a meaningful basis for segmenting some markets; in part, this arises from the fact that it is no longer so strongly related to income groups. For example, it is often the case that those in the skilled manual group (C2) earn higher incomes than their lower- or even intermediate-management counterparts (C1 or B) in industry. Such groups are often in a position to purchase products and services that were once 'traditionally' the prerogative of the upper social grades.

This increasing concern regarding the poor predictive power of many of these more conventional demographic bases for segmenting consumer markets, coupled with improvements in data collection and analysis methods, has led to the development in recent years of newer, and some would suggest more powerful, bases for segmenting consumer markets, such as personality or so-called lifestyle/psychographics segmentation.

Historically, China's markets have had a fairly simple structure concerning segmentation: at the top, a small premium segment served mainly by foreign companies, with solid margins and sometimes rapid growth; and at the bottom, a large, low-end segment served by Chinese companies offering lower-quality, undifferentiated products, that carry prices 40–90 per cent below the premium products in that segment. These companies often lose money – if there is rigorous accounting. Between the two is the good enough segment, where reliable enough products at low enough prices appeal to China's fast-growing mid-level consumers. Indeed, the good enough segment is growing faster than either the premium or low-end segments (Gadiesh et al., 2007)

Subculture

Besides belonging to a workplace environment, individuals are members of a variety of subcultures. These subcultures are groups within the overall society that have peculiarities of attitude or behaviour. For a subculture to be of importance for segmentation purposes, it is likely that membership of it has to be relatively enduring and not transient, and that membership of the subculture is of central importance in affecting the individual's attitudes and/or ultimate behaviour.

The major subcultures used for segmentation purposes are typically based on racial, ethnic, religious or geographic similarities. In addition, subcultures existing within specific age groupings may be treated as distinct market segments. For example, targeting members of the youth hip-hop culture has certain implications for the marketing of, say, clothing.

6.4.2 Personality characteristics

Personality characteristics are more difficult to measure than demographics or socio-economics. They are generally inferred from large sets of questions, often involving detailed computational (multivariate) analysis techniques. Perhaps the main value of personality measures lies in creating the background atmosphere for advertisements and, in some instances, package design and branding.

Lifestyle characteristics

This research attempts to isolate market segments on the basis of the style of life adopted by their members. At one stage these approaches were seen as alternatives to the social class categories discussed above.

Lifestyle segmentation is often referred to as *psychographics*. It is based on the fact that individuals have characteristic modes and patterns of living that may influence their motives to purchase selected products and brands. For example, some individuals may prefer a 'homely' lifestyle, whereas others may see themselves as living a 'sophisticated' lifestyle. Although there is much evidence to support the idea of this form of segmentation, in its earliest applications it proved to be disappointing in practice. However, more recent applications are proving that it now has much to commend it.

Lifestyle segmentation is concerned with three main elements: activities (e.g. leisure activities, sports, hobbies, entertainment, home activities, work activities, professional work, shopping behaviour, housework and repairs, travel and miscellaneous activities, daily travel, holidays, education and charitable work); interaction with others (e.g. self-perception, personality and self-ideal, role perceptions – as mother, wife, husband, father, son, daughter, etc. – and social interaction, communication with others, opinion leadership); and opinions (on topics such as politics, social and moral issues, economic and business–industry issues, and technological and environmental issues).

The approaches to consumer market segmentation that have been described so far have all been *associative*; that is, they are used where we feel that differences in purchasing behaviour/customer needs may be associated with them. If, say, we use social class or lifestyle to segment a market, we are assuming that purchasing behaviour is a function of social class or lifestyle. Most of the problems with using such associative bases tend to be related to the issue of the extent to which they are truly associated with, or are a reflection of, actual purchasing behaviour. Because of this, many marketers believe that it is more sensible to use *direct* bases for segmenting markets. As mentioned, such bases take actual consumer behaviour as the starting point for identifying different segments and are often referred to as *behavioural* segmentation bases.

Examples of some of the more frequently used behavioural bases in consumer markets include those described below.

6.4.3 Occasions for purchase

Attitudinal characteristics attempt to draw a causal link between customer characteristics and marketing behaviour. Here, segments are identified on the basis of differences in the occasions for purchasing the product.

Usage segmentation

Here, a distinction may be made between 'heavy', 'light' and 'non-user' segments. The usage segmentation concept is more useful in some markets than in others. In the soap market, for instance, it is noted that heavy users of soap account for 75 per cent of purchases. However, heavy users account for nearly half the population and constitute a very diverse group. By contrast, bourbon whisky is consumed by around 20 per cent of adults only, and heavy users account for 95 per cent of consumption, making this a much tighter target market.

Benefit segmentation

Benefit segmentation takes the basis of segmentation right back to the underlying reasons why customers are attracted to various product offerings. As such it is perhaps the closest means yet to identifying segments on bases directly relevant to marketing decisions. Developments in techniques such as conjoint analysis make them particularly suitable for identifying benefit segments.

This is a very meaningful way to segment a market. The total market for a product or service is broken down into segments distinguished by the principal benefits sought by each segment. For example, the market for shampoo includes the following benefit segments, which can be clearly observed from manufacturers' advertisements:

- cleanliness
- protection from dandruff, greasiness, dryness, and so on
- reasons of scalp medication
- reasons of well-being.

A 'benefits sought' basis for segmentation can provide useful insights into the nature and extent of competition, and the possible existence of gaps in the market.

Behavioural segmentation

The most direct method of segmenting markets is on the basis of the behaviour of the consumers in those markets. Behavioural segmentation covers purchases, consumption, communication and response to elements of the marketing mix. The study of purchasing behaviour has centred on such issues as time of purchase (early or late in the product's overall life cycle) and patterns of purchase (the identification of brand-loyal customers).

Innovators

Because of their importance when new products are launched, innovators (those who purchase a product when it is still new) have received much attention from marketers. Clearly, during the launch of new products, isolation of innovators as the initial target segment could significantly improve the product's or service's chances of acceptance in the market. Innovative behaviour, however, is not necessarily generalizable to many different product fields. Attempts to seek out generalized innovators have been less successful than looking for individual innovators in a specific field. Generalizations seem most relevant when the fields of study are of similar interest.

Opinion leaders can be particularly influential in the early stages of the product life cycle. Recording companies, for example, recognize the influence that DJs have on the record-buying public and attempt to influence them with free records and other inducements to play their recordings.

While innovators are concerned with initial purchase, loyalty patterns are concerned with repeat purchase; as such they are more applicable to repeat purchase goods than to consumer durables, though they have been used in durables markets (see the example of Volkswagen below).

This direct approach is based on the extent to which different customers are loyal to certain brands (brand loyalty) or possibly to certain retail outlets (store loyalty). Identifying segments with different degrees of loyalty enables a company to determine which of its customers or prospective customers may be brand- or store-loyal prone. Such a market segment is a very attractive one on which to concentrate future marketing efforts. Once they are convinced of the relative merits of a brand or supplier, such customers are unlikely to transfer their allegiance.

Where existing brand loyalty is already strong in a market, the would-be new entrant is faced with a particularly difficult marketing problem. In such a situation, it may be necessary to identify and target the non-brand-loyal segment.

Volkswagen, the German car manufacturer, has used loyalty as a major method for segmenting its customer markets. It divided its customers into the following categories:

- First-time buyers, and
- Replacement buyers:
  - **a** model-loyal replacers
  - **b** company-loyal replacers
  - **c** switch replacers.

These segments were used to analyse performance and market trends, and for forecasting purposes.

In the context of e-marketing, companies such as Site Intelligence have devised methods of segmenting website visitors and purchasers using combinations of behavioural (visits) and demographic characteristics.

Exhibit 6.1: *The use of occasion-based segmentation at Coca-Cola*

Typical segmentation approaches fall short of what is needed to grow sales and profits because they segment on what customers *currently do*, instead of what customers *will do*. Occasion-based segmentation identifies opportunities for growth based on the occasion when the product or service is used. In many categories, like beverages, the same consumer can experience a wide variety of needs, based on the situation. For example, you get up in the morning and you drink coffee and orange juice; at lunch you drink iced tea or a soft drink; in the afternoon maybe diet soda or perhaps a coffee from Starbucks; for dinner you may drink water and, later that night, perhaps juice again. Throughout the day the same person experiences many different needs and then makes beverage choices based on those needs. Coca-Cola has identified the psychological needs that drive those choices, and has positioned its brand to be the preferred choice, because this allowed it to segment the opportunity in a way that was consistent with how consumers use the category.

Source: adapted from Zyman and Singleton (2004)

6.5 Segmenting business markets (B2B)

The imperative to divide the market into different segments in order to offer products that match differing needs is at the very heart of both B2B and B2C marketing and is called market segmentation. The strength, width and depth of the segmentation demands will vary from industry to industry and from country to country depending on factors that often change and which are discussed later in this chapter. Only if the varying and diverse benefits demanded by different industries and organizations are known can products and services be offered with benefits that will satisfy these many disparate needs.

The basic approach to segmentation, targeting and positioning does not differ greatly between consumer and organizational markets. As one might expect, segmenting industrial product markets introduces a number of additional bases for segmentation, while precluding some of the more frequently used ones in consumer product markets.

6.5.1 The hierarchical approach to B2B segmentation

This approach was developed by Wind and Cardozo (1974) and is illustrated in Fig. 6.2. Basically, the approach calls for industrial markets to be segmented in two stages. The first stage includes formation of macro segments, based on the characteristics of the organization. The second stage involves dividing these macro segments into micro segments, based on the characteristics of the decision-making units (DMUs).

This hierarchical approach enables an initial screening of organizations and selection of these macro segments, which on the basis of organizational characteristics provide potentially attractive market opportunities. Organizations that may have no use for the given product or service can be eliminated. Starting with the grouping of organizations into homogeneous macro segments also provides a reduction in total research effort and cost. Instead of examining detailed buying patterns and attempting to identify the characteristics of the DMU in each organization individually, such analysis is limited only to those macro segments that passed the initial screening.

Once a set of acceptable macro segments has been formed, the marketer may divide each of them into micro segments, or small groups of companies, on the basis of similarities and differences among DMUs within each macro segment. Information for this second stage will come primarily from the sales force, based on sales people's analysis of situations in particular companies or from specially designed market segmentation studies.

This concept of successively combining industrial market segmentation bases giving, hopefully, more and more precise and hence meaningful segments is taken even further in the model developed by Shapiro and Bonoma (1984). Their 'nested' approach is shown in Fig. 6.3.

This approach identifies five general segmentation bases, which are arranged in the nested hierarchy shown, moving from the outer nests towards the inner. The segmentation bases (criteria) also move from macro to micro criteria. The bases are: demographics, operating variables, purchasing approach, situational factors and personal characteristics of the buyer. We now examine each of these in turn.

Demographics

This category represents the outermost nest, which contains the most general segmentation criteria. These variables give a broad description of the segments in the market, and relate to

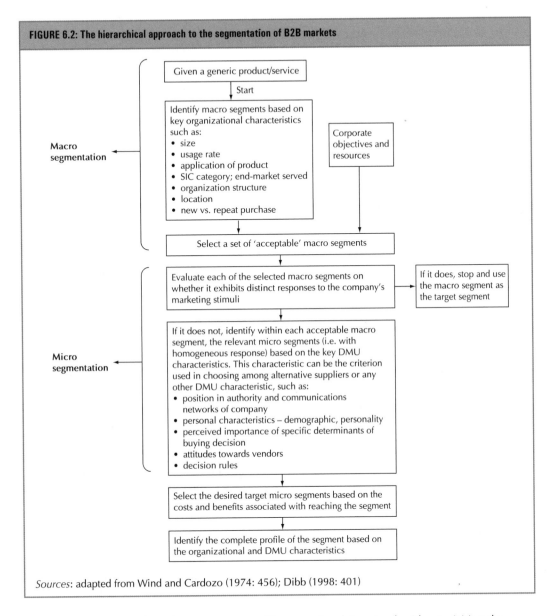

FIGURE 6.2: The hierarchical approach to the segmentation of B2B markets

Sources: adapted from Wind and Cardozo (1974: 456); Dibb (1998: 401)

general customer needs and usage patterns. They can be determined without visiting the customer, and include industry and company size, and customer location.

Demographic characteristics of companies can be a useful starting point for business segmentation; indeed, they characterize the approaches most commonly used by business marketing companies. Factors that can be considered here include demographics such as industry type, customer size and location, but also operating variables such as customer technology and capabilities, different purchasing policies and situational factors including product application.

Factors such as the Standard Industry Classification (SIC) provide a first stage of analysis, both for identifying target industries and subdividing them into groups of companies with

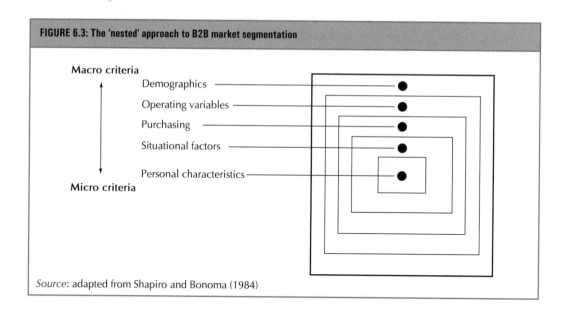

FIGURE 6.3: The 'nested' approach to B2B market segmentation

Source: adapted from Shapiro and Bonoma (1984)

different needs or different approaches to buying. This may be the basis for vertical marketing to industry sectors. Retailers and hospitals, for example, both buy computers, but they will have different applications and different buying strategies.

Size may also be highly significant if, for instance, small companies have needs or buying preferences that are distinctly different from those of larger companies. Typical measures would be variables such as number of employees and sales turnover. Size may be very significant because it impacts on issues such as volume requirements, average order size, sales and distribution coverage costs and customer bargaining power, which may alter the attractiveness of different segments as targets. Company size may be analysed alongside other demographics.

Operating variables

The second segmentation nest contains a variety of segmentation criteria called 'operating variables'. These enable more precise identification of existing and potential customers within demographic categories. Operating variables are generally stable and include technology, user/non-user status (by product and brand) and customer capabilities (operating, technical and financial).

The customer's stage of technology development will impact directly on its manufacturing and product technology, and hence on its demand for different types of product. Traditional factories operating mixed technologies and assembly methods require different product and subassembly inputs (e.g. test equipment, tooling, components) compared to the automated production unit. High-technology businesses may require very different distribution methods (e.g. Marks & Spencer requires suppliers to have the capability to co-operate in electronic stock control and cross-docking to avoid retail stockholding). Increasingly, high-technology companies require that their suppliers are integrated into their computer systems for all stages of the purchase process.

Purchasing approaches

One of the most neglected but valuable methods of segmenting an industrial market involves customers' purchasing approaches and company philosophy. The factors in this middle segmentation nest include the formal organization of the purchasing function, the power structure, the nature of the buyer/seller relationship, purchasing policies and purchasing criteria.

How customers organize purchasing may also identify important differences between customers. For example, centralized purchasing may require suppliers to have the capability to operate national or international account management, while decentralized purchasing may require more extensive field sales operations. Depending on a supplier's own strengths and weaknesses, the purchasing organization type may be a significant way of segmenting the market.

Situational factors

Up to this point the model has focused on the grouping of customer companies. Now it moves to consider the tactical role of the purchasing situation. Situational factors resemble operating variables, but are temporary and require a more detailed knowledge of the customer. They include the urgency of order fulfilment, product application and size of order.

Customers might divide, for example, into: those who want single supply sources versus those who want to dual-source important supplies; public-sector and similar organizations where bidding is obligatory versus those preferring to negotiate price; those actively pursuing reductions in their supplier base compared to others. Indeed, the model proposed above of the customer's relationship requirements as a basis for segmenting may be even more useful in the business market, where the demand for partnership between suppliers and customers characterizes many large companies' approaches to purchasing.

The product application can have a major influence on the purchase process and criteria, and hence supplier choices. The requirements for a small motor used in intermittent service for a minor application in an oil refinery will differ from the requirements for a small motor in continuous use for a critical process.

An added complication in business markets, however, is the DMU. Many business purchase decisions are made or influenced by a group of individuals rather than a single purchaser. Different members of the DMU will often have different perceptions of what the benefits are, both to their organization and to themselves.

In the purchase of hoists, for example, the important benefit to a user may be lightness and ease of use, whereas the purchasing manager may be looking for a cheaper product to make his or her purchasing budget go further. Architects specifying installations for new plant may perceive greater benefit in aesthetically designed hoists, and maintenance personnel may look for easy maintenance as a prime benefit.

Buyers' personal characteristics

People, not companies, make purchase decisions, although the organizational framework in which they work, and company policies and needs, may constrain their choices. Marketers for industrial goods, like those for consumer products, can segment markets according to the individuals involved in a purchase in terms of buyer/seller similarity, buyer motivation, individual perceptions and risk-management strategies.

Business goods markets can be segmented by issues such as:

- *buyer/seller similarity* – compatibility in technology, corporate culture or even company size may be a useful way of distinguishing between customers
- *buyer motivation* – purchasing officers may differ in the degree to which they shop around and look at numerous alternative suppliers, and dual-source important products and services, as opposed to relying on informal contacts for information and remaining loyal to existing personal contracts
- *buyer risk perceptions* – the personal style of the individual, intolerance of ambiguity, self-confidence and status within the company may also provide significant leverage.

6.5.2 The notion of segments and 'good' segmentation

Technically speaking, segmentation means grouping together similar customers. The results of segmentation performed by a given company depend on the quality of the information available and on the company's own characteristics (in particular, technological and organizational abilities), and the types of decision it wishes to make. Thus, market segmentation can vary according to how the company sees the market, and whether it is for the present or a future offer. Indeed, it may be the case that two competitors in the same market can produce two different market segmentations. Above all, segmentation helps to identify closely related (similar) customer groups. Statistically speaking, the aim is to minimize intragroup variance (to create sufficiently 'homogeneous' groups) and to maximize intergroup variance (to create groups that are different from each other). This means it is also an intellectual process (and/or statistical, if statistical data analysis techniques are used), which aims to give the company a simplified representation of its market, by incorporating the aspects of customer behaviour and the market dynamics that can affect it. Such a representation is always a simplification. This is necessary to make the market understandable and the segmentation usable. Therefore, the process must lead to a well thought out and controlled summary of the initial information.

Thus, the segment is by convention a group of 'customer units', although a market – a population – can be divided into an almost infinite number of segments. Each segment must have an operational 'reality' for the company, meaning that the company can define a suitable, autonomous and coherent marketing strategy for each group. The process depends on the market in question. The complexity of the segmentation is proportional to market volume, value and heterogeneity, which command the number of variables taken into consideration by the process. In other words, the quality depends on the work performed and how this complexity was managed and 'summarized'.

Thus, we can talk of 'good segmentation' as having led to the creation of homogeneous segments, all different between themselves, with a specific and identified competition, large enough to be profitable and operational. It thus justifies a differentiation in the offers, and/or in access to the market, and/or in the marketing process. It therefore affects both the supply strategy and customer approach, making it the key to the marketing process.

Exhibit 6.2: *Cadbury's segmentation strategy in chocolate confectionery*

The Cadbury brand name has been in existence since 1824 when John Cadbury opened his first shop in Birmingham, England. Cadbury's market share grew in 2003 to 7.2 per cent of the world chocolate market, making it the fourth largest global chocolate brand after Mars, Nestlé and Hershey Foods. Cadbury's core markets are currently the UK, Ireland, Australia and New Zealand. The Cadbury brand is very well known in these markets and consumers have established patterns of chocolate consumption.

Market research shows that women purchase almost two-thirds of all confectionery, but eat just over half of what they buy themselves as they are the gatekeepers when making purchasing decisions for the rest of the family. By targeting the gatekeeper with a new product the chances of a successful launch are increased.

Cadbury has identified three key segments in chocolate confectionery.

1   *Take home* confectionery is generally purchased in a supermarket for later consumption in and out of the home. Here consumers make more rational decisions and consider the price of the product, the value they place on the brand and the quantity purchased.
2   The *gift* segment of the market contains products that are purchased for everyday gift occasions such as Valentine's Day, birthdays and Christmas. The core drivers in making a purchasing decision in this segment are 'need a token of appreciation', 'need a romantic gesture' and 'need to celebrate a special occasion'.
3   *Impulse* purchases are typically products bought for immediate consumption. The core drivers for this type of purchase are indulgent and immediate consumer needs such as 'need filling up', 'need a light snack', 'feel like indulging' and 'need some energy'.

In general, the impulse market accounts for 50 per cent of total chocolate sales; 80 per cent of these sales are made on an impulse basis. Research has found that growth in the impulse market is driven by changes in lifestyle that are affecting the way we eat and an increasing demand for convenience. Snacking has become a part of everyday life and chocolate has become a unique impulse category because it is eaten throughout the day rather than specifically at mealtimes. The peak times for confectionery eating are late morning, late afternoon, after school and during the evening.

Changing lifestyle patterns, eating on the go and impulse snacking do already and continue to play a pivotal role in the confectionery market. Continual snacking, or 'grazing', has replaced traditional mealtimes for many people. The Cadbury product range addresses the needs of each and every consumer, from childhood to maturity, from impulse purchase to family treats. For example, an analysis of the 'gift' sector highlights the importance of developing innovative products to address specific markets. Cadbury designs products to coincide with Christmas, Easter, Valentine's Day, Mother's Day and Father's Day, and other calendar landmarks. Cadbury uses marketing strategies such as the 'Choose Cadbury' strategy to encourage a link between chocolate and these events, ensuring there is a Cadbury chocolate product suitable and available for every occasion.

Sources: adapted from www.cadbury.com; www.business2000.ie; www.cadburyworld.co.uk; Mortimer, R. (2004) Cadbury's purple reign, *Brand Strategy*, 186: 28–30; Jardine, A. and Wentz, L. (2004) Cadbury adopts umbrella strategy, *Advertising Age*, 75(34): 23; Parry, C. (2004) Cadbury leads the way with Dairy Milk, *Marketing Week* (*UK*), 27(30): 24–6.

6.6 Segmenting (screening) international markets and countries

6.6.1 Selecting target countries

The assessment of international marketing opportunities usually begins with a screening process that involves gathering relevant information on each country and filtering out the less desirable countries. A 'top-down' model for selecting foreign markets is shown in Hollensen (2004: 232). This model includes a series of four filters to screen out countries. The overwhelming number of market opportunities makes it necessary to break the process down into a series of steps. Although a company does not want to miss a potential opportunity, it cannot conduct extensive market research studies in every country of the world.

The screening process is used to identify good prospects. Two common errors of country screening are (1) ignoring countries that offer good potential for the company's products, and (2) spending too much time investigating countries that are poor prospects. Thus, the screening process allows an international company to focus efforts quickly on a few of the most promising market opportunities by using the published secondary sources available.

The first stage of the selection process uses macro variables to discriminate between regions and countries that represent basic opportunities, and countries with little or no opportunity or with excessive risk. Macro variables describe the total market in terms of economic, social, geographic and political information. Often macroeconomic statistics indicate that the country is too small, as demonstrated by its gross national (or domestic) product. It may be that the gross national product seems large enough, but the personal disposable income per household may be too low. Political instability can also be used to remove a country from the set of possible opportunities.

In the second stage of the selection process, variables are used that indicate the potential market size and acceptance of the product or similar products. Often, proxy variables are used in this screening process. A *proxy variable* is a similar or related product that indicates a demand for your product.

The third stage of the screening process focuses on micro-level considerations such as competitors, ease of entry, cost of entry and profit potential. Micro-level factors influence the success or failure of a specific product in a specific market. At this stage of the process, marketers may be considering only a small number of countries, so it is feasible to get more detailed, up-to-date information via primary data-collection methods like specific potential customers. During the screening process the focus switches from potential market to actual market and, finally, to company profitability.

The market screening process requires a significant amount of effort. Once the target country has been selected, there is a tendency to focus on the selected markets and ignore the rejected countries. However, the world market is continually changing, and countries that were rejected last year may provide significant opportunities next year.

6.6.2 Selecting global segments

Increasing numbers of industries are global. To succeed in this environment companies have to shift from a domestic perspective to considering the world as the arena of operations both with respect to consumer markets for products and services and resources markets for raw materials, research and development (R&D), manufacturing, and human and capital resources.

The globalization of industries is also accompanied by trends towards regional economic integration: the European Union (EU), NAFTA and the various other efforts towards regional integration in Asia and Latin America. The implication for segmentation of these developments is that management has to consider portfolios of segments that include:

- global segments
- regional segments
- segments within specific countries.

Added to this complexity is the need to consider as the unit of analysis not just countries but countries by mode of entry, since both the risk and attractiveness of a country depend on the mode of entry. The selection and implementation of a portfolio of segments, which includes global segments, regional segments and segments within countries (by mode of entry), requires a significant amount of information on all relevant markets around the world. The creation and maintenance of such a data/knowledge base is not a trivial undertaking and is one of the major obstacles to the development of global segmentation strategies. The creation of processes for the development and maintenance of country, regional and world databases is a high-priority undertaking for all global firms, yet the development of effective segmentation can take place even without such databases if the company will proceed in an iterative bottom-up and top-down segmentation. This process involves three bottom-up steps (contrary to the previous top-down model of country selection):

1 segmentation of the market in each country (by mode of entry)
2 examination of the resulting segments in all the selected countries to identify common segments across countries – clustering of country segments
3 creation of a global portfolio based on various clusters of segments.

The resulting portfolio of segments should be compared to a desired (top-down) conceptual portfolio of segments. The comparison and contrast of the two portfolios should be driven by the concept of global operation, which balances the need to develop strategies that best meet the needs of the local markets (given the idiosyncratic market, competitive and environmental conditions), while at the same time trying to achieve economies of scale and scope by focusing on cross-country segments in a number of markets.

6.6.3 Governmental buying and segmenting

A large number of international business transactions involve governments. For example, governments handle 80 per cent of all international trade of all agricultural products. The US government buys more goods and services than any other government, business, industry or organization in the world. Selling to governments can be both time-consuming and frustrating. Governmental buying processes tend to be highly bureaucratic.

Governments make it harder for a foreign company to sell to them; many place their own domestic firms ahead of foreign operations. Also, negotiating with foreign governments can be a very formal process. Understanding cultural differences is essential in order not to overstep boundaries.

Government procurement processes vary very much from country to country.

6.6.4 Targeting strategies

Having evaluated the relative attractiveness of different market segments we are now in a position to select a targeting strategy. A company can select from three broad strategies with respect to targeting. These are *undifferentiated* target marketing, *differentiated* target marketing and *concentrated* target marketing (see Hollensen, 2003: 331).

6.6.5 Positioning strategy

The final stages of the STP process involve the development of positioning strategies, together with a supporting marketing mix. In their seminal work in this area, Ries and Trout (1981) suggested that positioning is essentially 'a battle for the mind'. In other words, positioning takes place in the mind of the customer. For example, let us assume that a company seeks to enter the market for 'instant coffee', in which there are already competitors producing brands A, B, C, D, E, F and G. The company must establish what the customers believe to be the appropriate attributes when choosing between brands in this market, and the perceived position of existing competitors with respect to these attributes. If we imagine that the important attributes have been found to be 'price' and 'flavour', a possible positioning map (also called a brand map) might be drawn up, like the one shown in Fig. 6.4.

With this information, the company must decide where to position its product within the market segment. Possibilities are contained within the box, the parameters of which, in the example shown in Fig. 6.4, are low to medium price per gram and low to medium flavour. Perhaps a caffeine-free product could also be considered? Such a product would give the new brand distinctiveness, as opposed to positioning it next to another and fighting head on for market share.

The most appropriate position for the new coffee brand depends on a number of factors. For example, as outlined earlier, we must assess the relative attractiveness of a particular position in a market for the new brand compared to our resources and competencies in the company. Of course, it is also important to consider whether the number of customers in the chosen position is large enough to generate sufficient profit. Similarly, and related to this, we must assess the relative strengths of existing competitive brands in the market and whether we want to tackle this competition head on or not. Finally, we must consider what our objectives for the new product are, particularly with regard to brand image.

Once we have assessed brand positioning in the market and determined where we wish to position our products and brands, the final step in the process of segmentation, targeting and

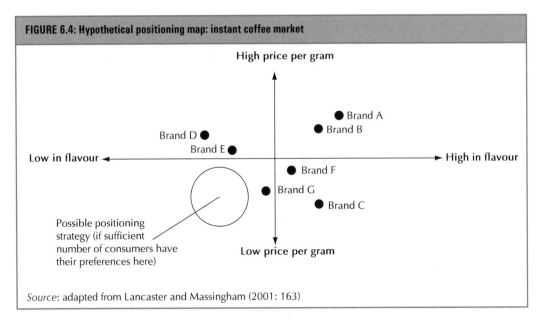

FIGURE 6.4: Hypothetical positioning map: instant coffee market

Source: adapted from Lancaster and Massingham (2001: 163)

positioning involves the design of marketing programmes, which will support the positional strategy in selected target markets. In our instant coffee example, the company must therefore determine what price, flavour (product), distribution and promotional strategy will be necessary to achieve the selected position in the market.

Although positioning is particularly crucial when developing and launching a new product for a market, it is also relevant to the management of existing products and brands. Because markets evolve and change over time – including, for example, changes in customer tastes, competition, and so on – the marketer must continuously assess the effectiveness of existing positioning strategies for products and brands. Often, existing brands will need to be repositioned to reflect changing market dynamics.

6.7 Difficulties of implementing segmentation in the organization

It is important to preface this review of implementation difficulties by explaining what is meant by segmentation implementation. For the purposes of this discussion, implementation difficulties arise when the segmentation process has failed to generate a solution that can be put into practice. This means that, for whatever reason, it has not been possible for the business concerned to use the segmentation scheme to develop suitable and distinct marketing mixes for different customer groups: the developed segmentation scheme has not been actioned effectively.

6.7.1 The main problems

According to Dibb and Simkin (2001) the main problems are those described below.

Infrastructure barriers

All aspects of segmentation can suffer when a company's infrastructure is inappropriate or too inflexible to deal with the process. These difficulties encompass anything to do with the corporation's culture, structure or resources acting as a segmentation barrier. For example, the marketing function in a business with a particularly entrenched organizational structure may fail in its attempts to implement segmentation if it has not secured the commitment of senior managers. Similarly, a business lacking the financial resources to collect appropriate market data will also have problems adopting a segmentation approach.

Many infrastructure difficulties relate to people issues. They arise because the business is devoting insufficient human resources to the segmentation process or because the individuals involved lack the required skills and experience to carry it out. Poor communication between functions and inadequate commitment from senior management also can cause problems.

Segmentation process issues

Despite an extensive segmentation literature, there is surprisingly little practical help available to those wishing to apply a market segmentation approach. Whereas many managers are familiar with the segmentation, targeting and positioning (STP) notion of marketing segmentation, they often express surprise about the lack of simple, practical advice available to them on how to proceed.

Implementation barriers

The underlying assumption of academic segmentation is that new solutions can simply be substituted for existing segmentation schemes. In practice, it is rarely simple for a business to make wholesale changes to its segmentation. Even assuming that the necessary resources are available to carry out a segmentation project, the planning and implementation of the process are constrained by a number of practical and operational concerns.

6.7.2   What should be done about the problems?

The requirement for appropriate marketing skills does not end with the identification of a segmentation solution. Businesses must continue to allocate appropriate personnel and resources if suitable marketing programmes are to be developed. Care must be taken to ensure that these programmes closely match the segments identified.

Dibb and Simkin (2001) show the benefits of a good fit between a segment solution and the marketing programme designed to implement it. This view should then be used to build a more appropriate and simpler segmentation structure, allowing the business to develop marketing programmes that match customer requirements more closely.

Summary

Segmentation is an operation of classification. It aims to provide management with a representation of the markets that is designed to help them make choices. This representation is the result of a process founded on a simplification of the initial data. The result depends on the variety and quality of data available.

In segmentation, targeting and positioning, we are seeking to identify distinct subsets of customers in the total market for a product. Any subset might eventually be selected as a market target, and on that basis a distinctive marketing mix will be developed:

- a better understanding of customers, their needs and wants
- a better understanding of competition and the kind of competitive advantage to pursue
- a more effective use of company resources
- the development of more effective marketing plans.

In order to secure these advantages, the base(s) used for segmentation should fulfil the following criteria.

- *Measurability/identifiability*: the base(s) used to segment a market should ideally lead to ease of identification (who is in each segment) and measurability (how large is each segment).
- *Accessibility*: the base(s) used to segment a market should ideally lead to marketers being able to reach selected market targets with their marketing efforts.
- *Substantiality*: the base(s) used to segment markets should ideally lead to segments that are sufficiently large for it to be worthwhile serving them as distinct market targets.
- *Meaningfulness*: the base(s) used to segment markets must lead to segments that have different preferences/needs and show clear variations in market behaviour/response to marketing efforts.

The overall differences between segmentation in B2B and B2C markets were identified and highlighted.

Many variables exist as bases for *consumer segmentation* (B2C), ranging from behaviour to attitudes to background characteristics. The most commonly used characteristics are product and brand usage, and demographics/socio-economics, primarily because of the ease of obtaining this sort of data from secondary sources. Ultimately, however, for a segmentation scheme to be useful to marketing management it should seek not only to describe differences in consumers but also to explain them. In this respect attitudinal segmentation can offer better prospects.

Many ways to segment *business markets* (B2B) can be identified at both the macro and micro level, including by geographical location, industry sector, type of industry, organization size, products and services sold, the buying situation, and the culture of the company. Group and individual differences were identified and reasons given for when and how this information should be used in the segmentation process. It is highly probable that more than one way to segment a market will be used, perhaps using geographical location, industry sector, organizational size and types of product marketed.

Finally, segmentation is the first part of the so-called STP process, which consists of:

- *segmentation* – identifying the most productive bases for dividing a market, identifying the customers in different segments and developing segment descriptions
- *targeting markets* – evaluating the attractiveness of different market segments, parts of segments (niches) or groups of segments, and choosing which should be targets for marketing

● *positioning* – identifying the positioning of competitors (in the market and the target segments or niches), to develop the company's own positioning strategy.

Questions for discussion

1 What stages are involved in market segmentation?
2 Under which conditions, if any, might segmentation be unnecessary and unwise?
3 Why should marketers go beyond demographic variables when segmenting consumer and business markets?
4 Can market segmentation be taken too far? What are the potential disadvantages of over-segmenting a market? What strategy might a company pursue when it believes that the market has been broken into too many small segments?
5 Which variables or descriptors might be most appropriate for segmenting the market for the following products and services? Explain your reasoning.
   a DVD players
   b portable computers
   c games for PCs and consoles
   d holidays
   e wind turbines.
6 Segmentation leads to differentiated marketing. How might a company avoid producing too many varieties of a product?
7 Under what circumstances would a marketer want to change a product's positioning?

References

Dibb, S. (1998) Market segmentation: strategies for success, *Marketing Intelligence & Planning*, 16(7): 394–406.

Dibb, S. and Simkin, L. (2001) Market segmentation – diagnosing and treating the barriers, *Industrial Marketing Management*, 30: 609–25.

Gadiesh, O., Leung, P. and Vestring, T. (2007) The battle for China's good-enough market, *Harvard Business Review*, September: 81–9.

Hollensen, S. (2003) *Marketing Management.* London: Financial Times/Prentice Hall.

Hollensen, S. (2004) *Global Marketing; A Decision-oriented Approach*, 3rd edn. London: Financial Times/Prentice Hall.

Hooley, G., Saunders, J. and Piercy, N. (2004) *Marketing Strategy and Competitive Positioning*, 3rd edn. London: Financial Times/Prentice Hall.

Lancaster, G. and Massingham, L. (2001) *Marketing Management*, 3rd edn. New York: McGraw-Hill.

Ries, A. and Trout, J. (1981) *Positioning: The Battle for your Mind.* New York: McGraw-Hill.

Shapiro, B.P. and Bonoma, T.V. (1984) How to segment industrial markets, *Harvard Business Review*, May–June: 104–10.

Wind, Y. and Cardozo R. (1974) Industrial market segmentation, *Industrial Marketing Management*, 3: 456.

Zyman, S. and Singleton, D. (2004) Segmenting opportunity, *Brand Strategy*, June: 52–3.

CASE STUDY 6: TAG HEUER

The Swiss watchmaker is segmenting and penetrating the Indian market

At present, Swiss-made watches are completely dominating the worldwide luxury watch market contributing almost 100 per cent share. These watches are exported to most of the developed countries. However, rising incomes in emerging markets have led to a new category of affluent young professionals with high purchasing power. These countries have become a potential opportunity for ultra expensive watch manufacturers.

Generally, the total watch market can be divided into the following price segments:

- mass price market: under €50
- middle price market: €50–299
- upper price market: €300–999
- luxury price market: €1,000 and above.

Furthermore, there is the 'Horlogerie' market with high complications and jewellery. Watches are priced €10 000 and above. Examples of brands are Patek Philippe, Zenith, Jaeger-LeCoultre, and so on.

Traditionally considered a male domain, women are also driving up sales now. Women are more fashion-oriented. Luxury watchmakers are trying their best to design the female equivalent of their most popular watch models. Women change watches more frequently – they seem to appeal to quartz instead of mechanic, because then they do not need to set the hour right before wearing. Women are also attracted by jewellery pieces (diamonds, etc.). Another notable trend is the integration of new technology and the use of unconventional materials in luxury watches. Also, all major brands are trying to raise their price levels by repositioning their products.

The world demand of luxury watches in the different world regions is shown in Table 6.3.

Region	Regional market share (%)	Main countries (%)
Europe	44	UK (14), Germany (12), Italy (10), France (8)
USA	43	
Asia	13	China (6), Japan (5), India (2)
Total	100	

TABLE 6.3 World demand of luxury watches in main regions
Source: adapted from World Watch Report 2009: Industry Report of Watches and Watchmakers (WWR)

Rolex dominates the world luxury watch market (approximately €20 bn in manufacturers' selling prices) with approximately 40 per cent of market share, followed by Omega (15–20 per cent of market share), TAG Heuer (15–20 per cent of market share), Breitling, Cartier, Bulgari, Chopard, Ebel, Girard-Perregaux, Jaeger-LeCoultre, Longines and Patek Philippe.

Counterfeit products remain a problem in the industry. The lost value of this part represents 5–10 per cent of the total world market for luxury products. The main market for counterfeit goods is still the USA, representing over 66 per cent of global demand. Eighty per cent of demand for counterfeit products is for Rolex only. The remaining 20 per cent is divided up between the other 24 brands analyzed. Japan is the only country in which there are more searches for counterfeit goods on Omega than Rolex.

Background of TAG Heuer

Founded by Edouard Heuer in 1860 at Saint-Imier, in the Swiss Jura, TAG Heuer has now been in the vanguard of Swiss watchmaking for nearly 150 years. Soon after Edouard Heuer set up the company's first workshop in Switzerland, it patented the first chronograph mechanism and followed that up with a series of inventions that shaped the future of watches.

From the first patent for a chronograph mechanism in 1882, Heuer has written some of the finest chapters in watchmaking history. By 1966 Heuer had developed the Microtimer, the first one-1,000th of a second chronograph. And the company is still pioneering today. This has made TAG Heuer the inescapable reference brand in motor sports.

TAG Heuer's first ambassador of the brand was Jo Siffert and first sponsoring contract was also signed with this Swiss driver, who became a friend of Steve McQueen while teaching him driving skills on the set of the movie *Le Mans*. McQueen wore the Heuer Monaco chronograph in the movie that made the timepiece an icon of the brand.

After the Swiss-based Techniques d'Avant Garde group took over TAG Heuer from the Heuer family in 1984, Christian Viros was hired as chief executive officer (CEO) to save the company from financial difficulties. The company had been hit by the recession at the beginning of the 1980s and the TAG Heuer brand was seen more as associated with scientific and timing instruments than a luxury brand. CEO Christian Viros transformed TAG Heuer into a lifestyle brand by concentrating on design and marketing. But his masterstroke was focusing on an association with sports. The sports watch market was a new niche and Viros cornered it with advertisements featuring stars such as French skiing champion Luc Alphand and Formula 1 racing driver Ayrton Senna.

This strategy remains to this day. In addition to celebrities such as Uma Thurman and Brad Pitt (only from 2005 to 2008), its 'faces' include Tiger Woods, Maria Sharapova, Formula 1 world champions Kimi Räikkönen and Lewis Hamilton and more recently Leonardo DiCaprio. The company further exploits these associations when Formula 1 drivers test new prototypes during races, submitting them to extreme G-forces, vibration and shock.

In 1985, TAG Heuer became the chronograph of the McLaren team and won several Formula 1 world championships on the wrists of Niki Lauda, Alain Prost, Ayrton Senna and Lewis Hamilton. At the same time, it became the official timer of the Formula 1 World Championship, timing to the thousandth of a second, before becoming the official timer of the Indy 500 in 2004, timing to the ten-thousandth of a second – a feature that today remains unequalled.

Venture capital firm Doughty Hanson bought the business in the mid-1990s and later cashed out in a public flotation before luxury goods conglomerate Louis Vuitton Moët Hennesy (LVMH) bought the company for around US$800 m in 1999.

In 2000 Jean-Christophe Babin was appointed CEO. He has reduced the product range from 800 to 200 lines in the past four years and is looking more closely at women's watches. Babin has also segmented the watch models into 'families'. Babin is also behind other successes like Heuer models brimming with nostalgia and images.

Today, TAG Heuer is still an independent division under LVMH and considered a star brand of the group.

The number of employees in TAG Heuer in their headquarters and factory in Switzerland is 350; another 2000 (including LVMH watch and jewellery staff) are employed worldwide in subsidiaries located in the most dynamic markets:

- Central Europe (Germany, Austria, Netherland, Sweden and Denmark)
- LVMH Montres & Joaillerie France SA
- LVMH Relojera y Joyeria España SA
- LVMH Watch & Jewelry Italia Holding S.p.A
- LVMH Watch & Jewellery (UK) Ltd.
- LVMH Watch & Jewellery Far East Ltd., Middle East Branch, Dubai
- TAG Heuer Moscow Office Russia
- TAG Heuer Switzerland
- LVMH Watch & Jewellery Hong Kong Ltd.
- LVMH Watch & Jewellery Australia Pty. Ltd.
- LVMH Watch & Jewellery Singapore Pte. Ltd
- LVMH Watch & Jewellery Malaysia SDN BHD
- LVMH Watch & Jewellery Taiwan Ltd.
- LVMH Watch & Jewellery India Pvt Ltd.
- LVMH Watch & Jewellery USA Inc.
- LVMH Watch & Jewellery Canada Ltd.
- LVMH Watch & Jewellery Caribbean and Latin America
- Agents in Latin America, South Africa, CIS states, Koreas, Greece, and so on.

TAG Heuer's world marketing strategy

By sponsoring sports where technology and accuracy are paramount, TAG has polished its reputation for precision while positioning itself as a luxury brand appealing to early achievers. Until now TAG's target market is college-educated 30–40-year olds. Every year approximately 3 per cent of them buy a new luxury watch, costing €1,000 or more.

The female market is a potential growth market for TAG Heuer. Historically, TAG Heuer only sold 20 per cent of its watches to women, but it is now on its way to 40 per cent. Women buy more watches for themselves than men. If it wants to double its female buyers, it needs strong female communication and female endorsers. This is why Maria Sharapova and Uma Thurman have been integrated. Their determination, talent, success and strong character fit well with the brand values of TAG Heuer, so they can help in gaining market share for TAG Heuer in a segment where it is underrepresented. At the end of 2008, Uma Thurman's contract came to an end and was not renewed due to the economic crisis, which has also been the main reason why since 2009 TAG Heuer has decided to concentrate on core business. Even if the 'women strategy' remains in place, the choice was made to concentrate on acquired market shares. The existence of a second female ambassador was set 'entre parenthesis' until the world economy shows signs of growth again.

The three main characteristics of TAG Heuer's world marketing strategy are:

1   TAG's average watch price is now approximately €1,500.
2   As a result of its brand positioning, TAG Heuer's revenues steadily increased from just €25 m in 1988 to over €1 bn in 2008.
3   With over 8,000 retailers globally stocking TAG, its annual sales of around 900 000 watches (2008) give it a 15–20 per cent share of the world luxury watch market.

Perhaps the best proof of TAG's success is that, having homed in on the lower end of the luxury market, it opened this sector up to watches from fashion brands such as Diesel, Fossil and Calvin Klein. TAG's greatest challenge to come could be differentiating itself from these newcomers as well as the upper end of connoisseur's timepieces. This recent strategy of the brand is also reinforced with the launch of the luxury line Grand Carrera in 2007 (priced at €3000–5000), which increases the average retail price and further differentiates from 'fashion' watches, supported by an intensive communication of know-how and heritage.

One of the main challenges for TAG Heuer's communication strategy is to be well represented on the Internet. However, brand advertising on official websites is no longer enough. The social networks are gaining marketing power: Facebook has now nearly 200 million members. According to the World Watch Report 2009, Cartier is dominating Facebook with 30 000 fans, followed by TAG Heuer (18 500), Rolex (17 500), Bulgari (14 300) and Breitling (13 600). On YouTube 100 million videos are viewed monthly. Videos uploaded by fans are now taking up 38 per cent of brand visibility.

TAG Heuer's celebrity endorsement strategy

Since becoming CEO and president of Swiss watch company TAG Heuer 10 years ago, Jean-Christophe Babin has put together a portfolio of global and local brand ambassadors and endorsers.

According to the Global Watch Report from 2009, the top luxury watches ambassadors in the industry are these:

● Omega is the highest ranked brand – 17 per cent of total Internet searches. Omega uses the 'Michael Phelps effect': The US swimmer who beat the Gold Medal record in a single Olympics (eight medals) in the 2008 Beijing Olympic Games.
● Six of TAG Heuer's ambassadors are ranked in the top 20. At the top of the line is golfer Tiger Woods, who garners 15 per cent of Internet searches, followed by Bollywood star Shah Rukh Khan (7 per cent), Formula 1 racing driver Lewis Hamilton (4 per cent), actor Leonardo DiCaprio (3 per cent), tennis star Maria Sharapova (3 per cent) and the late actor Steve McQueen (2 per cent).

TAG Heuer has enjoyed success through creating bespoke products for local markets, endorsed by local ambassadors such as Bollywood star Shah Rukh Khan, who is the main reason for the TAG Heuer growth in India. Yao Ming (the US-based Chinese basketball player) helped TAG Heuer to grow the brand in China (contract from 2005 to 2006) and enabled the company to catch up with competitors who have been in this market much longer than TAG Heuer.

TAG Heuer's ambassadors are encouraged to participate in product development. The company does not sign a contract with anyone who is not interested in going into product development with TAG Heuer. This is what makes TAG Heuer ambassadors different from those of any other brand.

Tag Heuer is now starting to look for new markets and for the last 2–3 years it has been active in the Indian market. Here are some facts about this market.

The Indian watch market

India is one of the world's largest markets for watches, with volume sales of more than 55 million units per year. Women account for two-thirds of watch purchases in India. The annual sales of watches in India is growing at 8 per cent per year and has accounted for almost Rs50 bn in 2009, of which Rs12 bn belongs to the upper-middle segment. For this upper-middle segment, with unit prices between Rs50 000–60 000, the ever-increasing target population is currently about 100 million people. Since a total of 20–25 watches are sold per 1,000 inhabitants each year in India (compared with 100 watches per 1,000 inhabitants each year in developed countries), the potential for growth is quite large.

Competition in Indian watch market

By initially protecting its industry totally and only then opening its markets slowly to foreign competition, India has been able to build its own watch manufacturing sector. Indian watchmaking was long dominated by the state-run HMT, which produced robust mechanical watches with a classic design and designed to last a lifetime, but HMT missed the opportunities offered by the quartz revolution. Then came the giant Titan, which now has 7,000–8,000 sales outlets and controls 50 per cent of the total watch market. Titan is now flooding the market with models following international styles and offers watches at highly competitive prices.

Now that the Indian market is wide open to imports, it will be extremely difficult for domestic players to maintain sustainable growth. Only price, innovation and continuous enhancement of brands can protect them from foreign competition.

Swiss manufacturers have developed a four-pronged strategy for the Indian market: to remove myths from the Indian mind that Swiss watches are only for the 'super rich'; to introduce watch faces suitable for the Indian market; to market their products in the same category as jewellery; and not to touch on anything that decreases the products' 'snob' value.

Japanese manufacturers are feeling under pressure from the Swiss, as a result of the latter's plans to market watches as *objets d'art* rather than as mere gizmos.

Taiwanese and Hong Kong/Chinese products are available in the grey market, and include sleek, sporty, electronic gizmos available at very competitive prices.

TAG Heuer's marketing strategy in India

In 2008, TAG Heuer launched three standalone stores in big Indian cities. At present (in 2009), Mumbai and Delhi account for a third of the company's business in India. However, now TAG Heuer plans to multiply its presence in the country through multi-branded outlets in the smaller cities. TAG Heuer worldwide president and CEO Jean-Christophe Babin thinks that is where the next phase of demand will come from.

Questions

1 How would you segment TAG Heuer's watch market?
2 What is the target group for TAG Heuer watches in India?
3 How should TAG Heuer position its watches among the (potential) customers?
4 Do you agree with TAG Heuer's strategy of penetrating smaller cities in India?

Sources: World Watch Report 2009: Industry Report of Watches and Watchmakers (WWR); Priyanka Joshi (2009): *Tag Heuer Looking Beyond the Metros*, Mumbai, 5 October. Available online at www.business-standard.com/india/news/tag-heuer-looking-beyondmetros/372141/; *The Independent* (2005): Branding: TAG Heuer: Famous faces for watches; what could you do with a star line-up that included Brad Pitt, Uma, 12 September; *The Smart Money: Perfect Timing*, March 2007. Available online at www.bmivoyager.com/2007/03/01/perfect-timing/; www.tagheuer.com

Marketing mix decisions I: product

07

❖ LEARNING OBJECTIVES

After studying this chapter you should be able to do the following:

❖ Define the terms 'product' and 'product levels'.

❖ Discuss the differences between services and goods.

❖ Explain the different product differentiation strategies.

❖ Discuss the steps in new product development (NPD) processes.

❖ Explain the different product stretching strategies.

7.1 Introduction

So far, we have discussed the analysis that precedes, and is essential to, the development of detailed marketing programmes designed to meet corporate and strategic marketing objectives. In this and the following chapters, we consider strategic decisions concerned with planning and implementing elements of the marketing mix (i.e. product, price, promotion and place decisions). In this chapter, we start with the *product* element of the marketing mix.

Exhibit 7.1: *Harley-Davidson's 'total experience' product (HOG)*

Typically, there is more to an experience than merely the product itself. Outstanding service companies pay attention to the complete experience that customers have from the first contact with the organization onwards. The more customer-focused manufacturing organizations have also learned this lesson. When people become Harley-Davidson customers, they buy into a brand experience and a way of life. Harley managers and dealers often refer to their business as 'fulfilling dreams through the experience of motorcycling'. An illustration of the company's appreciation of the total customer experience is its successful sponsorship of the Harley Owners Group (HOG).

Harley-Davidson established HOG in 1983 in response to a growing desire by Harley riders for an organized way to share their passion and show their pride. By 1985, 49 local chapters had sprouted around the USA, with a total membership of 60 000.

Rapid growth continued into the 1990s, and in 1991 HOG officially went international, with the first official European HOG rally in Cheltenham, England. Worldwide membership numbered 151 600, with 685 local chapters.

As the 1990s continued, HOG expansion spread into Asia, including new chapters in Singapore and Kuala Lumpur, Malaysia. By 1999, worldwide membership had hit the half-million mark, and the number of local chapters totalled 1,157. Today, more than 900 000 members make HOG the largest factory-sponsored motorcycle organization in the world, and it shows absolutely no signs of slowing down.

Source: adapted from www.harley-davidson.com

7.2 Product mix decisions

In order to illustrate the range of decisions that the product strategy encompasses, it is useful to consider the hierarchy of related decisions from product item to product mix elements.

The first level of product decisions concerns individual products or services that a company manufactures and markets. A *product item* is, then, by definition a separate product entity, identified by a certain design quality, features, packaging and branding. Individual product items that are closely related in some way to another are classed as *product lines*. The *product mix* (see Fig. 7.1) then constitutes the sum of individual product items and product lines.

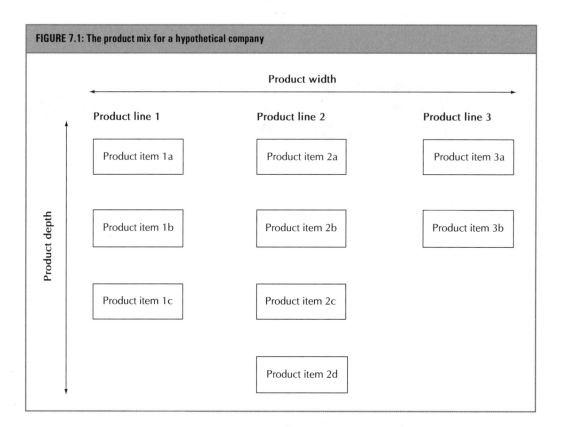

FIGURE 7.1: The product mix for a hypothetical company

The hypothetical company in Fig. 7.1 manufactures and markets three product lines (= product width). Product depth refers to the number of product items in each line – 3, 4 and 2, respectively – with the average being 3. By looking at Fig. 7.1 a strategic assessment of a company's product offering can be made. For example, the product width could be extended by adding more product lines. The same could be applied to the product depth.

Decisions about new products should reflect consistency with existing product lines in relation to previously determined marketing objectives set for product provision in specified markets. Hence, the addition to the width of the mix and the depth within each product line should be compatible with the planned long-term marketing strategy, based on a set of evaluation criteria so that the decisions taken are rational and not purely emotional or opportunistic. Product mix strategy involves the management of existing successful products, the elimination of obsolete or non-profit-making ones, and the development and introduction of new products. Each of these elements of product strategy and management is important to the achievement of company objectives.

7.3 Different product levels

The core product is the basic element of the company's offer to its customers. It has to be right in order for customers to consider the other elements. The core of the offer is exemplified by a product or service in its simplest form: the long-distance telephone call, the bank account, the hotel room or the flight to Paris. Because, as I have stressed before, there is often little in the core product or service that distinguishes one company's offer from another's, gaining any form of competitive advantage at this level is particularly difficult. In the case of tangible products, the quality of a company's product may, because of technological advances, easily be replicated by competitors. An example is the electronics industry where most consumers are unable to discern any real differences across brands of stereo systems, TV sets or laptop computers.

The situation is compounded in those situations where there is in fact no difference in the offerings of competing companies. In many industries today, at the level of the core product, their offerings are indeed all the same.

This situation, where competitive advantage is gained at the level of the core product, is widely known today as *commoditization* because the products and services involved have been reduced to the status of commodities. Whenever we have a situation where the customer does not perceive any difference across suppliers, we have commoditization.

Such a situation brings about two important results. First, it becomes extremely difficult to convince the customer that our product is better than the competition's. Second, when nothing is done to differentiate the core product or service, customers will default to using price as the differentiating factor. This situation is obvious in many industries where the customer simply does not see any value in the core product because it is indistinguishable from those offered by others. In the classic definition of commodities, that is why consumers will often buy household products like flour and sugar based on the lowest price, and why we have petrol price wars and a very large percentage of customers will shop around for the lowest rates for car insurance and home mortgages.

7.3.1 Support services

This is the level where companies add services that are intended to create value for the customer by reducing non-monetary costs. Services such as deliveries, repairs, installation, warranties and payment plans help to differentiate a company and provide added value for customers by reducing psychological sources of irritation, time and energy costs. A customer who buys a home theatre system will appreciate the delivery of the components, the warranty, repair service and other support services. Because the technology and features are quite similar in a given price range, the manufacturer will differentiate its product by these added service features. The customer will then choose a specific brand or vendor based on the support services provided and how important these are to him or her. These services are easily replicated by the competition, however, and what was a differentiating factor can become a commodity in the marketplace.

Enhancing the core product through the addition of services is a very sound strategy, but many of the services and enhancements that we may consider adding are, as mentioned above, easily copied by the competition and have in fact become standard equipment in the value proposition of many companies: we all expect furniture retailers to deliver, and auto and appliance manufacturers to offer warranties.

At the technical performance level, companies strive to deliver on their promises and establish themselves as leaders in 'service excellence'. They are becoming more aware of this level as a driver of customer satisfaction because it is more difficult to achieve and for the competition to replicate. There is a positive relationship between customers' evaluations of service quality and assessments of service value. Customers evaluate service quality in five underlying dimensions: tangibles, reliability, responsiveness, assurance and empathy. Four of these five are dimensions of relationship growth and are directly related to the customer's overall perception of value.

Achieving excellence at this level depends on many factors. Top management commitment is essential since time and money must be spent in order to develop processes and technologies, as well as to attract, retain and train staff to perform at the highest level. The payback from this investment comes from the customer's perception of increased value. Customers who value excellence in service will be more satisfied and will tend to remain loyal.

To create value at this level, a company can improve its performance and provide superior service. This increases what the customer gets because they can rely on the company to deliver on time and produce exactly what was promised. Thus, value is added through the addition of controls and systems to ensure that service is completed as and when it was said it would be. The company does whatever it takes to get it right. Some companies are now so confident of their ability to deliver for their customers that they are offering service guarantees.

In addition, companies can reduce the psychological cost to customers by making it easier for them to obtain information and advice. Many businesses now offer emailing or toll-free customer telephone lines, which allow customers to request service, seek advice on the use of a product or obtain information about where to take it for servicing.

Customers will decide whether to continue their patronage of some companies based largely on how they are handled by members of staff. Even when all aspects of the core product and its delivery are quite acceptable or even superb, poor treatment by staff can cause a customer to go elsewhere. For obvious reasons, customers prefer employees who are friendly, helpful, understanding, personable, courteous and empathetic. The interaction with staff influences the customer's assessment of the psychological costs associated with the interaction. Customers who are treated with respect, empathy and genuine concern will perceive psychological costs as low and benefits high, and will have a better view of the overall value of the interaction.

Exhibit 7.2: *Dell's online service programme*

Dell was one of the first companies to put its products on the Internet, launching www.dell.com in 1994. Currently, it is one of the highest volume Internet commercial sites in the world. The company receives 40 million visits per quarter to its websites in different countries. About 50 per cent of Dell's sales are currently web-enabled, with another 50 per cent of Dell's technical support activities occurring online.

When ordering online, customers are able to design a computer to meet their own needs. The web page immediately displays the price of the chosen system. As well as being able to customize the product, customers can track the progress of the order as it is produced and delivered. This can help them see the stages of the process and the likely delivery times. If changes are made in the specification, customers can see the price change immediately. A range of payment options is offered and, if customers wish, they can pay online. They can also check online the status of their computer as it moves through various production and test stages in the factory. A full after-sales support service is also offered over the Internet. Customers can access pages that give detailed instructions on how to resolve questions and issues. Information on new upgrades is also sent via email to customers.

Dell has created many features and services online to help the customer see the whole purchasing process clearly. Customers can create and view their service records online. This includes product support, shipment and delivery dates. Each purchase comes with a service tag code, which can track the model bought and its service requirements. This allows Dell customer service representatives to handle requests quickly and efficiently.

This level of 24-hour customer service and fast response time helps Dell build strong customer relations, which of course is crucial for the company in its understanding of consumer needs. It is also a very cost-effective way of providing sales and support – cost savings that can be passed on in the form of better prices to customers.

Source: adapted from www.dell.com, www.business2000.ie

7.4 Product differentiation

Product differentiation seeks to increase the value of the product or service on offer to the customer. Levitt (1986) has suggested that products and services can be seen on at least four main levels. These are the core product, the expected product, the augmented product and the potential product. Figure 7.2 shows these levels in diagrammatic form. Differentiation is possible in all these respects.

At the centre of the model is the *core, or generic, product*. This is the central product or service offered. Beyond the generic product, however, is what customers expect in addition: the *expected product*. When buying petrol, for example, customers expect the possibility of paying by credit card, the availability of screenwash facilities, and so on. Since most petrol forecourts meet these expectations, they do not serve to differentiate one supplier from another.

At the next level Levitt identifies the *augmented product*. This constitutes all the extra features and services that go above and beyond what the customer expects, to convey added value and hence serve to differentiate the offer from that of competitors. The petrol station where, in the self-serve 2000s, one attendant fills the car with petrol while another cleans the windscreen, headlamps and mirrors, is going beyond what is expected. Over time, however, these means of distinguishing can become copied, routine and ultimately merely part of what is expected.

Finally, Levitt describes the *potential product* as all those further additional features and benefits that could be offered. At the petrol station these may include a free car wash with every fifth fill up. While the model shows the potential product bounded, in reality it is bounded only by the imagination and ingenuity of the supplier.

In the past suppliers have concentrated on attempts to differentiate their offerings on the basis of the core and expected product, such that convergence is occurring at this level in

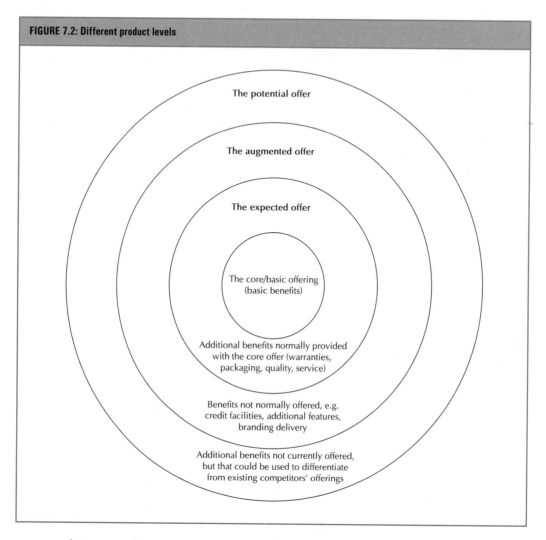

FIGURE 7.2: Different product levels

The potential offer

The augmented offer

The expected offer

The core/basic offering
(basic benefits)

Additional benefits normally provided
with the core offer (warranties,
packaging, quality, service)

Benefits not normally offered, e.g.
credit facilities, additional features,
branding delivery

Additional benefits not currently offered,
but that could be used to differentiate
from existing competitors' offerings

many markets. As quality control, assurance and management methods become more widely understood and practised, delivering a performing, reliable, durable, conforming offer (a 'quality' product in the classic sense of the word) will no longer be adequate. In the future there will be greater emphasis on the augmented and potential product as ways of adding value, creating customer delight and hence creating competitive advantage.

7.4.1 Differentiating the core and expected product

Differentiation of the core product or benefit offers a different way of satisfying the same basic want or need. It is typically created by a step change in technology, the application of innovation. For example, in mobile telephone technology, SMS messages represent a 'new' way of communicating.

7.5   Differentiating the augmented product

Differentiation of the augmented product can be achieved by offering more to customers on top of existing features (e.g. offering a lifetime guarantee on videotape rather than a one- or two-year guarantee) or by offering new features that are of value to customers. There are two main types of product feature that can create customer benefit; these are performance features and appearance features. Analysis of product features must relate these features to the benefits they offer to customers.

7.5.1   Quality

A prime factor in differentiating the product or service from that of competitors is quality. Quality concerns the fitness for purpose of a product or service. For manufactured products this can include the durability, appearance or grade of the product, while in services it often comes down to the tangible elements of the service, the reliability and responsiveness of the service provider, the assurance provided of the value of the service, and the empathy or caring attention received (see Parasuraman et al., 1988). Quality can reflect heavily both on raw materials used and the degree of quality control exercised during manufacture and delivery. Of central importance is consumer perception of quality, which may not be the same as the manufacturer's perception.

Quality has been demonstrated by the profit impact of market strategy (PIMS) project to be a major determinant of commercial success. Quality was shown to have a greater impact on return on investment (ROI) level and to be more effective at gaining market share than lower pricing.

Closely related to perceptions of quality are perceptions of style, particularly for products with a high emotional appeal (such as cosmetics). In fashion-conscious markets, such as clothes, design can be a very powerful way of differentiating.

7.5.2   Packaging

Packaging, too, can be used to differentiate the product. Packaging has five main functions, each of which can be used as a basis for differentiation.

1   Packaging *stores* the product, and hence can be used to extend shelf life or facilitate physical storage (e.g. Tetra Paks for fruit juice and other beverages).
2   Packaging *protects* the product during transit and prior to consumption, to ensure consistent quality (e.g. the use of foil packs for potato crisps to ensure freshness).
3   Packaging *facilitates* use of the product (e.g. applicator packs for floor cleaners, wine boxes, domestic liquid soap dispensers).
4   Packaging helps *create an image* for the product through its visual impact, quality of design, illustration of uses, and so on.
5   Packaging helps *promote* the product through eye-catching, unusual colours and shapes, and so on. Examples of the latter are the sales of the Absolut Vodka brand.

7.5.3 Branding

A particularly effective way of differentiating at the tangible product level is to create a unique brand with a favourable image and reputation. Brand and company reputation can be powerful marketing assets for a company.

The brand name or symbol is an indication of pedigree and a guarantee of what to expect from the product – a quality statement of a value-for-money signal. Heinz Baked Beans, for example, can command a premium price because of the assurance of quality the consumer gets in choosing the brand.

A great example of a brand that has a strong product/service competitive advantage is Dell. Dell takes orders straight from customers and builds each customer's personal computer according to demand. This means that customers get exactly what they want. Dell also gives its customers a fast, convenient service that other companies cannot match, including three-day delivery of PCs with all custom software preloaded. No other computer company can do what Dell does.

Branding is also a highly defensible competitive advantage. Once registered, competitors cannot use the same branding (name or symbol).

To a software product vendor deciding the technology strategy and focus, legal protection of the product's special features is critical. If strong protection is difficult to obtain, the only way to maintain competitiveness is to pursue rapid innovation and bring out a continuous stream of upgrades that maintain the product's uniqueness. For software service companies, intellectual property rights are less important. Companies rarely own the rights to the services they develop or to the knowledge generated during development. Thus, they lack the experience and processes to handle intellectual property rights appropriately for a product development plan.

7.5.4 Product complementarity

Software product companies expend a lot of effort developing products that complement, support or enhance the functionality of existing and established products. By leveraging the potential for products to complement one another, vendors can gain larger market size and make it more costly for customers to switch. For example, the initial success of i2 Technologies (a supply-chain solution provider) was due not only to its product's unique functionality, but also to how well the product complemented the leading enterprise resource planning (ERP) products. (ERP products provide companies with one comprehensive computer system that will integrate all the functions or tasks of the computer systems used by different departments or business units.)

According to Fig. 7.1, the last level of the product is the 'potential offer', but it is more or less impossible to differentiate benefits not currently offered.

7.6 Brand equity

It is recognized that marketing, as a discipline, sometimes uses and adapts concepts derived from other disciplines. The concept of added value can most notably be found in economics, accounting and marketing literature, and there is a distinct integration of ideas among these three disciplines. As far as marketing is concerned, the greatest degree of alignment is with the accounting literature. The concept of added value has evolved over time in the marketing literature such that there is much variation in the interpretation of the term. This variation in usage within marketing can be confusing, and the way that added value is used in marketing is incompatible with the accounting vocabulary.

What marketers call added value would be better termed 'added value agents'. Added value agents are the factors that create and help realize added value. Much marketing activity is based around managing added value agents, the outcomes of which are represented by added value itself. Added value agents are many and various, but branding is of major importance and gets significant coverage in the marketing literature. Clearly there is a relationship between what marketers and accountants call added value. By managing added value agents, marketers can significantly increase the added value that accrues to the organization.

An attempt to define the relationship between customers and brands produced the term 'brand equity' in the marketing literature. The term began to be used by US advertising practitioners in the early 1980s and led to academic interest. The concept of brand equity has been debated in both the accounting and marketing literature, and has highlighted the importance of having a long-term focus within brand management. Although there have been significant moves by companies to be strategic in the way that brands are managed, a lack of common terminology and philosophy within and between disciplines persists and may hinder communication.

Basically, brand equity refers to the value of a company's brand names. A brand that has high awareness, and perceived quality and brand loyalty among customers, has high brand equity. A brand with strong brand equity is a valuable asset.

Brand equity, like the concepts of brand and added value, has proliferated into multiple meanings. Again, accountants tend to define brand equity differently from marketers, with the concept being defined both in terms of the relationship between customer and brand (consumer-oriented definitions), or as something that accrues to the brand owner (company-oriented definitions). Brand equity can be defined as:

● the total value of a brand as a separable asset – when it is sold or included on a balance sheet
● a measure of the strength of consumers' attachment to a brand
● a description of the associations and beliefs the consumer has about the brand.

The first of these is often called brand valuation or brand value, and is the meaning generally adopted by financial accountants.

Table 7.1 illustrates the process of valuing a brand. The first step is to forecast brand sales, operating margins and cash flow over a reasonable period, such as five years. It is important that the forecasts are based solely on brand sales and not any unbranded products that may be produced in parallel. Here brand sales are predicted to grow at 5 per cent a year, the operating margin is 15 per cent, the tax rate 30 per cent and net investment is estimated at 50 per cent of incremental revenue. The second step is to calculate the percentage of the earnings that accrue from the use of the brand name. A brand name creates value by adding emotive associations, over and above the product, that lead to additional sales or higher prices. There are a variety of methods for estimating this increment, depending on the type of brand and its market. Where the brand operates by enhancing the margin, the most direct approach is to compare the operating margin on the brand with the estimated margin on similar unbranded products. This difference, that is ($OM_{branded} - OM_{unbranded}$), should be attributable to the company's unique assets: its brands, patents, channel partnerships, and so on. In heavily branded markets, any residual earnings will be predominantly due to brands; in high-technology markets other intangible assets may be more critical. In Table 7.1 the margin on unbranded products is estimated at 7 per cent, implying that earnings from intangibles account for 8 per cent of sales (i.e. 15–7 per cent). In this market, since there are no quality differences, it is assumed that the brand premium accounts for this residual. The brand cash flow associated with this premium in any one year is then:

$$CF_{brand} = \text{Sales } (OM_{branded} - OM_{unbranded})(1 - \text{tax rate})$$

		Year				
	Base	**1**	**2**	**3**	**4**	**5**
Sales	250.0	262.5	275.6	289.4	303.9	319.1
Operating margin	37.5	39.4	41.3	43.4	45.6	47.9
NOPAT (net operating profit after taxes)	26.3	27.6	28.9	30.4	31.9	33.5
Net investment		6.3	6.6	6.9	7.2	7.6
Cash flow		21.3	22.4	23.5	24.7	25.9
Brand cash flow = CF_{brand}		**14.7**	**15.4**	**16.2**	**17.0**	**17.9**
Discount factor ($r = 12\%$)		0.893	0.797	0.712	0.636	0.567
Discounted cash flow		13.1	12.3	11.5	10.8	10.1
Cumulative present value						57.9
Present value of continuing value						84.5
Total brand value (brand equity)						**142.4**

Source: adapted from Doyle (2000)

For example, the brand cash flow for year 1 would be calculated like this:

Year 1: $CF_{brand} = \text{Sales } (OM_{branded} - OM_{unbranded})(1 - \text{Tax rate})$

$\Leftrightarrow CF_{brand} = 262.5 \ (15\% - 7\%) \ (1 - 0.3) = 14.7$

TABLE 7.1 Valuing the brand (£m)

The final step is to estimate the brand discount rate. This will not be identical to the company's overall *cost of capital* since the brand's earnings may be more or less volatile than the average of the portfolio. The Interbrand Group, a pioneer of brand valuation methods, calculates the discount rate on the basis of a 'brand strength score', which measures the security that the brand name adds to the earnings stream. This rates such factors as the stability of the market, the brand's market share, its geographic spread, legal protection, and so on. In the example, the discount rate (= *r*) is calculated at *12 per cent*. The total brand value (brand equity) is then calculated by adding the cumulative present value with the estimate of present value of the future brand value. The total brand value is made up of two components: the present value during the planning period (cumulative present value = 57.9) and the value of the brand at the end of the planning period (present value of continuing value). Not surprisingly, since a brand normally has a longer lifetime, the present value of the continuing value (here set to 84.5 – not calculated as such) exceeds the value of the cash flow over the five-year planning period.

When marketers use the term 'brand equity', they tend to mean brand description or brand strength. Brand strength and brand description are sometimes referred to as 'consumer brand equity' to distinguish them from the asset valuation meaning. Brand description is distinct because it would not be expected to be quantified, whereas brand strength and brand value are considered quantified (though the methods of quantification are not covered by this chapter). Brand value may be thought to be distinct as it refers to an actual or notional business transaction, while the other two focus on the consumer.

Brand equity exists in the minds of various stakeholders, shareholders, employees, end users and distribution channels in particular. The customer/end user dominates most of the analysis and has been defined as the differential effect of brand knowledge on consumer response to the marketing of the brand.

Aaker (1991) describes five components of brand equity: brand loyalty, name awareness, perceived quality, brand associations, and a bundle of intellectual properties such as patents, trademarks and channel relationships.

7.7 The NPD process

Product development is the heart of the global marketing process. New products should be developed, or old ones modified, in order to fit new or changing customer needs on a global or regional basis. With the competition increasingly able to react quickly to new product introductions, an organization that adopts a worldwide approach is better able to develop products quickly, with basic specifications compatible on a worldwide scale. However, worldwide products should be adaptable in order to adjust features to unique market requirements whenever technically feasible. Some organizations design their products to meet major market needs and then make adjustments for smaller markets on a country-by-country basis. For example, Suzuki develops lead country models for the Far East that can, with minor changes, be made suitable for local sales in the majority of markets. Using this approach, Suzuki has been able to reduce its number of basic models considerably.

Some markets may require unique approaches. Some manufacturers enter developing markets, such as China, with cheaper products before selling them in more up-to-date versions.

A number of NPD frameworks have been developed to satisfy the needs of different organizations operating in different markets. Their goal is to bring products to market on time, to optimize business results by reducing cycle times and costs, and to manage the programmes according to agreed business plans over the products' life cycle. The majority of these NPD frameworks possess a number of similar important characteristics, which when executed in a balanced and effective manner significantly improve NPD performance. These characteristics generally include:

● use of a *structured development process*, providing the 'rules of the game', and describing entry and exit criteria between key programme milestones, primary tasks, schedules and resource assignments

- a team of senior executives, called a *review board,* which provides oversight of the programmes by resolving cross-project issues, setting project priorities, resolving issues and making 'go/kill' decisions
- use of *realization teams* (cross-functional execution teams), operating under a product 'champion' and reporting to the assigned senior management oversight board
- *phase or stage/gate reviews* at major development milestones, when funding, resources and project schedules are approved or rejected by the review board.

These activities are generally organized into distinct phases that are carried out sequentially by the realization teams and separated by 'stage/gate' reviews held by the review board (see Fig. 7.3).

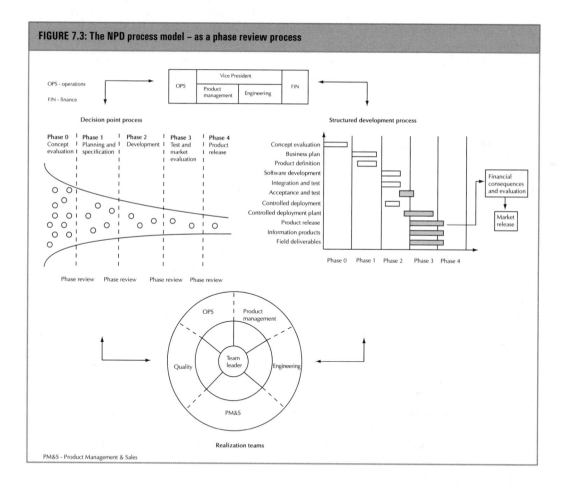

FIGURE 7.3: The NPD process model – as a phase review process

The phase review process can be viewed as a funnel, with many ideas entering at the concept phase and, through a series of screenings over the course of development, narrowed to a few appropriately resourced projects with a high likelihood of market success. At the conclusion of each phase, a review is held to determine the direction of the project: proceed ('go'), cancel ('kill') or redirect.

Exhibit 7.3: *The NPD process for a medicine*

The life cycle for new pharmaceutical products is defined mainly by the different phases of clinical trials, as shown in Figure 7.4.

FIGURE 7.4: New product development (NPD) for a medicine

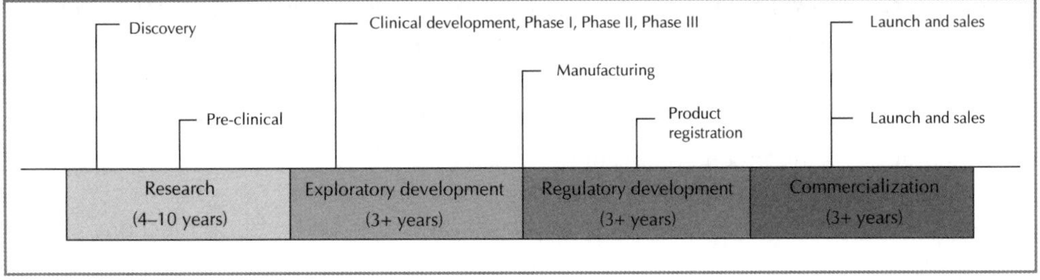

Phase I clinical trials (5–10 years pre-launch) are primarily designed to determine safe doses and administration methods (i.e. orally, intravenously, inhaled). These studies investigate how well the body metabolizes a drug and any side-effects that may result from increasing the dosage.

About two-thirds of drugs tested in Phase I continue to Phase II trials (3–5 years pre-launch). At this stage the drug is tested for efficacy. In most Phase II trials, one group of volunteers may be given the experimental drug while another control group will receive a placebo. Safety and effectiveness are examined in these trials. They do not give a final assessment of whether or not a particular drug will successfully treat an illness, although many patients may report experiencing same therapeutic benefits.

Phase III clinical trials (1–3 years pre-launch) are then performed on the proportion of drugs that demonstrated favourable profiles in earlier trials. These studies measure how well a drug works in a large number of people. This helps fine-tune dosage amounts and procedures to ensure a drug's safety and effectiveness. Once these studies are all successfully completed, a dossier is submitted to the appropriate regulatory authorities (e.g. the Food and Drug Administration in the USA) for approval.

Clinical studies sometimes require Phase IV trials (post-launch) to examine the long-term safety and effectiveness of a drug, and these continue after the launch of a new product.

As a new drug progresses from one phase of clinical research to another, these represent key go/kill decision points in committing further financial investment to product development. Here pricing information forms an important input for the product forecast, in the decision to progress development and guide allocation of resources within the company product portfolio. With possible resource limitations, tough decisions have to be made as to whether to progress one product or another.

Source: adapted from Hanlon and Luery (2002)

Structured development processes (SDPs) offer a framework consisting of terms that describe what needs to be done in development, and which allow them to be applied consistently across all projects. For this, an SDP must be used uniformly across the company, and compliance must be mandatory. In this way, it forms part of the organizational culture. 'Best in class' companies create guidelines around the SDP to ensure that major tasks are performed across all projects and that mistakes, once identified, are not repeated. The clarity offered in these documents concerning key cross-functional linkages and responsibilities ensures an effective overlap of activities, improved hand-offs between functional groups, setting of realistic and more achievable schedules, and improved planning and control.

The major activities commonly seen to be executed within a typical NPD framework, after the original idea has been screened and accepted by management, are to:

- develop and test the product concept
- formulate a marketing strategy
- analyse the impact on the business in terms of sales, cost and profit projections
- develop the concept into a product
- market test the product, and time its design and market strategy
- build and launch the product.

The SDP offers the guidance to execute these activities in the organization in an effective and co-ordinated fashion.

7.8   Brand stretching

Brand stretching – the use of an existing brand name for a new product in either an existing or a new product category – has been used extensively by many consumer goods organizations. The use of existing brand names to access new markets is based on the premise that established brands have high name recognition and significant consumer loyalty, at least parts of which will get transferred to the new product. Brand stretching, on the other hand, involves the use of an existing brand name for introducing new products in the same product category. Whereas both strategies help reduce the risk of failure for the new product, neither is available as a strategic option to product managers of generic or own-label brands. This is a consequence of the common assumption that own-label has little brand equity that they could possibly leverage. One possible way to partially overcome this constraint is through ingredient branding, whereby own-label brands use national brand ingredients and also prominently display this association in their promotions as well as on product packaging. An example would be Safeway Select Chocolate Chip Cookies with Hershey Chocolate Chips. This way, even a relatively obscure own-label brand can get instant recognition and potentially a more favourable consumer evaluation.

A major distinction between ingredient branding and brand/line stretching is that ingredient branding does not involve introduction of a new product by the national brand-owning company. The national brand simply lends its branded product to be used as one of the ingredients for the own-label brand product. The end product still has to be sold under the own-brand label. This has two important implications. First, unlike in the case of brand or line stretching, a company other than the one that owns the established brand stands to benefit from it. Thus, unless or until there are gains associated with this alliance for both the partners, it is not likely to happen. Second, the alliance product has two brand names associated with it: the own label for the product and the national brand for one of its ingredients. This is different from brand or line extensions where the national brand is typically the sole brand anchor for the new product.

An example of brand stretching in action is Kellogg's Special K Bar. Special K had built a reputation for tasty, nutritious breakfast cereals for people watching their figures. It was a relatively small functional stretch for the brand to offer a cereal bar. This met a real need by being tasty but having the same calories as just three potato crisps. The bar has added an incremental US$20 m to the brand's sales in the UK.

With a purely functional stretch like this, there is no need for a change in brand personality and tone, leading to a branding solution as follows:

● the *purchase brand* that people bought and had a relationship with could stay the same
● a simple *descriptor* name was used to introduce the new product
● Kellogg's provided an additional *endorsement* of quality and reliability.

Credibility depends on the stretch between current perceptions of the brand and the extension. The further the stretch, the more investment will be needed to overcome consumers' doubts and achieve trial. Big stretch *is* possible, but the level and duration of support needed may make a new brand a better alternative. Not one, but two dimensions need to be considered: functional and emotional. Taken together, these help highlight the boundaries of brand stretch and guide the optimum branding approach.

Emotional stretch occurs when the personality, tone and style of the extension are different from those of the master brand. As with people, this is more difficult than changing jobs (i.e. functional stretch). A *sub-brand* allows more emotional stretch than a simple descriptor (e.g. Bacardi Breezer versus Bacardi Lime and Soda). Here, the extension starts to break out of the master brand's universe and take on more of its own personality. Like a son or daughter, the sub-brand shares the same family values and name, but has a life of its own. Launching a totally new brand, possibly with some low-key *endorsement*, gives even more stretch but less leverage of the master brand (Fig. 7.5).

7.9 Co-branding and ingredient branding

Co-branding is a long-term brand alliance strategy. It is an association between two independent brands so that the perceived value of the integrated offering is enhanced in the mind of the customer. According to this definition, the following characteristics constitute co-branding:

1   The participating brands should be independent before, during and after the offering of the co-branded product.
2   The companies that own the brands should implement a co-branding strategy on purpose.
3   The co-operation between the two brands must be visible to potential customers.

Before coming to this long-term co-branding alliance, the involved companies may have been through some stages (see Fig. 7.6).

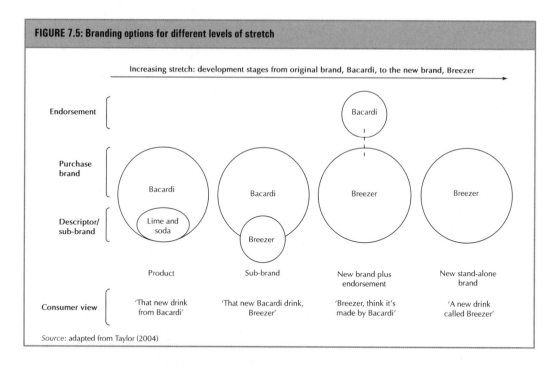

FIGURE 7.5: Branding options for different levels of stretch

Increasing stretch: development stages from original brand, Bacardi, to the new brand, Breezer

Endorsement

Purchase brand

Descriptor/ sub-brand

	Product	Sub-brand	New brand plus endorsement	New stand-alone brand
Consumer view	'That new drink from Bacardi'	'That new Bacardi drink, Breezer'	'Breezer, think it's made by Bacardi'	'A new drink called Breezer'

Source: adapted from Taylor (2004)

FIGURE 7.6: Different stages of co-branding

Short term/ low investment

Long term/ high investment

Co-branding strategy	Characteristics
Product bundling	Combined offer of two or more products in a package with one total price, e.g. hardware + software + services
Advertising alliance/ joint sales promotion	Timely limited appearance of two independent brands in promotional activities, e.g. in one advertisement
Dual branding	Common usage of a store location, 'shop in shop' concept, e.g. Burger King (fast food) and Shell (petrol stations)
'Real' co-branding	A new brand is branded by two brands simultaneously

Basically, there are two different types of co-branding (see Figure 7.6).

1 *Horizontal co-branding*: production, distribution and marketing of a multibranded product by producers at the same level in the value chain. One example is the (hypothetical) mixed drink of Bacardi Rum & Coca Cola (see Fig. 7.7).

2 *Vertical co-branding* (*ingredient branding*): vertical integration of products made by producers at different levels in the value chain. In the special case, ingredient branding, key attributes of one brand are incorporated into another brand as critical ingredients (Erevelles et al., 2008).

FIGURE 7.7: Co-branding (horizontal and vertical)

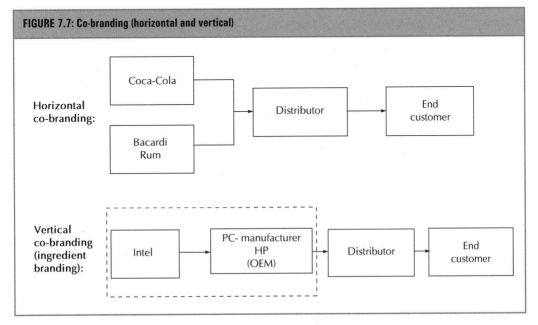

Ingredient brand alliances may be either supplier-initiated or manufacturer-initiated. In a supplier-initiated brand alliance, the supplier aims to establish its brand by the exposure of its brand name in the end product of the original equipment manufacturer (OEM). On the other hand, in a manufacturer-initiated brand alliance strategy, a manufacturer uses the established brand name of the supplier to enhance attitudes towards its own product. In some cases, a single brand can be involved in both a supplier- and manufacturer-initiated brand alliance. For example, the 'Intel inside' campaign was originally supplier-initiated. Cleverly, the 'Intel inside' campaign promoted the supplier's brand name itself rather than other aspects of the product. However, once Intel established its brand name, manufacturers of unknown brands started to use Intel's established brand name to enhance consumer perceptions for their own brands, making it a manufacturer-initiated brand alliance. As a result of Intel's enhanced visibility, unknown manufacturers, hoping to capitalize on Intel's brand name, entered the market, which in turn further enhanced Intel's sales.

7.10 Global branding

A global brand is one that expresses the same values in all its markets and owns a similar position *vis-à-vis* its competitors around the world. This creates several critical advantages, including:

- improved efficiency in costs for new product development and research and development (R&D) because their outputs create revenues globally and not just locally or regionally
- increased leverage with channel partners, especially in the packaged goods sector, which faces the constant parallel challenge of a consolidating and globalizing retail industry
- economies of scale in marketing communication because copy can be produced along identical guidelines, and even shared, across markets
- improved alignment across the organization, boosting speed to market, workforce flexibility and the sharing of best practices.

That is the theory, anyway. The reality often proves quite different. Almost all companies that own 'global' brands are actually struggling to achieve those theoretical economies of scope and scale. That is because most of them are mired in the same basic melodrama: 'central marketing' (or whatever the function is called) tries to establish a set of guidelines for the brand. Sometimes the guidelines are more assertive, explaining the 'core consumer', describing the 'brand pyramid', and so on. This brand guidebook is then distributed to the 'country organizations' (they may be divided by country or region), which almost invariably choose what they want to use from the book and ignore the rest. When the central organization pushes for greater adherence, the country managers respond with the classic refrain, 'But our market is different!'

Of course, the debate over local versus global brand execution is part of a broader set of challenges faced by global companies as they seek to strike a balance between central and regional management – a set of challenges for which there is no 'one size fits all' answer. When it comes to the brand execution debate, it has been found that the main stumbling block centres on the issue of global consumers. A brand is designed to communicate a set of messages and values to consumers, so the assertion 'Our brand should be global' implies that there must be some set of consumers in every country or market that has a common set of beliefs and motivations that the brand will target.

Global branding must be driven by collaboration among local markets, both with each other and with central marketing. Because local markets do face unique competitive challenges, each country organization should bring to the table data on its own market. This process can be facilitated, but not forced, by the central marketing function.

Summary

The first level of product decisions concerns the individual products or services that an organization manufactures and markets.

A *product item* is then by definition a separate product entity, identified by a certain design quality, features, packaging and branding. Individual product items that are closely related in some way to another are classed as *product lines* (product width). The *product mix* constitutes the sum of individual product items and product lines. Product width could be extended by adding more product lines. The same could be applied to product depth.

Decisions about new products should reflect consistency with existing product lines in relation to previously determined marketing objectives set for product provision in specified markets. Hence, the addition to the width of the mix and the depth within each product line should be compatible with the planned long-term marketing strategy.

Product mix strategy involves the management of existing successful products, the elimination of obsolete or non-profit-making ones and the development and introduction of new products. Each of these elements of product strategy and management is important to the achievement of company objectives.

The core product is the basic element of the organization's offer to its customers. It has to be right in order for customers to consider the other elements.

To create value, an organization can improve its performance and provide superior service. This increases what the customer gets because they can rely on the company to deliver on time and produce exactly what was promised. Thus, value is added through the addition of controls and systems to ensure that service is completed as and when the company said it would be. The company does whatever it takes to get it right. Some companies are now so confident of their ability to deliver for their customers that they are offering service guarantees. In addition, companies can reduce psychological costs to customers by making it easier for them to obtain information and advice.

Product differentiation seeks to increase the value of the product or service on offer to the customer. Products and services can be seen on at least four main levels. These are the core product, the expected product, the augmented product and the potential product. Differentiation is possible in all these respects.

A prime factor in differentiating the product or service from that of competitors is quality. Quality concerns the fitness for purpose of a product or service. For manufactured products this could include the durability, appearance or grade of the product, while in services it often comes down to the tangible elements of the service, the reliability and responsiveness of the service provider, the assurance provided of the value of the service, and the empathy or caring attention received. Of central importance is consumer perception of quality, which may not be the same as the manufacturer's perception. Closely related to perceptions of quality are perceptions of style, particularly for products with a high emotional appeal.

A particularly effective way of differentiating at the tangible product level is to create a unique brand with a favourable image and reputation. Brand and company reputation can be powerful marketing assets for a company.

An attempt to define the relationship between customers and brands produced the term 'brand equity' in the marketing literature. Basically, brand equity refers to the value of an organization's brand names. A brand that has high awareness, and perceived quality and brand loyalty among customers has high brand equity. A brand with strong brand equity is a valuable asset.

Product development is the heart of the global marketing process. New products should be developed, or old ones modified, in order to fit new or changing customer needs on a global or regional basis. With competition increasingly able to react quickly to new product introductions, an organization that adopts a worldwide approach is better able to develop products quickly with basic specifications compatible on a worldwide scale. However, worldwide products should be adaptable in order to adjust features to unique market requirements whenever technically feasible. Some organizations design their products to meet major market needs and then make adjustments for smaller markets on a country-by-country basis.

Brand stretching – the use of an existing brand name for a new product in a different product class – has been used extensively by many consumer goods organizations. The use of existing brand names to access new markets is based on the premise that established brands have high name recognition and significant consumer loyalty, at least part of which will get transferred to the new product. Brand stretching, on the other hand, involves the use of an existing brand name when introducing new products in the same product category.

Co-branding alliances are formed so that individual brands can co-operate in their marketing efforts for mutual benefits, and so that the perceived value of integrated offering is enhanced in the mind of distributors and end consumers.

Questions for discussion

1 What do you think is the 'total product' offered by McDonald's? How does that company's understanding of a product give it a comparative advantage over its direct competitors?
2 Suggest ways in which a computer manufacturer could add to its product offering to provide a more acceptable 'total product'.
3 From the company's perspective, what are the advantages and disadvantages of line and brand extensions?
4 What types of product might reach maturity more quickly than others? What are the implications for marketing planning?
5 How can you use research to support decisions about building brand equity?
6 For what kinds of product do you think customers need to be worldwide? Why?
7 In what ways does a product's packaging need changing when the product is being marketed in another country?
8 What factors decide whether a similar product can be marketed in different international markets and whether modifications are necessary?

References

Aaker, D. (1991) *Managing the Brand Equity: Capitalizing on the Value of the Brand Name.* New York: The Free Press.

Doyle, P. (2000) Valuing marketing's contribution, *European Management Journal*, 18(3): 233–45.

Erevelles, S., Horton, V. and Fukawa, F. (2008) Understanding B2C brand alliances between manufacturers and suppliers, *Marketing Management Journal*, 18: 32–46.

Hanlon, D. and Luery, D. (2002) The role of pricing research in assessing the commercial potential of new drugs development, *International Journal of Market Research*, 44: 423–47.

Levitt, T. (1986) *The Marketing Imagination*. New York: The Free Press.

Parasuraman, A., Zeithaml, V.A. and Berry, L. (1988) SERVQUAL: a multiple-item scale for measuring customer perceptions of service quality, *Journal of Retailing*, 64(1): 12–40.

Taylor, D. (2004) *Brand Stretch*. Chichester: John Wiley & Sons.

CASE STUDY 7: DYSON AIRBLADE

Penetrating the US hand dryer market with a new technology

In 2004 James Dyson went into the company's toilet, washed his hands, and dried them for 30 seconds under a conventional dryer. James Dyson thought that they were still not dry. James came to the conclusion that the main reason was that conventional hand dryers use conventional technology, some 60 years old. They dry by evaporation, using a heater and a blower, which uses quite a lot of energy. Two years later and £10 m used for product development, the Dyson Airblade came out in late 2006 in the UK market, launched as a completely new concept for a hand dryer. The Airblade blasts out air at 400 mph through a 0.3 mm gap, scraping water off the hands 'like a windscreen wiper'. Hands are completely dry in 10–12 seconds.

But, as the paper towel industry would rightly ask, what about spreading those nasty germs around? Dyson's answer is a HEPA filter, which it says removes 99 per cent of bacteria from the air, while the run-off water is treated by an iodine resin micro filter, which cleans the waste water and removes 99 per cent of bacteria.

The purchase price of the Dyson Airblade is three times more expensive than traditional dryers. However, Dyson says the Airblade costs up to 80 per cent less to run, and despite the higher purchase price, Dyson claims it will still cost at least 20 per cent less to own and run over a five-year period. Compared to paper towels in terms of cost, Dyson claims that if an average washroom uses 200 paper towels per day, then it costs £950 more to run annually than a washroom with an Airblade.

James Dyson and his company

It is impossible to separate the very British Dyson vacuum cleaner from its very British inventor. Together they are synonymous with innovation and legal battles against established rivals.

James Dyson was born in Norfolk in 1947. He studied furniture design and interior design at the Royal College of Art from 1966 to 1970 and his first product, the Sea Truck, was launched while he was still studying.

Dyson's foray into developing vacuum cleaner technology happened by chance. In 1978, while renovating his 300-year-old country house, Dyson became frustrated with the poor performance of his conventional vacuum cleaner. Whenever he went to use it, there was poor suction. One day he thought he would find out what was wrong with the design. He noted that the appliance worked by drawing air through the bag to create suction, but when even a fine layer of dust got inside, it clogged its pores, stopping the airflow and suction.

In his usual style of seeking solutions from unexpected sources, Dyson noticed how a nearby sawmill used a cyclone – a 30-foot-high cone that spun dust out of the air by centrifugal force – to expel waste. He reasoned that a vacuum cleaner that could separate dust by cyclonic action and spin it out of the airstream would eliminate the need for both bag and filter. James Dyson set out to replicate the cyclonic system.

Over the next eight years, Dyson tried to license his Dual Cyclone concept to established vacuum manufacturers, only to be turned down. At least two of these initial contacts forced him to file patent infringement lawsuits, which he won in out-of-court and in-court settlements. Finally in 1985, a small company in Japan contacted him out of the blue after seeing a picture of his vacuum cleaner in a magazine. Mortgaged to the hilt and on the brink of bankruptcy, Dyson took the cheapest flight to Tokyo to negotiate a deal. The result was the G-Force vacuum cleaner, priced at US$2,000, which became the ultimate domestic appliance status symbol in Japan.

In June 1993, using money from the Japanese licence, Dyson opened a research centre and factory in Malmesbury, Wiltshire. Here he developed the Dyson Dual Cyclone and within two years it was the fastest-selling vacuum cleaner in the UK.

Dyson was nearly bankrupted by the legal costs of establishing and protecting his patent. It took him more than 14 years to get his first product into a shop and it is on display in the Science Museum. Other products can be seen in the Victoria & Albert Museum, the San Francisco Museum of Modern Art and the Georges Pompidou Centre in Paris.

Dyson went on to develop the Root 8 Cyclone, which removes more dust by using eight cyclones instead of two. In 2000, he launched the Contrarotator washing machine, which uses two drums spinning in opposite directions and is said to wash faster and with better results than traditional washing machines.

In 2008 the company's sales reached £700 m, roughly two-thirds of which came from outside the UK, while pre-tax profit for the year was £150 m, up 32 per cent on 2007. Almost all the sales come from vacuum cleaners – a product in which Dyson has built large sales in the USA, Japan and Australia.

The US hand dryer market

Berkeley-based World Dryer Corp. held the top position in the US electric hand-drying market for 50 years. But the company now faces its stiffest competition ever as long-standing rivals and dryer-industry arriviste Sir James Dyson beat it to market with state-of-the-art machines that cut drying time by 50 per cent or more.

There are no official market share numbers for US hand dryers, and the long-time players – World, American and Excel Dryer Inc. – are private companies that do not release sales figures. IBISWorld Inc., a Los Angeles market research company, estimates the US hand-dryer market will be about US$60 m this year (see Table 7.2). The industry is in a good growth situation. Given the green transition, IBISWorld (2009) believes more restaurants, schools, businesses and malls increasingly will turn to hand dryers over paper towels. The US hand dryers have traditionally made up only 5 per cent of the drying market for the past 50 years – the rest was paper towels – but the machines' share has jumped to 10 per cent since the advent of high-speed dryers.

World Dryer, founded in 1948, was owned by Beatrice Foods in the 1970s. United Technologies Corp. bought it in 2000, then sold it in 2007 to current owner NewCastle Partners LLC, a Greenwich, Conn.-based private-equity company. It seems that World Dryer has relied for too many years on its strong name. Ten years ago, World Dryer had more than 50 per cent of the US market, but now it needs another technological leap to make up all the lost ground, because Excel Dryers and Dyson Airblade in particular are now getting close to World Dryer in terms of sales.

	Market share (%) – 2008
World Dryer (USA)	30
Excel Dryer (USA)	20
Dyson Airblade (UK)	20
American Dryer (USA)	15
Others	15
Total	100
Total market value (ex factory prices)	US$60 m

TABLE 7.2   The US hand dryer market (2008)
Source: adapted from Sterrett (2009)

The US market shifted significantly when Massachusetts-based Excel introduced its XLerator high-speed dryer in 2002, which cut drying time from the standard 30–40 seconds down to 10–15 seconds. Before the launch of the XLerator, World Dryer was probably six times the size of Excel Dryer, but now the two companies are quite close.

In 2007, Dyson entered the US market with its Airblade and American Dryer followed Excel with its Extreme Air, with a drying time of 10–15 seconds. World Dryer rolled out its high-speed model, the AirForce (drying time: 12 seconds – the same as for the Dyson Airblade), in 2008.

Standard high-speed dryers typically sell for US$300–400; Dyson's Airblade sells for US$1,200 (net price). The variable costs of making one Dyson Airblade are around US$750.

Questions

1   How would you characterize the product development process of Dyson's new Airblade?
2   Who are the key US customers of Dyson Airblade and how would you characterize their buying process?
3   What would be the key arguments for selling the Dyson Airblade into the US market?

Sources: Sterrett, D. (2009) Hand-dryer giant feeling the heat; World Dryer losing battle for hand-washers' hearts, minds, fingertips, *Crain's Chicago Business*, 19 October; IBISWorld (2009) The US hand-dryer market, IBISWorld Inc., Los Angeles.

CHAPTER 08

Marketing mix decisions II: pricing

❖ LEARNING OBJECTIVES

After studying this chapter you should be able to do the following:

❖ Discuss the importance of pricing decisions to the individual company.

❖ Explain the major steps in pricing decisions.

❖ Demonstrate how external factors influence pricing decisions.

❖ Explain how the product life cycle (PLC) can affect the price decision.

❖ Understand the advantages of using a differentiated price strategy across segments.

❖ Discuss the special problems in international pricing.

8.1 Introduction

Pricing is one of the most important marketing mix decisions, price being the only marketing mix variable that generates revenues. Pricing is not a single concept, but a multidimensional one with different meanings and implications for the manufacturer, the middleman and the end customer. Pricing strategy is of great importance because it affects both revenue and buyer behaviour. The whole pricing environment is, therefore, considered in this chapter; first, from the point of view of the company and its strategies and then from the perspective of the consumer. However, it must not be forgotten that there are other, external influences on pricing – not just from a company's competitors but also from government and legislation. Once these factors have been taken into account in this chapter, various pricing strategies are reviewed and some attention is given to how best to implement those strategies, how pricing levels can be adjusted, and how such tactics affect buyer behaviour and company revenue.

The multidimensional character of price should be taken into account for the pricing of products and services. Pricing involves the determination (and adjustment) of a price structure and price levels, as well as decisions on short-term price changes. A more effective, goal-oriented approach to pricing is needed that explicitly takes into account the role of price as a marketing mix instrument and as a profit generator. This provides a framework for effective, goal-oriented pricing, and helps highlight the major aspects and factors of the pricing decision.

Figure 8.1 provides a schematic overview of the steps involved in effective price decisions. At the same time, it illustrates the sections covered in this chapter.

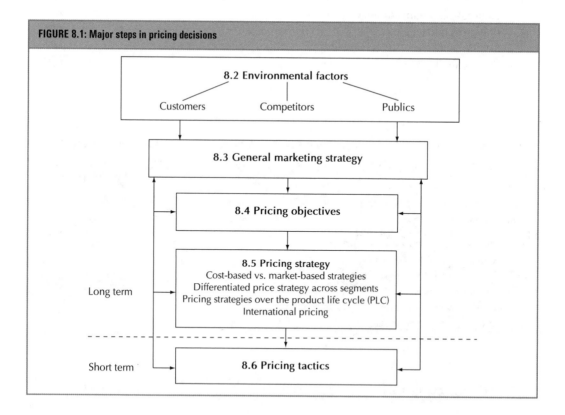

FIGURE 8.1: Major steps in pricing decisions

As the lines in Fig. 8.1 indicate, environmental characteristics influence each subsequent step, and feedback loops within one decision period and over time are bound to occur. In the following sections, the areas illustrated in Fig. 8.1 are analysed in more detail.

8.2 Environmental factors

8.2.1 Customers

A key parameter affecting pricing decisions is essentially customer-based. The upper limit to the price to be charged is set by the market unless, of course, the customer *must* purchase the product and we are the sole supplier. Effectively, then, at least in competitive markets, demand (i.e. the price that customers are both willing and able to pay) is a major consideration in the selection of pricing strategies and levels.

Ideally, the marketing manager needs to know the demand schedule for the products and services to be priced. This means that we must take into consideration the time factor (i.e. demand must be specified for a given time period). For example, it is conventional to distinguish between short, medium and long-run time horizons when discussing demand. Certainly demand can, and does, vary over these different time periods. The time period must be explicit when evaluating demand concepts in the context of marketing.

The ability of the purchaser to buy products and services according to income levels and purchasing power converts the buyer's needs and wants into actual purchasing. The economist refers to this willingness and ability to purchase as 'effective demand'. For an organizational buyer, the ability to purchase is directly related to budget requirements and constraints set on the purchaser.

Demand for a product or service, and indeed the price the customer is willing to pay, are related to the attributes of competitive products being offered. Demand for a product is therefore closely related to how the customer perceives the various attributes of competitive products. These attributes include physical/tangible attributes of the product or service in question: for example, quality features, packaging, and so on, and 'intangible' attributes, such as brand/corporate image and status.

So far, we have emphasized the complexity of consumer reactions toward prices, and the psychological factors affecting the role of price in the decision process. An even more important observation is the enormous heterogeneity in price reactions among potential buyers. This heterogeneity is already apparent at the level of price awareness and knowledge. In addition, consumers may evaluate prices differently because they are more or less informed about prevailing prices and product characteristics. Decision-makers should recognize these differences, and positively exploit consumer heterogeneity in the development of pricing strategies and tactics.

8.2.2 Competitors

The results of the pricing strategy will not only depend on consumer response, but also on the reaction of competitors. Competitive behaviour varies considerably with market structure, intensity of competition, and the existence and nature of significant competitive advantages.

Competitors' prices are therefore more decisive for own pricing decisions in markets with many undifferentiated competitors. Market structure and intensity of competition change over the PLC as new competitors enter the market and products become more homogeneous. Competition intensifies in most cases, and becomes especially severe in the maturity and decline stage, because sales growth can now only be accomplished at the expense of competitors' sales volumes.

Intense competition implies an increased likelihood of competitive reactions to pricing decisions (adjustments in price and/or other marketing mix variables). Besides market structure, the distribution of market shares, the sources and types of competitive advantage, and the marketing goals and strategies of competitors affect the likelihood and nature of competitive reactions. Competitive retaliation may attenuate pricing effects and sometimes provoke real price wars (prices are continually reduced, even to unprofitable levels). The analysis of competitive behaviour is therefore a prerequisite for effective pricing. Competitors respond to the actions of other market players by using those marketing variables that are their 'best weapons', such that price as well as non-price reactions should be monitored. Competitive response behaviour can be investigated in several ways, for example, by means of competitive response profiles.

Substantial deviations from competitors' price levels are feasible only through significant competitive advantages. The most important competitive advantages for pricing relate to costs and unique product values. Cost advantages exist when the product can be produced and/or distributed at a lower unit cost than competitors can achieve; they result from superior skills or resources.

Unique product value results from (tangible or intangible) product characteristics that are valued by consumers and differentiate the product from its substitutes. Unique product value reduces the price sensitivity of consumers, thereby enabling a company to set prices above the competitors' level without experiencing a considerable decrease in demand.

The most important considerations with regard to competitor pricing include:

- competitors' prices, including discounts, credit terms and terms of trade
- competitors' resources, especially financial
- competitors' costs and profit margins
- likely competitor responses to a company's pricing strategies and decisions
- likely potential competitors and barriers to market industry entry
- substitutes from other industries
- competitor marketing strategies, especially targeting, positioning and product differentiation.

Three of the most important competitor considerations that directly affect the extent to which an industry will be price competitive are:

1   the number of competitors
2   the degree of product differentiation between competitors
3   freedom of entry.

For example, where there is only one supplier (i.e. a monopoly), then the pricing decision-maker has substantial discretion over price. On the other hand, where products are undifferentiated, price competition is likely to be fierce. Finally, where competitors can enter an industry with relative ease, then the price setter will have less discretion over price and may be forced to set lower prices than might otherwise be the case, in order to deter new entrants.

8.2.3   Publics

In addition to customers and competitors, a number of other publics influence pricing decisions. The most important of these is government (legal constraints). Other individuals, groups or institutions may also have an impact on the pricing decision (e.g. financial institutions, workforce) but they are not discussed here.

A number of government laws set legal constraints on competitive pricing behaviour, consumer pricing, international pricing and (the control over) retailer pricing. Prohibited or restricted competitive pricing practices are price fixing, price discrimination and predatory pricing. Important legal constraints on consumer pricing are regulations against deceptive pricing and consumer price discrimination. Moreover, in specific product categories like pharmaceuticals or bread, governments exert direct price controls and establish ranges of legally acceptable consumer prices.

8.3 General marketing strategy

The pricing decision is only one part of the general marketing strategy. It must therefore be integrated with the other Ps of the global marketing mix (product, place, promotion). Price is the only area of the marketing mix where policy can be changed rapidly without large direct cost implications. However, this characteristic also results in the danger that pricing action may be resorted to as a quick fix instead of changes being made in accordance with the other elements of the overall international marketing strategy. It is important, then, that management realizes that constant fine-tuning of prices in international markets should be avoided, and that many problems are not best addressed with pricing action.

In addition to broader corporate objectives, pricing decisions must also reflect and support specific marketing strategies. In particular, pricing strategies need to be in line with market targeting and positioning strategies. Clearly, if a company produces a high-quality product or service aimed at the top end of the market and with a prestige image, it would not make much sense (indeed, it would probably be a major mistake) to set a low price on the product even if cost efficiency allowed this. Pricing must therefore be consistent with the other elements of the marketing mix and the selected positioning strategy.

8.4 Pricing objectives

As mentioned earlier, pricing decisions are salient to the achievement of corporate and marketing objectives. Hence, it is essential that pricing objectives and strategies are consistent with and supportive of these overall objectives. Environmental analysis provides crucial inputs for the specification of operational and attainable pricing objectives, which are in line with general company goals and strategies, and exploit the possibilities offered by the marketplace. Many pricing objectives can be pursued and these can be classified as follows:

- *profit-oriented objectives* (e.g. profit maximization, profit satisfaction, target return on investment)
- *cost-oriented objectives* (e.g. recover investment costs over a particular time period, generate volume so as to drive down costs)
- *demand/sales-oriented objectives* (e.g. sales growth or maintenance, market share growth or maintenance, use price of one product to sell other products in the line, build traffic), or
- *competition-oriented objectives* (e.g. be the price leader, discourage entry by new competitors, discourage others from lowering prices).

Companies may pursue more than one pricing objective; in such a case, pricing objectives should be mutually consistent, and priorities (or interrelationships) clearly defined. Managers often concentrate on cost-oriented pricing objectives because these can easily be translated into rules of thumb that simplify the pricing problem. In doing so, however, they disregard opportunities for profitable pricing based on factors other than cost.

8.5 Pricing strategy

Many different pricing strategies have been put forward by marketing academics and practitioners. Which of these are feasible in a given problem situation depends on three main factors (see also Fig. 8.1):

1 the characteristics of the environment
2 the general marketing strategy of the company
3 the pricing objectives of the company.

Some typical pricing strategies are highlighted below.

8.5.1 Cost-based versus market-based strategies

Cost-based pricing

The most widely used method for determining prices involves setting prices predominantly on the basis of the company's own costs. This method of pricing is often referred to as *cost-plus pricing*. In its simplest form, cost-plus pricing involves a company calculating average cost per unit and then allocating a specified mark-up, which may be related to rate of profit required by the company, to arrive at the selling price.

The major advantage of this method of pricing is its seeming simplicity. However, despite its widespread use by companies, it has long been severely criticized. The mechanics of cost-plus pricing involve calculating the variable costs per unit and adding to these an allocation of the total fixed costs. The first problem with cost-plus pricing is in both the calculation and allocation of these fixed costs. In many multiproduct companies the allocation of fixed and semi-variable costs to individual products is often arbitrary. In practice, total fixed costs are allocated on the basis of either a standard volume or a forecast level of output.

A second problem with cost-plus pricing is the determination of the mark-up. As mentioned earlier, often the percentage mark-up is derived from a predetermined target rate of profit or return. The problem with such predetermined mark-up rates, however, is that they take no account of demand conditions.

With these disadvantages there must of course be good reasons why cost-plus pricing still remains widely used by companies. The advantages are as follows.

- If competitors are using cost-plus pricing, and provided they have similar costs and mark-ups, it can lead to price stability.
- The pricing decision-maker does not have to consider the difficult (if essential) area of demand and price sensitivity.
- It is often claimed that because prices are directly related to costs it is 'fair' to both competitors and customers.

None of these potential advantages compensates for the fact that cost-plus pricing, certainly in its most rigid form, is not at all market-oriented, and can lead to significant strategic disadvantages in the market.

8.5.2 Market-based pricing

Market-based pricing moves away from the focus on costs and instead concentrates on what the price should be, seen in a combination of two perspectives:

1   What are competitors' prices for similar products?
2   What is the perceived value of the product to customers?

The first perspective is based on several assumptions, including that of product image and the position of the company as being the same or very similar to that of the competition. Although it is vital to consider competitors' prices, costs, and so on (as we have seen), this information should be used to influence pricing rather than as a 'formula' for setting it.

The basic idea underpinning the perceived value-based approach to pricing is that when customers purchase a product they go through a complex process of balancing benefits against costs.

A customer will not purchase a product where the costs are seen as being greater than the benefits. It is important to stress that the costs may include more than just the purchase price, and again it is the customer's perception of these costs that is used in the evaluation process. For example, in assessing the costs of, say, a new car it is not just the initial purchase cost, but also maintenance, insurance, petrol and perhaps depreciation costs that the purchaser may consider. In addition, just as there are psychological benefits so too are there psychological costs. For example, a new car purchaser may well consider the costs of 'loss of status' if he buys a cheap eastern European car.

For the pricing decision-maker, of course, the difficulty in this method of pricing is in measuring how the customer perceives the company's offer against the competition. Moreover, value perceptions may vary considerably among consumers, and even over usage situations.

Different customers may use the 'same' product in different ways and hence make different cost/benefit evaluations. If the customer makes such a trade-off between costs and benefits, it would seem sensible for the selling company to do the same. It is important to understand that the benefits involve a great deal more than the core attributes, and that in many choice situations it is the augmented product benefits that differentiate products.

8.5.3 Differentiated price strategy across segments

Any one price, even if it has been developed on the basis of market data in conjunction with overall marketing strategy, risks leaving a huge amount of money on the table. Because each customer – or, more realistically, each customer segment – makes a value/price judgement, developing an 'average' price at some midpoint along the spectrum of perceived value runs counter to the concept of aligning price and value. The result of this single 'average' price approach, represented in Fig. 8.2, is that the company ends up charging almost everyone the wrong price (Simon and Butscher, 2001).

For each of the customer segments that perceive more value than is represented by the single price, profit is being lost. On the other hand, the segments that perceive less value

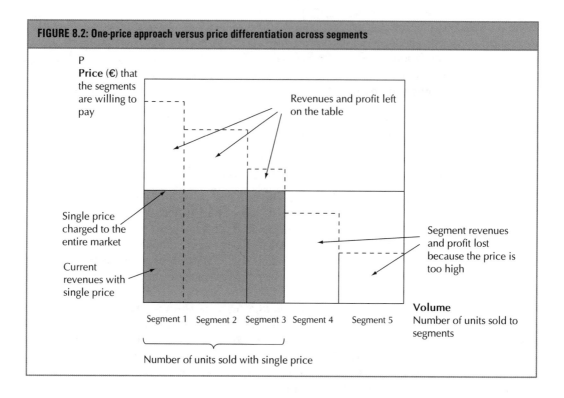

FIGURE 8.2: One-price approach versus price differentiation across segments

than is represented by the price simply will not buy the product. While effective marketing and sales communications may be able to move each segment's perception of value slightly, this will still capture only those segments whose perceived value is closest to the average price. At the high and low ends, substantial revenue and profit are being left on the table.

The ideal pricing strategy, then, should follow the natural segmentation of the market based on perceived value. By setting prices at or just below the value realized by each customer segment, a company will maximize revenue and profit. The role of marketing in this process is to identify the customer value segments and set prices accordingly. The role of sales is to maintain the differentiated pricing structure by selling on value, rather than just on price. To successfully implement differentiated pricing, marketing and sales must work together to understand customer needs and redefine the product/service offering in terms that intersect with these needs. This will maximize the perception of value. Often, definitions and perceptions of value differ within a single organization from one level of management to another. In such situations, success depends on identifying and targeting the level most likely to understand the full value of the complete product and service 'bundle' (Klompmaker et al., 2003).

8.5.4 Price bundling

Price bundling is marketing two or more products in a single package for a special price. Many physical goods and services unite a core product with a variety of supplementary products at a set price. This has become a popular marketing strategy. Examples include the sale of maintenance contracts with computer hardware and other office equipment.

Should such service packages be priced as a whole (referred to as the bundle), or should each element be priced separately? To the extent that people dislike having to make many small payments, bundled pricing may be preferable. But if customers do not like being charged for product elements they may not use, itemized pricing may be preferable.

Many companies offer an array of choices. Telephone subscribers, for instance, can select from several service options, ranging from paying a small monthly fee for basic service and then extra for each phone call made, or paying a higher flat rate and getting a certain number of local, regional or long-distance calls free. At the top of the scale is the option that provides business users with unlimited access to long-distance calls over a prescribed area – even internationally. Bundled prices offer a service firm a certain guaranteed revenue from each customer, while giving the latter a clear idea in advance of how much the bill will be. Unbundled pricing provides customers with flexibility in what they choose to acquire and pay for, but may also cause problems. For instance, customers may be put off by discovering that the ultimate price of what they want is substantially higher than the advertised base price that attracted them in the first place (Arora, 2008).

Auctions and Dutch auctions

The growth of the Internet has made customer-driven pricing models feasible on a large scale. In terms of price customization, auctions and Dutch auctions come close to the ideal situation in which every customer pays exactly the maximum of what he is willing to spend (Simon and Butscher, 2001). Auctions are an ancient form of pricing in which interested parties bid for a product that is for sale and have the chance to increase their original bid as other bidders top it. The product is typically sold to the party that in the end places the highest bid (there are alternatives where the second highest bid wins). Auctions require that all bidders are either physically present at the site of the auction or can participate via telephone or another technology. The Internet has made auctions a tool for the masses, as it enables everybody around the world with access to the Internet to participate in an auction on an auction website such as eBay or QXL. Auctions are becoming more and more popular in business-to-consumer, business-to-business and consumer-to-consumer scenarios.

Auctions are the best pricing strategy to extract the maximum 'willingness-to-pay' for a product that currently exists in the market, as determined by the highest bid. Of course, the highest bidder may have been willing to pay an even higher price.

In Dutch auctions, the starting price is an amount slightly above the highest price a seller thinks he can achieve. The price then begins to drop and the first customer to signal their willingness to buy at the current price gets the sale. Similar to regular auctions, this pricing system permits extraction of the maximum willingness-to-pay for a product that currently exists in the market, as it creates competition between customers. A customer could wait for the price to drop below their personal price limit, but then has to take the risk of another customer snatching the sale.

In order to make either auction form effective, however, it must be ensured that a large enough number of customers can and will participate in the auction. The participating audience should be an exact mirror of a company's entire market or, ideally, all its potential customers should participate. The Internet is an excellent way to achieve this, but, depending on what market a company is in, this might mean that it has to enable access to the auction through different technologies. For example, if its market has a low Internet penetration (i.e.

small businesses, low-income consumer segments, etc.), it will have to allow access to the auction via mobile phone, conventional telephone, and the like.

8.5.5 Pricing strategies in the PLC

As we have already seen, the competitive situation for a product changes throughout its life cycle. Each different phase in the cycle may require a different strategy. Pricing plays a particularly important role in this respect. Some of the ways in which price may be used at various stages of the PLC will now be examined. Once again, it should be noted that considerable care should be taken in interpreting the possible strategic implications of each of the life cycle stages.

Pricing in the introductory stage of the life cycle

With an innovatory product its developers can expect to have a competitive edge, at least for a period of time. With innovatory new products, a company can elect to choose between two extreme pricing strategies (Lancaster and Massingham, 2001):

1   *price skimming* – introducing new products at a high price level
2   *price penetration* – introducing new products at a low price level.

Price skimming

The setting of a high initial price can be interpreted as an assumption by management that, eventually, competition will enter the market and erode profit margins. The company therefore sets the price high so as to 'milk' the market and achieve the maximum profits available in the shortest time period. This 'market skimming' strategy involves the company estimating the highest price the customer is willing or able to pay, which will involve assessing the benefits of the product to the potential customer. This strategy has in the past been used successfully by companies marketing innovative products with substantial consumer benefits.

After the initial introduction stage of the product, the company will tend to lower the price of the product so as to draw in more price-conscious customers. When a company adopts this kind of strategy the following variables are usually present:

● demand for the product is high
● the high price will not attract early competition
● the high price gives the impression to the buyer of purchasing a high-quality product from a superior company.

Price penetration

The setting of a low price strategy, or 'market penetration strategy', is carried out by companies whose prime objective is to capture a large market share in the shortest time period possible.

The conditions that usually prevail for penetrating pricing to be effective include:

● demand for the product is price sensitive
● a low price will tend to discourage competitors from entering the market
● potential economies of scale and/or significant experience curve effects.

Exhibit 8.1: *Pricing research in the early stage of pharmaceutical product development*

In early stages of drug development the product profile is highly uncertain. Only the mechanism of action, data on basic efficacy and safety at different doses will be in the process of being established. At this stage it may be difficult for physicians to comment on the value of product benefits, as these are not yet well defined. To a large extent, pricing research at this stage has to be qualitative in nature and tries to establish a sensible range of possible values (ceiling and floor prices), given possible best case and safety scenarios (Fig. 8.3).

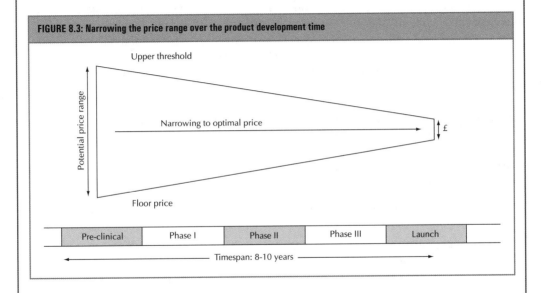

FIGURE 8.3: Narrowing the price range over the product development time

Narrowing the price range

Conducting pricing research with such a wide divergence from existing prices and price expectations requires approaching respondents with mind-sets that can think beyond the day-to-day drug budgeting and cost constraints. One should therefore try to establish an initial price range that, over time, research will narrow down to the optimal price.

In early-stage research a qualitative approach involving in-depth interviews with opinion leaders who may act, or have acted, as advisers to government authorities, together with a few clinicians, is usually a good starting point from which to define the upper price limits and potential reference compounds. However, price acceptability will depend on product performance that at this stage of development will still be largely unknown.

One approach at this stage is to undertake some benchmarking or price referencing with respondents in relation to existing drugs on the market (not necessarily within the same therapy area) in order to be able to gauge the range of acceptable prices. This is particularly important for new chemical entities. The competitive environment must also be examined as the prices can vary widely.

Source: adapted from Hanlon and Luery (2002)

8.5.6 International pricing

Geographic pricing

Geographic pricing becomes an issue when a company serves geographically distant markets and transportation constitutes an important component of transaction costs. Depending on the competitive conditions in these markets and on the threat of entry, it may be more profitable to charge either uniform standardized prices in all markets or locally adapted prices.

Price setting within individual country markets is driven by typical corporate issues and objectives. Also, the major problem areas in international pricing have been meeting local competition, cost, lack of competitive information, distribution and channel factors, and government barriers.

Multinationals tend to make pricing decisions close to each market's prevailing conditions, but the relationship is symbiotic: co-ordination and strategic direction come from headquarters, yet short-term pricing decisions are made locally.

Price escalation

In preparing a quotation, the international marketer must be careful to include unique export-related costs as well as normal costs shared with the domestic side of the business, such as:

- the cost of modifying the product for foreign markets
- operational costs of the export operation (e.g. subsidiary costs) – personnel, market research, additional shipping and insurance costs, communications costs with foreign customers, and overseas promotional costs
- foreign market entry costs – tariffs and taxes, commercial credit and political risks associated with a buyer in a different market, and foreign exchange risks.

The combined effect of clear-cut and hidden costs causes export prices to accelerate. Price escalation can result in different-sized price increases across markets. Customers who shop around for lower prices, or distributors unhappy about their margins in certain markets, might force a marketer to abandon a market altogether. International marketers combat price escalation through accurate information and creative strategies such as the following methods, which emphasize cutting costs.

- *Reorganize the channel of distribution*: eliminate some distribution levels. However, shortening the value chain might incur other new costs such as new intermediaries' demands for better discounts.
- *Adapt the product*: use less expensive ingredients or unbundle costly features. Remaining features, such as packaging, can also be cheapened. If price escalation causes differentials between markets that customers might discover, alter the product by changing styling and packaging, for example.

- *Emphasize non-price benefits*: quality, after-sales service, warranties, and so on (not necessarily price concessions) can add to the value the customer receives, or at least perceives, from your offer.
- *Assemble or produce the product overseas*: through foreign sourcing, the exporter may receive an additional benefit to lower cost – duty drawbacks.

Transfer pricing

Transfer (intracorporate) pricing is the pricing of sales to members of the multinational corporate family. With rapid globalization and consolidation across borders, estimates have up to two-thirds of world trade taking place between related parties, including shipments and transfers from parent company to affiliates, as well as trade between alliance partners. Transfer pricing must be managed in a world of varying tax rates, foreign exchange rates, governmental regulations, and other economic and social challenges. Allocating resources among multinational units requires central management to achieve the following objectives:

- competitiveness in the international marketplace
- reduction of taxes and tariffs
- management of cash flows
- minimization of foreign exchange risks
- avoidance of conflicts with home and host governments
- allaying of internal concerns, such as goal congruence and motivation of subsidiary managers.

The Euro and the 'price corridor'

The advent of the Euro illustrates how all companies will need to re-examine the positioning of their businesses. The potential advantages of a single-currency in Europe are considerable, but it also threatens businesses of all nationalities, sizes and types. More production and operating strategy decisions will be made on the basis of true cost differentials – proximity to specific inputs, materials, immobile skills or niche customers, for example. Consolidation will be the norm for many national business units whose existence was in some way perpetuated by using different currencies.

Intracompany transaction pricing – pricing among company business units and headquarters – becomes more troublesome with currency consolidation. Transparency allows tax authorities to easily enforce transfer price uniformity. If discrepancies among markets are not justified by market differences such as consumption preferences, competition or government interference, parallel importation may occur. Parallel imports into affluent markets will force prices to their lowest level as buyers simply go to the cheapest available source. For example, Portugal may influence prices in Germany through parallel imports and centralized buying power.

The price corridor solution

The recommended approach following the introduction of the Euro is a 'price corridor' – a range within which national prices vary. A company sets the maximum and minimum prices that country organizations can charge – enough to allow flexibility as a result of differences in price elasticities, competition and positioning, but not enough to attract parallel imports that may start at price differences of 20 per cent and higher. The corridor would be much narrower for easily transportable items like photographic film than for immobile products such as industrial machinery. This approach moves pricing authority away from country managers and into the hands of regional management, and requires changes in management systems and incentive structures. In Europe, as in future regional currency consolidations, manufacturers will do well to compromise between individually market-optimized prices and a uniform regional price. Uniformity will occur over time as consumers and national economies slowly adjust.

Global pricing contracts (GPCs)

As globalization increases, customers will put pressure on suppliers to accept GPCs. Purchasers may promise international markets, guaranteed production volumes and improved economies of scale and scope, but what if they fail to deliver or if suppliers' global price transparency inspires them to make unrealistic demands? Suppliers must make three key decisions: whether to pursue a GPC, how to negotiate the best terms, and how to keep a global relationship on track. It has been found that the best tool for suppliers is solid information on customers. Good information can help a supplier make a sensible counter-proposal to demands for the highest levels of service at the lowest price.

Exhibit 8.2: *Barbie clothing: a case of brand stretching at high-end prices*

Mattel, the world's number one toy maker, has about 16 stand-alone stores in Japan selling Barbie clothes that are geared towards adults. It hoped to expand to 20 stores by the end of 2004. Barbie herself has always been a fashion icon and so creating her own label perhaps seemed only logical. Now Mattel also wants to penetrate the US home market. In June 2004, it showcased a new Barbie brand of vintage T-shirts, cocktail dresses, shoes and coats in New York at the International Licensing show.

The USA will see a limited debut of the line, with a few select pieces. The heritage of the Barbie brand in the USA is very sensitive and Mattel wants to reposition the Barbie brand as a fashion icon, not just a kitsch concept.

In July 2004 Mattel launched a Barbie vintage-style T-shirt inspired by the 1959 Barbie, priced at US$40–60 at the high-end department store chain Nordstrom.

Source: adapted from Bhatnagar (2004)

8.6 Pricing tactics

This section makes the following distinction between pricing strategies and pricing tactics: *pricing strategies* determine long-term price structure and price levels, and their evolution over time in response to long-term changes in the environment, while *pricing tactics* consist of short-term price decisions (mostly price reductions from the normal or long-term level) to induce immediate sales increases or to respond to short-term changes in the environment. Part of the confusion that may arise between the two stems from the fact that the same set of instruments and actions can serve both strategic and tactical purposes. This is, for instance, true for the use of price deals.

8.6.1   Price promotions

The measurement of sales promotion effects has generated a great deal of interest in recent years. While a variety of promotional activities is available, the bulk of sales promotion actions take the form of either a straight price cut or a more indirect price reduction. Typical of such price promotions is their temporary character; a large portion of the observed sales increase stems from brand switching.

All in all, temporary price reductions have about the weakest positive long-term effects of any below-the-line activity since they appeal to rational (financial) arguments rather than building brand image or franchise. While the evidence of positive long-run implications for brand sales is limited, there are indications that price deals lead to purchase acceleration and stockbuilding, followed by sales dips in the post-promotion period. In other words, sales promotions may partly 'borrow sales from the future'. More importantly, frequent price cuts may reduce the consumer's willingness to buy the product at the regular price and eventually damage product image.

So far, the discussion has implicitly concentrated on the impact of promotions directed at consumers. Manufacturers spend increasingly large budgets on trade promotions (i.e. temporary price cuts aimed at retailers). While the impact of trade promotions bears similarities to that of consumer promotions, their (long-run) implications are even more complex. Nevertheless, they may generate effects that extend over a longer period of time.

Summary

A whole set of complex factors affects pricing decisions, making this in fact one of the most complex and difficult areas of market planning. Pricing decisions are more than just a 'mechanical' exercise of adding margins for profit onto costs. Price setting must become an integral part of the marketing strategy of the company and must be consistent with corporate and marketing objectives and other elements of the mix. In addition to these inputs to pricing decisions, the marketer must consider demand, cost and competitors.

Based on environmental factors (customers, competitors and publics) and general marketing strategy, the major components of pricing decision-making are:

- pricing objectives (long term)
- pricing strategies (long term)
- pricing tactics (short term).

Companies use price skimming (high prices) as a pricing strategy for a new product when the product is perceived by the target market as having unique advantages. Penetration pricing means charging a relatively low price to capture a large market share.

The basic idea of price differentiation is simple: charge every market segment the price it is willing to pay. The Internet has made customer-driven pricing models feasible on a large scale.

As a product moves through its life cycle the management usually sets prices high during the introductory stage. Later on, as competition intensity increases, prices are likely to decrease.

In international pricing, companies have the possibility of using a 'price corridor'. A price corridor defines the range within which prices across borders may vary. This price corridor needs to be set as narrow as possible in order to avoid the threat of parallel imports.

Pricing tactics are short-term, fine-tuning pricing techniques. They include various sorts of discounts, promotional pricing and other special pricing tactics.

Questions for discussion

1 Why do customers sometimes believe high prices indicate high-quality products?
2 How does competition affect a company's prices? Briefly describe a major competitor-based pricing approach.
3 What could be the strategy behind having another pricing strategy outside the 'main season' (off-peak pricing)?
4 What are the drawbacks to using penetration pricing as the main strategy in entering a new market?
5 We know that several factors influence consumer responses to prices. What psychological factors should marketers keep in mind when using consumer-oriented pricing? Describe each factor.
6 Many companies enter a market as price leaders, but end up dominating the lower end of the market. What may be the reasons for this?
7 In what ways is the role of pricing in the international market (a) similar to and (b) different from the role of pricing in the domestic market?
8 What influence do distribution strategies have on international price setting?
9 Outline an international pricing strategy that offers a 'win-win' outcome for both manufacturer and importer.
10 Discuss the circumstances when one global price for all international markets is (a) the most appropriate course of action, and (b) an inappropriate course of action for a company.

References

Arora, R. (2008) Price bundling and framing strategies for complementary products, *Journal of Product & Brand Management*, 17: 475–84.

Bhatnagar, P. (2004) Wanna dress like a Barbie? *CNN Money*. Available online at money.cnn.com.

Hanlon, D. and Luery, D. (2002) The role of pricing research in assessing the commercial potential of new drugs development, *International Journal of Market Research*, 44(4): 423–47.

Klompmaker, J.E., Rodgers, W.H. and Nygren, A.E. (2003) Value, not volume, *Marketing Management Journal*, June: 45–8.

Lancaster, G. and Massingham, L. (2001) *Marketing Management*, 3rd edn. Maidenhead: McGraw-Hill.

Simon, H. and Butscher, S.A. (2001) Individualized pricing: boosting profitability with a high art of power pricing, *European Management Journal*, 19(2): 109–14.

CASE STUDY 8:   BANG & OLUFSEN

Is the image justifying the price level in a time of recession?

Founded in 1925 in Struer, Denmark, Bang & Olufsen a/s is one of the oldest manufacturers of home entertainment in the world. Its products are often seen as synonymous with good design of technology-based products. The technology itself is rarely groundbreaking but the quality of materials and the user interfaces are second to none.

The company itself is very small, employing 2,500 people in its research and development, manufacturing and marketing divisions. Most retailing of the product is carried out through an independent dealer network. The product range is small and the prices are generally seen as high. The company has won innumerable design awards and its products appear in the industrial design collections of museums all over the world. That it has managed to survive at all is testament to the clarity of the vision laid down by its founders in 1925 – where quality was to be the driving force behind everything that the company does.

Currently, Bang & Olufsen is world renowned for its distinctive range of quality audio, video and multimedia products that represents its vision: courage to constantly question the ordinary in search of long-lasting experiences. Bang & Olufsen manufactures a highly distinctive and exclusive range of TVs, music systems, loudspeakers, telephones and multimedia products that combine technological excellence with emotional appeal. Bang & Olufsen products are sold by over 1,000 dealers in more than 70 countries in an extensive network of retail stores.

A study was carried out in 2008 by an independent UK brand research company, Superbrands, which questioned more than 2,000 UK consumers on the list of the 'coolest brands' on the market and Bang & Olufsen came fourth after Aston Martin, Apple iPod and YouTube. Further down the list came Google, PlayStation and Apple.

Background information: Bang & Olufsen's history

Peter Bang and Svend Olufsen, two engineers with a shared interest in radios, founded the company in 1925. Their first product, a radio working on alternating current (AC), was developed in the attic of the Olufsens' manor house in Struer, where the family still lives today. From the outset their focus was on quality and innovation. In 1939 they launched the first radio with a Bakelite cabinet and by 1952 the company had launched its first commercial TV set. In 1974, it achieved yet another first with its launch of the world's first colour TV with a remote control.

When Denmark joined the European Free Trade Association in 1960, Bang & Olufsen seized the opportunity to grow its international sales in nearby markets. Bang & Olufsen was exported to the UK for the first time in 1963.

Though well known in Denmark, it knew it would be hard work to be recognized elsewhere. Its strategy was to create a visual identity that would be immediately recognizable anywhere in the world. It did that so successfully that, in 1979, 11 Bang & Olufsen products were selected for the permanent collection of New York's Museum of Modern Art.

By 1993, after diminishing sales and earnings, Bang & Olufsen completed a radical restructure, and the company, under a new and aggressive management team, began the process of making a remarkable turnaround from the brink of disaster. Following a massive restructuring programme, Bang & Olufsen was looking for significant growth opportunities in new export markets. The main European markets were well established and it was assumed that there was limited opportunity for double-digit growth; therefore it was decided to focus on the agency-run markets and push some serious expansion into the Asian region.

Core business areas

A/V business

The A/V business, Bang & Olufsen's core business area, is expected to face a challenging year – as has been the case since mid-December 2007. The Group expects a decline in turnover in the A/V business in 2008 and expects growth to resume during the second half of 2009 at the earliest. This is, in part, owing to the fact that the timing of the launches of the new products is such that the products are not expected to be able to create a foundation for turnover growth until the second half of 2009.

Of the product launches planned for 2008, the following should be mentioned: a new audio concept designed to set new standards for enjoying music in the home. The concept is an important step in the new way of living with, and experiencing, music in the converging digital world. The product combines the very best from Bang & Olufsen's long tradition of producing sublime audio systems with the digital world of the present and future. Also in the second half of 2008, the BeoVision 8 family has been increased by a 40-inch version.

The A/V business covers at DKK3.7 bn around 90 per cent of Bang & Olufsen's total turnover. Three single markets – Denmark, Germany and the UK – account for almost 30 per cent of turnover of the A/V business. In May 2008 there were 822 B1 shops (shops dedicated exclusively to Bang & Olufsen's products) worldwide accounting for 81 per cent of the A/V turnover, and a further 421 shop-in-shop (shops with a dedicated sales area for Bang & Olufsen's products).

Business-to-business

Bang & Olufsen Enterprise, which covers the Group's sales to luxury hotels across the world as well as construction projects in the Middle East and Asia, posted a particularly satisfactory development in turnover from DKK96 m in 2007 to DKK155 m in 2008. This equates to an advance of 61 per cent. The positive development is partly owing to significant growth in the Middle East and Asia, including the installation during the financial year of Bang & Olufsen products in the largest hotel project ever in Macau, China.

The financial year under review also continued to see a good intake of orders for delivery in the years ahead. In the new financial year, Enterprise will intensify its sales efforts in the Middle Eastern region. Towards the end of the financial year, it was decided, therefore, that Enterprise's daily management and its recently appointed director should be based in Dubai in order to grow the market in the area.

Bang & Olufsen's products are now represented in more than 200 five-star hotels worldwide. Synergies from marketing, PR and local events between Bang & Olufsen's retailers and these prominent hotels are particularly positive and offer significant potential for all parties.

Automotive

Turnover for Bang & Olufsen Automotive for the financial year 2008/9 was €23.2 m against €16.4 m in 2007/08, an increase of 41 per cent. During the year, the partnership with Audi was extended to include six Audi models so that Bang & Olufsen sound systems are now available for Audi A4, Audi A5/S5, Audi R8 and – during the autumn – for Audi Q5. An even more advanced Bang & Olufsen sound system is available for Audi A8/S8 and Audi Q7.

The previously announced partnership with Aston Martin has also proceeded according to plan and the first audio systems were delivered in November 2008. Aston Martin sells 10,000 cars per year of which each DBS and DB9 Aston Martin model will be equipped with a B&O Beosound system. Automotive has established an office in the Munich area in order to enhance its support to its German partners and to improve the recruitment of individuals with experience in the sector.

Bang & Olufsen ICEpower a/s

ICEpower specializes in audio power conversion solutions. It develops dedicated solutions for driving consumer and professional speakers, automotive audio, mobile/portable devices and home theatre systems.

Turnover for Bang & Olufsen ICEpower a/s for the financial year 2007/8 totalled DKK118 m against DKK117 m in 2006/7. As its achievements included a new contract with Samsung, ICE power's technology will continue to be incorporated into many of Samsung's new mobile phone models.

Target customer groups and price strategy

Bang & Olufsen products are marketed as 'lifestyle' products, and are carefully targeted at middle and upper-class customers who are educated, well-to-do, cultivated in their interests and highly individualistic and self-motivated. Bang & Olufsen often refers to Mercedes Benz as its primary competitor, and perceives that it is competing for upper-middle-class discretionary dollars. Its designs attract both men and women with a combination of high technology, spectacular and often a Danish modern styling, excellent performance and extremely functional integration into the typical upper-middle-class home.

In 1968, Danish consumer electronics manufacturer Bang & Olufsen bore the slogan: 'Bang & Olufsen, for those who discuss design and quality before price'.

While other brands focus on exotic techniques and components in their products, thereby limiting themselves to customers who want to understand technology such as frequency range and the finer art of speaker cables, Bang & Olufsen always had a more 'high-brow' approach. The company seeks customers with money and good taste, who own a nice home and car and are willing to spend money to achieve the same quality for their audio and video equipment, long before design-widescreen TVs became fashionable.

So while Bang & Olufsen's competitors make one product for the many, Bang & Olufsen makes a few select products for the clearly defined few. It is therefore 'broad appeal' versus 'individual needs'.

Design alone, of course, did not create Bang & Olufsen's international reputation. Design in itself was never a goal, only a means. 'Design is a language', so it was said. It was in the first half of the 1970s that Bang & Olufsen developed a deep understanding of the concept of design. It was clear to the company's management team that design without a basic idea – a concept – would become both superficial and transient.

In parallel with the design, Bang & Olufsen therefore developed a new marketing and communication strategy — a 'lifestyle'-oriented strategy aimed at a smaller, but more international target group. Along with all other aspects of Bang & Olufsen's communication with the public, selected retail prices match the general message of exclusivity. For example, retailing for US$93 000, Bang & Olufsen's 103-inch BeoVision 4 (this unit is only available for special order) commands a premium price over other TV alternatives. The company targets a very limited segment (niche) of the world population, and can command these prices due to documented premium quality and sustainability of its products.

Competition

There are not many competitors in the same price range as Bang & Olufsen. One of the most important competitors in the premium segment is German, *Loewe*, which produces and distributes home entertainment systems such as TVs, digital video disc (DVD) players and recorders, audio components and other consumer electronics products. The company operates primarily in Europe. It is headquartered in Kronach, Germany and employs about 1,000 people.

The company recorded revenues of €374 m in the fiscal year ended December 2008, as compared to the revenues of €372 m in 2007. The company's operating profit was €28.5 m in the fiscal year ended 2008, an increase of 35 per cent over 2007.

Developments in the Bang & Olufsen's markets: 2007, 2008 and 2009

The Group began the financial year 2007 as planned, culminating in its best ever November sales. Since mid-December 2007, turnover has been volatile, and, by the end of that financial year, order intake was lower than for the same period in the previous year. 2008/9 as a whole, however, saw growth in markets such as Expansion Markets, including Russia, the Middle East, Asia Pacific, Switzerland and France, as well as in business areas like Automotive and Enterprise. However, this has been far from sufficient to compensate for the decline in turnover in the large traditional markets such as Denmark, Germany and the UK. This development has continued during 2009.

The global financial crisis has made selling its products difficult for Bang & Olufsen. The company generates about 90 per cent of its revenue in foreign markets. Even among its bread-and-butter luxury clients, the company saw sales slip in 2008 and slide further in 2009. And while its sales figures were steadier in emerging markets, such as the East and Russia, Bang & Olufsen logged considerable decreases in established European markets. In 2008/9 this development resulted in a negative net profit (after tax) of €51 m (see Table 8.1). In 2010 the situation looks a little better as some of Bang & Olufsen's middle-range products start to take off.

EUR	2008/9 (€m)	2007/8 (€m)	2006/7 (€m)	2005/6 (€m)	2004/5 (€m)
Net turnover	372	546	583	563	499
Net profit (after tax)	(51)	15	50	40	35
Number of employees (end of year)	2,051	2,579	2,520	2,422	2,331

TABLE 8.1   Bang & Olufsen's financial development over the last five years

Bang & Olufsen's new strategy plan

In the present demanding financial environment, Bang & Olufsen faces a number of challenges at home as well as on both its traditional markets and expansion markets. In October 2008 the management of Bang & Olufsen responded to these challenges by presenting an overall strategy plan for the Group's future development and operations:

- In order to reduce its costs following the sharp decline of the company's sales and announcing significant losses, Bang & Olufsen in October 2008 announced 300 layoffs in Denmark. It will abandon the development of new mobile phones, MP3s and stand-alone systems like DVD2 and HDR2 and instead focus on high-quality audio and video products as well as sound systems for the automotive industry.
- While defending and continuing servicing the traditional markets, Bang & Olufsen will increase the number of shops in growth markets like South Africa, the Middle East and Russia, as well as China, Japan and other Asian markets. In key growth markets, for example Russia and China, Bang & Olufsen management aims to more than double the number of B1 shops.
- Finally, to ensure more effective support for, and development of, Bang & Olufsen's dealer network, the present seven regional sales organizations worldwide – which until now have operated as independent units with their own back office and service functions – will be replaced by a more efficient global sales organization to ensure a consistent approach.

While the new overall strategy plan has been received reasonably well by banks and investors, Bang & Olufsen's master dealer with exclusive rights for Bang & Olufsen's products in Russia and Ukraine strongly disagrees with the planned increased numbers of Bang & Olufsen's shops in Russia. He argues that six years ago Bang & Olufsen's products were sold in 35 shops in Moscow. Currently, there exist only three exclusive Bang & Olufsen shops in the city selling better than the combined 35 shops six years ago. The Russian master dealer worries that the perceived exclusive brand of Bang & Olufsen will be diluted and will negatively affect sales if a larger number of Bang & Olufsen shops are opened in Moscow. According to the master dealer, the Bang & Olufsen brand is for the absolute Russian elite all living in Moscow. Seventy-five per cent of Bang & Olufsen's Russian turnover is generated in Moscow by the three shops. Twenty retail shops outside of Moscow generate the remaining 25 per cent of turnover.

Also, an increased number of Bang & Olufsen shops in China, the Middle East and Asia Pacific will raise the demand for Bang & Olufsen a/s in Denmark to provide better support and logistics as well as increase focus on servicing the needs of its worldwide dealerships.

Questions

1 Describe Bang & Olufsen's general pricing strategy. What does the company's positioning have to do with its pricing strategy and its distribution strategy?

2 Should Bang & Olufsen alter its prices, given that the financial crisis still has negative effects on consumer spending and strong price pressures from rivals?

Sources: www.bang-olufsen.com

Note

The author wants to thank Christian Wibroe Warming for his input to this case.

Marketing mix decisions III: distribution

❖ *LEARNING OBJECTIVES*

After studying this chapter you should be able to do the following:

❖ Explain how distribution patterns affect the various aspects of international marketing.

❖ Understand the variety of distribution channels and how they affect cost and efficiency in marketing.

❖ List the functions, advantages and disadvantages of various kinds of middlemen.

❖ Explain the different stages in the design of channel structure.

❖ Understand how distribution channels can be managed internationally.

9.1 Introduction

A product must be made accessible to the target market at an affordable price. Distribution decisions deal with the problems of moving products from points of origin to points of consumption. Often referred to as the *place* variable, distribution decisions are directed at ensuring that the right product is in the right place at the right time and in the right quantities. The creation of place, time and possession utility for a select group of customers located in a specific geographic location provides the focus of the logistics manager's efforts. The distribution network is referred to as a *marketing channel* – a team of marketing institutions that directs a flow of goods and services from the original producer to the final consumer.

Getting the product to the target market can be a costly process if inadequacies within the distribution structure cannot be overcome. Forging an aggressive and reliable channel of distribution may be the most critical and challenging task facing the international marketer.

9.2 The role of the intermediary

Channel intermediaries (e.g. wholesalers and agents) essentially solve the problem of the discrepancy between the various assortments of goods and services required by industrial and household consumers, and the assortments available directly from individual producers. In other words, manufacturers usually produce a large quantity of a limited number of products, whereas consumers purchase only a few items of a large number of diverse products. Middlemen reduce this discrepancy of assortments, thereby enabling consumers to avoid dealing directly with individual manufacturers in order to satisfy their needs. This is shown in Fig. 9.1.

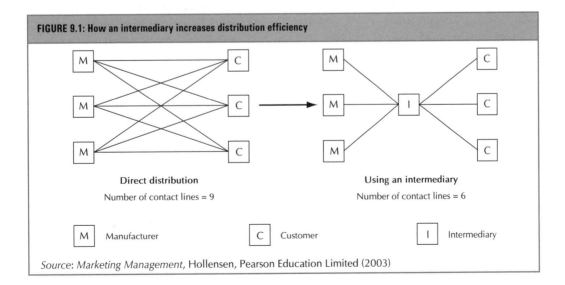

FIGURE 9.1: How an intermediary increases distribution efficiency

Direct distribution
Number of contact lines = 9

Using an intermediary
Number of contact lines = 6

M   Manufacturer

C   Customer

I   Intermediary

Source: *Marketing Management*, Hollensen, Pearson Education Limited (2003)

The middlemen may participate in the performance of any or all of the marketing flows (i.e. ownership, physical possession, information, financing, risk taking, negotiating, ordering and payment). However, the rationale for a wholesaler's existence boils down to the 'value-adding' functions he or she performs for the suppliers and customers he or she serves, as illustrated in Fig. 9.2.

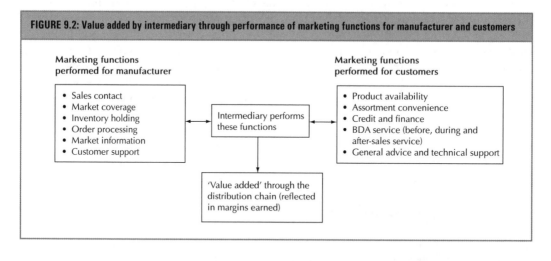

FIGURE 9.2: Value added by intermediary through performance of marketing functions for manufacturer and customers

9.3 Entry mode strategy

Once the company has chosen its target markets abroad (as discussed in Chapter 6) the question arises as to the best way to enter those markets. An international market entry mode is an institutional arrangement necessary for the entry of a company's products, technology and human capital into a foreign country/market.

Figure 9.3 shows the classical distribution systems in a national consumer market. A company may choose among entry modes within three entry mode categories, and in Fig. 9.3 one example from each of the three categories is shown:

1 export modes – here the distributor is shown as an example
2 intermediate modes – here the joint venture is shown as an example
3 hierarchical modes – here a sales subsidiary is shown as an example.

The chosen market entry mode can be regarded as the first decision level in the vertical chain that will provide marketing and distribution to the next actor in the vertical chain; in Fig. 9.3 this actor is the retail chain. This chapter also takes a closer look at the further distribution systems at the single national level.

Some companies have discovered that an ill-judged market entry selection in the initial stages of a company's internationalization can threaten its future market entry and expansion activities. Since it is common for companies to have their initial mode choice institutionalized over time, as new products are sold through the same established channels and new markets are entered using the same entry method, a problematic initial entry mode choice can survive through the institutionalization of this mode. The inertia in the shift process of entry modes delays the transition to a new entry mode. The reluctance of companies to change entry modes once they are in place, and the difficulty involved in so doing, makes the mode of entry decision a key strategic issue for companies operating in today's rapidly internationalizing marketplace.

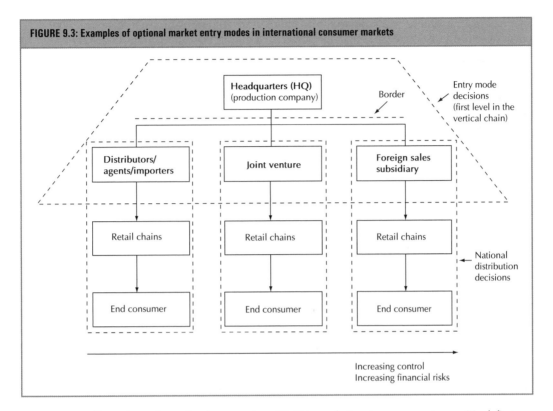

FIGURE 9.3: Examples of optional market entry modes in international consumer markets

For most small- and medium-sized enterprises (SMEs) market entry represents a critical first step, but for established companies the problem is not how to enter new emerging markets, but how to exploit opportunities more effectively within the context of their existing network of international operations.

There is, however, no ideal market entry strategy, and different methods might be adopted by different companies entering the same market and/or by the same company in different markets. The same company may also use a combination of entry modes for a specific market (multiple-channel approach).

As shown in Fig. 9.3 three broad groupings emerge when one looks at the assortment of entry modes available to the company when entering international markets. There are different degrees of control, risk and flexibility associated with each of these different market entry modes. For example, the use of hierarchical modes (investment modes) gives the company ownership and thereby high control, but committing heavy resource to foreign markets also represents a higher potential risk. At the same time, heavy resource commitment creates exit barriers, which diminish the company's ability to change the chosen entry mode in a quick and easy way. So the entry mode decision involves trade-offs, as the company normally cannot have both high control and high flexibility.

Each of the three categories of entry mode is described in more detail below.

9.3.1 Export modes

Export modes are the most common method used for initial entry into international markets. The company has to decide which functions will be the responsibility of the external international distributor and which will be handled by the company itself. Arnold (2000) suggests seven guidelines for managing the relationship to the international distributor.

1 Select distributors – don't let them select you.
2 Look for distributors capable of developing markets, rather than those with a few obvious customer contacts.
3 Treat local distributors as long-term partners, not temporary market-entry vehicles.
4 Support market entry by committing money, managers and proven marketing ideas.
5 From the start, maintain control over marketing strategy.
6 Make sure distributors provide you with detailed market and financial performance data.
7 Build links among national concerns at the earliest opportunity.

Manufacturers get the most out of their international distributors if they let them do what they do best: implementing the local marketing strategy.

9.3.2 Intermediate modes

Intermediate entry modes are distinguished from export modes because they are primary vehicles for a closer transfer of knowledge and skills between the partners in a strategic alliance. They are distinct from the hierarchical entry modes in that there is no full ownership (by the parent company) involved, but ownership and control can be shared between the parent company and a local partner. This is the case with the (equity) joint venture.

9.3.3 Hierarchical modes

Here the company owns and controls the foreign entry mode (e.g. the sales subsidiary, as illustrated in Fig. 9.3). The degree of control that the headquarters (HQ) would like to exert over the subsidiary will depend on how many and which value chain functions are transferred to the subsidiary. By using hierarchical modes, transactions between independent actors are substituted by intra-organisation transactions, and market prices are substituted by internal transfer prices.

Many factors should be considered in deciding on the appropriate market entry mode. Hollensen (2004) discusses these different factors and how they influence the entry mode decision.

9.4 Designing and managing the channel structure

Once having considered and chosen the overall market entry strategy for a given foreign market, the management then needs to turn its attention to the task of designing the company's channels of distribution within a given country. *Channel design* is the process of developing new channels where none had existed before, or making significant modifications to existing channels. The process of channel design and the management of it can be broken down into seven basic stages or phases:

1 setting distribution objectives
2 specifying the functions that need to be performed by the channel
3 considering alternative channel structures

4 choosing an 'optimal' channel structure
5 selecting the intermediaries
6 motivating the channel members
7 evaluating channel member performance.

We now look at each of these in turn.

9.4.1 Setting distribution objectives

Distribution objectives refer to what the company would like its channel strategy to accomplish in terms of how, when and where its products and services are provided to its target markets.

At the stage of channel design, distribution objectives need to be stated explicitly so that they can be made operational. Usually this means expressing the distribution objectives in quantifiable terms such as: within 12 months we would like to have XYZ cereal distributed in 80 per cent of the supermarkets in which consumers of this product are likely to shop.

Distribution objectives must also take into account the company's broader marketing and corporate objectives so that there are no inconsistencies. A manufacturer of a luxury product, for example, would have to pay close attention to whether distribution objectives that seek to broaden the availability of its products would detract from the exclusive image of the goods.

Designing and managing distribution channels does not, of course, take place in a vacuum. All the other variables of the marketing mix are also in operation: hence, channel strategy needs to be co-ordinated with the marketing mix. Such co-ordination should help reduce strategies and actions in the four areas of the marketing mix that work at cross-purposes. Ideally, good co-ordination should enhance the effectiveness of the company's overall marketing mix strategy by creating synergies among the marketing mix variables rather than the debilitating incongruencies that can result from neglecting this important issue. To achieve such co-ordination, management needs to be aware of and sensitive to the many possible interfaces and relationships of channel strategy with product, price and promotional strategies.

9.4.2 Specifying the functions that need to be performed by the channel

The following factors should be considered as detailed distribution functions, which should be performed by the distribution channel.

- *Product and services flow* (*from manufacturer to final customer*): inventory management, product transportation, product modification and after-sales service, customizing a product for the specific needs of clients/distributors, providing technical service, product maintenance and repair, procedure and handling of returned products, promoting product availability, packaging, specific packaging requirements, evaluating new products, and so on.
- *Communication flow* (*from manufacturer to final customers*): sales promotion to final consumers, information about product features, advertising, providing sales force, packaging information, loyalty programmes, website participation, traceability information, and so on.

- *Information flow (from customers to manufacturer)*: sharing knowledge of local market, scanning data (access to computer data), complaints via website/service line, order frequency, order formats consideration, arrange information about consumption, and so on.
- *Payments and financial flows*: conducting credit checks on final consumers, billing customers, caring for specific customer orders, arranging for credit provisions, price guarantees, financing, and so on.

This step provides a detailed overview of the chain and the distribution channels for a specific company. Management must therefore try to be as comprehensive and precise as possible in spelling out just what functions need to be performed to attain the distribution objectives.

9.4.3   Considering alternative channel structures

The form or shape that the channel of distribution takes to perform the distribution functions is the channel structure. Unless a direct channel structure from manufacturer to final customer is used, the structure will include some combination of independent intermediaries such as wholesalers, retailers, agents and brokers.

Management needs to be concerned with three dimensions of channel structure:

1   the length of the channels
2   the intensity at the various levels
3   the types of intermediary involved.

With regard to channel length, in developed countries management usually has only three or four options for the distribution of consumer goods ranging from direct up to possibly three levels of intermediaries. In channels for industrial products, the range of choice for levels in the channels is usually even more restricted.

The intensity dimension, which refers to the number of intermediaries to be used at each level of the channel, is usually characterized as:

- *intensive distribution* – where as many intermediaries as possible are used
- *selective distribution* – where the number of intermediaries to be used is limited through more careful selection
- *exclusive distribution* – where only one intermediary is used in a given geographical territory.

With regard to the types of intermediary to be used at each level in the channel structure, this can vary quite widely depending on the industry in question.

Decisions involving any of the dimensions of channel structure, particularly those of intensity and type of intermediary, should be guided by channel strategy and the distribution objective being pursued, in order to avoid channel structures that are inappropriate to the strategy and objective. For instance, if a company's objectives and strategy stress high levels of attention and service for final customers, this would generally be far more difficult to attain with an intensive distribution structure than with a more selective one because the very large numbers of channel members involved in intensive distribution would be harder to monitor and control than a small group of carefully chosen ones.

9.4.4 Choosing an 'optimal' channel structure

In practice it is not possible to choose an optimal channel structure in the strictest sense of that term. However, it is possible to choose an effective and efficient channel structure that can meet the company's distribution objectives.

Many different approaches have been suggested over the years for choosing such a channel structure. The most popular are *judgemental* and *heuristic approaches* that rely on managerial judgement augmented by some data on distribution costs and profit potentials.

Of course, in the process of applying its best judgement, management also needs to take into consideration a number of key variables that are usually relevant when choosing channel structure. The most basic of these are:

- market variables
- product variables
- company variables
- intermediary variables
- behavioural variables
- external environmental variables.

The location of final customers, the number of customers and their density, together with their patterns of buying behaviour, would all be key *market variables*.

Factors such as bulk and weight, unit value, newness, technical versus nontechnical, and perishability are *product variables* that are frequently important.

The financial capacity of the company, its size, expertise and desire for managerial control are some of the most important *company variables*.

Cost, availability and services provided are indicative of significant *intermediary variables* that management needs to consider.

Factors such as the potential of particular channel structures to reduce conflict while maximizing power and communications effectiveness are critical *behavioural variables* for management to consider.

Finally, variables such as economic conditions, socio-cultural changes, competitive structure, technology and government regulations can all be important *environmental variables* to consider when choosing channel structure.

9.4.5 Selecting the intermediaries

The selection of intermediaries who will become channel members can be viewed as the last phase of channel design (choosing the channel structure), or as an independent channel management area if selection is not undertaken as part of an overall channel design decision. In any case, the selection of channel members essentially consists of four steps:

1 developing selection criteria
2 finding prospective channel members
3 assessment of the prospective channel members against the criteria
4 converting prospective channel members to become actual channel members.

Developing selection criteria

Each company should develop a set of criteria for selecting channel members that is consistent with its own distribution objectives and strategies. Obviously, then, there is no universal list of selection criteria that would be applicable for all companies under all conditions. As a general rule, however, there is a basic guiding principle, or heuristic, that most companies can use, which can be stated as follows: the more selective the company's distribution policy, the more numerous and stringent the criteria used for selection should be, and vice versa.

Thus, the list of criteria for a company practising highly selective distribution might include such factors as the prospective channel member's reputation, competing product lines carried and management succession. A company using very intensive distribution might use little more than one criterion consisting of the ability of the prospective channel members to pay the manufacturer for the products it ships to them.

Finding prospective channel members

The search for prospective channel members can utilize a number of sources. If the manufacturer has its own outside field sales force, this is generally regarded as the best source because of the sales force's knowledge of prospective channel members in its territories.

Other useful sources include final customers, trade sources, advertising and trade shows. Usually, a combination of several of these sources is used to find prospective channel members whether these are at wholesale or retail levels.

Assessment of the prospective channel members against the criteria

Once the group of prospective channel members has been identified, they need to be assessed against the criteria to determine those who will actually be selected. This can be done by an individual manager (such as the sales manager) or by a committee. Depending on the importance of the selection decision, such a decision might well include top management even up to and including the chairman of the board if the selection decision is of great strategic importance.

Converting prospective channel members to become actual channel members

The key issue of concern here is to recognize that the selection process is an interaction process. Not only do producers and manufacturers select intermediaries or various agents, but these intermediaries also select producers and manufacturers. Indeed, quite often it is the intermediaries, especially large and powerful distributors and wholesalers, who are in a powerful position when it comes to selection. Consequently, the manufacturer seeking to secure the services of quality channel members has to make a convincing case that carrying its products will be profitable for the channel members. Given the sophistication of today's retailers and wholesalers, owing to the excellent computerized information systems they use, manufacturers must make their cases very carefully and thoroughly to win the acceptance of such channel members.

9.4.6 Motivating the channel members

Motivation in the context of channel management refers to the actions taken by the manufacturer to secure channel member co-operation in implementing the manufacturer's channel strategies and achieving its distribution objectives. Because the manufacturer's efforts to motivate channel members take place in the inter-organizational setting of the marketing channel, the process is often more difficult and certainly less direct than would be the case for motivation in the intra-organizational setting of one company.

Motivation management in the marketing channel can be viewed as a sequence of three steps:

1 learning about the needs and problems of channel members
2 offering support to channel members to help meet their needs and solve their problems
3 providing ongoing leadership.

Although the stages in the motivation process are sequential, the process is also iterative because of the continuous feedback from stages two and three.

Learning about the needs and problems of channel members

As mentioned earlier, channel members, as independent businesses, have their own objectives, strategies and operating procedures. But also as independent businesses they have their own needs and problems, which might be quite different from those of the manufacturer. Hence, if the manufacturer seeks strong co-operation from the channel members, it is incumbent on that manufacturer to discover the key needs and problems of channel members in order to be able to help meet those needs and solve those problems. This is not a simple or straightforward task for the manufacturer because the range of needs and problems of channel members can be legion. Small channel members may be overburdened with inventory, lack modern information systems, and need better managerial skills and newer ideas for competing against giant retailers. On the other hand, large retailers may face problems of how to reduce costs to operate profitably on small gross margins while being forced to carry larger and larger inventories as wholesalers disappear from the channel and new products proliferate. At the same time, wholesale channel members may be in desperate need of finding ways of competing successfully against power-buying retailers and customers who seek direct sales from the manufacturers. This list could go on and on for different channel members in particular industries, times and circumstances.

In order to foster better communication between manufacturer and channel member, an advisory committee consisting of representatives from wholesale and/or retail-level channel members and key executives from the manufacturer meets on a regular basis (such as twice a year) in some neutral location. This type of close interaction between manufacturer and channel member can generate the kind of constructive dialogue needed to uncover channel member needs and problems, which may not emerge in the normal course of business.

Offering support to channel members

Offering support to channel members to help meet their needs and solve their problems can be done in a variety of ways, from an informal 'hit and miss', *ad hoc*, approach through to formal and carefully planned partnerships and strategic alliances.

The *ad hoc* approach, also called co-operative support, is the most common in loosely aligned traditional channels. Basically, advertising dollars, promotional support, incentives, contests and a host of other *ad hoc* activities are offered by the manufacturer to initiate channel members' efforts to push the manufacturer's products.

Partnerships and strategic alliances, in contrast, represent a more substantial and continuous commitment between the manufacturer and channel members. Support provided by the manufacturer is based on extensive knowledge of the needs and problems of the channel members, and tends to be carried out on a longer-term basis, with specific performance expectations that have been carefully worked out by the manufacturer in conjunction with channel members.

Providing ongoing leadership

Even a well-conceived motivation effort, based on a thorough attempt to understand channel member needs and problems, together with a carefully articulated support programme, still requires leadership on a continuing basis to achieve effective motivation of channel members. In other words, someone has to be in charge to deal with the inevitable changes and unforeseen problems that arise, such as new forms of competition, technological developments and government regulations. While the manufacturer cannot always assume the leadership role and immediately deal with any problems, it is important that support should be available to provide direction and input over the long term instead of only while a new motivation programme is being developed and then quickly left to channel members to deal with on a day-in-day-out basis.

9.4.7 Evaluating channel member performance

The evaluation of channel member performance is necessary to assess how successful the channel members have been in implementing the manufacturer's channel strategies and achieving distribution objectives. Evaluations require the manufacturer to gather information on the channel members. The manufacturer's ability to do this will be affected by:

- the degree of control of channel members
- the importance of the channel members
- the number of channel members.

Usually, the higher the degree of control, the more information the manufacturer can gather, and vice versa.

With regard to the importance of channel members, if the manufacturer relies heavily on them for the distribution of its products, it will tend to put more effort into evaluation than those who do not rely heavily on independent channel members. Finally, when large numbers of channel members are used, such as in intensive distribution, evaluation tends to be much more cursory than when smaller, more carefully selected channel members are used. The actual performance evaluation essentially consists of three steps:

1   developing performance criteria
2   evaluating channel members against the performance criteria
3   taking corrective action if necessary.

Developing performance criteria

Although a wide variety of performance criteria can be used to evaluate channel members, by far the most commonly used are:

- sales performance
- inventory maintenance
- selling capabilities
- attitudes
- competitive products handled
- growth prospects.

Of course, this list can be supplemented to fit the particular circumstances of the manufacturer. The relative importance of each criterion may also vary considerably based on the policies of a particular manufacturer.

Evaluating channel members against criteria

The use of a list of criteria to evaluate channel members can be done in an informal, judgemental fashion or by using a more formal quantitative approach. In the former approach, criteria are used as a general benchmark of what the manufacturer is seeking. Channel members are then assessed against this list based on qualitative managerial judgements. In the latter approach, formal weighting schemes can be developed to specify precisely the importance of criteria relative to each other. Formal scoring systems such as a scale of 1–10 can then be used to rate each channel member against each criterion. It is then possible to arrive at an overall quantitative performance index for each channel member by multiplying the criteria weights by the scores and adding up the results.

Taking corrective action

The management purpose behind evaluation is not only to monitor performance but also to take the necessary action to improve the performance of those channel members that are below standard. Thus, an integral part of the evaluation process is to have a set of pre-planned steps to be taken to help channel members meet or exceed performance expectations. Termination of the relationship with the channel member should be the very last step in this pre-planned corrective process.

Exhibit 9.1: *Dell's disintermediation in the distribution chain*

Dell is the world's leading direct computer systems company, with 34 400 employees in 34 countries around the globe. At Dell, the traditional supply chain has two fundamental characteristics: *disintermediation* and *real-time production*. Dell sells directly to its customers, cutting out the middleman, the distributor and retailer. When a layer that exists between two other layers is removed like this, it is known as disintermediation. Dell manufactures the products and then sells them directly to the customer, thus it creates disintermediation – the outside retailer is cut out of the process. This reduces time and costs in the process and also ensures that Dell is better positioned to understand its customers' needs.

In this way, Dell's supply chain costs are reduced on the storage side, too, by the efficient relationship between orders and production. Each individual PC that is ordered is only manufactured *after* the order has been received and using only the freshest raw materials, which are delivered to the factory several times a day. This is known as just-in-time (JIT) production, or real-time production. There is no warehouse for either raw components or finished goods. Each PC has been paid for by, and built for, a specific customer before it is shipped.

Real-time production ensures that no costs are incurred from rising inventory stocks. Output is always driven by actual customer demand. Each individual product is created with the latest technology and each is custom-made to the customer's precise specifications.

Source: adapted from www.dell.com

9.5 Global distribution channel design

In every country and in every market, urban or rural, rich or poor, all consumer and industrial products eventually go through a distribution process. The *distribution process* includes the physical handling and distribution of goods, the passage of ownership (title) and – most important from the standpoint of marketing strategy – the buying and selling negotiations between producers and middlemen, and between middlemen and customers.

A host of policy and strategic channel-selection issues confronts the international marketing manager. These issues are not in themselves very different from those encountered in domestic distribution, but the resolution of the issues differs because of different channel alternatives and market patterns.

Each country market has a *distribution structure* through which goods pass from producer to user. Within this structure are a variety of middlemen whose customary functions, activities and services reflect existing competition, market characteristics, tradition and economic development.

In short, the behaviour of channel members is the result of the interactions between the cultural environment and the marketing process. Channel structures range from those with little developed marketing infrastructure, such as those found in many emerging markets, to the highly complex, multilayered system found in Japan.

Traditional channels in developing countries evolved from economies with a strong dependence on imported goods. In an *import-oriented*, or *traditional*, *distribution structure*, an importer controls a fixed supply of goods and the marketing system develops around the philosophy of selling a limited supply of goods at high prices to a small number of affluent customers. In the resulting seller's market, market penetration and mass distribution are not necessary because demand exceeds supply and, in most cases, the customer seeks the supply from a limited number of middlemen. Obviously, few countries fit the import-oriented model today.

Currently, few countries are so sufficiently isolated that they are unaffected by global economic and political changes. These currents of change are altering all levels of the economic fabric, including the distribution structure. Traditional channel structures are giving way to new forms, new alliances and new processes – some more slowly than others, but all are changing. Pressures for change in a country come from within and without. Multinational marketers are seeking ways to profitably tap market segments that are served by costly, traditional distribution systems. Direct marketing, door-to-door selling, hypermarkets, discount houses, shopping malls, catalogue selling, the Internet and other distribution methods are being introduced in an attempt to provide efficient distribution channels.

Some important trends in distribution will eventually lead to greater commonality than disparity among middlemen in different countries. Wal-Mart, for example, is expanding all over the world – from Mexico to Brazil and from Europe to Asia. Avon is expanding into eastern Europe, Mary Kay Cosmetics and Amway into China, and Lands' End has made a successful entry into the Japanese market. The effect of all these intrusions into the traditional distribution systems is a change that will make discounting, self-service, supermarkets, mass merchandising and e-commerce concepts common all over the world, and that elevates the competitive climate to a level not known before.

9.5.1 The global channel design process

The actual process of building channels for international distribution is seldom easy, and many companies are halted in their efforts to develop international markets by their inability to construct a *satisfactory system* of channels.

Despite the special characteristics of each individual country's channel structure, it can still be possible to identify what middlemen should be used for in a country to ensure that the strategic objectives of the marketing mix – the target segmentation and the desired product positioning – are reached. To do this requires an analysis of what the important functions in the channel network are (identification of what the key success factors are as they relate to channel choice) and then ensuring that the chosen intermediaries in each country measure up to those criteria.

To identify the channel requirements, the natural first step is to decide whether any of the firm-specific advantages (FSAs) and competencies are uniquely lodged in the distribution channels to be used.

Key success factors and FSAs may vary across countries. For example, many of the convenience products sold in western markets (packaged foods, cigarettes, soft drinks, etc.) require intensive distribution coverage, precisely because customers want them to be conveniently available.

If the firm cannot find relevant distribution partners, it might invest in a dedicated network in order to supply the market. This is usually a big investment question and, as we have seen, there is no certainty of success. When the market is sufficiently large, as the US market almost always is, it might pay for the company to develop its own distribution network. But where the market is smaller and the gains consequently less, the investment might not be worth the risks involved.

The following sections go through the different stages in designing the global channel network (Baker, 2000):

- selection of the right international distributors
- contracting with the chosen distributor
- motivating middlemen (channel tie-up)
- co-ordination and control
- terminating contracts with distributors.

9.5.2 Selection of the right international distributors

Construction of the middleman network includes seeking out potential middlemen, selecting those who fit the company's requirements and establishing working relationships with them. In international marketing, the channel-building process is hardly routine. The closer the company wants to get to the consumer in its channel contact, the larger the sales force required.

The search for prospective middlemen should begin with a study of the market and determination of criteria for evaluating middlemen servicing that market. The checklist of criteria differs according to the type of middlemen being used and the nature of their relationship with the company. Basically, such lists are built around four subject areas: productivity or volume, financial strength, managerial stability and capability, and the nature and reputation of the business. Emphasis is usually placed on either the actual or potential productivity of the middleman.

Finding prospective middlemen is less of a problem than determining which of them can perform satisfactorily. Low volume or low potential volume hampers most prospects, many are under-financed, and some simply cannot be trusted. In many cases, when a manufacturer is not well known abroad, the reputation of the middleman becomes the reputation of the manufacturer, so a poor choice at this point can be devastating.

The screening and selection process itself should include the following actions: an exploratory letter including product information and distributor requirements in the native language sent to each prospective middleman; a follow-up to the best respondents for more specific information concerning lines handled, territory covered, size of firm, number of sales people, and other background information; check of credit and references from other clients and customers of the prospective middleman; and, if possible, a personal check of the most promising companies.

Experienced international marketers suggest that the only way to select a middleman is to go the country in question in person and talk to ultimate users of the product to find who they consider to be the best distributors. Visit each possible middleman before selecting one to represent you; look for one with a key person who will take the new product to their hearts and make it a personal objective to make the sale of that line a success. Further, international marketers stress that if you cannot sign up one of the two or three customer-recommended distributors, it might be better not to have a distributor in that country because having a worthless distributor will cost you time and money every year.

9.5.3 Contracting with the chosen distributor

Once a potential middleman is found and evaluated, there remains the task of detailing the arrangements with that middleman. So far the company is in a buying position; now it must shift into a selling and negotiating position to convince the middleman to handle the goods and accept a distribution agreement that is workable for the company. Agreements must spell out the specific responsibilities of the manufacturer and the middleman, including an annual sales minimum. The sales minimum serves as a basis for evaluation of the distributor; failure to meet sales minimums may give the exporter the right of termination.

Some international marketers recommend that initial contracts be signed for one year only. If the first year's performance is satisfactory, they should be reviewed for renewal for a longer period. This permits easier termination and, more important, after a year of working together in the market, a more workable arrangement can generally be reached.

9.5.4 Motivating middlemen (channel tie-up)

The level of distribution and the importance of the individual middleman to the company determine the activities undertaken to keep the middleman motivated. On all levels there is a clear correlation between the middleman's motivation and sales volume. Motivational techniques that can be employed to maintain middleman interest and support for the product may be grouped into five categories: financial rewards, psychological rewards, communication, company support and corporate rapport.

Where channel members are available to provide the functions necessary, they may still be unwilling to sign on with the new product unless special trade allowances bigger than those offered by the competition are made. There are reasons for making sure at this stage that the best units available are tied into, and it is customary for new entrants to pay a premium to established dealers to get them to accept the new product. For example, when Japanese car manufacturers entered the US car market they offered higher dealer margins than had been customary for that size of car.

The thrust behind signing up good distributors and dealers is not only that sales will be high, but also that they are the ones most likely to sustain the FSAs identified as necessary for the competitive success of the manufacturer.

Being human, middlemen and their sales people respond to psychological rewards and recognition of their efforts. A trip to the parent company's home or regional office is a great honour. Publicity in company media and local newspapers also builds esteem and involvement among foreign middlemen.

In all instances, the company should maintain a continuing flow of communication, in the form of letters, emails, newsletters and periodicals, to all its middlemen. The more personal these are, the better. One study of exporters indicated that the more intense the contact between the manufacturer and the distributor, the better the performance from the distributor. More and better contact naturally leads to less conflict and a smoother working relationship.

Finally, considerable attention must be paid to the establishment of close rapport between the company and its middlemen. In addition to the methods noted earlier, a company should be certain that the conflicts that arise are handled skilfully and diplomatically. Bear in mind that, all over the world, business is a personal and vital thing to the people involved.

9.5.5 Co-ordination and control

The extreme length of channels typically used in international distribution makes control of middlemen especially important. Marketing objectives must be spelled out both internally and to middlemen as explicitly as possible. Standards of performance should include sales volume objective, market share in each market, inventory turnover ratio, number of accounts per area, growth objective, price stability objective and quality of publicity. Cultural differences enter into all these areas of management.

The more involved a company is with the distribution, the more control it exerts. A company's own sales force affords the most control, but often at a cost that is not practical. Each type of channel arrangement provides a different level of control; as channels grow longer, the ability to control price, volume, promotion and types of outlet diminishes. If a company cannot sell directly to the end user or final retailer, an important selection criterion for middlemen should be the amount of control the marketer can maintain.

9.5.6 Terminating contracts with distributors

When middlemen do not perform up to standard or when market situations change, requiring a company to restructure its distribution, it may be necessary to terminate relationships. In some parts of the world (e.g. in the European Union (EU)) the distributor often has legal protection that makes termination difficult. In other parts of the world (e.g. the USA) it is usually a simple action regardless of the type of middlemen: they are simply dismissed.

It is vital to secure competent legal advice when entering into distribution contracts with middlemen. But as many experienced international marketers know, the best rule is to avoid the need to terminate distributors by screening all prospective middlemen carefully in the first place. A poorly chosen distributor may not only fail to live up to expectations but may also adversely affect future business and prospects in the country.

Exhibit 9.2: *De Beers is controlling distribution in China*

A short history of diamonds in China and the rest of the world

Ancient Greeks and Romans believed diamonds were the tears of the gods and splinters from falling stars. In the East, some tradition is present with, for example in India, the first diamonds mined over 4,000 years ago and largely used by Hindus as the eyes of some of their statues. They considered diamonds as symbols of power. However, in China, no such history is present and no positive preconceptions exist.

Diamonds have no roots in China, in terms of either culture or production. In Chinese culture, the colour white is considered unlucky and is linked with misfortune. Diamonds are viewed as white, therefore it is understandable that they have never been celebrated or even emphasized in Chinese history. Neither is China a diamond-producing country, so it would seem reasonable that the Chinese have little knowledge of diamonds.

Despite this background, however, diamonds occupy an important position in the minds of Chinese consumers today. In China, diamonds are now considered symbols of honour, luck, wealth, status and power (which is much like the current western perception of diamonds).

De Beers worldwide and in China

The De Beers Group was established in 1888 and since its initiation has been involved in all aspects of the diamond industry, including exploration, mining, recovery, sorting, valuation and marketing. The group comprises two main wings: De Beers Consolidated Mines Ltd and De Beers Centenary AG. The mining division focuses on the group's South Africa-based operations and activities, while De Beers Centenary AG administers those operations that are outside South Africa. An important arm of this operation is the Diamond Trading Company (DTC), based in the UK, which markets nearly two-thirds of the world supply.

▶

Since the late 1930s the DTC has developed and implemented some of the most effective promotional campaigns in the history of advertising (such as 'A Diamond is Forever' – recognized as the most effective slogan of the last millennium by *Advertising Age*).

For 100 years, throughout (largely) western economies, De Beers has driven the market to the extent that consumers currently equate diamonds with tradition, love and romance.

De Beers itself owns and operates mines that produce over 43 per cent of the total world value of rough-cut diamonds, and for over a century the De Beers Group has had *de facto* control over nearly 75 per cent of the rough-cut diamond market (through an international diamond cartel). Globally, De Beers spends about US$200 m a year in the promotion of diamonds, based on the assumption that the company will be the primary beneficiary of such efforts. De Beers controls both sides of the consumption chain: supply and demand. Its mission in the Chinese market has been to cultivate and stimulate market demand, and serve the ultimate consumption market.

Indeed, De Beers' source of power in controlling diamond prices no longer comes from rough diamond production alone but from a complex network of marketing, sales and production arrangements that are all controlled and operated by the company. Such is the power and market coverage of De Beers that the company is viewed as totally dominating the market, even more so in China than in other parts of the world.

The De Beers policy of controlling supply and demand for diamonds is also rehearsed fully elsewhere. Of more interest to strategic marketers, though, is the decision by De Beers to pursue a two-pronged strategy of (1) improved branding and market control, and (2) market expansion into under-exploited markets.

In terms of branding and market control, in mid-2000 De Beers launched its 'Supplier of Choice' initiative, which aims to supply service to only those clients that are included in the DTC distribution channel, aided by a new identity known as the 'Forevermark'. In terms of market expansion, in 1999 the USA accounted for 48 per cent of retail diamond consumption, Japan 14 per cent, Europe 12 per cent, Asia-Pacific 10 per cent, Asia-Arabia 11 per cent and others 5 per cent. In this regard, China is clearly an underdeveloped market.

Before De Beers' entry in 1993 the Chinese market's underdevelopment was largely due to historical reasons and the fact that China does not produce and thus have experience of diamonds. There was little market demand and, in turn, jewellers had little motivation to push diamond sales. Consequently, as part of its market-driving approach, De Beers in China has proactively created purchase desire and developed specific market demand.

Creation of market demand for diamonds

By using an explicit market-driving strategy (see, e.g., Jaworski et al., 2000; Harris and Cai, 2002) diamonds' retail value in the Chinese market had increased from US$169 m in 1993 to US$800 m in 2002.

Currently, De Beers divides the Chinese market into two main segments: female diamond jewellery and diamond wedding rings. Each of these segments has individually tailored promotional campaigns and in-store point-of-sale themes. Similar to the case in other countries, the wedding ring segment accounts for one-quarter of sales, while female diamond jewellery accounts for very nearly three-quarters of sales. Interestingly, De Beers estimates that significantly less than 5 per cent of the female population in China owns a piece of diamond jewellery.

How has De Beers created this development? It is changing customer preferences for diamonds

De Beers focused on modifying the existing preferences of customers. This manifestation of De Beers' tactic of changing customer perception of diamonds centres on a long-term education process, which De Beers' employees view as the 'education' of potential customers via 'rational information' to 'subjective association'. The supply of 'rational information' centres on educating the Chinese market in terms of what De Beers labels the '4Cs': cut, carat, colour and clarity. This process is viewed as fundamental to helping Chinese consumers choose suitable diamonds, while also achieving continuously increasing exposure of diamond images and the De Beers brand.

Changing 'subjective associations' pivoted on establishing in Chinese culture similar views regarding diamonds to those held in the West (and rather similar to those most Chinese consumers *currently* ascribe to diamonds).

Sources: adapted from www.debeers.com; www.diamonds.net; www.forevermark.com; Jaworski, B., Kohli, A.K. and Sahay, A. (2000) Market-driven versus driving markets, *Journal of the Academy of Marketing Science*, 28(1): 45–54; Harris, L.C. and Cai, K.Y. (2002) Exploring market driving: a case study of De Beers in China, *Journal of Market-Focused Management*, 5(3): 171–96

9.6 Multiple channel strategy

Distribution channels can be seen as sets of interdependent organizations involved in the process of making a product or service available for consumption or use. When making channel choices, firms can choose from a wide variety of alternatives. It should be noted, however, that companies are increasingly using a multiple channel strategy for most or all of their products.

A multiple channel strategy is employed when a company makes a product available to the market through two or more channels of distribution. This strategy was expected to become the most popular channel design in the 1990s. The increasing popularity of this strategy results from the potential advantages provided: extended market coverage and increased sales volume; lower absolute or relative costs; better accommodation of customers' evolving needs; and more and better information. This strategy can also, however, produce potentially disruptive problems: consumer confusion; conflicts with intermediaries and/or internal distribution units; increased costs; loss of distinctiveness; and, eventually, increased organizational complexity (Valos, 2008).

A special case of multiple channel marketing is often referred to as *dual marketing*, where the same product is sold to both consumer and business customers at the same time (Biemans, 2001). For instance, in selling mobile phones, fax machines and audio equipment,

Philips Electronics is confronted with a lot of similarities and overlap between both markets. For instance, small business owners also shop in consumer outlets and focus on price differences, while ignoring the differences in product functionality offered on both markets. Therefore, Philips uses different product versions, sales channels, prices and communication methods in an effort to tailor its offering to both groups of customers. In addition, it is faced with a continuous struggle to adapt the internal organization of the marketing function to the dynamics of the marketplace.

The use of dual marketing is also stimulated by a convergence of consumer marketing and business marketing. At the same time, consumers have become increasingly knowledgeable about products and product functions, such as personal computers and the health implications of food ingredients, making them more open to *rational* selling arguments. Finally, new interactive technologies allow companies to build one-to-one relationships with customers, whether these are large companies or individual consumers.

Although it is often impossible to completely separate the channels used for both markets, a supplier can enhance the differences between them by offering different versions of the same product and charging different prices. The success of this strategy depends on the extent to which the distribution channels can actually be separated.

9.6.1 Managing multiple channels

In managing multiple channels, companies demarcate products and models by channel, thus minimizing direct comparison. The demarcations, of course, work only when there are meaningful differences among products. Unfortunately, consumers do not come neatly segmented into such airtight compartments. There is considerable movement between segments and across purchases. Moreover, with accelerating product life cycles, proliferation of products and fragmentation of customer segments, multiple channel approaches are often the only way to provide market coverage. Different customers with different buying behaviours will seek the channels that best serve their needs.

Options are not, however, a perfect solution. Customers can infiltrate from other segments by patronizing both the full-service channel and the low-price channel (see Fig. 9.4). As long as higher price fairly reflects higher service, customers will be loyal to a particular channel, but if the service is unnecessary or can be obtained at a lower cost, customers will cross to the low-price channel. In some businesses, presales service is a public good that customers can avail themselves of without making a purchase. For example, a customer can get a full-function demonstration at a high-street computer store and then buy the product from a low-cost mail-order retailer on the Internet. The customer thus gets a free ride on the full-service channel.

Multiple channels are most prevalent in fast-changing market environments. When the product market matures slowly, the channel has time to adapt to changes in customer buying patterns. Even if multiple channels are necessary to reflect market plurality, each channel is clearly specialized to serve a specific buying pattern. Crossovers are less common. Discount stores in the late 1970s and early 1980s were clearly targeted to the value-conscious shopper, and the service-conscious shopper continued to patronize the speciality stores. The two channels often stocked, displayed and sold different brands and attracted a very different clientele. This does not occur in more dynamic industries. Computer models that start out in speciality stores end up with the catalogue retailers in under six months. Early buyers may not face channel dissonance, but latecomers always do. While later buyers may seek the

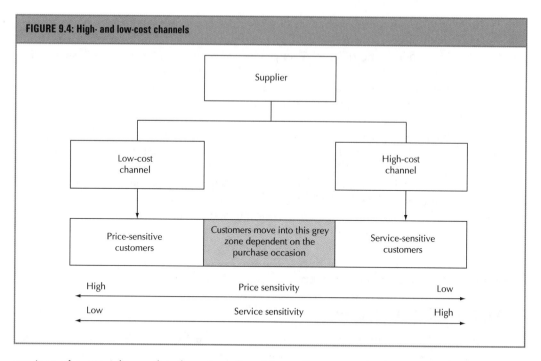

FIGURE 9.4: High- and low-cost channels

services of a speciality outlet, the price offered by a discount outlet is too tempting to pass up. Moreover, in dynamic environments, customers' shopping and buying behaviours, buying criteria and segments change frequently.

In coping with turbulence, channel diversity pays, but only if the arrangements are treated as options. Further, they must decide what to do with options as the market stabilizes.

9.6.2   The trend towards hybrid multiple channels

In a hybrid multiple distribution channel, the marketing functions are shared by the producer and the channel intermediary. The former usually handles promotion and customer-generation activities, whereas the intermediary is in charge of sales and distribution (Gabrielsson et al., 2002).

Another model is illustrated in Anderson et al. (1997). Both the supplier and its channel partners divide up the execution of the channel functions. The supplier performs some functions, such as sales negotiation and order generation, while its channel partners deliver physical distribution and order fulfilment. Other channel members might specialize in functions such as after-sales service. The members work together, with certain members specializing in certain functions (see Fig. 9.5). The difference between the hybrid and conventional channels is the horizontal task allocation. A team of channel partners (including the supplier), each specializing in a few tasks, satisfies the customer's total needs. In the conventional channel, the hand-offs are vertical; each member performs the full channel functions that its immediate customers require.

The trend towards functional specialization (and therefore horizontal channels) is driven by customers' desire to receive products and services in the most cost- and time-efficient manner possible. If channel functions have to be unbundled and sourced separately, customers, especially large ones, will be willing to accept that.

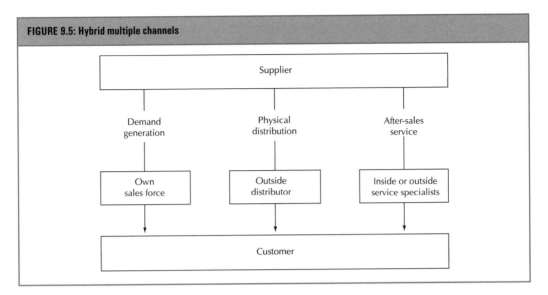

FIGURE 9.5: Hybrid multiple channels

In the PC industry, multiple channels are often used. In addition to the sales channel strategy, the PC producer must also consider a great variety of channel intermediaries at each channel level. (The vocabulary used in this instance, in respect of the channel members, is specific to the PC industry.) Channel intermediaries can be classified into distributors, resellers and retailers. By definition, distributors usually do not sell directly to end customers but use either resellers or retailers as intermediaries. Resellers can be further divided into dealer chains (or corporate resellers); local dealers; indirect fax, telephone or Internet resellers; and value-added resellers, which add software and services to the industrial organizations, whereas retailers sell to consumers through retail outlets. However, because the definitions of intermediary types vary greatly from industry to industry, and even from company to company, it is more important for a producer to consider the functions a particular intermediary can perform than to pay attention to labels *per se*. The sales channels target a variety of customers. In this example, they are divided into two broad groups: consumers (which includes people who buy the PCs from a personal budget); and business organizations from the different worlds of industry and services (Gabrielsson et al., 2002).

Multiple channels, in the context of international business, have not previously been the object of an explicit study; the conventional view has been to consider channel decisions from a single channel viewpoint. Therefore, the multiple sales channel strategy alternatives, choice and development discussed here contribute by narrowing this research gap (see also Gabrielsson, 1999); for example, Figs. 9.4 and 9.5 contribute by presenting the channel alternatives in relation to international marketing operation modes. Note too that this example has applied and developed the existing internationalization process and other theories, constructs and concepts in examining the multiple sales channels.

9.6.3 The Internet and the growth of multiple channel strategies

The Internet has turbocharged the growth of multi-channel companies, enabling them to leverage their existing assets, brands and customer bases for revenue and profit growth. Key to this leverage is correctly determining the strategic role of the online channel in combination with all other channels.

Here are a few important ideas on how multi-channels (and pure plays for that matter) can build competitive advantage (Vishwanath and Mulvin, 2001).

- *Define the Internet's role in your channel and operational portfolios*: the Internet means different things to different companies: a new channel, a place to unload slow-moving inventory, a customer service resource, a cost-reduction tool, a customer acquisition channel, or all the above. Identifying where the Internet can help your business and where investment will pay off the most is the first step in extracting value from this flexible tool. Next you need to integrate the offline and online functions, both to cut costs and to raise service levels for customers. Only then can the natural advantages of multi-channels over both online pure plays and bricks-and-mortar companies be translated into profit.

- *Identify and cater to your most profitable customer segments*: whether you plan to make a large investment in the Internet or simply place 'a check in the box', you need to understand which groups of customers are providing the bulk of your profits, and how the Internet can best improve your offering for those customers. You can also learn to avoid unwanted customers: having the best website on the Internet will not do you any good if you are attracting unprofitable or fickle customers. Once you understand your best customers, you can execute a marketing plan to attract and retain new ones, and serve existing ones better. Basically, this is about which customers you want to court in all media, and how. The Internet represents just one important facet of this plan.

- *Invest in execution*: as we have seen, the companies that 'cash in' on their Internet sales sites best enjoy customer conversion rates up to eight times the industry average. Retention rates for online companies vary widely too. Differences in performance are achieved by being world-class in a small number of key areas: targeted, accurate and cost-efficient marketing; an intuitive, fast and easy-to-use site; sufficient product information available on the site, with non-Internet back-up options for customers; timely and accurate shipping; and a quick and simple transaction process. The companies that execute on these factors have seen significant improvements in their online performance; these improvements translate into profits that can be reinvested in their online presence.

- *Take risks, but remain flexible*: the multi-channels have the pure-play dotcoms (and the venture capitalists who funded them) to thank for many early lessons and forward steps that we now take for granted: the dotcoms educated consumers, created awareness of the Internet, demanded and paid for infrastructure development, and dragged the bricks-and-mortar companies into the online arena far faster and further than they would otherwise have come. They also bore the brunt of some costly mistakes: it was dotcoms, for instance, that felt most acutely the disappointments of online advertising. Partly as a result, the pure plays are now on the wane, and the mantle of online leadership has passed to the multi-channels. It will not be easy for multi-channels to sit back and watch any more, and then just invest in the safer bets, so managers of multi-channel retailers will have to adjust their approach to investing in the Internet: they will have to become the risk takers and, like the pure plays before them, will have to place a number of bets, carefully monitor them to see which are panning out and redirect spending as their learning progresses.

9.7 Grey (parallel) distribution

Development in logistics coupled with floating exchange rates and widely different prices in different countries have led to the emergence of 'grey' trade through (parallel) distribution channels.

9.7.1 Grey distribution

Grey trade is the parallel distribution of genuine goods by intermediaries other than authorized channel members. Grey marketers are typically brokers who buy goods overseas either from the manufacturer or from authorized dealers at relatively low prices and then import them into a country where prevailing prices are higher. The grey marketers sell the merchandise at discounted prices in direct competition with authorized local distributors, often advertising the lower prices openly in print media and direct mail. The practice is not illegal *per se*, except under certain circumstances, but the activities tend to disturb existing trading relationships and are usually fought against by manufacturers as well as authorized distributors.

The World Wide Web has drastically increased grey market potential for both domestic and foreign goods. As an information medium, it raises a customer's awareness of special offers that were initially designed to be limited to specific regions, countries or classes of customers such as original equipment manufacturers (OEMs). Web-based grey marketers can also advertise merely by using a product's brand name or model number on their websites and waiting for search engines to direct consumers there. (Grey trade tends to serve as an arbitrage mechanism, equalizing prices between markets in different countries.)

The conditions necessary for grey market activity are similar to those in arbitrage, in which the same financial security is sold at the same time at different price levels in different financial markets. In either foreign or domestic grey marketing, the price differentials across markets must be great enough to justify the costs associated with buying a good in one market and selling it in another. However, unlike financial securities, a grey marketer may have significant transportation and holding costs, and deal with goods that have different brand names, are labelled in different languages and need to be modified to meet a particular country's safety standards. The basic principle is that significant price differences between markets are the stimuli for grey marketing.

The sources of foreign grey marketing are based largely on the need to charge different prices to different countries or regions based on wealth, excise taxes, competitive environments or government price caps in certain markets (such as on pharmaceutical products in the EU). Unfortunately, some of the goods exported to foreign countries are trans-shipped back to the original country. Unauthorized resellers can purchase goods from authorized resellers or manufacturers in a foreign country. Foreign wholesalers or manufacturers are aware that goods will be shipped to the original country.

Three main factors motivate entrepreneurs to engage in grey marketing:

1 *Wide price discrepancies*: there are substantial price differences between national markets, because of currency fluctuations for example.
2 *Limited availability*: there is limited availability of certain models or versions in one market. Demand outstrips supply and is likely to push local prices even higher relative to other markets. Certain Mercedes-Benz and Porsche models, for example, are unavailable in the USA, as was originally the case with some Lexus models in Japan, and this

stimulated grey trade. Localization requirements, such as local certification of emissions controls on cars, have a dampening effect, but with sufficient margins grey traders will invest in conversion equipment (although sometimes the buyer gets stuck with that job).

3 *Inexpensive logistics*: transportation and importation can be accomplished with relative ease. The increased availability of global modes of transportation and the added services offered by carriers and freight forwarders have meant that logistics problems are usually few. Grey traders can use independent middlemen.

Figure 9.6 shows some of the ways in which grey traders infiltrate the global distribution of Japanese watches; two export markets – China and Europe – are used as examples. The Japanese companies (here Seiko is used as an illustration) export watches to the importer, often a sales subsidiary, in the various countries. From there the watches are shipped to the distributors and then on to retailers. These are the authorized channels where the company offers merchandising support and sales training, and in turn demands service support.

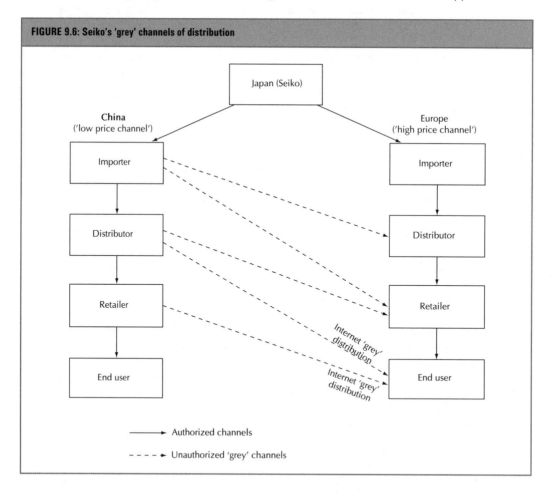

FIGURE 9.6: Seiko's 'grey' channels of distribution

As can be seen in Fig. 9.6, the grey trade arises from several sources. Some of the distributors in price-competitive markets, such as China, will divert part of their shipment to more lucrative markets. They may sell directly to unauthorized (or even authorized) European or US distributors or retailers, getting higher prices that more than offset any transportation charges. Alternatively, Japanese distributors and retailers backed by a strong yen can go abroad to get watches from overseas distributors or retailers for sale at home.

9.7.2 Difficulties associated with grey market sales

While the grey market can lead to additional short-run sales revenues for manufacturers, the potential disruption is generally long term in nature, as described below.

Difficulty in developing and maintaining a global image

Grey marketing can generate problems for organizations seeking to build a global brand. With traditional channels, a marketer controls which product version is sold in a given country. In contrast, with grey market goods, products with different tastes, consistencies and sizes may be sold in a country where the product was never intended to be resold. For example, chocolate made for the UK market tends to be sweeter than chocolate sold in the rest of Europe. In other European markets with very warm climates, chocolate contains chemicals to retard melting, and this affects taste. Thus, says Benady (2003), two chocolate bars sold in the same country – one on the grey market, the other through traditional channels – may have different tastes.

Less control over an organization's overall marketing strategy

The grey market can result in an organization having less control over its marketing strategies. As stated earlier, because grey marketers are unauthorized dealers, manufacturers have no control over their selection or continuance. The traditional rewards and sanctions used by an organization to control its distributors are not present. Ironically, an organization's internal sales force is typically rewarded for the increased sales that lead to grey marketing.

Grey market activity can also affect other areas of market planning, such as an organization's new product introduction plans. Forecasted sales in a market may not be realized when there is a sudden influx of grey goods. Roll-out campaign plans for new product introductions might have to be changed if grey traders introduce a product prematurely, as happens frequently with movie videos and popular music.

Coca-Cola, for example, was forced to bring forward the product launch date for its Vanilla Coke in the UK after discovering that the product had been sold in London and the south-east six months prior to its official launch date. The goods had been imported from Canada via the grey market.

Not all effects are negative, however. It is also possible to gain some advantages because grey trade tends to enlarge the market for a product through lower prices.

Erosion of an organization's traditional pricing strategy

The low prices offered by grey marketers may cause consumers to view the authorized reseller's price as being too high. And while an authorized dealer may be contractually obliged to run a complete service facility, purchase a manufacturer's full product line, participate in co-operative advertising and handle product recall responsibilities, grey marketers typically do not have to meet any of these obligations. Unfortunately, such augmented services may mean little to a price-conscious consumer. Continued low prices on grey market goods can also devalue a brand name whose image is associated with premium prices, as well as undermine a manufacturer's established list price and discount structure.

Problems in obtaining support from authorized resellers who 'play by the rules'

The grey market can generate difficulty in obtaining support from authorized dealers, who are particularly resentful of the pricing structure differences if a significant degree of free-riding occurs. With free-riding, customers visit authorized dealers for product information and then buy cheaper goods from grey market dealers. As a result, the latter benefit from the advertising, display and sales support of the authorized dealers. According to a recent KPMG study, 81 per cent of the information technology (IT) distributors surveyed said that their competitive position would improve if all grey market activities were eliminated (KPMG, 2003).

The legal liabilities problem usually involves warranties that cannot be honoured and performance criteria that cannot be fulfilled. These problems are especially acute for pharmaceutical products because of the potential harm involved: taking medication that has expired or whose dosages are meant for adults can severely harm children, for instance.

Erosion of a brand's image

The erosion of a brand's image due to grey market activity may be the result of frequent sales at a low price, the existence of instructions in a foreign language, the absence of replacement parts for foreign goods, poor product quality (due to problems in the way foreign goods are stored and handled), and lack of manufacturer control over reseller selection. Because grey market sales are made through unauthorized channel members that have never been evaluated by their suppliers, some grey marketers can engage in unscrupulous behaviour, such as selling factory-remanufactured goods as new, repairing goods with parts manufactured by independent firms, selling supplies not made by the manufacturer and improperly adapting products to meet national safety standards.

9.7.3 Channel strategies for limiting grey market activity

Proactive strategies

These are designed to limit grey distribution even before the activity starts. The two most important proactive strategies are as follows:

1 *Reduce price differences across markets*

   Because both domestic and foreign grey market activity are forms of market arbitrage, one obvious deterrent is to reduce the price differentials between market areas and adjust an organization's quantity discount schedule to prevent trans-shipping. For example, there is no economic reward for grey marketing when the price difference between two market areas is so small that it is less than shipping and inventory holding costs. An extreme example of a strategy to eliminate grey market activity is the LVMH Moët Hennessy – Louis Vuitton decision to price its TAG Heuer and Christian Dior watches the same worldwide. According to the organization's chairman, this strategy 'will dry out temptations for the grey market' (Shashidhar, 2002).

2 *Differentiate products sold to different markets*

A second strategy is to differentiate products sold to different markets: have products tailored to meet a region's unique regulatory requirements; use foreign labels; assign unique product numbers and names to foreign products. This provides legal rights in foreign grey market cases and reduces the consumer attraction of grey market goods. Set up a cross-border programme; for example, Canon uses different names and model numbers for cameras sold in lower-priced European and Asian markets.

Other proactive strategies

- Manufacturers can deter grey market goods by carefully checking their new and existing distributors. For example, they can employ cargo inspection organizations to verify that foreign shipments are actually delivered to their specified location. They can also conduct compliance audits on an unscheduled basis to verify that goods have actually been sold to local final consumers.
- Manufacturers can also track down trans-shippers through a product's serial number, warranty card information and factory rebate data. Some manufacturers and wholesalers take a more aggressive position and employ 'shoppers' to purchase products from unauthorized resellers. Manufacturers and wholesalers should make resellers aware that they carefully monitor all reselling activity and will take away distributor or dealer status from authorized representatives that trans-ship goods. Most Japanese camera makers, for instance, use different model numbers and introduce slight differences in features between their Asian, North American and European markets. By stressing features and model numbers in the advertising, their global advertising copy can remain uniform with the same brand name (Minolta, Canon, Nikon) while at the same time alerting buyers when a grey import does not correspond to an 'authentic' model.
- Ironically, even as the web stimulates grey market activity, it also makes surveillance relatively easy. For example, manufacturers can easily search the web to determine the extent of sales by unauthorized resellers and the nature of price discounts, as well as the names and locations of grey marketers. They can also purchase grey market goods on the web to determine their condition and possibly trace their origin.
- Manufacturers can use their marketing information systems to monitor above-average purchases by specific wholesalers and retailers. Some manufacturers even hire investigators to approach wholesalers and retailers with offers to buy merchandise for diversion. Despite the importance of these deterrents, audits of channel partners are apparently rarely carried out.
- Consumer education and the use of rebates are two demand-side means of reducing grey market activity. Wella warns consumers not to buy its products outside of professional beauty supply stores and licensed beauty salons. According to its website (www.wellausa.com), 'diverted products usually pass through ... many hands, travel great distances, [and] have been marked up 5 to 6 times before they finally make their way onto the retailer's shelves'. As a result, products are often old or damaged. Likewise, Kodak uses its website (www.kodak.com) to report that it is 'unable to govern the conditions under which these products are shipped. Film is very sensitive to heat and humidity, which means by the time a gray market film reaches you, it may be an inferior product'. A more constructive solution is to go on the attack and create stronger reasons for customers to patronize authorized dealers. This might involve aggressive price cutting,

but other measures should be considered as well. Supporting authorized dealers in offering innovative credit plans, improved service and other customer-oriented initiatives is a possible tactic. Caterpillar, the heavy machinery company, helped authorized dealers develop customized warranties that the individual buyer could tailor to their own special needs. Manufacturers also support their dealers by regionalizing their offerings, and, as mentioned above, by differentiating model features and numbers between trade areas to make it possible to spot grey imports and restrict servicing liability.

9.7.4 Reactive strategies

The reactive strategies for fighting grey marketing once it has occurred are largely legal in nature. Many defences are most applicable when grey marketers sell goods that differ materially from the manufacturer's domestic goods, or when they seek to confuse customers. Trademark and state consumer protection laws can provide a basis for protecting manufacturers in such cases.

Legal actions, of course, may be quite costly and are not always successful. Suing grey marketers for breach of contract is difficult to enforce for two reasons: first, some grey market distributors may also be good customers for authorized products; second, in breach-of-contract cases, lost income due to diminished sales of lower prices must be proved.

A more drastic measure is to search for grey imports at the grey traders' outlets in the importing country and then ask the dealers – or help them – to get rid of their inventory. Organizations sometimes attempt simply to destroy grey merchandise in the stores. This kind of 'search and destroy' action requires a substantiated legal justification, such as an illegal change in the valid dates, or improper packaging, and is more common for counterfeit goods.

9.8   Logistics

Logistics involves all activities required to plan and move items from a material or manufacturing source to the point of consumption. While logistics has been defined as a discipline of its own, it is important to note that it is also a critical component of a company's marketing capability. The right product, price and promotional mix are useless without dependable and timely product availability (place, or distribution). Timely availability creates value by allowing customers to purchase products or services where desired and if appropriate arrange delivery when and where desired. For a customer, availability or timely availability is as important as price and assortment.

While the role of logistics has not always been visible and well defined in commercial enterprises, transportation, inventory storage and customer service have always been performed. However, top management did not always fully understand the strategic importance and competitive impact of integrated logistics. Wide acceptance of enterprise operating philosophies such as just-in-time (JIT), total quality management, customer satisfaction and customer responsiveness served to enhance the role of logistics in achieving competitive advantage. A well-planned and well-executed logistics effort can achieve timely shipment arrival, undamaged product and satisfied customers at the lowest attainable total cost. Both the professional and popular press recognize the role of logistics in serving customers effectively.

Simply stated, customers expect nine 'rights' in any transaction:

1 the right product
2 the right quantity
3 the right quality
4 the right location
5 the right time
6 the right form
7 the right price
8 the right packaging
9 the right information.

Logistics plays a major role in achieving each of these customer expectations. The participants involved in logistical process management include wholesalers, distributors, retailers and third-party service providers necessary to provide warehousing, transportation and a wide range of other value-added services. The transportation service decision includes a selection of transport modes and providers. The managerial aspect of logistics includes scheduling and execution of activities to respond to customers and facilitate shipments. Management or execution activities include order processing, selection and shipment. Measurement includes monitoring activities to ensure performance both satisfies customers and deploys the firm's resources effectively. Typical measures include customer service level, cost, productivity, asset utilization and quality.

Although not specifically stated, the discipline also includes activities related to recycling, returns handling and product recall.

9.8.1 The logistics value chain

The logistics value chain links all activities required to support profitable transactions as a single process linking a business with its customers. In some situations the value chain is owned by a vertically integrated firm, which controls all activities from raw material procurement to retail sales. Such vertical integration is found in the petroleum industry where firms control product value added from the drill to retail sales.

The more common value chain involves a number of independent firms such as material suppliers, manufacturers, wholesalers, retailers and logistics service firms. Due to the potential efficiency and effectiveness benefits, most companies linked together in a value chain seek to integrate some behaviours. Such collaboration is what distinguishes a traditional channel of distribution from a value chain.

A traditional channel of distribution comprises multiple chain members each attempting to optimize their individual performance. For example, each channel member may seek to minimize inventory investment rather than co-ordinate activities to reduce overall value chain inventory. The integrated value chain perspective attempts to co-ordinate value chain activities in an effort to reduce redundancy and duplication. It is the degree of collaboration in joint planning and co-ordinated operations that differentiates a traditional channel of distribution and an integrated value chain.

Value chains facilitate a combination of value-added flows. The primary three are inventory, information and financial flows. Information flow consists of sales activity, forecasts, plans and orders, which must be refined into deployment, manufacturing and procurement plans.

Another observation is that normal inventory flow towards end customers must at times be reversed. Product recall capability is a critical competency to accommodate increasingly rigid safety standards, product expiration and responsibility for hazardous material. Reverse logistics is also necessary due to the increasing number of laws prohibiting disposal and encouraging recycling of containers and packaging materials. Reverse logistics does not usually enjoy the scale economies characteristic of outbound movement. However, reverse movement capability is a social responsibility that must be accommodated in logistical system design.

Retailers and wholesalers typically link physical distribution and procurement activities even though no change in product form typically occurs. Nevertheless, wholesalers and retailers are key contributors to the value-added process. Wholesalers develop assortments of products from multiple manufacturers, allowing retailers to purchase desired end combinations in smaller quantities. Retailers make a broad range of products conveniently available to customers. Such sorting and positioning is an essential element of the value-added process.

9.8.2 Logistics activities

While it is appropriate to consider the logistics process across an integrated value chain, it is also useful to identify the major work required to accomplish the logistics mission. Traditional organizations incorporate four areas of logistics functionality:

1 customer service
2 transportation
3 inventory management
4 distribution operations.

Even though many companies have integrated the logistics process with other internal units, and externally with suppliers and customers, these work areas remain at the heart of the logistics value chain. Each of these work areas is described below.

Customer service

Customer service manages the primary interface between a company and its customers from an order fulfilment perspective. Customer service includes order taking and modification, order status inquiry and customer problem resolution. Customers expect the company's customer service activity to be capable of providing accurate information regarding product availability, delivery time, product substitution, pricing and product customization options.

Transportation

Transportation controls product movement from manufacturing sites to distribution facilities to customers. The responsibilities include selecting the type of carrier, scheduling, routing and freight payment. In addition to managing the firm's shipping activities, transportation is responsible for monitoring carrier performance. Logistics is responsible for improving transportation service levels while simultaneously decreasing overall cost. The transportation management objective is to minimize total costs associated with all movements from suppliers to the final customer.

Inventory management

Inventory management consists of monitoring inventory levels and requirements at manufacturing plants and distribution facilities. The objective is to maintain enough inventory to satisfy customer demand while minimizing total asset deployment. Leading-edge firms gather knowledge regarding sales, customer demand, customer promotion plans, delivery times and replenishment cycles so that inventory can be synchronized with demand.

Distribution operations

Distribution operations have responsibility for the physical facilities and activities that take place at the distribution facilities used by a firm. The facilities include the buildings, offices, communications equipment, storage racks and material handling equipment. The activities include product receipt, storage, order selection and shipment. The distribution operations objective is to minimize expenses for receiving, storing and shipping product from a distribution facility. The historical operations focus has been to minimize the variable cost associated with handling or moving a product. A more comprehensive focus is to reduce assets required to support logistics while simultaneously increasing operating flexibility. Reduced assets remove distribution facilities and handling equipment from a company's books.

9.9   The internationalization of retailing

In spite of the power and sophistication of large-scale retailers, the process of internationalization has been slow and painful. In addition to legal, linguistic and logistical problems, it is difficult to export even the most successful of retail concepts into other markets. As noted earlier, competitive structures differ greatly and there are still major differences in consumer tastes and preferences. Difficult or not, the internationalization of retailing is, however, gaining in importance.

9.9.1   Motives for internationalization

The pressures towards and reasons for internationalization are diverse, but may be summarized as 'push', 'pull' or 'facilitating' factors.

- *Push factors* include the maturity or saturation of home markets, domestic trading restrictions, unfavourable economic conditions, rising costs, adverse demographic changes and imitation of trading styles.
- *Pull factors* include more enlightened corporate philosophies, perceptions of growth opportunities abroad (niche or underdeveloped markets), established bridgeheads in other countries and imitative 'bandwagon effects'.

- *Facilitating factors* include the lowering of political, economic and perceived barriers between countries, the broader vision of senior management, an accumulation of expertise, the ability to assess other retailers' international moves and the improvement of communication technologies.

The particular mix of these factors often determines the most appropriate route to internationalization. Also relevant is the availability of capital, the level of understanding of market needs within other countries, and the compatibility of the domestic trading format(s) with those needs (Doherty, 2007).

Prior to the 1980s, retailing was essentially a localized, domestic industry and thus retail operations were long considered poor candidates for international expansion. However, for the past two decades or so, retailers in mature markets have expanded their operations into overseas markets as a means for strategic growth. Retailers from Europe, the USA and Japan are now breaking into the developing markets of Asia, eastern Europe, and South America as the next step of their retail format expansion. A number of US-based retail giants, including Wal-Mart, Sears, Gap and Home Depot, have entered international markets in recent years. A similar trend is also evident in Europe, with the development of the EU. European retailers derive a relatively large proportion of their turnover from operations outside their home market.

The internationalization of retailing has produced very diverse styles of operation, ranging from global to multinational. Global retailers such as Benetton vary their format very little across national boundaries, achieving the greatest economies of scale but showing the least local responsiveness. Multinationals, on the other hand, tend to develop or acquire a diversity of formats internationally, usually achieving rather lower benefits from integration. A middle course may be termed 'transnational' retailing, whereby a company seeks to achieve global efficiency while responding to national needs, opportunities and constraints. Some of the more recent developments by Marks & Spencer could best be described as transnational, recognizing that even the most successful retail formats within the domestic market may require adaptation to suit markets aboard.

Cross-border alliances have become a major element of international retail co-operation and expansion in recent years. The European Retail Alliance (ERA) and Associated Marketing Services (AMS), for instance, link retailers across Europe and open opportunities for many forms of co-operation, including purchasing, sourcing, logistics, product development, promotion and political lobbying.

Summary

Marketers must get their goods into the hands of consumers and must choose between handling all distribution or turning part or all of it over to various middlemen. Distribution channels vary depending on target market size, competition and available distribution intermediaries. It is evident that the international marketer has a broad range of alternatives for developing an economical, efficient, high-volume international distribution system.

The creation of globally co-ordinated channels has to start with a clear understanding of how the FSAs depend on distribution channel design. Key elements in distribution decisions include the functions performed by middlemen. The process of channel design and management of it can be broken into seven basic stages:

1 setting distribution objectives
2 specifying the functions that need to be performed by the channel
3 considering alternative channel structures
4 choosing an 'optimal' channel structure
5 selecting the intermediaries
6 motivating the channel members
7 evaluating channel member performance.

Parallel distribution and grey trade create control problems for the global firm and resellers, but can have some positive aspects too.

Global logistics are important determinants of financial performance, and their efficiency has been improving dramatically.

The wholesale and retail structure of a local market reflects the country's culture and economic progress, and the way business is done in that country; but new channel modes may be successful if timing and conditions are right.

Although international middlemen have become more numerous, more reliable and more sophisticated over the past decade, traditional channels are being challenged by the Internet, which is rapidly becoming an important alternative to many market segments. Such growth and development offer an ever wider range of possibilities for entering foreign markets.

Questions for discussion

1 Why is global distribution more difficult than domestic distribution?
2 What are the factors that affect the length, width and number of marketing channels?
3 Why might a company choose not to use an intermediary in its efforts to reach its customers?
4 From the manufacturer's and the customer's perspective, how might a long channel be beneficial?
5 Suggest three products that might benefit from intensive distribution, and explain how this might be achieved.
6 What are the advantages and disadvantages for a clothing manufacturer of making products available via their own website or, alternatively, via a mail-order catalogue sent out to known customers?
7 Why is a good logistics strategy especially vital for foods and high-technology products?
8 What are the advantages and disadvantages of a company establishing its own distribution in the international market, and what forms might this take?

9 How do the characteristics of the final consumers influence the structure of international distribution channels?

10 How does international physical distribution differ from international channel distribution?

References

Anderson, E., Day, G. and Rangan, V.K. (1997) Strategic channel design, *Sloan Management Review,* Summer: 59–69.

Arnold, D. (2000) Seven rules of international distribution, *Harvard Business Review,* 2(6): 131–7.

Baker, M. (2000) *IEBM Encyclopedia of Marketing.* London: Thomson Learning.

Benady, D. (2003) Selling you a new past, *The Independent,* 21 October, p. 18.

Biemans, W. (2001) Designing a dual marketing program, *European Management Journal,* 19(6): 670–7.

Doherty, A.M. (2007) The internationalization of retailing, *International Journal of Service Industry Management* 18(2): 184–205.

Gabrielsson, M. (1999) Sales channel strategies for international expansion – the case of large companies in the European PC industry. Doctoral dissertation, Helsinki School of Economics and Business Administration.

Gabrielsson, M., Kirpalani, V.H.M. and Luostarinen, R. (2002) Multiple channel strategies in the European personal computer industry, *Journal of International Marketing,* 10(3): 73–95.

Hollensen, S. (2003) *Marketing Management.* London: Financial Times/Prentice Hall.

Hollensen, S. (2004) *Global Marketing: A Decision-oriented Approach,* 3rd edn. London: Financial Times/Prentice Hall.

KPMG (2003) *The Grey Market – a KPMG Study in Cooperation with the Anti-Gray Market Alliance.* Available online at www.kpmg.co.uk/industries/t/pubs.cfm.

Shashidhar, A. (2002) *Top Swiss Watch Brands Cost the Same Worldwide – LVMH Gears to Check Grey Market, Business Line* – Internet Edition, 5 October. Available online at www.blonnet.com.

Valos, M.J. (2008) A qualitative study of multi-channel marketing performance measurement issues, *Journal of Database Marketing & Customer Strategy Management,* 15(4): 239–48.

Vishwanath, V. and Mulvin, G. (2001) Multi-channels: the real winners in the B2C Internet wars, *Business Strategy Review,* 12(1): 25–33.

CASE STUDY 9: HENNES & MAURITZ (H&M)

Successful fashion retailer with one brand store concept

Company background and history

Erling Persson founded Hennes in Vasteras, Sweden in 1947. Later, the company acquired the hunting and men's clothing chain of stores, Mauritz Widforss, in 1968, and changed its name to H&M Hennes & Mauritz (H&M) (www.hm.com).

Expanding out of its home country during the 1960s, the company developed its network in Norway (1964), Denmark (1967), Switzerland (1978), Germany (1980), the UK (1976) and the Netherlands (1989). The company was listed on the Stockholm Stock Exchange in 1974.

H&M introduced cosmetics to its product portfolio in 1975 and expanded into London in the following year. Also in 1976, the company introduced its teenage clothing stores under the Impulse brand. By the end of the 1970s, H&M moved into Switzerland and Germany. It also introduced baby clothes at about the same time.

In 1980, H&M started its mail-order catalogue business by purchasing the mail-order company, Rowell.

H&M further expanded its operations in the 1990s by expanding into Belgium (1992), Austria (1994) and Luxembourg (1996). It began selling its products over the Internet in 1998. By this time, the company had also consolidated its men's, women's, children's and teens' stores under the H&M brand. H&M expanded into the USA and Spain in 2000.

Further international expansion occurred in 2003. In the same year, H&M opened its first stores in Portugal, the Czech Republic, Italy and Poland. H&M's German subsidiary acquired The Gap – Deutschland in 2004. In order to further strengthen H&M's buying function, the company divided its buying department into two different functions: a buying division and a production division. Also in 2004, the company expanded into Slovenia and Canada, by opening two stores in Slovenia (one of which is in the capital Ljubljana) and six in Toronto (Canada). Later that year, H&M signed a contract for its first store in Ireland (this store opened in March 2005). It also opened its first store in Hungary in 2004.

In 2005, the company opened approximately 145 new retail stores primarily in Germany, the USA, the UK, Poland and Spain. It also closed 20 stores in 2005. H&M expanded its online sales outside the Nordic region and began online sales in the Netherlands in 2006. H&M was chosen to sponsor Madonna's world tour in 2006. Also during the year, H&M opened two stores in Dubai and its first store in Japan.

With a view to rejuvenating its brand name, the company signed Madonna in 2007 to create a fashion line 'M by Madonna'. In the same year, H&M opened its first store in China to tap the expanding Asian market. The company also launched its new concept store, Collection of Style (COS), in the UK.

The company opened its first store in Tokyo, Japan in September 2008. Two months later, in November 2008, the company opened its second store at Harajuku, Japan. H&M, in collaboration with Comme des Garçons, launched its autumn collection in Japan ahead of all other stores worldwide. In the same month, the company collaborated with Matthew Williamson to design its summer collection.

In December 2008, H&M entered into a franchise agreement with Match Retail to open H&M stores in Israel by 2010. In February 2009, the company signed an agreement to open its first store in Seoul, South Korea during spring of 2010. H&M opened its first store in Moscow, Russia in March 2009.

H&M business strategy

H & M Hennes & Mauritz AB (H&M) is engaged in designing and retailing of fashion apparel and accessories. The company offers a wide range of fashion apparel, cosmetics, footwear and accessories for men, women, children and teenagers. Wide geographical presence enables the company to diversify its business risk. However, declining consumer confidence due to the sluggish economic conditions across the world poses a threat for the company. Dampening consumer confidence would adversely affect the company's business operation and profitability.

Basically, the H&M strategy is to offer customers quality fashion at best prices, through a strong procurement and designing strategy.

The company offers a wide range of quality fashion merchandise for men, women, teens and children at an affordable price. The company has a strong centralized design team of over 100 designers. The design team is responsible for providing innovative product design by striking a good balance between basic garments and latest fashions. It enables H&M to design clothes for all kinds of customer groups and provides a greater choice of merchandise to its customers.

H&M sourcing strategy

The strong procurement strategy of the company helps it to provide fashion at a relatively low price. The company procures its merchandise from a number of suppliers located primarily in the Asia and Europe region. The company has about 20 local production offices in that region to maintain contacts with the suppliers. The production offices procure quality product from various vendors. The production office is also involved in product quality testing such as chemical and laundry tests in association with external laboratories. The centralized product procurement strategy with higher economies of scale enables the company to negotiate with the vendors to get quality merchandise at the best price. The company subsequently passes the price benefit to its customers to ensure the best price in the industry. This in turn helps the company to generate higher customer footfall thereby supporting its revenue growth rate.

H&M internationalization strategy

H&M has market presence across 33 countries with over 1,700 stores. The company operates primarily in Europe, North America and Asia. H&M has segmented its business operation based on its geographic presence to provide quality service across its stores and to support its business growth. In the financial year 2008, the company entered Japan and set up franchise operations in Egypt, Saudi Arabia, Bahrain and Oman. A wide geographical market presence enables the company to diversify its business risk. Furthermore, a wide market presence enhances the brand awareness of the company.

H&M has expanded in recent years in Europe, the USA, Asia and the Middle East, and has extended Internet and catalogue sales to more countries.

The business expansion plan in new and existing markets provides an opportunity for the company to consolidate its business operation in the respective regions (such as in Europe, North America and Asia), which in turn would help H&M in attaining economies of scale.

In 2008, a net total of 196 stores were opened. In 2009 H&M opened 225 stores, mostly in the USA, France, Italy, Spain, the UK and Germany.

H&M collaboration with well-known designers

H&M, in collaboration with various designers, offers a wide range of fashion merchandise to its customers. Starting in 2004, the company has collaborated with Karl Lagerfeld followed by numerous well-known designers including Stella McCartney, Viktor & Rolf and Roberto Cavalli. H&M's collaboration with designers enables it to provide a wide choice of fashion designs to its customers. Furthermore, the collaboration strategy also helps H&M to reach a larger customer base by leveraging the designer's popularity.

Fashion retailer competitors in the world market

The fashion industry is highly competitive resulting in increasing profit margin pressures among fashion retailers. H&M faces tough competition from speciality retailers, department stores, mall-based retailers and e-retailers. Because of the company's slightly lower price point, it directly competes against the discount retailers in the fashion merchandise categories. If discounters were to further increase their discount, it would increase pressure on H&M's retail pricing.

The three major world fashion retailers are: GAP Inc., Inditex/Zara and H&M. In the following the business models of H&M's two main worldwide competitors (GAP and Inditex/Zara) are described and compared with H&M's business model.

Gap Inc.

Gap Inc. (www.gapinc.com) is a US clothing and accessories retailer based in San Francisco, California, and founded in 1969 by Donald Fisher and Doris F. Fisher.

The company sells its products for men, women and children under five primary brands: the namesake Gap banner, Banana Republic, Old Navy, Piperlime and Athleta. Gap Inc. has approximately 150 000 employees and operates over 3,100 stores worldwide (September 2009). Gap also has franchise agreements with unaffiliated franchisees to operate Gap and Banana Republic stores in Asia, Europe and Middle East. Gap also markets its products to US customers through four websites – Gap.com, bananarepublic.com, oldnavy.com and Piperlime.com.

Gap Inc. remains the largest speciality apparel retailer in the USA, although it has recently been surpassed by the Spanish-based Inditex Group as the world's largest apparel retailer, in terms of turnover. Despite its publicly traded status, the founding Fisher family remains deeply involved in Gap Inc.'s business. Donald Fisher served as Chairman of the Board until 2004; when he stepped down, he was succeeded by his son, Robert J. Fisher.

Inditex/ZARA

Inditex/Zara (www.inditex.com) is a fashion retail chain of the Inditex Group owned by the Spanish businessman, Amancio Ortega, who also owns brands such as Massimo Dutti, Pull

2008 – figures	Inditex-Zara (Spain)	Gap, Inc. (USA)	H&M (Sweden)
Net sales (€m)	10,410	10,150	8,680
Net profits (€m)	1,250	677	1,500
Growth in sales (%) compared to 2007	+ 9	− 10	+ 13
% International sales (outside home country)	Inditex: 66 Zara: 70	19	93
Number of employees	90,000	150,000	53,500
Number of stores and global reach	Inditex: 4,359 stores in 73 countries Zara: 1,520 stores in 72 countries	3,100 stores in 24 countries	1,740 stores in 34 countries
Business model and production	High degree of vertical integration – mainly own production facilities	Partial vertical integration – control over design, distribution and sales – production is outsourced	Partial vertical integration – control over design, distribution and sales – production is outsourced
Promotion and advertising	Only 0.3% of turnover. The store is the main promotional tool	3–3.5% of turnover spent on advertising	4% of turnover spent on advertising
Brand portfolio	*8 brand stores*: Zara, Pull and Bear, Massimo Dutti, Bershka, Stradivarius, Oysho, Zara Home and Uterqüe	*5 brand stores*: Gap, Banana Republic, Old Navy, Piperlime and Athleta	*1 brand store*: Single format

TABLE 9.1   Comparison of the three main global competitors in fashion retailing (end of 2008)

and Bear, Oysho, Uterqüe, Stradivarius and Bershka. The Inditex group (which Zara belongs to) is headquartered in La Coruña, north-west Spain, where the first Zara store opened in 1975. It is claimed that Zara needs just two weeks to develop a new product and get it to stores, compared with a two-month industry average. Zara has resisted the industry-wide trend towards outsourcing fast fashion production to low-cost countries. Zara's most unusual strategy is its policy of zero advertising; the company prefers to invest a percentage of revenues in opening new stores instead.

At the beginning of 2009 Zara (Inditex) had 89 000 employees. During 2008, 573 establishments were opened around the world, including five new markets (Ukraine, South Korea, Montenegro, Honduras and Egypt).

Zara is a vertically integrated retailer. Unlike similar apparel retailers, Zara controls most of the steps in the supply chain: it designs, produces and distributes. Fifty per cent of the products Zara sells are manufactured in Spain, 26 per cent in the rest of Europe, and 24 per cent in Asian and African countries and the rest of the world. So while some competitors (e.g. H&M and Gap Inc.) outsource all production to Asia, Zara makes its most fashionable items at a dozen company-owned factories in Spain and Portugal. Clothes with a longer shelf life, such as basic T-shirts, are outsourced to low-cost suppliers, mainly in Asia and Turkey.

Questions

1   What are the main differences in the business models of the three main players in the fashion retailing industry?
2   Evaluate H&M's retail distribution strategy compared with that of its competitors.
3   H&M is planning to launch a range of textiles for interior decorating under the H&M home concept. Initially, the company plans to sell H&M home merchandise through its e-commerce portal. Do you think this new concept is a good idea? Why/Why not?

Sources: www.hm.com; www.gapinc.com; www.inditex.com

Marketing mix decisions IV: communication

Chapter contents

❖ LEARNING OBJECTIVES

After studying this chapter you should be able to do the following:

- ❖ Discuss the role of communication in the marketing mix.
- ❖ Describe the main elements of the promotional mix.
- ❖ Identify the local market characteristics that affect the advertising and promotion of products.
- ❖ Explain the five steps in developing an international advertising campaign.

- ❖ Discuss the role of the new media: mobile marketing, viral marketing and social media.
- ❖ Understand the importance of personal selling in international marketing.
- ❖ Explain the considerations and steps in designing and managing an international sales force.
- ❖ Discuss how to design compensation systems for an international sales force.
- ❖ Explain the principles of multi-channel customer management.

10.1 Introduction

Without an effective marketing communications programme, a marketing strategy will fail. Target customers must be made aware of the product and its benefits, be continually reminded of these benefits, and stimulated to take action. Building awareness, message comprehension and interest are essential phases in building a high level of customer response.

Effective communication is the core aim of most promotion decisions. The marketing manager's job is to combine various forms of promotional activities to effectively communicate specific messages concerning the company and its market offering to targeted consumers, channel partners, company shareholders and the general public. This promotion mix consists of such communications activities as advertising, sales promotion, personal selling, public relations (PR) and direct marketing.

A business's total marketing communications programme is called the 'promotional mix'. This consists of a blend of advertising, personal selling, sales promotion and PR tools. The following sections describe the six key elements of the promotional mix (see Table 10.1) in more detail, and from an international marketing perspective in particular.

Mix element (section number)	Advantages	Disadvantages
Advertising (10.2) Any paid-for or non-personal communication of ideas or products in the prime media (i.e. TV, newspapers, magazines, billboard posters, radio, cinema). Advertising is intended to persuade and to inform. The two basic aspects of advertising are the message (what you want your communication to say) and the medium (how to get your message across)	● Good for building awareness ● Effective at reaching a wide audience ● Repetition of main brand and product positioning helps build customer trust	● Impersonal – cannot answer all customer questions ● Not good at getting customers to make a final purchasing decision
Sales promotion (10.3) Providing incentives to customers or to the distribution channel to stimulate interest and demand for a product	● Can stimulate quick increases in sales by targeting promotional incentives on particular products ● Good short-term tactical tool	● If used over the long term, customers may get used to the effect ● Too much promotion may damage the brand image
Public relations and sponsorship (10.4) The communication of a product, brand or business by placing information about it in the media without paying for the time or media space directly. PR communicates via a news release to definable news media in the hope of secondary exposure to a target audience through an editorial mention earned by the newsworthiness of the subject matter	● Often seen as more 'credible' – since the message seems to be coming from a third party (e.g. magazine, newspaper) ● Cheap way of reaching many customers – if the publicity is achieved through the right media	● Risk of losing control – cannot always control what other people write about your product

▶

Mix element (section number)	Advantages	Disadvantages
Internet promotion (10.5) The Internet represents a change away from a push strategy towards a pull strategy in which the manufacturer communicates directly with the customer. Examples of mix elements are banner ads, sponsorships, interstitials (TV-like commercials), mobile marketing (m-marketing) and viral marketing	• Interactive communication with customers • Reduced global advertising costs • Access to directories that guide people to visit the site	• The promoted product cannot be touched (important for tangible products, not important for intangible products) • Online advertising messages are often perceived in a local context, and should be adapted to the local environment; this will increase total advertising costs
Direct marketing (10.6) Communicates person to person, but through an intervening channel, such as the post (direct mail), the telephone, e-mail or social media, guaranteeing exposure to a selected individual within a target market. For many years, the only form of direct marketing in use was direct mail	• Person-to-person interactive communication • Direct exposure to selected individuals within a target market • Messages can be targeted	• Higher cost per recipient, but cheaper than 'personal selling'
Personal selling (10.7) Oral communication with potential buyers of a product with the intention of making a sale. Personal selling may focus initially on developing a relationship with the potential buyer, but will always ultimately end with an attempt to 'close the sale'	• Highly interactive – lots of communication between the buyer and seller • Excellent for communicating complex/detailed product information and features • Relationships can be built up – important if closing the sale may take a long time	• Costly – employing a sales force has many hidden costs in addition to wages • Not suitable if there are thousands of important buyers

TABLE 10.1 Advantages and disadvantages of each element of the promotional mix

10.2 Advertising

Of all the elements of the marketing mix, decisions involving advertising are those most often affected by cultural differences among country markets. Consumers respond in terms of their culture, its style, feelings, value systems, attitudes, beliefs and perceptions. Because advertising's function is to interpret or translate the qualities of products and services in terms of consumer needs, wants, desires and aspirations, the emotional appeals, symbols, persuasive approaches and other characteristics of an advertisement must coincide with cultural norms if an advertisement is to be effective.

Global advertising can be defined as advertising that is more or less uniform across many countries, often, but not necessarily, in media vehicles with global reach. In many cases complete uniformity is unobtainable because of linguistic and regulatory differences between nations, or differences in media availability.

In contrast, *multidomestic advertising* is international advertising deliberately adapted to particular markets and audiences in terms of message and/or creative execution.

Several problems traditionally face the decision-maker in global advertising. One is how to allocate a given *advertising budget* among several market countries. Another is the *message* to use in these various markets. A third is what *media* to select. Even before tackling these management decisions, however, the advertiser needs to define the *objectives* of the advertising in the different countries.

Reconciling an international advertising campaign with the cultural uniqueness of markets is the challenge confronting the international or global marketer. The basic framework and concepts of international advertising are essentially the same wherever used. Five steps are involved (Baker, 2000):

1 strategic objectives
2 message creation
3 media selection
4 advertising budgeting
5 executing the campaign.

Of these five steps, developing messages almost always represents the most daunting task for international marketing managers, so that topic is emphasized here. The nuances of international media are then discussed. Advertising agencies are ordinarily involved in all five steps and are thus the subject of a separate section.

10.2.1 Strategic objectives

Most managers approach global advertising with the intention of using the global reach of media and the similarity of message to enhance the awareness and unique positioning of the brand or product. The boost to the *brand image* and global brand equity is usually the most immediate benefit. When the target market involves global consumers, the ability to reach these customers in many places throughout the world helps sustain a positive image of the brand. The traveller who recognizes a brand advertised in a foreign resort location may pay more attention to it there than he or she would at home. Global advertising helps create goodwill.

Unilever is introducing a new product-line extension, Dove Shampoo, in East Asian markets; and Russia's national airline Aeroflot is seeking to upgrade its quality image. Such marketing problems require careful marketing research, and thoughtful and creative advertising campaigns in country, regional and global markets, respectively.

Intense competition for world markets and the increasing sophistication of foreign consumers has led to a need for more sophisticated advertising strategies. Increased costs, problems of co-ordinating advertising programmes in multiple countries, and the desire for a broader company or product image causes multinational companies (MNCs) to seek greater control and efficiency without sacrificing local responsiveness.

10.2.2 Message creation

The effectiveness of promotional strategy can be jeopardized by so many factors that a marketer must be certain that no controllable influences are overlooked. Those international executives who understand the communications process are better equipped to manage the diversity they face in developing an international promotional programme.

In the international communications process, each of the seven identifiable stages listed below can ultimately affect the accuracy of that process. The process, then, consists of the following stages.

1 *An information source*: an international marketing executive with a product message to communicate.
2 *Encoding*: the message from the source converted into effective symbolism for transmission to a receiver.
3 *A message channel*: the sales force and/or advertising media that convey the encoded message to the intended receiver.
4 *Decoding*: the interpretation by the receiver of the symbolism transmitted from the information source.
5 *Receiver*: consumer action by those who receive the message and are the target for the thought transmitted.
6 *Feedback*: information about the effectiveness of the message that flows from the receiver (the intended target) back to the information source for evaluation of the effectiveness of the process.
7 *Noise*: uncontrollable and unpredictable influences, such as competitive activities and confusion, which detract from the process and affect any or all of the other six factors.

Noise comprises all other external influences, such as competitive advertising, other sales personnel, and confusion at the receiving end, which can detract from the ultimate effectiveness of the communication. Noise is a disruptive force that can interfere with the process at any stage and is frequently beyond the control of the sender or the receiver.

Unfortunately, the process is not as simple as just sending a message via a medium to a receiver and being certain that the intended message sent is the same one perceived by the receiver.

For good reasons, message creation and language translation are the aspects most consistently and thoroughly discussed in the literature on global advertising. Even experienced advertising people commit mistakes with ease.

Message translation is complicated because of the cultural diversity among the various countries of the world. Language difference is only the most obvious manifestation of this diversity.

10.2.3 Media selection

Although nearly every sizeable nation essentially has the same kinds of media, there are a number of specific considerations, problems and differences that are likely to be encountered from one nation to another. In international advertising, an advertiser must consider the availability, cost, coverage and appropriateness of the media.

If message creation needs the collaboration of the agency and the advertiser (to ensure a unified positioning theme), media selection is one area where the agency and its local representative rule. The reason for this is primarily expertise. Local knowledge of the availability of media alternatives is absolutely necessary so that the optimal media, given the constraints, are chosen. It might be possible to direct an advertising campaign from overseas as far as budgeting, message creation and general direction go, but the media choices must be negotiated and made locally.

Rates of media usage are determined by a number of factors such as availability of commercial TV and radio, Internet, level of economic development, literacy rates, religion, and so on, and reflect directly, of course, the actual media selection decisions made by the advertisers and agencies for the country in question.

What type of media to select hinges (within availability constraints) very much on the objectives and target segment(s) of the campaign.

For *awareness*, TV serves well in many countries where it is generally available. In markets with lower rates of TV penetration, radio can often be used to supplement TV advertising. TV in most cases has the advantage of a high attention value, especially in countries where it is relatively rare.

Once the media types have been decided upon, the particular vehicles to be used within each type are usually selected on the basis of some efficiency criterion such as cost per mille (CPM). The use of an efficiency criterion requires information about how much advertising in a vehicle costs and how many people (in the target market) will be reached. Here a major problem is encountered in many markets. The available audience measurements are either incomplete (lacking audience demographics, for example), unreliable or even nonexistent at times. It can be very hard to find accurate figures.

10.2.4 Advertising budgeting

In domestic markets, a common method for advertising budgets is percentage of sales: setting a certain percentage of last year's sales as next year's budget. The figure arrived at can be adjusted by considering a changing competitive situation, increasing growth objectives or a squeeze on company profits; but percentage of sales has the advantage of establishing a stable and predictable expenditure level tied to revenues. The percentage chosen can be calibrated against the industry average ratio of advertising-to-sales, making for easy comparisons with competitors.

Although *percentage of sales* is popular among companies from most countries, it is not a very useful method for setting *global* advertising budgets. Even if total worldwide revenues can be used as a base, it is not clear what the appropriate percentage would be. Which country's industry average should be used as a starting point, for example? Different countries show widely different levels of advertising-to-sales ratios for the same industry, depending on media availability, competitive situation, and so on. Since the percentage of sales approach sets advertising on the basis of past sales, it is of little use when a shift from multidomestic to global advertising is contemplated. *Competitive parity* approaches, where advertising budgets are set on the basis of what competitors spend, are also of less relevance in global advertising. The main difficulty is in identifying the appropriate parity to actual and potential competitors from different countries, many of which have very different firm-specific advantages (FSAs) and market presence. Competitive parity is most appropriate when the major global competitors are from the same countries, as with Coca-Cola and Pepsi-Cola, or Sony, Matsushita, Sharp and other Japanese players in consumer electronics.

Budgeting for global advertising typically involves some version of the so-called *objective–task method* favoured domestically by more sophisticated marketers. In this method the objectives of the advertising are first made explicit and quantified, after which the requisite media spending to reach the required exposure levels is specified. Although precise calibration of spending is difficult because of the uncertainty in gauging worldwide audiences of media vehicles, the basic logic is sound. After the initial specification of the job to be done by advertising (target percentages for awareness, for example, or certain reach and frequency figures), the creative solutions and the media schedules likely to attain the desired levels are developed.

This is work requiring the expertise of an advertising agency with a global network. The budgeting done for global advertising involves an unusually large amount of agency input, since assessing the feasibility and cost of global campaigns requires input from the local branches in the agencies' global network. Partly for this reason, the drive towards global advertising is often spearheaded by an agency with global reach.

10.2.5   Executing the campaign

The drive towards global advertising has to a large extent been initiated by global advertising agencies that have developed worldwide networks of subsidiaries or affiliates.

Advertising, being so close to the cultural traditions of a country, was for a long time one of the more decentralized decisions in the multinational company. Headquarters would perhaps be setting the budget, but the basic positioning strategy would be determined by the local subsidiary and approved by headquarters. When it came to execution, including message creation and especially media selection, the advertising agency and its local branch were the prime movers.

The global advertiser, aiming to gain some benefits from a unified approach, has to take charge of this process more effectively. Positioning strategy has to be unified across countries and the unique selling propositions of the brand made clear – and the same – everywhere. That is the strategy part. As for execution, the global advertising manager needs to work closely with local personnel in the subsidiaries and in the agency network to get consensus on a message that transcends borders, reflects the brand accurately and has punch everywhere. As for media, although the agency must still be the main actor, the global advertiser will want to make sure that cost factors such as media discounts are properly taken into account. While doing all this, the global advertiser also needs to keep an open eye and open mind to suggestions from the local people, to quickly diffuse information through the various local affiliates, and to be flexible enough to change when new information and market research suggest this is necessary.

10.2.6   Standardization or adaptation of global advertising

The global advertiser faces a complex task. The communication has to be appropriate for each local market, while at the same time there is a need to co-ordinate campaigns and control expenditures across the globe. Because of the varying media availability in different countries, and the differing effectiveness of global media, the feasible channels for advertising will differ. But customizing the advertising to each individual country leads to increased costs and unwieldy control procedures.

The advertisements can be identical, usually with localization only in terms of language voiceover changes and simple copy translations. Pan-European advertising featuring Exxon gasoline's tiger in the tank and Marlboro cigarettes' cowboy are examples. In some cases the identical advertisement or commercials can be used without any translation at all. Levi's, the jeans manufacturer, uses cartoons with rock music and unintelligible, vaguely Esperanto-sounding vocals in one commercial where the Levi's-wearing hero rescues a beautiful woman from a burning building, an easily comprehended message. In other cases the commercials simply carry subtitles. IBM shows Italian-speaking nuns discussing the pros and cons of Internet surfing with subtitles translating the conversation: global advertising with a local touch. It might be assumed that global products and brands need global advertising. This is often true. Campaigns for Diesel, Club Med, Benetton and Reebok are very similar across continents. But there is often a need to do some local adaptation of global campaigns. For example, a global product and brand such as Levi's jeans targets specific segments with different appeals in each local market, since the positioning of the product and brand varies as the target markets differ.

Sometimes a brand's global campaign has misfired and the company has retreated to a more multidomestic adaptation. Parker Pen, a globally recognized US brand name, shifted to global advertising in the mid-1980s only to return to multidomestic advertising after sales slumped badly; the result was successful. The cause of the failure had been lack of co-operation on the part of the company's country subsidiaries, whose previously successful campaigns were discontinued.

In summary, global advertising is most powerful under the following conditions:

- the *image* communicated can be identical across countries
- the *symbols* used carry the same meaning across countries
- the product *features* desired are the same
- the *usage* conditions are similar across markets.

If all these conditions hold, as they do in the case of the airlines, global advertising is a natural. When one or more are not fulfilled – as in the case of Levi's – even standardized products may need adapted multidomestic advertising. If the conditions are not right, global advertising will fail, which helps explain why there is still so much controversy about global versus multidomestic advertising.

Exhibit 10.1: *Adaptation of Danone's international advertising*

From small beginnings, Danone has grown to become a global business that makes yoghurts, yoghurt drinks and fromage frais, designed to make it easy for all the family to live a healthier life. Today the Danone Group is the largest producer of fresh dairy products in the world. It produces 18 million tons of cheese, yoghurts and other dairy products per day.

Danone now employs in excess of 100 000 people worldwide and has a turnover of €15 000 m (2004). It is the world market leader in the dairy products market, where it controls 15.5 per cent. It is also market leader in the bottled water market with its Volvic and Evian brands, and number two in sweet biscuits with Jacobs and Lu.

Danone has adapted its advertising messages to suit different European market expectations. In France, yoghurt is typically sold plain, a symbol of good health. Fruit and flavourings come later, as advertising emphasizes the health aspect. In the UK, the product is often associated with indulgence: fruit adds to the pleasure of eating yoghurt. In Spain or Portugal, where fruit is abundant, consumers prefer plain yoghurt, eaten as much by children as by adults. In Italy, consumers prefer blended yoghurt, while flavoured varieties are positioned for very young children. Advertising messages are therefore adjusted accordingly to reflect these preferences.

Source: adapted from www.danone.com; www.business2000.ie

10.2.7   Consolidation of advertising agencies

As advertising agencies expanded their global reach, many advertisers started to centralize their advertising spending and appointed a single company as the global agency. This meant that many smaller agencies lost accounts as large companies consolidated their advertising spending. As a result, smaller agencies merged and became part of larger global networks. According to researchers, the emphasis on pan-regional campaigns is mainly due to the emergence of regional groupings and trading blocs.

Local agencies are often preferable (and sometimes the only ones willing to accept the assignment) when the account is small. The reason is that global agencies, owing to their sheer size, tend to neglect smaller accounts.

A breed of generalist 'integrated marketing communications agencies' has recently developed, threatening to reduce the traditional full-service advertising agency's role to provider of one specialist service among many, and starting a reversal of the trend towards multiple delegation.

10.3   Sales promotion

Sales promotion communicates via a variety of promotions not encompassed by any of the definitions above, each aiming for exposure to a target audience and some furthermore offering an incentive to respond actively.

Sales promotions are marketing activities that stimulate consumer purchase and improve retailer or middleman effectiveness and co-operation. They are short-term efforts directed to the consumer or retailer to achieve such specific objectives as consumer product trial or immediate purchase, consumer introduction to the store, gaining retail point-of-purchase displays, encouraging stores to stock a product, and supporting and augmenting advertising and personal sales efforts.

As is the case with advertising, the success of a promotion may depend on local adaptation. Further, research shows that responses to promotions can vary across promotional types and cultures. Major constraints are imposed by local laws, which may not permit premiums or free gifts to be given. Some countries' laws control the amount of discount given at retail, others require permits for all sales promotions. In markets where the consumer is hard to reach because of media limitations, the percentage of the promotional budget allocated to sales promotions may need to be increased. In some less-developed countries, sales promotions constitute the major portion of the promotional effort in rural and less accessible parts of the market.

10.3.1 Different types of sales promotion

Price-based promotions

Discount pricing and sales

Discounting is a widely used form of promotion in a range of markets. It is only effective where the additional sales volume will compensate for the lost revenue, and in markets where a reduction in price will not be interpreted as a reduction in quality. Discounts are a relatively expensive form of promotion in that they provide a price reduction for all consumers, regardless of their price and promotion sensitivity. Discounting also carries with it the danger that it will undermine the consumer's expected reference price, so that they come to expect discounting and will resist a return to 'normal' prices.

Money-off coupons

Coupons are a very popular form of promotion, particularly in fast moving consumer goods (FMCG) markets. Coupons can be delivered by direct mail, in stores, as inserts in publications or on packages. The traditional disadvantages of couponing are in the logistical effort of the redemption-handling process, and consumer resistance to the need to physically clip and carry coupons. New technology may overcome all these problems with innovations such as barcode scanning for coupons, and 'smart cards' for consumers that store information about coupon entitlements.

Improved payment terms

Interest-free credit and 'buy now, pay later' offers make purchase easier for consumers, and may reduce the real cost of purchase, while allowing the price to stay constant. Special payment terms are popular for relatively expensive consumer durables such as cars and domestic appliances.

Product-based promotions

Product samples

Samples are frequently used to encourage product trial for products such as foods, drinks and toiletries. There are a variety of methods of delivering samples, including direct mail, inserts within publications or packages, and sampling points inside stores. Sampling is a relatively expensive form of promotion, which often involves a high degree of wastage. It can also be difficult to assess its effectiveness, since there is no way to establish whether those who receive samples later go on to purchase (unless the sample is accompanied by a coupon).

Multipacks and multibuys

Offers of 'three for the price of two' are a useful means of getting consumers to stock up on a particular brand. Banding multiple product units or complementary products together can now be accomplished electronically through the use of electronic point-of-sale (EPoS) systems, rather than banding them together physically.

Improved product quality or features

Major consumer durables such as cars or new homes are often marketed with additional free features such as a car stereo or a free fitted kitchen.

Opportunity-based promotions

Competitions

Competitions are a very versatile promotional tool that can be aimed at consumers, intermediaries or the sales force. Selecting the right prize can help to reinforce the brand's image. The limited number of winners and known cost of prizes generally make competitions a very cost-effective form of promotion, and one that can appeal to a wide range of consumers.

Promotional information

A great deal of promotional activity involves providing prospective customers with information that assists their purchasing process. The information provided can also be put into an entertaining and informative format that reinforces the image of the brand and its advertising. Some companies issue information with little in the way of a direct 'selling' message, which aims to educate consumers and hopefully make them likely to act in the company's favour. For example, Procter & Gamble's introduction of Ariel detergent in Egypt included the *Ariel Roadshow*, a puppet show that was taken to local markets in villages, where more than half of all Egyptians still live. The show drew huge crowds, entertained people, informed them about Ariel's better performance without the use of additives, and sold the brand through a distribution van at a nominal discount. Besides creating brand awareness for Ariel, the roadshow helped overcome the reluctance of rural retailers to handle the premium-priced Ariel.

There are many benefits of using sales promotions, but they also have limitations. They will neither compensate for fundamental weaknesses in the rest of the marketing mix, nor revive the fortunes of an outdated brand, and overuse can be counterproductive. Many companies fail to integrate sales promotions with the rest of the marketing strategy and mix.

10.4   Public relations (PR) and sponsorship

10.4.1   PR

Creating good relationships with the popular press and other media to help companies communicate messages to their publics – customers, the general public and government regulators – is the role of *PR*. The job consists not only of encouraging the press to cover positive stories about companies, but also of managing unfavourable rumours, stories and events. Effective damage control – actions taken to limit spillover into negative public opinion – requires both good PR and timing.

Corporate communications staff at headquarters and their counterparts in the various host countries serve as promoters of the corporation to various stakeholders interested in the company's foreign expansion. These stakeholders can include a wide variety of groups: stockholders, employees, customers, distributors, suppliers, the financial community, media, activist groups, the general public and government.

PR companies' billings in the international arena have been growing at double-digit rates for some years. Handling such international PR problems as global workplace standards is big business for companies serving corporate clients such as Mattel Toys, McDonald's and, of course, Nike. Fast growth is also being fuelled by the expanding international communications industry. New companies need PR consultation in order to build an international profile.

10.4.2 Sponsorship

With the advent of global media the possibilities for global sponsorships are opening up. Sponsoring the soccer World Cup or the Olympic Games by plastering a brand name on bleachers and piggybacking on TV broadcasts has helped companies establish a strong identity in the global marketplace. It is somewhat unsettling, however, to see newspaper pictures of the star-studded national soccer team of Brazil and find that it is sponsored by Nike. Global promotion knows no boundaries.

The global reach of sporting events, which has created opportunities for products to become associated with globally recognized sports stars, has made these stars rich as well as famous. Soccer player David Beckham, for instance, receives more money from endorsements than from playing soccer.

The use of well-known athletes has its downside, though. When the superhuman perfection of the stars is called into question – the cases of O.J. Simpson and Magic Johnson come to mind – sponsorship can be a liability rather than an asset. Athletes do not last for ever either; as part of its efforts to streamline marketing costs in order to compete more effectively in the athletic footwear industry Nike has ceased sponsoring a number of star athletes, including former world number one tennis player Pete Sampras.

Exhibit 10.2: *Snickers sponsors key sporting events*

Snickers and Mars are two of the largest confectionery 'single bar' brands in the world. At a local level, Snickers' manufacturer Masterfoods Ltd in Ireland invests heavily in maintaining and strengthening its brand image. In the case of Snickers, Masterfoods has found that one of the most effective and targeted marketing tools at its disposal is the sponsorship of key sporting events, the strategy being to position it squarely as an energy booster – it is 'the big eat when you are hungry'.

Sources: adapted from: www.masterfooods.com; www.mars.com; www.business2000.ie

10.4.3 Celebrity endorsement

A recent estimate indicates that approximately 25 per cent of US commercials use celebrity endorsers (Silvera and Austad, 2004). In support of this practice, research indicates that celebrity endorsements can result in more favourable advertisement ratings and product evaluations, and can have a substantial positive impact on financial returns for the companies that use them. One possible explanation for the effectiveness of celebrity endorsers is that consumers tend to believe that major stars are motivated by genuine affection for the product rather than by endorsement fees. Celebrities are particularly effective endorsers because they are viewed as highly trustworthy, believable, persuasive and likeable. Although these results unequivocally support the use of celebrity endorsers, other research suggests that celebrity endorsements might vary in effectiveness depending on other factors like the 'fit' between the celebrity and the advertised product.

10.5 Internet promotion

The Internet is considered to be a global channel of communication, but advertising messages sent out via this medium are often perceived in the local context by the potential customer. Herein lies the dilemma that often causes the results of Internet promotion to be weaker than anticipated.

Traditional media have two capabilities: building brands and direct marketing. In general, most promotional forms are useful for one or the other. The Internet, however, has the characteristics of both broadcast mass media and direct response advertising.

In the traditional model of communications in the marketplace, there are clear distinctions between the sender, the message and the recipient, and control of the message is with the sender. In 'market space', control of the message is shared between sender and receiver because of the interactivity of the medium, the ability of the medium to carry a message back in reply to that sent, and the impact of the information technology (IT) on time, space and communication. The above impacts on the feedback loop are built into the Internet and hence give rise to interference. In general, however, this interference is more likely to be from Internet clutter than from external sources.

The web represents a change away from a push strategy in international promotion – where a producer focuses on convincing an intermediary to represent the products or services, or a distributor to stock its goods – and towards a pull strategy, in which the producer communicates directly with the customer. In this transition process promotional and other transaction costs are reduced. The feature that differentiates the Internet from other promotional vehicles is its interactivity. This results in the special feature that the Internet combines: the attributes of both selling and advertising. Interactivity facilitates a completely new approach to reaching potential customers. Unlike TV, for example, where the consumer passively observes, with the web there is an active intention to log on to the Internet, and a greater degree of attention to content as a result. With the Internet the potential customer has a high-involvement approach to advertising. A continual stream of decisions is demanded from the user: each click represents a decision and therefore the web is a very high-involvement medium. In addition, unlike traditional media, the web is a medium by which the user can 'click through' and obtain more information or actually purchase a product. Web advertisements can be, and often are, targeted to a user profile that in turn affects the way the message will be received. Increasingly, advertisements displayed on the web are specific to user interests and appear as these interests are revealed while the user navigates the web.

In order to provide value to the potential international customer, and hold their interest, a website must be attractive and user-friendly. This involves an appealing design, being available in the buyer's language (or one with which the buyer is likely to be familiar) and being aesthetically aware in terms of colours and backgrounds used (taking into account buyers' cultural norms). A site should be easy to navigate, contain the information that the buyer is likely to want and be easy to access.

The most common form of advertising on the web (as opposed to advertising the existence of a website) is banners across the top of commercial sites, known as 'banner ads' (Fletcher et al., 2004).

10.5.1 Effective online advertising strategies

An effective advertising strategy for online advertising aims to target the right advertisement message to the right person at the right time (Kumar and Shah, 2004).

Who to advertise to

Is online advertising for everyone? Experienced marketers will tell you that advertisement design depends on the type of product or service being sold and the desired target segment. Let us dig a layer deeper and divide the desired target segment into first-time visitors to the company's website, registered users and general information seekers. There is bound to be some overlap across these segments. However, this form of segmentation can provide useful insights when designing online advertising. Based on the user segment, a website can be programmed to respond appropriately. For example, every first-time visitor to a website can be made to see the same advertisement. Visitors identified as information seekers may be shown useful content instead of products and services, and registered users may see a customized advertisement message based on their profiles. Technologically, it is feasible to identify the type of user visiting a website by studying their browsing behaviour through clickstream data and by using files known as 'cookies' (a cookie is a piece of code that is retained on a computer user's hard disk, which enables a website to store information that can be retrieved later – the user's ID, preferences for that site, and so on).

How to advertise

After identifying the user or the website visitor, the next step is determining how to advertise or what format to use for advertising. There are several different formats currently being used for Internet advertisements. Interestingly, the form of advertising chosen by online marketers is undergoing a rapid transformation. What was previously dominant has now fallen out of favour, and what had been weak has now grown strong. The type of advertisement chosen should be directed towards not only 'pushing' the message across but also 'pulling' the customer to click deeper into the website by designing advertisements that contribute to the overall website experience. For example, a website with too many pop-up advertisements on its first page runs the risk of driving the user away.

What to advertise

People use the Internet to seek information as well as products and services. Marketers can be creative and design advertisements that simply offer helpful information to the user. For example, a user browsing for a digital camera may be offered useful tips and pointers on how to get the best results from digital photography. Non-commercial advertising like this may not have a short-term financial gain but may definitely contribute to a superior browsing experience leading to customer loyalty and repeat visits from the user.

If the customer's profile or past purchasing history is known, it is possible to predict future purchase behaviour. For example, let's assume that a user purchased a home appliance online. Given this information and the profile of the user (perhaps she is a woman, aged 30–40), it is possible to predict what she is most likely to buy next. The company can programme this information into its website code and the next time this user is detected returning to the website there will be an advertisement ready and waiting for her with the desired content. If deployed properly, this approach can help marketers to cross-sell products through combinations of online advertisement messaging.

When to advertise

The first three dimensions of the advertising strategy discussed so far will be rendered ineffective if the timing is not right. In the case of offline media, one can proactively call up the customer or send him or her a direct mailing at a specific time with a customized advertising message. However, these rules do not apply online; in the case of the Internet, users may decide to go online and visit the website during working hours, in the middle of the night or whenever they feel like it. Therefore, timing, in the Internet context, would refer to the time from the instant a user is detected online.

So when should the advertisement be triggered? As soon as the user comes online, after he or she has browsed for a while, or at the time of the first purchase? Studies conducted with Internet advertisement timings have indicated that generally response (clickthrough) to pop-ups is greater when the advertisement appears immediately after the user enters the site. However, the results could vary greatly depending on the user segment and the user's information-seeking purposes.

Amazon.com employs a subtle form of advertisement in real time. Basically, while performing a search for a particular book, the search also throws up a list on the side or bottom of the page of relevant books that may complement the book the user was originally considering for purchase. Also, when a user logs on to the site, Amazon pulls up their purchase history and profile to proactively suggest books or items that they may have a latent propensity to purchase next.

Where to advertise

It is crucial to make Internet advertisements visible at vantage points that maximize their hit rate with the intended target segment. Unlike other forms of media, where one can pick a well-defined spot within a finite set of possibilities, cyberspace offers an infinite number of possibilities across thousands of portals, search engines and online publishers, as well as multiple possibilities within the vendor's website. Identifying the perfect spot may seem like searching for a needle in a haystack.

There are two ways to tackle this. The first is to take the easy way out. Follow intuition and place advertisements at obvious locations, such as frequently visited portals and search engines. This is not, however, a cost-effective solution. A more sophisticated approach involves analysing the browsing pattern of an Internet user on a company's website using the website's log files. Analysis of these files can help model the browsing behaviour of a random visitor to the website. Based on this information, Internet advertising displays may be placed at appropriate locations. Marketing managers can also leverage this model to sell complementary products to potential users. For example, a department store such as Marks & Spencer may advertise cosmetics on the page where a user is buying fragrances online. An electronics store like Best Buy may advertise the latest CD releases on the page listing different audio systems.

However, this form of analysis is limited to advertising within the company's website. A more advanced research approach involves modelling browsing behaviour at multiple websites using clickstream data. Information analysed in this manner renders a total view of a customer's online habits before purchase consideration. Such information is invaluable to marketers who are interested in knowing when and where they are most likely to find their potential customers and, based on that information, how they should place Internet advertisements in order to pull in the relevant customers to their site.

Online performance tracking (metrics)

Having designed an online advertising strategy, the next critical step is to track its performance. Traditional offline media (radio, TV and print advertisements) have well-defined and well-researched metrics in place that can accurately measure advertising effectiveness. For example, there are many years of research testimony to show what a TV commercial can do; Internet advertisements have a long way to go on this front.

Some of the most commonly used measures include:

- *clickthroughs* – the number of times that users click on an advertisement
- *cost per click* – the amount spent by the advertiser to generate one clickthrough
- *cost per action/lead* (*CPA/L*) – the amount spent by the advertiser to generate one lead, one desired action, or simply information on one likely user; the advertiser pays an amount based upon the number of users who fulfil the desired action
- *cost per sale* (*CPS*) – the amount spent by the advertiser to generate one sale; here, the advertiser pays an amount based upon how many users actually purchase something.

Increasingly, a large number of marketers claim to be optimizing their online campaigns using the 'CPS' metric, but it is clear that they are looking at sales (through online advertisements) as strictly margin transactions. The problem with this approach is that, while each individual transaction may look profitable to start with, this may not necessarily hold true over the lifetime duration of the customer. Similarly, initial returns that seem to be unprofitable may translate into very profitable transactions when measured over the lifetime value of the customer.

Therefore, customer lifetime value (CLV), which may be defined as the measure of expected value of profit to a business derived from customer relationships from the current time to some future point, is perhaps the most relevant of all metrics (see also Chapter 11). It provides a direct linkage on a customer-by-customer basis to what is most important for any company: profits. Marketing spend and the outcome of advertisements guided by lifetime value measures would yield the most superior decision support system for a marketer. As companies become increasingly customer-centric, a switch to a CLV metric and building of buyer loyalty will become inevitable.

10.5.2   Building buyer loyalty

Using the web as a vehicle for building loyalty on the part of international buyers involves a number of different stages (Fletcher et al., 2004), as described below.

Attract

Attract clients to visit the website. They do so on a voluntary basis and will not come simply because a site has been created. To create awareness of a site, it is necessary to use banner ads and links to other sites.

Engage

Engage visitors' attention. This is necessary in order to get the visitor to a site to participate and encourage interaction. Most sites fail as promotional mediums because they are boring and have poorly presented material. In this regard, the content of the site is most important.

Retain

Retain the visitor's interest in your site. This is important to ensure repeat visits to the site and the creation of a one-to-one relationship between the company and its potential overseas customers. One way of achieving this is by persuading the customer to provide information on their requirements so that the company can customize its offering and thereby increase switching costs.

Learn

Learn about the client and their preferences. This is enabled by providing on the site an easy-to-use facility for feedback and comment. The use of cookies can assist in this.

Relate

Adopt a deliberate policy of building relationships with site visitors. This is achieved by providing value-added content, by tailoring the product/service to the needs of each customer and promising customized delivery.

10.5.3   The web as a customer acquisition tool

Attracting visitors to a company's website is a big step, but it is only the first: turning them into buyers is a bigger challenge, and one at which many online sellers fail. The average sales conversion ratio across online B2C merchants is just 1.8 per cent (Vishwanath and Mulvin, 2001).

Companies lose potential customers at different stages in the purchasing process (see Fig. 10.1). The stages at which customers lose interest can be summarized under the following headings:

- homepage
- product search
- after product found
- shopping cart
- failure to repeat purchase.

One reason for defection that applies throughout each of these stages is unacceptable download times.

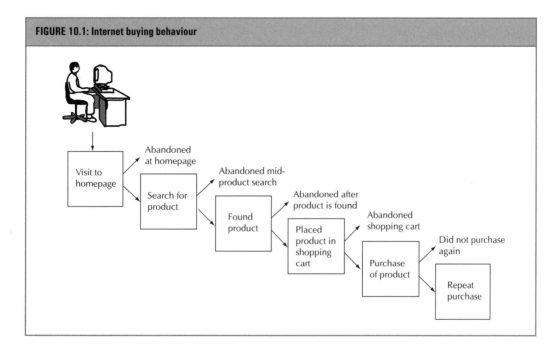

FIGURE 10.1: Internet buying behaviour

We now look at each of these stages in turn.

Abandoned at homepage

There are many reasons why a visitor may take one look at your homepage and decide to leave. Errant advertising is a leading cause.

Established 'clicks-and-mortar' companies have an advantage over pure plays in attracting visitors. People know from experience what the company sells. But even well-established brands can lose a significant percentage of their homepage visitors. Often, it is poor design features such as slow download time or confusing navigation that drive them away.

Abandoned mid-product search

Customers who leave the website while they are still perusing merchandise typically do so when they cannot find what they are looking for. Perhaps the selection is too limited or the shopper has run out of gift ideas. Best-practice merchants such as Victoria's Secret overcome such problems by feeding the visitor suggestions ('We think you'll also love …'), directing them to the recipient's wish list, or promoting online gift certificates.

Abandoned after product is found

Even after online customers find what they are looking for, many stop short of making a purchase. There are many reasons for this: for example, net shoppers who decide not to purchase gifts online may want to actually see the physical product before buying it. Tiny pictures and incomplete product information keep many browsers from buying online. Out-of-stock items and high prices are also deterrents. To stem the tide of customer defections at this stage of the buying process, some online merchants, such as Lands' End, offer a live chat feature so shoppers can get their questions answered on the spot.

Abandoned shopping cart

The foremost reason customers abort an online shopping trip is a cumbersome checkout process. Other reasons include excessive shipping costs and concerns about credit-card security or making returns. In this final moment of reckoning, multi-channel companies whose offline business has already established a strong brand and loyal customers are less likely to lose out on the sale. Retailers must have an efficient checkout process that minimizes the amount of information shoppers have to enter and closes the sale as quickly as possible.

Failure to repeat purchase

What is better than a new customer? A repeat customer, since repeat shoppers tend to spend more. One of the main reasons why customers do not return is delivery problems.

As the customer expectations are very high in this regard online marketers must make or buy a back-end system that will meet or exceed customer needs. Managing customer expectations is also important. In the case of stockouts or back orders, it is better to give shoppers the bad news *before* they submit an order rather than to send a follow-up email, as some e-retailers do. While the result may be a lost sale, preserving the customer relationship is more profitable in the long run.

Unacceptable download times

Another factor in customer abandonment that is relevant at all points in the transaction chain is slow download and server response times. Five seconds is considered the current 'breaking point' for page downloads, above which customers will go elsewhere. Even this number would seem to be on the high side – the top 10 online retailers all have download times under two seconds. Meanwhile, consumer expectations are continually rising. Companies that decline to make the necessary investments to keep their websites fast may see declines in sales and retention; but they should be careful how they invest in their sites – fancy graphics and interactivity features designed to simplify the purchase process can actually slow down transaction times, especially since many potential customers do not have high bandwidth. Even if the servers are adequate, a data-rich website (such as one with lots of images, flash capabilities or sound) may render your site maddeningly slow and impractical for a large percentage of your potential customers. The key for retailers is to find the balance between the site's marketing impact, its functionality, and the ability of company and consumer infrastructure to handle the content.

10.5.4   Viral marketing

Another example of cost-effective Internet promotion for online customer acquisition is *viral marketing*, which can be defined as a marketing technique that seeks to exploit pre-existing social networks to produce exponential increases in brand awareness, through viral processes similar to the spread of an epidemic. It is word-of-mouth delivered and enhanced online; it harnesses the network effect of the Internet and can be very useful in reaching a large number of people rapidly. From a marketing perspective, it is the process of encouraging individuals to pass along favourable or compelling marketing information they receive in a hypermedia environment.

Unlike traditional advertising viral is not an interruptive technique. Instead, viral campaigns work the Internet to deliver exposure via peer-to-peer endorsement. Viral campaigns, whether ultimately liked or disliked, are often welcomed by the receiver. The act of forwarding electronic messages containing advertising is voluntary rather than a paid testimonial or a mass advertising campaign and thus may be viewed more favourably by the recipient. The focus is on campaigns containing material that consumers want to spend time interacting with and spreading proactively.

Successful viral campaigns are easily spread. The key is to get your customers to do the hard work for you by recommending your company or its promotional offers to friends and colleagues, who in turn will recommend it to their friends, and so on. An effective viral marketing campaign can get your marketing message out to thousands of potential customers at phenomenal speeds.

When creating a campaign marketers should evaluate how people will communicate the message or campaign to others.

10.5.5   Mobile marketing

Mobile marketing, or m-marketing, should be considered within the context of m-business and m-commerce. Emerging from recent developments in communications technology, m-business represents 'mobile' business and refers to the new communications and information delivery model created when telecommunications and the Internet converge. Thus, m-marketing is defined as the application of marketing to the mobile environment of smart phones, mobile phones, personal digital assistants (PDAs) and telematics. M-marketing is characterized by both the interaction with the World Wide Web and the location-specific context, which enhances communication and delivery of information. Marketing communication and information can be delivered to mobile devices via voice-activated portals, or 'vortals', text applications such as SMS, using email (the current I-mode application), and via web-mediated delivery using the 3G spectrum.

M-commerce combines the power and speed of the Internet with the geographic freedom of mobile telephony in terms of receiving and transmitting data and, importantly, the ability to conduct transactions. The emerging capacity to communicate with any individual, from any place, over any network and to any device, regardless of time or geographical location, provides enormous potential for marketers. For this reason, the impact on marketing strategies for direct marketers needs to be addressed.

The emphasis on real-world interactions is paramount and creates a compelling difference between m-applications and traditional web-based delivery. The mobile environment is not suitable for surfing the net, sorting through large and random accumulations of information requiring large amounts of time; therefore, information needs to be in small 'packets', and products and applications should be developed around business models that are likely to deliver real value using the unique features and immediacy of mobile interactivity to target customers. Volvo was the first company to use direct m-marketing in Australia to launch the Volvo S60. This successful campaign using wireless hand-held palm pilots highlights the potential for targeting appropriate segments cost effectively by using opt-in email (Mort and Drennan, 2002).

10.6 Direct marketing

Direct marketing is defined by the Direct Marketing Association (DMA) as 'an interactive marketing system that uses one or more advertising media to effect a measurable response and/or transaction at any location'. It is a more encompassing concept than direct sales, which simply refers to sales from the producer directly to the ultimate consumer, bypassing the channel middlemen. Direct marketing is not so much a promotional tool as a new distribution channel, but it grew out of direct mail, which is a traditional advertising medium. The traditional direct mail promotions of various products often offered 'direct response' options, including requests for more information, redeemable money-off coupons, and participation in contests and lottery draws. It was only a small step to a completed sale, and especially since credit cards have become common, direct mail has grown into an important promotion *and* sales channel.

The traditional direct marketing medium is *mail order*, with catalogues and sales offers sent directly to individual households, which customers then order via email. The names and addresses are drawn from various lists – in the beginning often from subscription lists of newspapers and magazines but, currently, more often from commercial data banks that can screen for key words and develop lists of qualified prospects. In recent years, *telemarketing*, selling via the telephone, has grown, and so has direct-response television (DRTV), where TV commercials will list telephone numbers that allow viewers to call and make purchases.

With the growing presence of the Internet, direct marketing has become a very important channel. There is no doubt that the Internet has changed the way people communicate. For many, email has virtually replaced traditional letters and even telephone calls as a first choice for communication. Every day, billions of email messages are sent out. This has also influenced our way of doing business.

10.6.1 Email marketing

Done well, email marketing can be the most cost-effective communications tool you have. It is fast, inexpensive and effective, and its response rates are many times that of direct mail. Unfortunately, however, the email marketing landscape is littered with examples of marketers getting labelled as spammers, annoying customers, violators of privacy laws and worse.

A major strength of direct email is its ability to qualify leads. Appropriate software allows the company to track who is reading and responding, along with the types of response. This enables the company to segment the audience accordingly, targeting future communications based on recipients' self-reported priorities.

The following is an example of a checklist for launching a successful email marketing campaign (Linkon, 2004):

- *Solid planning*: have clear and measurable objectives, and plan your campaign as if it was a space shuttle launch.
- *Excellent content*: standards are higher with email, so make sure you are offering genuine value to the subscriber.
- *Appropriate and real 'from' field*: this is the first thing recipients look at when they are deciding whether or not to open an email.
- *Strong 'subject' field*: the next place recipients look before deciding whether to open an email is the subject field. Make it compelling.
- *Right frequency and timing*: do not overwhelm your audience. Do not send emails Friday to Monday or outside normal business hours.
- *Appropriate use of graphics*: do not get carried away. If graphics add real value and aren't too big, use them. However, save most of them for your website.
- *Lead with your strength*: do not bury your best content or offer. Make sure it is at the top or at the email equivalent of 'above the fold'.
- *Shorter is better*: nobody reads a lot these days, and they read even less in email than elsewhere.
- *Personalize*: use just three or four elements of personalization and your response rates can improve by 60 per cent. Try to go beyond just the first name. Learn about your subscribers.
- *Link to your website*: this is where richness of content and interactivity can really reside. Tease readers with the email so they will link to your website. Advertising can also be incorporated, serving the same role as the initial email: to create a desire in the audience for more information. The website catch page is crucial to this tactic and is often where many companies falter when integrating traditional advertising with online promotions. Let us say, for instance, that you are in the market for a small hand-held video camera and come across a magazine advertisement for exactly the product you need. The advertisement offers a web address, but when you go there you find the company's general website. It takes more than a dozen clicks before you find the product mentioned in the advertisement. You have gone from elation to frustration. A website catch page should fulfil your promise to the audience that when they go to the address, they will receive information on the offer that brought them there. From the catch page you can invite them to click to a more general website to make a donation, send a letter, sign a petition, learn who has endorsed your effort, or learn more about related causes, sales or promotions.
- *Measure and improve*: the ability to measure basics such as open and clickthrough rates is one of the main advantages of email marketing, but do not stop there: also track sales or other conversions. Learn from what works and make the necessary adjustments.

10.6.2 Social media and social networking

Social media encompasses a wide range of online, word-of-mouth forums including social networking websites, blogs, company-sponsored discussion boards and chat rooms, consumer-to-consumer email, consumer product or service ratings websites and forums, Internet discussion boards and forums, and sites containing digital audio, images, movies, or photographs, to name a few.

While Facebook, YouTube, MySpace and Twitter continue to dominate social media in the USA and some other countries, the global scene tells a different story. In Germany, Russia, China and Japan, the most visited social networking site is not Facebook but homegrown rivals.

Social networking as communication tools has two interrelated promotional roles (Mangold and Faulds, 2009):

1   Social networking should be consistent with the use of traditional integrated marketing communication (IMC) tools; that is, companies should use social media to talk to their customers through such platforms as blogs, as well as Facebook, MySpace or Twitter groups. These media may be either company-sponsored or sponsored by other individuals or organizations.

2   Social networking is enabling customers to talk to one another. This is an extension of traditional word-of-mouth communication. While companies cannot directly control such consumer-to-consumer (C2C) messages, they do have the ability to influence the conversations that consumers have with one another. However, consumers' ability to communicate with one another limits the amount of control companies have over the content and dissemination of information. Consumers are in control; they have greater access to information and greater command over media consumption than ever before.

Marketing managers are seeking ways to incorporate social media into their IMC strategies. The traditional communications paradigm, which relied on the classic promotional mix to craft IMC strategies, must give way to a new paradigm that includes all forms of social media as potential tools in designing and implementing IMC strategies. Contemporary marketers cannot ignore the phenomenon of social media, where available market information is based on the experiences of individual consumers.

The impact of the interactions among consumers in the social media space on the development and execution of IMC strategies is illustrated by the following points (Mangold and Faulds, 2009):

- The Internet has become a mass media vehicle for consumer-sponsored communications. It now represents the number one source of media for consumers at work and the number two source of media at home.
- Consumers are turning away from the traditional sources of advertising: radio, TV, magazines and newspapers. Consumers also consistently demand more control over their media consumption. They require on-demand and immediate access to information at their own convenience.
- Consumers are turning more frequently to various types of social media to conduct their information searches and to make their purchasing decisions.
- Social media is perceived by consumers as a more trustworthy source of information regarding products and services than corporate-sponsored communications transmitted via the traditional elements of the promotion mix.

10.7 Personal selling

Because of the importance of personal factors in selling, it is not surprising to find that good salesmanship varies across countries. Personal selling is usually the least global of all the marketing activities.

When a company wants to have more control than with independent distributors and takes over distribution in a country, it will usually end up establishing its own sales force. Doing this in a foreign country requires faith in the market and considerable resources. But some companies, especially those for which the selling function is a key success factor, have decided to take the plunge, and have done it successfully.

Structuring and managing a sales force (Cateora and Graham, 2004) involves:

- designing the sales force
- recruiting marketing and sales personnel
- selecting sales and marketing personnel
- training for international marketing
- motivating sales personnel
- designing compensation systems
- evaluating and controlling sales representatives.

We now look at each of these in turn.

10.7.1 Designing the sales force

Based on analyses of current and potential customers, the selling environment, competition, and the company's resources and capabilities, decisions must be made regarding the numbers, characteristics and assignments of sales personnel. All these design decisions are made more challenging by the wide variety of pertinent conditions and circumstances in international markets.

After decisions have been made about how many expatriates, local nationals or third-country nationals a particular market requires, then more intricate aspects of design can be dealt with, such as territory allocation and customer call plans.

Many things can differ across cultures: length of sales cycles, the kinds of customer relationship, and types of interaction with customers.

10.7.2 Recruiting marketing and sales personnel

The number of marketing management personnel from the home country assigned to foreign countries varies according to the size of the operation and the availability of qualified locals. The largest personnel requirement abroad for most companies is the sales force, recruited from three sources: expatriates, local nationals and third-country nationals. A company's staffing pattern may include all three types in any single foreign operation, depending on qualifications, availability and a company's needs.

The advantages and disadvantages of the three types of international sales force are summarized in Table 10.2.

Category	Advantages	Disadvantages
Expatriate (person sent out from home base – HQ)	• Greater control is possible from home base (HQ) • Knowledge about product, technology, history and management policies • High service levels • Willing to learn as it is often training for later promotion	• Highest costs • High training costs • Lack of local cultural understanding • High staff turnover
Host country (local person)	• Economical, 'good' solution • Best cultural knowledge • High market knowledge • Local language skills • Access to local network of relevant decision-makers	• Needs product training • May be held in low esteem • Importance of language skills declining • Difficult to ensure loyalty
Third country	• Allows regional coverage • Cultural sensitivity • Language skills • Economical • May allow sales to country in conflict with the home country	• May face identity problems • Income gaps • Needs product training • Blocked for promotion in the company • Resources needed for loyalty assurance

TABLE 10.2 Advantages and disadvantages of international sales force types

10.7.3 Selecting sales and marketing personnel

To select personnel for international marketing positions effectively, management must define precisely what is expected of its people. A formal job description can aid management in expressing long-range needs as well as current needs. In addition to descriptions of each marketing position, the criteria should include special requirements indigenous to various countries.

International personnel require a kind of 'emotional stability' not demanded in domestic positions. Regardless of location, these people are living in cultures dissimilar to their own; to some extent they are always under scrutiny and always aware that they are official representatives of the company abroad. They need sensitivity to behavioural variations in different countries, but they cannot be so hypersensitive that their behaviour is adversely affected.

Managers or sales people operating in foreign countries need considerable breadth of knowledge of many subjects, both on and off the job. The ability to speak one or more additional languages is always preferable.

An international sales person must have a high level of flexibility, whether working in a foreign country or at home. Expatriates working in a foreign country must be particularly sensitive to the habits of the market; those working at home for a foreign company must adapt to the requirements and ways of the parent company.

Cultural empathy is also clearly part of the basic orientation because it is unlikely that anyone can be effective if they are confused about their environment. Finally, international sales and marketing personnel must be energetic and enjoy travel.

Selection mistakes are costly. When an expatriate assignment does not work out, a great deal of money has probably been wasted in expenses and lost time. Getting the right person to handle the job is also important in the selection of locals to work for foreign companies within their home country.

10.7.4 Training for international marketing

Many companies send their new sales representatives into the field almost immediately upon hiring them, after only a cursory training programme. The rationale is that time is best spent prospecting and meeting with customers, rather than sitting in a training centre (Crittenden and Crittenden, 2004). It is true that detailed training can be costly and may result in lost opportunities when a seller is not in the field. Yet effective long-term sellers must not only have appropriate personal characteristics, but must also know and identify with the company and its products, understand customer buying motives, and be prepared to make an effective sales presentation, counter initial resistance, and close the sale. Moreover, to be successful, the seller has to know how to develop and maintain the records necessary to process orders, service customers and cultivate repeat sales.

The nature of a training programme depends largely on whether expatriate or local personnel are being trained for overseas positions. Training for expatriates focuses on customs and special foreign sales problems that will be encountered, whereas local personnel require greater emphasis on the company, its products, technical information and selling methods.

The Internet now makes some kinds of sales training much more efficient. Users can study text on-screen and participate in interactive assessment tests.

Companies may also need to devote resources towards training the trainers. Top sellers who move into positions where they also manage other representatives do not necessarily have the appropriate skills, mind-set or disposition to train others.

10.7.5 Motivating sales personnel

Motivation is especially complicated because the company is dealing with different cultures, different sources and different philosophies. Selling is hard, competitive work wherever it is undertaken, and a constant flow of inspiration is needed to keep personnel functioning at an optimal level. National differences must always be considered in motivating the marketing force.

Communications are also important in maintaining high levels of motivation; foreign managers need to know that the domestic office is interested in their operations, and, in turn, they want to know what is happening in the parent country. Everyone performs better when well informed. However, differences in language, culture and communication styles can make mutual understanding between managers and sales representatives difficult.

10.7.6 Designing compensation systems

Developing an equitable and functional compensation plan that combines balance, consistent motivation and flexibility is extremely challenging in international operations. Besides rewarding an individual's contribution to the company, a compensation programme can be used effectively to recruit, develop, motivate or retain personnel.

International compensation programmes also provide additional payments for 'hardship' locations and special inducements to reluctant personnel to accept overseas employment and to remain in the position. The compensation plans of companies vary substantially around the world, reflecting the economic and cultural differences in the diverse markets served.

It is difficult to design compensation programmes that motivate sales forces without financially ruining a company. The sections below take a closer look at some of the payment plans available.

Straight salary

Perhaps the simplest reward system for sales people involves paying a fixed amount each pay period. The major benefits to a company of paying by salary are greater control over wage levels and generally lower compensation for field sales people. With a salary plan, wages are a fixed cost to the company, and the proportion of wage expense tends to decrease as sales increase.

Straight salary is common in industrial selling where service and engineering skills are important. It is also effective when sales people spend their time calling on retailers to set up displays, take inventory and arrange shelves. 'Pharmaceutical detail' people, for example, are not expected to make direct sales and are paid a salary to strengthen relations with doctors and pharmacists. Because pay is not tied directly to performance, salary systems are often criticized for failing to provide incentives for extra effort.

Straight commission

A straight commission plan rewards people for their accomplishments rather than for their time. Also, sales people who are paid commission typically make more money than they do with other wage programmes. Higher wages tend to attract better qualified applicants and provide a strong incentive to work hard. Despite some obvious advantages, straight commission also has a number of drawbacks. The major problem is that sales managers have little control over sales people working on commission, and non-selling activities are likely to be neglected. Sales people working on commission are likely to be tempted to sell themselves rather than the company, as well as to service only the best accounts in their territories. Because sales people's wages are directly related to sales to particular accounts, sales people are often reluctant to have their territories changed in any way.

Combination plans

The most common compensation plan combines a basic salary with a commission and/or bonus. The basic salary provides sales people with income security and the commission and/or bonus offers an added incentive to meet the company's objectives. If a company wants a modest incentive, a plan could be designed so that 70 per cent of the compensation is salary and 30 per cent is earned by commissions or bonuses. Companies that need more push to move their products could raise the incentive portion to 50 per cent or more.

10.7.7 Evaluating and controlling sales representatives

In evaluation and control of sales representatives in the USA, emphasis is often placed on individual performance, which can easily be measured by sales revenues generated (often compared with past performance, forecasts or quotas). However, in many countries the evaluation problem is more complex, particularly in relationship-oriented cultures (e.g. in some European and Asian countries) where teamwork is favoured over individual effort.

Performance measures require closer observation and may include the opinions of customers, peers and supervisors. On the other hand, managers of sales forces operating in relationship-oriented cultures may see measures of individual performance as relatively unimportant.

10.8   Push and pull strategies

The distinguishing features of push and pull strategies are illustrated in Fig. 10.2 (note that both the wholesaler and the retailer are contained in the 'Distributor' box).

FIGURE 10.2: Push and pull strategies

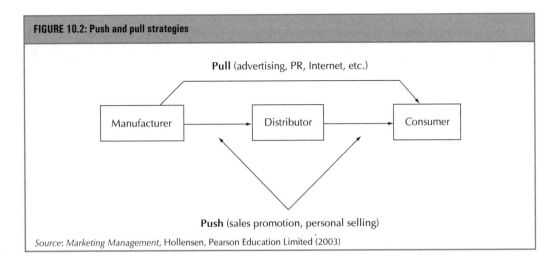

Source: *Marketing Management*, Hollensen, Pearson Education Limited (2003)

10.8.1   Push strategy

A push promotional strategy makes use of a company's sales force, and trade promotion activities create distributor demand for a product. The producer promotes the product to wholesalers, the wholesalers promote it to retailers, and the retailers promote it to consumers. A good example of push selling is mobile phones, where the major handset manufacturers, such as Nokia, promote their products via retailers such as Carphone Warehouse. Personal selling and trade promotions are often the most effective promotional tools for companies such as Nokia, for example, offering subsidies on handsets to encourage retailers to sell higher volumes. With this type of strategy, personal selling, sales promotion and trade promotion are the most likely promotional tools.

10.8.2   Pull strategy

A pull selling strategy is one that requires high spending on advertising and consumer promotion to build up consumer demand for a product. If the strategy is successful, consumers will ask their retailers for the product, the retailers will ask the wholesalers, and the wholesalers will ask the producers.

A good example of a pull is the heavy advertising and promotion of children's toys, mainly on TV. Consider the recent BBC promotional campaign for its new pre-school programme

Fimbles. Aimed at 2–4-year-olds, 130 episodes of *Fimbles* have been made so far, and they are featured every day on digital children's channel CBeebies as well as BBC2.

As part of its promotional campaign for *Fimbles*, the BBC has agreed a deal with toy maker Fisher-Price to market products based on the show, which it hopes will emulate the popularity of *Tweenies* (another successful TV series for young children). Under the terms of the deal, Fisher-Price develops, manufactures and distributes a range of *Fimbles* products, including soft, plastic and electronic learning toys, for the UK and Ireland.

In 2001, BBC Worldwide (the commercial division of the BBC) achieved sales of £90m from its children's brands and properties. The demand created from broadcasting *Fimbles* and a major advertising campaign were likely to pull demand from children and encourage retailers to stock *Fimbles* toys in stores for Christmas 2002.

Exhibit 10.3: *Donald Trump launches a fragrance for men*

In September 2004 Donald Trump announced a deal with Aramis and Designer Fragrances, a division of the Estée Lauder Company, to market his new business venture: Donald Trump, The Fragrance.

At the launch, Donald Trump said, 'My new partnership with Aramis and Designer Fragrances is huge. They are leaders in the industry. Donald Trump, The Fragrance, will be the best men's scent available and the must-have gift for the holidays.'

A spokeswoman for Estée Lauder said that the top note, or scent, of the cologne contains citrus notes with hints of mint, cucumber and black basil. The core note is made from an exotic plant – which the company keeps secret – that provides a green effect with woody undertones, rounded out with spicy, peppery accents. The finish comes from exotic woods and has earthy, herbaceous and spicy notes.

The geometric glass bottle in which the fragrance is sold is tall, slim and clear, and comes wrapped, of course, in gold packaging.

Aramis president Fabrice Weber said, 'We are confident that men of all ages want to experience some part of Mr Trump's passion and taste for luxury. People want to know him on every level.'

If you had responsibility for setting up an advertising plan for the Trump fragrance, what would your proposals be?

Source: adapted from Hargreaves (2004)

10.9   Combining communications and distribution: multi-channel customer management (MCCM)

Companies are moving towards the world of multi-channel integration where we will see an increasing integration between *distribution channels* (through which products or services reach customers from suppliers, including transfer of title) and *communication channels* (through which customers and suppliers communicate with each other before, during and after distribution channels do their work).

A broad definition of the term 'multi-channel customer management' (MCCM) is: 'Multi-channel customer management is the use of more than one channel or medium to manage customers in a way that is consistent and co-ordinated across all the channels or media used.'

Note that this definition does not say that customers are managed in 'the same way', as different channels may be best used for different tasks. For example, in a complex, technical, business-to-business environment, a sales person may offer the best way to explain the product, meet objections, deal with queries and set up initial contacts, while the web or a call centre might be used for reordering or checking progress with delivery. Also, it may be that channels are used in a differentiated manner; for example, if a person wants to buy tickets for last-minute cancellations by other customers (anything from flights to equipment orders), they are referred to an auction website as other channels cannot support this kind of interaction cost-effectively. Many companies are in a transition phase in terms of channel management:

- they are moving away from channels dedicated to restricted tasks and not communicating with each other, but are not certain how far to move towards channels that all work with the same data and to the same objectives
- they have seen some of the disadvantages of having different, and possibly incompatible, technology platforms for each channel, but are not certain of the benefits of moving to a single platform
- they have been through the process of setting up dotcoms as separate web channels
- separate web channels often had their own objectives, management, staff and systems, usually experienced escalating costs, provided a customer experience that was very different from that of other channels, and in some cases created brand damage and increased customer churn.

A multi-channel strategy is one that provides numerous customer touchpoints – the points at which products and services are purchased or serviced – across several distribution channels, such as:

- direct channels; for example, telephone, Internet, mobile telephone (voice, SMS) and interactive TV (iTV)
- counter and kiosk service in branch networks or retail outlets – partnerships and alliances – sales force
- service force.

In some cases, these may be supported by broadcast media in which the customer is not necessarily identified (e.g. TV, radio, press and some web applications).

10.9.1 Why is MCCM important now?

There are two main reasons for the current importance of MMCM:

1 *Developments in new channel technology*: increasing reliability and speed of storage and telecommunications technology, convergence of voice, video and data.
2 *Customer requirements and expectations*: some (not all) customers expect technology and processes to be used to manage them more consistently across channels.

Although it is now easier to ensure that every channel dealing directly with a given customer has the latest data on the state of interaction between supplier and customer, and follows related, connected processes, this is neither cost-free nor without technical problems. In particular, it should be noted that the companies for whom it is suggested that MCCM will yield the most benefits are those for whom achieving it is most problematic. They have the largest customer bases, the most complex lines and the longest history of systems development, with many business-critical systems that support the process of customer management being quite old. This applies, for example, to many companies in the financial services, logistics and manufacturing industries.

10.9.2 Drivers of multi-channel customer management

The seven factors discussed below are causing companies to focus on MCCM.

Customer demand

Customers' desire for convenience has partly fuelled the increasing requirement for multi-channel integration. Increased customer expectations translate to a demand for 24/7 high-speed access and choice in how they interact with a company. Customers often have strong preferences for using a specific channel for particular kinds of interaction; for example, they may use the in-store channel to commit to a buying decision, while using the more convenient online channel for exploring options.

Strategic competitive advantage and differentiation

Products can be copied within days (some fashion retailers can copy a design from the catwalk and get it on to the high street within a week). Pricing can be undercut within minutes. Apart from branding, MCCM is one of the few customer-facing differentiators that can deliver true sustainable competitive advantage.

Channel costs

Maintaining channels (including marketing, advertising and managing the channels themselves) can typically account for around 40 per cent of a company's costs. Channels tend to be managed and maintained in silos, with multiple infrastructures, management teams, technology and, possibly, different marketing strategies. The potential sharing and reuse of people, process and technology that can be achieved through an integrated channel strategy can, however, help improve an organization's channel cost structure. Furthermore, the mapping of high-value customer usage and preferences can help identify channel areas of overinvestment and channels that are not providing their optimum rate of return (ROI), consequently pinpointing those channels that require some form of disinvestment and asset reallocation.

Allowing customers to manage relationships

Badly executed customer relationship management (CRM) – as, sadly, many CRM implementations are – can result in the organization trying to control customers almost against their will through specific channels at specific times in the buying cycle. Customers can end up being made to feel like cattle being herded. Customer satisfaction and sales plummet. The term 'customer-managed relationship' (CMR) recognizes the possibility of the customer being in control and the idea that it is the supplier's job to nurture and service the relationship.

Convergence of channel roles

Traditionally, channels were usually silos with most, if not all, of the functions required in the customer-buying cycle being fulfilled through one channel. Now, at many companies, several channels are used during each customer-buying cycle and these need to be designed, maintained and measured appropriately.

Increased variety in customers' channel use patterns

Those who synchronize their distribution channels will preserve or gain market share. Research has shown that multi-channel shoppers in the financial services and retail sectors represent an increasingly large proportion of the attractive buying population. Furthermore, in the retail banking sector, multi-channel customers are 25–50 per cent more profitable than those using one channel, while retail shoppers who use multi-channel purchasing spend 2–4 times more than those who purchase through a single channel. These findings are reinforced by the Boston Consulting Group (BCG), whose research revealed that European retailers who have an offline presence and manage an integrated Internet channel enjoy a disproportionate market share, and that online satisfied customers spend 71 per cent more and transact 2.5 times more than dissatisfied ones (Stone, 2002).

Providing the target high-value multi-channel customer segment with increased convenience through integrated channel management thus not only encourages customer lock-on and brand loyalty, but results in improved customer lifetime value.

Regulatory pressure

In some sectors (e.g. financial services, the public sector) government has a strong interest in the cost-effectiveness and quality of channel use, particularly where high channel costs lead to customers apparently getting poor value or even to customers being excluded or disenfranchised.

10.9.3 Benefits of and problems with MCCM

The benefits

The benefits of MCCM are numerous. These include benefits that work *through customers*, ones that work *for customers* and ones that work *through efficiency*, as described below.

The benefits for companies working with MCCM are:

- the identification and capture of opportunities for increasing value per customer
- increased convenience and an improved experience, reducing customer churn rates and increasing their motivation to buy more from the supplier
- the ability to leverage an established brand, creating positive impacts on brand perception and mitigating the risk of brand damage, increasing the incentive for customers to stay and buy more
- increased efficiency through the sharing of processes, technology and information

- increased organizational flexibility
- increased efficiency in dealing with business partners, so they can reduce their costs
- increased efficiency in exploiting customer data to identify customer needs, possibly indicating new paths for growth.

The benefits for customers are:

- increased choice in the way they can interact
- the ability to switch easily between the various channels, when it suits them and wherever they want to, depending on their preference and the type of interaction, whether it be the exploration or purchase of a product or service.

For the supplier, channel integration helps facilitate the sharing of customer data across channels to create a more complete customer profile, which will help maximize cross-selling opportunities.

Problems

Multi-channel integration does not come without its challenges, however. Problems experienced by companies include:

- heavy investment in unconvincing multi-channel strategies and technologies that result in a poor ROI
- problems in bringing together and standardizing data about customers or resulting from interactions with them
- problems unifying different systems that may have very different data models
- difficulties in reducing or abolishing organizational boundaries.

10.9.4 Managing MCCM

Determining channel functionality

Careful thought needs to be given to the use of each channel in multi-channel programmes – 'one channel fits all' is no longer the case. Car buyers do not just visit their local dealer any more, and TV buyers no longer just go down to their local electrical store. Research shows that many customers use multiple channels throughout the buying cycle; some channels are used to research while others are used to purchase or service.

If a company decides to adopt a multi-channel strategy, it must consider whether all its channels should offer the same range of products and services, and whether all channels should support all functionality areas. If necessary, one channel can perform all three functions: online retailers or bricks-and-mortar retail outlets, for example.

It is essential to define the role of the various channels and how they interact. This helps identify and clarify target customer usage and preferences. Customer experience should be the starting point for defining required channel functionality.

Consistency

Suppliers should plan for consistency of their brand, customer information and the customer experience across different channels. Channel synchronization may be used to deliver a consistent customer experience. Consumers can become frustrated when suppliers' online channels sell only a selection of their offline products or services, or different products or services altogether. Many suppliers, however, offer either the same or fewer product categories online as in other channels. In order to improve consistency in the product/services offering, suppliers should stage online product rollouts, first focusing on depth in their core product/services categories, then adding breadth through new complementary products and, finally, once the depth and breadth of products online reach critical mass, suppliers should introduce less obvious categories and services, both on- and offline. Alternatively, the on- and offline channels should be clearly positioned as different.

Consistency in customer service and promotions

Services and promotions can be integrated across channels. Companies can use various strategies to achieve this: merging mailing lists to target email and catalogue promotions better; launching cross-channel loyalty programmes to increase customer retention; rewarding customers for whichever channel they complete their transaction within; and using bricks-and-mortar stores to provide local services to improve customer convenience for online shoppers. Examples of the latter include accepting returns in-store from online shoppers and offering in-store pick-up to get online shoppers to favour them. Where companies fail to integrate services and promotions across channels, this will shift the balance of business elsewhere as customers' expectations are not met.

Pricing

In making the transition from single- to multi-channel approach, companies face the challenge of pricing issues (i.e. can they charge different prices to their customers for the same product on- and offline?). Many believe that charging different prices for the same product from the same company is not feasible; customers expect to be charged the same price whether purchasing online or offline, whether or not it is more cost-effective for a supplier to sell online. The argument of suppliers is that a universal pricing strategy is not realistic, as offline customers must inevitably pay a premium for the added satisfaction of the in-store shopping experience. Therefore, in developing a channel strategy, companies must give consideration to the very real consumer pricing expectations: consumers expect prices to be competitive, whichever website they purchase from, and regardless of whether the site is a pure Internet operation or an online channel as part of a wider multi-channel operation.

Organizational issues

Multi-channel integration requires a new organizational model – one that adapts people, processes and technology to meet this co-ordinated approach to channel management. Redefining the organization, and the processes and technology that support it, to meet the multi-channel challenge, requires strong support from the chief executive and the senior management team. They need a clear vision of how channel integration will generate business value for the organization and where the main changes need to be in the organization. Decisions will need to be taken on the size of team and the skills needed to ensure the necessary resources and flexibility. Employees must have the right skills to understand increasingly sophisticated customers, analyse customer preferences and create value from these customer relationships.

An organization is unlikely to get it right first time, so it is vital to measure, monitor and review channel integration programmes. Financial measures are important, but they are a blunt instrument in a multi-channel world where not all channels are used to fulfil or close the deal. Instead, a balanced scorecard approach is needed in which a mixture of relevant strategic and operational measures are applied. This includes customer-focused measures, innovation and learning measures, and process measures, all of which drive the financial and value measures. Profit rather than sales targeting should be used (sales targeting focuses on promoting volume at the expense of profits and the quality of the customer base, while profit targeting focuses on contribution rather than volume and provides a basis for prioritizing multi-channel offers).

Consideration should be given to how to measure employees. They should be judged on customer profitability (present or ideally estimated future), and organizations must train their employees to develop the right skills in order to create the necessary company relationship. Organizational processes must be redefined to overcome organizational barriers, reduce operational costs, increase efficiency and improve the cross-channel customer's experience. Organizational structures can be a barrier to multi-channel integration when a company is product- or function-focused rather than customer-focused.

While developing a new organizational model for multi-channel integration, organizations should consider cross-channel opportunities generated through channel co-operation. Online co-operation of retailers with their manufacturers can enhance sales through referrals.

The power of manufacturers online lies in their ability to affect retailers' sales, both on- and offline. Consumers will take what they have learned while visiting manufacturer websites and spend their money in bricks-and-mortar stores and via catalogues. A bricks-and-mortar employee is unlikely to divert customers to a low-cost web channel if this reduces their bonus entitlement. Consequently, single-channel metrics should be replaced with cross-channel metrics. This may include crediting one channel for purchases through another channel, or rewarding different customer service representatives for their shared involvement in resolving a customer inquiry.

An example of a five-stage 'road map' for formulating a multi-channel strategy is as follows.

1 Analyse the industry structure; use market mapping and intermediation analysis.
2 Define channel chains to describe how channels combine to serve customers through their lifetime; consider both current and potential combinations and fit with customer life cycle.
3 Compare value proposition; use the channel curve to test whether a channel innovation will win market acceptance.
4 Set channel strategies; consider strategic options and the channel mix using the classic channel choice portfolio matrices for prioritizing.
5 Determine channel tactics; consider organizational structure, human resources (HR) and reward systems, as well as project management and IT.

A starting point could be to transform yesterday's cost-intensive call centre into today's multi-channel customer interaction centre (CIC). The CIC is the first line of communication with customers and its 'hub-like' quality means that all customer touchpoints and departments connect to it. The solution can include call recording on a sampling basis, searchable tagging to route intelligence about customers to where it is needed most, and the ability to monitor any call at any time from any location. Another advantage is the ability to build and maintain a data-rich profile of each customer such that, even if a customer leaves and then returns, the company is able to view and maintain a complete record of the relationship.

Summary

Despite the pitfalls of standardized and translated messages, global advertisements have become an important alternative to adapted multidomestic advertising. For the global marketer, faced with increasing spending needs in all markets, a co-ordinated effort with synchronized campaigns, pattern standardization and unified image across trade regions is usually more effective and cost-efficient than multidomestic campaigns. The major problem facing international advertisers is designing the best messages for each market served. The potential for cross-cultural misunderstandings is great in both PR and in the various advertising media. The availability and quality of advertising media also vary substantially around the world.

Advances in communication technologies (particularly the Internet) are causing dramatic changes in the structure of the international advertising and communications industries.

Building an effective international sales force constitutes one of the international marketer's greatest concerns. The company's sales force represents the major alternative method of organizing a company for foreign distribution and, as such, is in the front line of a marketing organization.

The importance of personal selling to the achievement of company marketing objectives, and to the efficiency of the exchange process, must not be underestimated. Sales people provide information on their products and services, use persuasion and sales skills to obtain and sustain a competitive advantage, and are responsible for building a relationship between a supplier and its customers. These activities are fundamental to both customer satisfaction and the competitiveness of the company.

Consumers are becoming ever more multi-channel in behaviour – using specific channels at various stages of the interaction process. Consequently, companies must understand their customers' expectations, in particular their customers' interaction preferences and patterns of behaviour across different channels, particularly for those segments that are critical to the company's future. They must improve channel performance for these segments rather than trying to be all things to all customers.

Questions for discussion

1 How does the standardized versus localized debate apply to advertising?
2 Comment on the opinion that 'practically speaking, neither an entirely standardized nor an entirely localized advertising approach is necessarily best'.

3 How does each stage in the communications process require modification when communicating in international markets?

4 Why do more companies not standardize advertising messages worldwide? Identify the environmental constraints that act as barriers to the development and implementation of standardized global advertising campaigns.

5 Identify and discuss the problems associated with assessing advertising effectiveness in foreign markets.

6 Compare domestic communication with international communication. Explain why 'noise' is more likely to occur in the case of international communication processes.

7 Is international personal selling a reality? Or is all selling national, regardless of who performs it?

8 What is the role of PR in global marketing?

9 Evaluate the 'percentage of sales' approach to setting advertising budgets in foreign markets.

10 Why are trade shows (exhibitions) an ideal medium for the exporter to introduce products in the international market?

11 How can trade shows (exhibitions) be used as a vehicle for researching opportunities in the international market?

12 When would you use a technical seminar in preference to a trade show (exhibition)?

13 Identify and discuss the problems associated with allocating the company's promotion budget across several foreign markets.

14 What effect will the Internet have on international marketing communications?

References

Baker, M. (2000) *IEBM Encyclopedia of Marketing.* London: Thomson Learning.

Cateora, P.R. and Graham, J.L. (2004) *International Marketing,* 12th edn. Maidenhead: McGraw-Hill.

Crittenden, V.L. and Crittenden, W.F. (2004) Developing the sales force, growing the business: the direct selling experience, *Business Horizons,* 47(5): 39–44.

Fletcher, R., Bell, J. and McNaughton, R. (2004) *International e-Business Marketing.* London: Thomson Learning.

Hargreaves, S. (2004) Trump: The Fragrance, *CNNMoney.* Available online at money.cnn.com.

Hollensen, S. (2003) *Marketing Management.* London: Financial Times/Prentice Hall.

Kumar, V. and Shah, D. (2004) Pushing and pulling on the Internet, *Marketing Research,* 16(1): 28–33.

Linkon, N. (2004) Using e-mail marketing to build business, *TACTICS,* November: 16.

Mangold, W.G. and Faulds, D.J. (2009) Social media: The new hybrid element of the promotion mix, *Business Horizons,* 52: 357–65.

Mort, G.S. and Drennan, J. (2002) Mobile digital technology: emerging issues for marketing, *Journal of Database Marketing & Customer Strategy Management*, 10(1): 9–23.

Silvera, D.H. and Austad, B. (2004) Factors predicting the effectiveness of celebrity endorsement advertisements, *European Journal of Marketing*, 38(11/12): 1509–27.

Stone, M. (2002) Multichannel customer management: the benefits and challenges, *Journal of Database Marketing*, 10: 39–52.

Vishwanath, V. and Mulvin, G. (2001) Multi-channels: the real winners in the B2C Internet wars, *Business Strategy Review*, 12(1): 25–33.

CASE STUDY 10: SUNTORY WHISKY

'For relaxing time, make it Suntory time'

Company history and background

Shinjiro Torii founded Suntory in 1899 under the name Torii Shoten wine store. In 1907 Akadama Port Wine, a sweet grape wine, was introduced. The Torii Shoten store was named Kotobukiya later in 1921. The group opened Japan's first whisky distillery, known as Yamazaki Distillery, in 1923 and launched the nation's first whisky, Suntory Shirofuda (now called Suntory White), in 1929. The Suntory Whisky expanded its business overseas in 1931. In 1936, the group opened Yamanashi Winery, later renamed Tomi no Oka Winery. In 1961 the Suntory Museum of Art was established.

Currently, the Suntory Group (Suntory) is a Japanese company with diversified operations. The Group is one of the leading producers and distributors of alcoholic and non-alcoholic beverages in Asia. The Group operates in Japan, Asia Pacific, the Americas and Europe. Its headquarters are in Osaka, Japan and its employees total nearly 22 000 as at 31 December 2008.

Suntory, being a privately owned company, does not announce its financial results in the public domain. However, the Group recorded revenues of JPY1 513 000 m (approximately US$15 130 m) during the financial year ended December 2008, an increase of 1.2 per cent over 2007.

Suntory operates three lines of business: food and non-alcoholic beverages; alcoholic beverages; and restaurants, sports, flowers and services. Each of these business lines represents a separate business unit. In January 2009, Suntory announced a switch to a holding company structure effective from April 2009. Under the new structure, the Group started operating soft drink, health food, alcoholic beverage and wine operating companies, a beverage manufacturing company, a liquor sales company and a business support company, all under the holding company, Suntory Holdings Limited.

This case focuses on Suntory's alcoholic beverage business, called *United Spirits Limited* (*USL*), especially the whisky business.

The alcoholic beverages business is involved in the production of alcoholic beverages such as beer, cocktails, whisky, liqueurs, spirits, wine and shochu (Japan's traditional distilled spirits). The Group conducts a global wine business in co-operation with foreign wineries such as Chateau Lagrange winery, Chateau Beychevelle in France, Weingut Robert Weil in Germany and Tokaj Hetszolo in Hungary. The Group's other brand, Midori, is established as a global brand and operates in the Americas, Australasia, Europe and Asia.

Suntory whisky in Japan and abroad

Suntory gained fame after its whisky was featured in the film *Lost in Translation* in 2003, starring Bill Murray as Bob who is in Japan to make a whisky commercial for Suntory. In one scene the Japanese director of the scene speaks rapidly in Japanese to Bob, giving him instructions on how he wants Bob to be in the commercial. The scene ends with Bob making the final and famous statement: 'For relaxing time, make it Suntory time.'

As Suntory's whisky operation has now taken over 60 per cent of Japan's whisky market, it has a similar position in Japan as Jack Daniel's has in the USA. For a large Japanese company like Suntory, it is not unusual to pay multimillion dollars to hire an ageing US actor to promote the company's famous product to Japanese consumers, who are fascinated by the US Hollywood stars.

Whisky, whether domestic or imported, is a very popular drink among Japanese consumers, perhaps even more popular than Sake. The term 'Sake' can actually mean all types of alcohol in general.

As you see in *Lost in Translation*, in Japan alcohol is much more socially accepted and exposed in public compared to in the USA; vending machines sell alcohol on the street, whisky advertisements are everywhere and Bill Murray gets lost in translation while making TV commercials of the whisky.

Drinking has been a big part of Japanese society for centuries. The history of Japanese whisky-making goes back to the early twentieth century. Masatake Taketsuru was the first person to bring the whisky distillation techniques home from Scotland in 1917, after learning the art of blending at the University of Glasgow. He established the Nikka company in 1934.

Shinjiro Torii of Suntory was the first person to build a distillery, in 1923. His goal was to produce a whisky that goes well with Japanese traditional food. He also sought a steady balanced taste that could not be broken by diluted water. As a result, 'Mizu-wari' became a common way of drinking whisky; 'mizu' means water and 'wari' refers to 'to cut' or 'on the rocks.' Mizu-wari whiskies are usually taken with a meal instead of before or after the meal as in western countries.

Because Japanese learned whisky-making from the Scots, it is spelt 'whisky' without an 'e' as in the Scottish way, unlike US bourbon whiskey or Irish whiskey, spelt with an 'e' with some exceptions.

The world whisky market

On a global basis, consumption of whisky represents approximately 10 per cent of all spirits consumption in the world. During the last five years the sectors driving spirits growth were mainly the dark spirits (whisky, brandy, cognac and dark rum). This trend is expected to continue in the coming five years, with most growth coming from local products in emerging markets, especially India.

As shown in Table 10.3, Asia is the leading region in the world whisky consumption.

	Total volume Millions of litres	Volume – Litre per capita	Total value – €m (retail selling prices)	Value – € per capita (retail selling prices)
World	1,623	0.2	22,372	3.3
Asia Pacific (India and China, etc)	795	0.2	7,041	1.9
Australasia (Australia and NZ)	22	0.9	804	15.1
Eastern Europe	34	0.1	997	3.0
Latin America	93	0.2	2,188	3.8
Middle East and Africa	42	0.0	568	0.5
North America	342	1.0	4,956	14.7
Western Europe	293	0.6	5,815	12.1

TABLE 10.3 World whisky[1] consumption – retail sector (2008) in different parts of the world
Source: adapted from Euromonitor.com
[1] The whisky category includes: single malt Scotch whisky, blended Scotch whisky, bourbon/other US whiskey, Canadian whisky, Irish whiskey, Japanese whisky and other whisky.

Company	Market share (2008) %
UB Group (India)	18
Pernod Richard Groupe (France)	16
Fortune Brands Inc. (USA)	13
Brown-Forman Group (USA)	6
Jagatjit Industries Ltd. (India)	5
William Grant & Sons Ltd. (UK)	3
John Distilleries Ltd. (India)	3
Allied Blenders & Distillers Plc (India)	2
Constellation Brands Inc (USA)	2
Suntory (Japan)	2
Rest	30
Total	100
Total volume/value in the world market	Volume: 1,623 million litres Value: €22,372 m

TABLE 10.4 Global market shares of whisky consumption (Top 10)
Source: adapted from www.euromonitor.com

The future growth in whisky consumption is also expected to come mainly from the emerging countries in Asia (India and China). India is the biggest whisky market of the world. Table 10.4 shows the global market shares of the world's largest whisky producers.

Since 2002 new whisky producers have entered the Top 10 list, mostly from India. The world's largest whisky producer is the Indian United Breweries (UB) group, which is also India's largest spirits company, with a portfolio of 140 brands. In May 2007, the UB Group completed the acquisition of the world's sixth largest Scotch whisky producer, Whyte & Mackay. This acquisition helped the UB Group move from being the world's second largest whisky producer to being the leading one in 2008.

Though Suntory has a leading position in the Japanese whisky market, the brand has fallen on the worldwide Top 10 from position 7 in 2002 to 10 in 2008.

Questions

1　How could Suntory have made better use of the 'endorsement value' for Suntory whisky, which was featured in the film *Lost in Translation*?
2　How can Suntory make a comeback in the Top 10, from its current position (no. 10) in the world whisky market? Which communication tools should be utilized and in which combination?

Sources: www.suntory.com; www.euromonitor; Tabuchi, H. and Wassener, B. (2009) Japanese beverage rivals may join to form a giant, *New York Times*, 13 July.

PART 03

Implementing and Managing the Marketing Plan

Part Contents

Developing and managing customer relationships

❖ LEARNING OBJECTIVES

After studying this chapter you should be able to do the following:

❖ Discuss loyalty, satisfaction and perception of value as determinants for development of the customer relationship management (CRM) strategy.

❖ Understand how CRM, one-to-one marketing and global account management (GAM) differ from each other.

❖ Explain how customer lifetime value (CLV) can be measured.

11.1 Introduction

Simply put, marketing is all about *creating value* for customers. Currently, many companies profess to be dedicated to value creation or adding value for their customers. The sad fact, however, is that few really understand their customers well enough to know exactly how they should go about creating or adding value in ways that customers will recognize and appreciate. Many organizations fall into the trap of attempting to create value for customers, using as a definition management's own view of what the customer wants.

Customer relationships may be viewed as long-term customer commitment or loyalty, which results from the fact that customers are satisfied not only by the organization's products and services, but also by how they are treated by it and its employees, and are made to feel as a result of their contact and association with the organization.

Long-standing customer relationships represent an organization's most valuable assets, assets that will pay dividends well into the future. By knowing how much equity really resides in its customer relationships, an organization can have a very good understanding of how these relationships will pay returns to shareholders in the future through their contribution to a stream of revenue on which the organization can rely.

The measurement of concepts such as service quality, customer satisfaction and customer relationship equity has to be tied directly to strategy. Many organizations have established a corporate strategy of 'relationship marketing' (RM) on the premise that they will achieve success through the creation and enhancement of customer relationships.

11.1.1 About this chapter

This chapter is structured as illustrated in Fig. 11.1, which shows the forces (as discussed in Sections 11.2, 11.3 and 11.4) that determine the subsequent strategies:

- customer relationship management (CRM) (Section 11.5)
- one-to-one marketing (Section 11.6)
- global account management (GAM) (Section 11.7).

It is important to understand that all three management concepts are part of the same RM paradigm.

In Section 11.8 we examine how to create long-term customer value and how to measure customer lifetime value (CLV).

11.2 Loyalty

Loyalty, like so many other concepts that we encounter when discussing consumer psychology and marketing, is a state of mind. As is implied above, loyalty is a subjective concept, one that is best defined by customers themselves. There are, of course, *degrees* of loyalty: some customers are more loyal than others, and customers are very loyal to some organizations and less loyal to others. Some customers may be loyal to more than one organization or brand within a product or service category. This is particularly so where to give one organization all of one's business simply does not make sense, as in the case of restaurants. Very few people will be completely loyal to one restaurant to the point where it

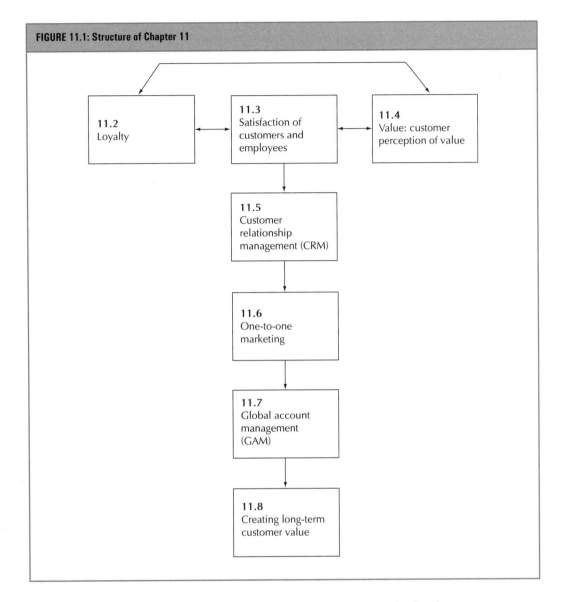

FIGURE 11.1: Structure of Chapter 11

is the only restaurant they would ever patronize. But is possible to be loyal to a restaurant, or even to have a relationship with it, and yet visit it very infrequently.

Consumers and businesses will define loyalty in many different ways. Often longevity of customer patronage and repeat buying are used by businesses as proxies for loyalty. In other cases, loyalty is equated with or even defined as the percentage of total spending in the product or service category.

What are the main components of loyalty? Time, continuity and duration of the connection are indicators of loyalty, but these alone cannot lead us to conclude that a customer is loyal. A customer may patronize a business for many years without really being loyal to that business. Some bank customers, for instance, may deal with a bank for many years; however, if we look more closely at their financial services buying behaviour, we may find that they have recently purchased products from other financial institutions. Many may, in fact, be reluctant customers, feeling themselves locked into a relationship that they would really like to change.

Artificial or spurious loyalty illustrates a situation where customers appear to be loyal because they continue to do business with the organization, but these patterns of buying behaviour mask the reality. That reality is often defined by negative attitudes and feelings of frustration because customers, despite the fact that they continue to buy, wish they could move their business elsewhere. Such customers are not loyal, they are trapped.

This brings us to another aspect of loyalty that demands attention: *share of wallet*. When we assess a customer's loyalty, it is imperative that we consider the share of the customer's overall business we have secured for our products and services. If we think of our own dealings with, for example, hotels, airlines and retailers, it is obvious that we spread business around, often within a set of alternatives. This gives rise to situational loyalty, a sense of loyalty within bounds. We may be loyal to a certain restaurant in one market or for one occasion, and another restaurant at a different time or place.

The 'share of wallet' measure of customer loyalty is valid only in situations where spreading business around is feasible. Obviously, if we give all our electricity business to the local power company, it is not relevant to talk about spreading business.

Where a competitive marketplace operates, and products and services are bought regularly and frequently, the customer's share of wallet represents a reasonable indicator of loyalty. In other cases, where the range of products and services is much less homogeneous or comparable, the calculation of share of wallet as an indicator of loyalty is much less useful. This is the case in retail clothing and in situations where products and services are bought very infrequently. Many companies are not, however, in a position to make even a rough estimate of the share of a customer's wallet they enjoy. They do not know what total amount the customer spends with their organization and have no way of knowing what he or she is spending elsewhere.

Another measure of loyalty is the willingness of the customer to recommend a company to friends, family members and associates. Customers who are satisfied to the point of being prepared to refer others to an organization are demonstrating their loyalty. Satisfied customers will be more likely to tell others about their experiences and to recommend the business. Loyal customers want to see the business thrive to the point where they feel a sense of ownership towards the organization. They feel comfortable making a recommendation because they know that a friend or family member will not be disappointed.

Genuine customer loyalty cannot exist in the absence of an emotional connection. It is this evidence of emotion that transforms repeat buying behaviour into a relationship. Until the customer feels some sense of attachment or closeness to a service provider or other organization, then the connection between the customer and the organization is not taking on the characteristics of a relationship. Customers themselves know, and are quite able to say, when there are stirrings of emotions between them and an organization, or between them and an individual service provider. At what point would they describe this as a relationship, though? Possibly never. They may reserve that word for close family and other personal ties. However, they will admit to feeling a certain closeness or attachment to an organization, and that they have a certain comfort level in dealing with it.

Customers demonstrate their loyalty to an organization or brand by making repeat purchases, buying additional products from it and recommending it to others. Longevity should not be misconstrued as loyalty. There are many organizations that customers have dealt with for many years, not because of an emotional connection or sense of loyalty, but because of convenience, price or inertia. By definition, these customers are not genuinely loyal. Their business is, in fact, vulnerable because their continued patronage is predicated not on any emotional connection that would bond the customer with the organization in a meaningful sense, but on negative incentives or barriers to exiting, or on the absence of a viable or attractive alternative. It may simply be too much trouble to switch!

11.3 Satisfaction of customers and employees

The length of time a customer has been doing business with a company is only one indicator of loyalty. Loyalty is, after all, very closely related to the concept of a relationship, as indicated above. Those individuals to whom we feel the closest are also those to whom we are the most loyal and who are probably most loyal to us. Genuine loyalty stems not from some artificial bond that makes it difficult for one of the parties to the relationship to leave; the foundation of loyalty is in sustained customer satisfaction; it is an emotional, attitudinal connection, not simply a behavioural one. To increase loyalty, we must increase each customer's level of satisfaction and sustain that level of satisfaction over time. To raise satisfaction, we need to add value to what we offer the customer. Adding value leaves customers feeling that they got more than they paid for or even expected. It does not necessarily mean lowering prices or providing more tangible product for their money.

Customers enter into purchase situations with certain expectations. Whether buying a car, a stereo or a vacation, attending a concert or donating to a charity, customers have ideas about how they want to feel when they complete the interaction and while they are using or experiencing the product or service. They have expectations for the purchase situation and for the performance and consumption of the product or service. To be satisfied, the customer must have both sets of expectations met.

Achieving the highest possible level of customer satisfaction is the ultimate goal of marketing. In fact, much attention has been paid recently to the concept of 'total' satisfaction; the implication being that achieving partial satisfaction is not sufficient to drive customer loyalty and retention. When customers are satisfied with how they have been handled during the purchase and how the product or service has performed, they are much more likely to come back to make additional purchases and to say good things to their friends and family members about the company and its products; they are also less likely to defect to competition. Sustained customer satisfaction over time leads to customer relationships that increase the long-term profitability of the company. Marketing is not about single transactions and 'making the sale'; it is about satisfying the customer over and over again. When customers are satisfied, additional sales will follow.

The concept of service as a component of the offer to the customer may be viewed from a number of different perspectives. The essence of what is offered may itself be a service, in that it is an intangible. Air travel is a service, as are hotel accommodation and a haircut. Service may also be defined very formally as the elements of the 'package' of goods and services that a company includes with the purchase of a tangible product, or a core service that enhances the total offering. These elements of the offer include repairs, delivery, installation and warranty, and represent aspects of service that are quite inseparable from the core product or service itself.

These are not, however, the aspects of service a customer refers to when stating that he or she is no longer going to deal with a company because its 'service' is poor. The customer here is usually referring to the level of service that he or she experiences dealing with the company and its personnel, either face to face or on the telephone. This concerns how the customer is handled and treated, how he or she interacts with staff, and what their experience with service provision has been. The customer is talking about the speed of service, the responsiveness and attentiveness of employees, and the convenience experienced.

In this representation, customer satisfaction is seen to be a function of the value created for the customer through the quality of service provided by a company and its employees. That satisfaction is seen as a major contributor to customer retention and, by extension, profitability.

Satisfied employees are more likely to provide superior levels of service; they stay longer with the company and have a greater sense of commitment to it and its customers. The concept of employee retention is as important, therefore, as customer retention, and is a major contributor to it. Employee churn is as much to be avoided as customer churn. Just as treating customers well leads to customer satisfaction, treating employees well leads to employee satisfaction. Thus, marketing and human resources meet.

When a company provides value for its employees, it improves the value that will ultimately be delivered to its customers. Employees want many of the same things from their jobs that customers want from businesses: satisfaction, respect, quality and value are all important in the workplace. Employees who feel satisfied with their jobs and with their employer are more likely to want that employer to succeed and will work harder to ensure success. This often translates into better relationships among employees and between employees and management. It is no secret that satisfied employees are more likely to deliver higher-quality service, both within the company and to external customers, than those who are not satisfied in their jobs.

For this reason, companies who wish to deliver superior service and increased satisfaction among customers must first focus on the quality of service being delivered within the company. This quality of service determines the satisfaction and loyalty of the employee. To improve satisfaction among employees, companies must improve the value the employee receives by working for them.

In a company where service to the customer is important, the most important marketing decision made by management is who to hire: not only those who work with customers or develop marketing programmes and advertising campaigns, but all the employees in a company are responsible in some way for the marketing of it. The way in which employees are treated and the level of employee satisfaction that results have an impact on customer satisfaction, retention, referral rates and overall profitability.

11.4 Value: customer perception of value

Many organizations attempt to add value, but if the customer does not feel that he or she is getting value, an organization's efforts will not pay off in the shape of increased levels of customer satisfaction. In addition, as we have just observed, different things are valued by different customers and in different contexts. We cannot make blanket statements about value and expect them to apply to all customers; because each customer brings a unique background, value system and level of expectation to their interaction with an organization, each one's notion of value and what adds value is also unique.

Value is a predictor of customer choice and loyalty. Buyers who are considering a purchase in a particular product or service category will consider their options and develop a 'consideration set' that consists of all the brands or models they will consider purchasing. The customer will purchase the product or service that he or she perceives to deliver the most value. This assessment of value in the products or services being considered, and the post-purchase evaluation of value received, may take place at a very subjective, or even subconscious, level. The customer will probably not weigh each element of the product or service offer and mentally calculate which offers the best value or whether value has been received; he or she may not even use the term value, but may simply decide to buy one product or another. However, the customer is making an implicit determination of value whenever he or she faces the inevitable trade-off that characterizes a purchase situation or a decision whether to stay with a supplier. It will be a judgement call – very appropriate terminology for a situation that is highly judgemental. The customer will weigh anticipated benefits against current and anticipated costs.

The simple definition of value as what customers get for what they give is broad enough to allow for the incorporation of many different types of benefits and costs. The concept of give versus get goes far beyond the basics of money and core product or service, however. The costs that the customer might give in the exchange situation with an organization include money, time, energy or effort, and psychological costs.

The value proposition focuses the attention of the organization on what it can offer the customer that would be valued and would, as a result, contribute to increased customer satisfaction. Organization must have a holistic view of their value proposition: that it is literally everything that it offers or is capable of doing for its customers. Conversely, the value proposition may be viewed as the collectivity of tools that the organization can use to create or add value for existing or prospective customers.

Consider for a moment how online retailers create value for their customers. They do so not only by providing a variety of products for sale, but also by making it convenient for customers to buy from them. They also create value by offering various delivery and payment options, allowing customers to track the progress of their orders online, offering book reviews, virtual dressing rooms and joint shopping trips with a friend, and making suggestions on what would look good with that pair of jeans, or what book by that same author you might like to read.

When we examine the value proposition, we must look at the entire offering an organization provides or is capable of providing to its customers. This offering goes beyond the core product or service. It has the potential to meet the higher-order needs of customers and to create value at a level much higher than product features, price discounts and support services. However, many organizations stop at this level for various reasons. Some do not see any long-term benefit in trying to meet their customers' higher-order needs. Others see the benefit but are unwilling to spend the money in the short term. Some organizations simply fail to recognize all the needs that a customer brings to the purchase situation and the opportunities that are presented.

Different segments of customers perceive value in different ways. Customers combine various elements of the value proposition in order to define the value from their perspective. As a result, what is considered valuable or an important element of the value proposition by one customer is not considered valuable by another. Value may be created in different ways, and it is critical that marketers really understand what forms of value are considered most important by the segments of the market in which the organization is interested. In fact, an extremely lucrative way in which to segment markets is on the basis of the forms of value that contribute to satisfaction for the various segments. However, it is critical, first, that marketers and others understand how the customer defines value.

In an attempt to break away from the narrow interpretation of value as a function of what is received for the price paid, four sources of value can be identified.

1   *Process*: optimizing business processes and viewing time as a valuable customer resource.
2   *People*: employees are empowered and able to respond to the customer.
3   *Product/service/technology*: competitive features and benefits of products and services, lowering productivity interruptions.
4   *Support*: being there when the customer needs assistance.

Different customer segments value different combinations of things in assessing the attractiveness of a service offering. In addition, customers will place different weights on various components of value in certain circumstances, buying principally on low price in some situations and paying more in different circumstances to buy from an organization that offers superior service or makes it easier for the customer to buy. Much of what may be considered impediments to value creation stems from the fact that customers view value in many different ways. They clearly know when value has not been added, or when some aspect of service that they valued has been removed.

Within customer value the goal should not be to increase customer loyalty across the board, but rather to acquire, retain and develop the most valuable customers. The first step is to understand the costs of acquiring and maintaining customers, and the value created by improvements in customer interactions. One can then create metrics such as customer lifetime value (CLV) and customer-level return on investment (ROI), which will help to identify the most valuable customers. Rather than focusing solely on customer retention or market share, the more effective approach is to track the share of high-value customers and analyse trends such as movement between service tiers. By developing metrics aligned with their customer value growth objectives, organizations can effectively analyse market trends and the effect of their initiatives on the bottom line (see Table 11.1).

Using the right value metrics will help focus the organization on the activities and investments that are growing customer value. Such metrics can align the efforts of both customer-facing and internal departments.

11.5   Customer relationship management (CRM)

CRM is a company-wide business strategy designed to optimize profitability, revenue and customer satisfaction by focusing on highly defined and precise customer groups. This is accomplished by organizing the company around customer segments, encouraging and tracking customer interaction with it, fostering customer-satisfying behaviours, and linking all processes of the company from its customers through its suppliers.

A company using a CRM system must view its customers comprehensively, understanding that they interact, either directly or indirectly, with all components of the internal business system, from suppliers and manufacturers to wholesalers and retailers.

Not these	But these
Market share	• Share of high-value customers • Tier movement among customers • Customer acquisition rate • Customer retention/turnover rate/tenure • Uptake of target programmes and promotions
Number of customers	• Customer-level ROI • Customer lifetime value (CLV) • Relationship depth • Number of accounts per customer • Product mix • Share of wallet • Spending from repeat customers
Number of employees	• Employee development (training) costs • Employee retention • Employee satisfaction • Staffing levels/mix for campaign and customer contact management
Direct costs	• Cost per acquisition • Campaign efficiency • Channel usage and channel migration • Cost of campaign/customer service by channel

TABLE 11.1   Customer-centric metrics for creating value

On the surface, CRM may appear to be a rather simplistic customer service strategy, but while customer service is part of the CRM process, it is only a small part of a totally integrated, holistic approach to building customer relationships. CRM is often described as a closed-loop system that builds relationships with customers.

To initiate the CRM cycle, a company must first establish customer relationships within the company. This may simply entail learning who the customers are or where they are located, or it may require more complex information on the products and services they are using. For example, a bank may find it very beneficial to determine all the services a customer is using, such as loans, savings accounts, investment instruments, and so on. Once the company identifies its customers and its popular products and services, it then determines the level of interaction each customer has with it.

Based on the company's knowledge of the customer and their interaction with it, the company can then acquire and capture all relevant information about the customer, including measures of satisfaction, response to targeted promotions, changes in account activity and even movement of assets.

Technology plays a major role in any CRM system. It is used not only to enhance the collection of customer data, as discussed later in this chapter, but also to store and integrate customer data throughout the company. Customer data are the actual first-hand responses that are obtained from customers through investigation or asking direct questions. These initial data, which might include individual responses to questionnaires, responses on warranty cards or lists of purchases recorded by electronic cash registers, have not yet been analysed or interpreted.

Data mining is an analytical process that compiles personal, pertinent and actionable data about the purchase habits of a company's current and potential customers. (Data mining will be examined in greater detail later in the chapter.) Essentially, data mining transforms customer data into customer information, which consists of data that have been interpreted and to which narrative meaning has been attached. The data are subjected to a pattern-building procedure that profiles customers on variables such as profitability and risk. Customers may be categorized as highly profitable, unprofitable, high risk or low risk, and these categories may depend on the customer's affiliation with the business.

11.5.1 Implementing a CRM system

Companies that implement a CRM system adhere to a customer-centric focus or model. Customer-centric is an internal management philosophy similar to the marketing concept discussed in Chapter 1. Under this philosophy, the company customizes its product and service offering based on data generated through interactions between the customer and the company. This philosophy transcends all functional areas of the business (production, operations, accounting, etc.), producing an internal system where all decisions and actions of the company are a direct result of customer information. A customer-centric company builds its system on what satisfies and retains valuable customers, while learning those factors that build long-lasting relationships with those customers.

A customer-centric company and its representatives learn continually from customers about ways to enhance their product and service offerings. Learning in a CRM environment is normally an informal process of collecting customer information through customer comments and feedback on product or service performance. Dell Computer, for example, learned from its customers that they were experiencing difficulties unpacking its computers. The packaging was so strong that customers were damaging the computers while trying to remove them from the box. Dell responded with a simpler, more efficient packaging design that allowed customers to disassemble the packaging material in one easy procedure.

The success of CRM – building lasting and profitable relationships – can be directly measured by the effectiveness of the interaction between the customer and the company. In fact, what further differentiates CRM from other strategic initiatives, such as one-to-one marketing and market development, is the company's ability to establish and manage interactions with its current customer base. The more latitude (empowerment) a company gives its representatives, the more likely it is that the interaction will conclude in a way that satisfies the customer.

CRM is a company-wide process that focuses on learning, managing customer knowledge and empowerment. It differs from one-to-one marketing in a very important way: one-to-one marketing is an individualized marketing method that utilizes customer information to build a long-term, personalized and profitable relationship with each customer; CRM is broad and systemic, whereas one-to-one marketing is focused and individualized. Some more aspects of one-to-one marketing are dealt with in the next section.

Exhibit 11.1: *Dell builds relationships with both customers and suppliers*

Dell attributes its success to the direct relationship business model it has pioneered. This model works with both customers and suppliers.

Dell's customer relationship model

There are no retailers or other resellers between Dell and the customer. Dealing direct allows Dell to better understand its customers' expectations. The first contact is typically through the telephone or via the Internet; in the case of large corporate customers, it is more typically via a face-to-face meeting. In either case, an experienced sales representative advises the customer on the best possible computer for their needs and takes the customer's order. This is then entered on to the system and the order is downloaded to the factory.

At the manufacturing plant, a team of Dell employees assemble and test the entire computer system that has been ordered. Rapid delivery, award-winning technical support, customer service and ongoing feedback help ensure the highest-quality experience for Dell customers.

The direct relationship model with customers is based on the following core principles:

- *Price for performance* – the company produces a range of high-performance products, which are competitively priced.
- *Customization* – every Dell system is built to order; customers get exactly, and only, what they want.
- *Service and support* – Dell uses knowledge gained from direct contact before and after sale to provide a good customer service.
- *Latest technology* – because a PC is assembled only when a customer orders it, the very latest technology can be used.

Dell's supplier relationship model

Dell has a strategic partnership with suppliers such as Intel and Microsoft. From the start the company decided it was better to buy in components rather than build them itself. By doing this, it can choose among the best providers in the world, often called best in class. This leaves Dell free to focus on what it does best: designing and building solutions for customers. It selects suppliers with the greatest level of expertise, experience and quality for any particular part.

Sources: adapted from www.dell.com; www.business2000.ie

11.6 One-to-one marketing

One-to-one marketing is the ultimate goal of a new trend in marketing that focuses on understanding customers as individuals instead of as part of a group. To achieve this, contemporary marketers are making their communications more customer-specific.

Most businesses today use a mass-marketing approach designed to increase their market share by selling their products to the greatest number of people. For many businesses, however, it is more efficient and profitable to use one-to-one marketing to increase customer share; in other words, to sell more products to each customer. One-to-one marketing is an individualized marketing method that utilizes customer information to build long-term, personalized and profitable relationships with each customer. The goal is to reduce costs through customer retention and increase revenue through customer loyalty. CRM, which was discussed in the previous section, is a related marketing strategy that takes a broader approach.

The difference between one-to-one marketing and the traditional mass-marketing approach can be compared to shooting a rifle and a shotgun. If you have a good aim, a rifle is the most efficient weapon to use. A shotgun, on the other hand, increases your odds of hitting the target when it is more difficult to focus. Instead of scattering messages far and wide across the spectrum of mass media (the shotgun approach), one-to-one marketers are now homing in on ways to communicate with each individual customer (the rifle approach).

As one-to-one marketing takes hold, it is no longer enough to understand customers and prospects by aggregate profiles. The one-to-one future requires that marketers understand their customers and collaborate with them, rather than use them as targets. In fact, many early one-to-one marketing efforts failed because marketers bombarded customers with irrelevant, one-to-one communications before making an effort to understand the customers. The fundamental challenge of one-to-one marketing currently is to combine the customer information gleaned from database technology with compelling marketing communications.

The one-to-one future is still a goal, not a reality, for most companies; but progress towards one-to-one marketing is evident in the increase in personalized communications and product customization. The battle for customers will be won by marketers who understand why and how their customers buy their products, and they will win them over one customer at a time.

Fundamentally, one-to-one marketing is no more than the relationship cultivated by a sales person with the customer. A successful sales person builds a relationship over time, constantly thinks about what the customer needs and wants, and is mindful of the trends and patterns in the customer's purchase history. A good sales person often knows what the customer needs even before the customer does! The sales person may also inform, educate and instruct the customer about new products, technology or applications in anticipation of the customer's future needs or requirements.

This kind of thoughtful attention is the basis of one-to-one marketing. Database technology provides the tools marketers need to 'get to know' their customers on a personal basis. Moreover, today's databases are capable of storing information about a company's customers, their purchasing history and their preferences, and then presenting it in a meaningful format that marketers can use to assess, analyse and anticipate customer needs.

Today's customers demand more choices; they seek to buy precisely what meets their needs and wants, and expect individualized attention. Technology now makes it possible for companies to interact with these customers in new ways, by allowing companies to create databases that pull data from, and feed information to, those interactions. Companies are using technology that makes it possible to tailor products, service and communications to meet those expectations.

Several forces have helped shape this new one-to-one focus on customers. They include the following.

- *A more diverse society*: a more diverse society has ruled that the one-size-fits-all marketing of yesteryear no longer fits. Consumers do not want to be treated like the masses. Instead, they want to be treated as the individuals they are, with their own unique sets of needs and wants. By its personalized nature, one-to-one marketing can fulfil this desire.
- *More demanding and time-poor consumers*: more direct and personal marketing efforts will continue to grow to meet the needs of consumers who no longer have the time to spend shopping and making purchase decisions. With the personal and targeted nature of one-to-one marketing, consumers can spend less time making purchase decisions and more time doing the things that are important to them.
- *Decline of brand loyalty*: consumers will be loyal only to those companies and brands that have earned their loyalty and reinforced it at every purchase occasion. One-to-one marketing techniques focus on finding a company's best customers, rewarding them for their loyalty and thanking them for their business.
- *Explosion of new media alternatives*: mass-media approaches will decline in importance as advances in market research and database technology allow marketers to collect detailed information on their customers – not just the approximation offered by demographics, but specific names and addresses. One-to-one marketing will increase in importance and offer marketers a more cost-effective avenue to reach customers.
- *Marketing accountability*: the demand for accountability will drive the growth of one-to-one marketing (see Section 11.7 on global account management (GAM)) and justify its continued existence.

11.6.1   One-to-one marketing and the Internet

Undoubtedly, one of the most important trends in the field of one-to-one marketing is the emergence of one-to-one marketing over the Internet. While marketers have overwhelmingly adopted the Internet and World Wide Web as a new channel for promotions and commerce, many marketers are capitalizing on the web's full set of interactive marketing capabilities. Internet companies are learning more about their customers and using this information to fine-tune their marketing efforts and build relationships with each customer on a more individual level.

One advantage of online one-to-one marketing is the ability to deliver personalized promotional messages to each customer visiting a company's website. Past customer transaction history, clickstream data and survey responses are used to identify buying patterns and interests. Based on information known about the customer visiting its site, such as colour and brand preferences, geographic location and past customer transaction data, the marketer can develop a targeted and personalized online promotion or custom catalogue. For example, Amazon.com creates a personalized experience each time the same customer visits its website. Customers are greeted by name and instantly provided with a customized web page offering book, music and DVD suggestions based on their past purchasing and viewing behaviour.

To fund the new mobile marketing technology, mobile operators are looking for ways to increase mobile data service revenue. Many operators believe advertising revenue is the best option. Therefore, information technology research firms are working to improve mobile marketing technology. In the future, mobile marketing will be able to target messages based on both individual customer profiles and customer location. For instance, when a customer arrives at the grocery store, a message could be sent to remind him or her to purchase laundry detergent or to pick up a copy of a newly released DVD at the media store next door.

Of course, mobile marketing is not that sophisticated yet, but marketers do know that the advantages of mobile marketing will include interactivity, personalization, location awareness and always being with the user. In addition, mobile marketing will need to be personalized and permission-based in order to be effective.

Increasingly, more and more companies are realizing that email is the ideal one-to-one medium, capable of establishing and building enduring customer relationships with highly targeted lists of prospects. This technique works in much the same way as offline one-to-one marketing campaigns.

One-to-one email marketing should be strictly permission-based; that is, consumers should 'opt in' or give their permission to receive email messages from a marketer. Amazon.com and other online booksellers ask customers to provide them with additional information about their likes and dislikes so that they can receive future book recommendations, but customers can indicate that they do not wish to receive these recommendations.

11.7 Global account management (GAM)

As a relatively new marketing phenomenon for supplier organizations, GAM is an organizational form employed by multinational/global supplier organizations and used to co-ordinate and manage worldwide activities of servicing a customer centrally by a managed team. GAM focuses on dealing with the needs of an important global customer (= global account = GA) in the B2B market – see Figure 11.2.

The development of a GAM relationship has a number of attributes that appeal to a global customer organization (Prashantham and Birkinshaw, 2008):

1 consistency in the application of policies throughout the world
2 co-ordination of marketing/selling activities to increase sales volume
3 effective utilization of marketing strategies and programmes in multiple locations
4 efficiency of management, in that there is a central contact for key accounts
5 establishment of a control mechanism relative to key accounts, to reduce the probability of account turnover
6 improvement in the two-way flow of communications with key accounts, thereby increasing the knowledge base in order to improve the quality of goods/services to these global clients
7 use as a means to pre-empt local/global competitors from securing business from these critical customers.

The co-ordination issues of short-run contracting also need to be assessed. In this situation, if a supplier is reactive in its relational behaviour, and forms a unilaterally dependent GAM relationship initiated and forced by the customer organizations, the supplier is motivated to

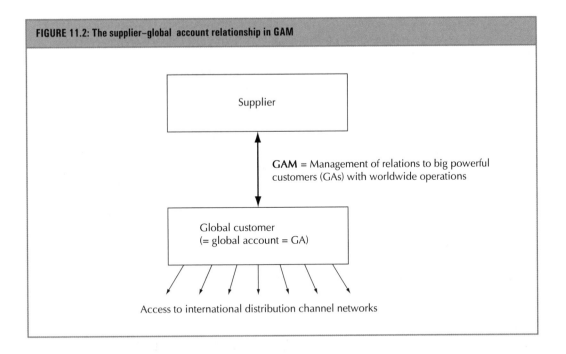

FIGURE 11.2: The supplier–global account relationship in GAM

Supplier

GAM = Management of relations to big powerful customers (GAs) with worldwide operations

Global customer
(= global account = GA)

Access to international distribution channel networks

adopt a defensive GAM strategy. The reactive short-run motivations to accept a GAM programme in spite of co-ordination issues are (Zupancic and Müllner, 2008):

- *pressure from key accounts to improve global consistency* – global customers may force the supplier to institute GAM to maintain their global 'preferred' supplier status
- *pressure to 'standardize' pricing on a global basis* – global customers may attempt to use GAM as a means to lower prices globally in the guise of inferring that there should be equity/commonality of pricing throughout the global network of customer organizations
- *as a reaction to losing key customer sales in select foreign markets* – due to the 'unevenness' of selling and marketing activities globally (i.e. loss of sales in a foreign market to local suppliers), any departure from a high level of service or account attention to a global customer may stimulate the centralization of the management of key accounts
- *the loss of key accounts due to major competitors utilizing the GAM organizational strategy* – the focal organization may feel compelled to form a GAM team to match or counteract the strategy of key competitors.

A more proactive posture on the part of the supplier is demonstrated when a more proactive strategic reason for forming a GAM relationship can be employed in spite of high customer demands for supplier adaptation. The perceived long-run benefits of this are:

- *the development of relational contracting with large, global customers* – the co-operation between customer and supplier into long-term global relationships has a number of positive outcomes that provide the foundation for the formation of GAM teams (Wilson and Millman, 2003)
- *increasing the long-term dependency of the customer on the supplying organization* – if the supplier becomes the preferred source for products worldwide, it is more difficult for

the customer to switch suppliers in one location; therefore, there is a tendency for the customer to become dependent on the supplier, shifting the balance of power in the relationship

- *development of synergistic strategies between the global customer and the supplier* – through the formation of the supplier–customer coalition, unique strategies can be implemented that are difficult for 'outside' competitors to duplicate due to the tacit knowledge developed in the relationship
- *development of a strategic 'fit' between the supplier and the customer* – to increase the effectiveness of the supplying organization, the supplier's strategies can be developed to be consistent with those of the key global account (e.g. providing the effectiveness/efficiency of co-ordinated and/or integrated strategies between the two organizations)
- *utilization of successful programmes throughout the world* – the GAM strategy allows the best strategies to be employed with key accounts throughout the world, thereby increasing their impact and reducing the cost of creating new programmes for each country/region
- *development of a network to increase global effectiveness and efficiency* – due to the relationship between supplier and customer, economies of scale, as well as of scope, can be utilized through the GAM strategy.

11.7.1　The power balance in GAM: the supplier–customer fit

The key strategic questions facing the supplier company are whether to create global accounts at all and, if the decision is made to do so, which customer relationships should be selected. In selecting the right customers to designate as global accounts, the two most important criteria are the balance of the power in the relationship and the potential for strategic synergy.

A professional buyer looking for standard worldwide pricing is, of course, looking for the lowest price to be applied everywhere. In most companies, the purchasing function is considerably more globally co-ordinated than the sales function, since it shows greater return to scale than the more execution-sensitive function of managing customer relationships. Therefore, it is surprising that so many global account relationships favour the customer at the expense of the supplier.

One key determinant of the balance of power in global account negotiations is the degree of internationalization of both the supplier and the buyer (see Fig. 11.2).

In the case of a customer's 'low' international co-ordination (as shown in Fig. 11.3), it may be difficult to talk about a global account (customer) at all. Consequently, the potential is also low or non-existent. In the 'price squeeze' area, the supplier with low internationalization has access to a global player with a widespread network, which results in a 'medium potential' but, as the supplier is 'under-globalized' in relation to the customer, the supplier will be in a rather vulnerable position. The supplier can end up servicing agreements in countries where it has no presence. For example, the supplier may receive a call demanding service from a customer at its plant in Thailand, although the supplier may not have any operation in that country; in such a case, rather than ignore the customer, this supplier may fly someone out from a neighbouring country, but this would be an expensive solution for the supplier.

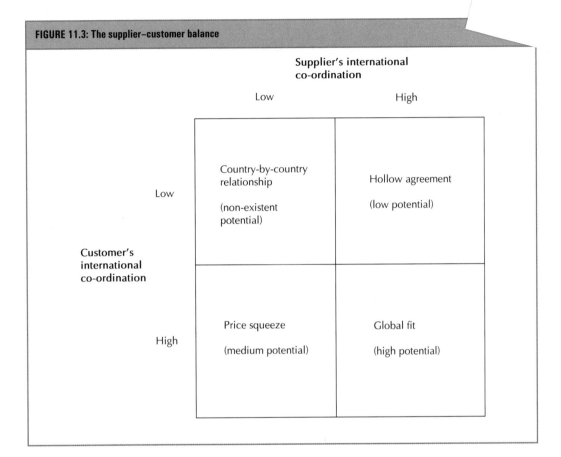

FIGURE 11.3: The supplier–customer balance

Supplier's international
co-ordination

	Low	High
Low	Country-by-country relationship (non-existent potential)	Hollow agreement (low potential)
High	Price squeeze (medium potential)	Global fit (high potential)

Customer's international co-ordination

In the 'price squeeze' area, suppliers will not always face demand for low prices. Many far-sighted customers will choose to build a win–win relationship with their suppliers rather than squeeze them on price in the short term. Furthermore, some suppliers are skilful at increasing their power over their customers in other ways. They may try offsetting the central buying power of customers by negotiating contracts locally. Many local decision-makers of large GAMs prefer good local service from the supplier to very low prices.

As shown in Fig. 11.2, the 'global fit' area is normally the alternative with the best potential. When the two sides are well matched in their internationalization, a GAM relationship can work very well.

11.7.2 Potential risks of entering GAM relationships

While the potential benefits associated with accepting a GAM relationship seem to be clear to the supplier, entering such a strategic arrangement is risky and should be prepared with the appropriate due diligence. The operational risks should be understood prior to adopting a GAM supply strategy. The issues/problems associated with the operational risks can be classified into the six categories described below (Harvey et al., 2003).

Motivational issues/problems

The motivation for adopting the GAM supply strategy may have potentially negative implications for the supplier. The specific motivational issues refer to: customer information, customer panels, GAM revenue/profit measures, and incentives and compensation for the GAM team. In an effort to illustrate some of the problems associated with a reactive rationale, a number of potential consequences can be hypothesized. First, if the basic orientation to GAM is instituted as a defensive measure to keep an existing global customer, the management's support of the GAM relationship/strategy will be conditional. If the GAM strategy does not involve (1) an internal champion, (2) extensive support by top management, or (3) key functional heads, the probability of the GAM supply strategy being effective over time is minimal. Second, if the GAM strategy is implemented with a short-run, reactive perspective, the supplier may become strategically 'trapped' into an organizational solution that is not consistent with other strategies or structural considerations in the company. The dependency on the global customer may accentuate the path dependency of the supplier, given the 'derived' growth in sales volume/profit due to the GAM strategy.

Structural issues/problems

There are a number of potential structural issues inherent in a GAM relationship, such as customer demands for: resources co-ordination in being serviced; single point of contact; and consistency in service quality and performance. The first and the most critical related problem is that the GAM solution can be perceived by the regional field operating managers as eviscerating their authority with the global customer, both at the national and the regional level. In particular, the supranational nature of the GAM team can blur the lines of authority as well as undermine the operating personnel's social capital with local representatives of the global account. This problem of overlapping authority is compounded by the fact that the local operating managers are frequently required to execute the policies/strategies formulated by the GAM team that may none the less conflict with established local practices. Therefore, to many experienced managers, the GAM structural design resembles a virtual matrix organization, with its attendant nightmares of parallel reporting, which are experienced by local and regional operating managers.

Relational richness

Another structural problem associated with GAM is that 'not all relationships with key customers are created equal' (i.e. there are different levels of relational richness in a GAM relationship). The concept of relational richness reflects the variation in the demands placed upon the supplier by the global customer, as well as the trust that it places in the supplier. The level of relational richness (i.e. how close the strategic intent/fit of two potential GAM members is) within a GAM relationship dictates, to a degree, the operating format of the policies/procedures for the supplier GAM team. Therefore, not all GAM relationships should be assumed to operate at the same level of supplier trust and commitment. As demand for the level of commitment and support to global customers can vary extensively, the interface at the boundary of the supplier organization needs to reflect the expected difference in 'service level'.

Personnel and team issues/problems

The personnel and issues influencing the supplier's GAM use include: the global account manager; the GAM support staff; the personnel evaluation policy; and the reporting processes. The GAM team's composition entails a number of interrelated problems that could translate into operating impediments for the supplier. First, neglect of the team composition issue could present an initial barrier to the team's effectiveness, as far as who should be placed on the team. The appropriate functional representation of the team is essential to (1) gain acceptance in the organization, (2) smooth reporting processes, and (3) provide the GAM team with the expertise to be able to address cross-functional issues that will be salient when servicing a customer globally. Also, the team's leadership and the selection of the appropriate members from the various functional areas present another set of problems.

A specific related problem that needs to be addressed in a timely manner is the degree of heterogeneity of team membership. On one hand, the need for broad representation, both functionally and relative to global background/experience, could cause too much heterogeneity on the team, reducing the team's effectiveness. On the other hand, to assemble a team that possesses global expertise, it may be necessary to integrate a wide range of experiences and national orientations. The heterogeneity issue may necessitate the movement of international managers to organization headquarters so that they can be GAM team members.

Conflict issues/problems within/between organizations

There are a number of potential conflict issues within the supplier organization that is pursuing the GAM strategy. The issues are those that drive the demand for GAM, including: price uniformity; terms-of-trade uniformity; and service in markets in which the company has no customer operations. If the conflict issues are not addressed in a timely fashion, they may expand into conflict areas. Several of these conflict areas have already been mentioned, but there are others that could affect the functioning of the GAM relationship. The first conflict area originates from regional operating managers who see the GAM strategy as an intrusion into their sphere of authority. The conflict over who has the authority to make decisions concerning the global customer is heightened due to the need for the local operating manager to execute the GAM team's strategy. In this case, the operating manager in the foreign marketplace has the responsibility, but not the authority, to countermand or modify the strategy dictated by the GAM team. The second conflict area encompasses varying perceptions of 'fit' with the global customer organization; the perception gap can create a great deal of conflict and pressure in the GAM relationship.

Issues/problems of increased cost and potential for depressed profits

As with any addition to the organization/management of an organizational layer, there is potential for increased costs. This is particularly germane when considering the implementation of a GAM strategy, in that the GAM team in effect duplicates the costs of existing functional personnel, both at the supplier headquarters and at local market level. The overlay of another group or team of managers both improves the functioning of the GAM relationship and increases supplier costs, particularly in the initial stages of the GAM programme's implementation. Specifically, significant costs will also be incurred in the development of the infrastructure to support the GAM team. This operating platform must be endowed with adequate resources dedicated to ensuring quality service to global customers. In many cases, if not most, this infrastructure will not only separate, but also stand apart from, the existing support mechanisms in the local markets. In addition, providing the GAM team (i.e. the global account manager and support staff) with the ability to effectively communicate not only with the global customer organization but also with the operating units in its own organization, will increase costs at headquarters level.

There can also be implicit costs associated with the implementation of a GAM strategy. These include costs related to: (1) increased length of time to make decisions; (2) resolving conflicts with the local operating units; (3) co-ordination of communications between operating units and the GAM team prior to communicating with the global customer; and (4) resolving additional myriad time-consuming issues relative to embarking on a new organizational strategy.

Exhibit 11.2: *International advertising agencies and their GAM strategies*

Major advertising agencies and other business service providers must co-ordinate their services internationally. Service complexes need to provide every possible means to encourage communication between offices and specialists. This will become critical as more companies form international account teams to serve multinational enterprises (MNEs).

Traditionally, advertising agencies go through a three-stage evolution internationally:

1   an imperial phase in which larger national agencies, mainly in the USA, follow major global accounts (GAs) clients (GM, Ford, IBM, Kodak) overseas and establish offices staffed by expatriates in major metropolitan centres
2   a nationalization phase in which large agencies retrench from full to partial ownership of local affiliate agencies
3   a transnational phase in which a network of international agencies are co-ordinated by a central holding company under a mix of full and partial ownership arrangements.

Cordiant plc (formerly Saatchi & Saatchi) is an example of the transnational form of a global advertising agency under a central holding company.

Sources: adapted from www.cordiant.com; Davis, T.R.V. (2004) Different service firms, different international strategies, *Business Horizons*, 47(6): 51–9

11.7.3   Step-by-step implementation plan for a GAM team

Once the GAM selection process has been established and the team members are assembled, the explicit mission and goals of the GAM team strategy concerning managing the GAM relationship can be established (see Fig. 11.4). There is an apparent paradox in selecting team members prior to the development of the team's mission and goals. But in reality, the team members must be a part of the initial charge of the team; therefore, it is recommended that the team be assembled first.

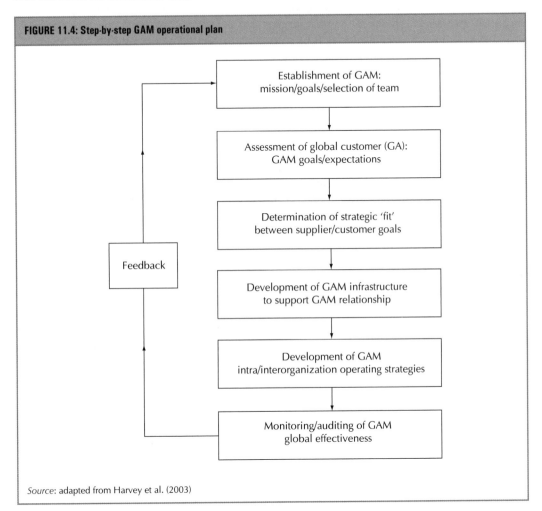

FIGURE 11.4: Step-by-step GAM operational plan

Source: adapted from Harvey et al. (2003)

Each global customer will have specific requirements and expectations about the handling of their business on a global basis. A GAM team member's input on customizing the team effort is particularly critical when they have tacit knowledge of the account or have worked with the global customer prior to the formation of the GAM team. Also, the goals of the GAM team should be explicit, in order to permit the team's performance to be measured and to allow it to adapt to changes in the GAM relationship (i.e. relational richness) over the stages of the relationship. Specifically, the goals of the GAM team need to reflect the team's varying requirements, which vary due to differences in operating procedures relative to the functional units, since these units need to 'execute' the GAM strategy at the local level. This co-ordination of activities between the GAM and the functional unit levels is one of the primary concerns of the supplier. Without this collaboration, the effectiveness and, ultimately, the success of the GAM programme will be jeopardized.

Developing an operating strategy explicitly related to fostering co-ordination between the two organizations in the GAM programme is an essential step in implementation of the GAM strategy. However, managing between organizations is one of the more difficult management tasks in the global marketplace. Most frequently, managers are trained to manage within their organizations, but with many GAM relationships, more and more of the key managers' time in the global network organization will be directed at obtaining co-operation/co-ordination with managers in organizations outside of their own.

Besides the interorganizational management format, the standard operating procedures for implementing the GAM strategy with key global customers must also be established in the supplier organization. Without the procedures clearly delineating the role of the GAM team and its mission, the support of operating managers for the GAM programme will be minimal. The likelihood of conflict over authority and responsibility is too great to be left to the chance that functional managers will bargain with the global customer in their markets.

The final stage of the GAM implementation/operating process is to institute an ongoing monitoring and auditing process to assess the direct and indirect impact of the GAM programme. This control process would have to elicit information from key managers in the global customer organization in order to validate the impact of the GAM supplier team. The central issue or problem related to the GAM control system is whether one system is effective when two organizations with different cultures are involved in a relationship spanning multiple national cultures.

As noted earlier, if the GAM relationship has no rationale other than sales, then the negotiations will focus on price, and the globalization of the relationship will result in pressure for volume discounts. The broadening of the relationship to include strategic development projects – such as new product development or customized service agreements – is the only way to make global accounts pay for suppliers. As with any sort of key account, the relationship shifts from price negotiations to strategic issues as you move through the customer's hierarchy. Currently, most global account managers are recruited from the sales organization, from positions as regional sales manager or national sales manager in a small country. However, this approach is misguided because a global account is very different from a portfolio of regional or national accounts. True, many regional account managers do make good global account managers, but they have to learn some new skills to make the transition: internal co-ordination, taking a long-term perspective, nurturing the account not milking it, understanding supply chain management (SCM), and so on. Therefore, some organizations have had good experiences by appointing senior line management as global account managers (Arnold et al., 2001).

11.8 Creating long-term customer value

Customer lifetime value (CLV) projects the future value of the customer over a period of years. One of the basic assumptions in any lifetime value calculation is that marketing to repeat customers is more profitable than marketing to first-time buyers. It is a well-known marketing fact that it costs more to find a new customer in terms of promotion and gaining trust than to sell more to a customer who is already loyal.

CLV has a number of uses: (1) it shows marketers how much they can spend to acquire a new customer; (2) it provides a level of profitable spending to retain a customer; and (3) it provides a basis for targeting new customers who look like a company's most profitable customers. Lifetime value analysis allows a company to identify its most valuable customers and profit from them over the long term by building relationships with them.

The increasing importance of the customer-centric approach to marketing is evident in the numerous CRM initiatives prevalent today, such as one-to-one marketing and database marketing. Most of these customer-centric marketing initiatives aim to increase the length of the customer life cycle as well as the value of the transaction between the company and the customer during each stage of the life cycle. More and more companies are focusing on nurturing customer relationships for a long lifetime of customers with the company and, subsequently, for higher profitability and growth. As a result of this approach, marketing activities and performance evaluations are increasingly being organized around relationships with customers rather than products. This has resulted in a totally different paradigm for making and evaluating marketing decisions. The focus on relationship management makes it extremely important to understand CLV because CLV models offer a systematic way of understanding and evaluating a company's relationship with its customers.

CLV models have a variety of uses in all kinds of business organization. Particular use of such models, however, will depend on the type of products and customers a company has. Companies that have few and identifiable customers might benefit from models that measure the lifetime value of individual customers, whereas those with large numbers of customers and with small sales to each customer might benefit from models that help segment the customer base on the basis of lifetime value.

CLV models can be very useful in helping companies make strategic as well as tactical decisions; that is, strategic decisions in terms of identifying who its customers are and their characteristics and which customers to go after in the long run, and tactical decisions in terms of short-term resource allocation among marketing variables and the focus of marketing activities.

CLV models help quantify the relationship of the company with its customers and subsequently allow it to make more informed decisions in a structured framework. CLV models also help a company to know who its profitable customers are, and customer profitability provides a metric for the allocation of marketing resources to consumers and market segments. Marketing efforts are best directed at the most profitable consumers.

The advent of the Internet has greatly increased the importance of CLV models. Many companies with a presence on the Internet do not have highly valued physical assets. Such companies can be valued correctly only when the value of their intangible assets is taken into account. Since the value of their customer base is the most important intangible asset that these companies have, understanding the lifetime value of the customers of these companies gives a more accurate picture of their potential.

The era of mass marketing is being replaced by an era of targeted marketing. Knowledge of CLV enables companies to develop customer-specific marketing programmes leading to an increase in the efficiency and effectiveness of such programmes. The Internet is undoubtedly a major instrument of such targeted marketing; the direct marketing concepts of CLV can be extended to be useful in interactive scenarios.

11.8.1 Problems in calculating CLV

The calculation of the CLV (see Fig. 11.5) is not problem-free. Most of these problems, however, can be solved successfully if the following two main issues are taken into consideration:

1   The company applying this method has to define clearly from the beginning the purpose of using CLV analysis and the expected benefits.
2   The problems raised by the CLV analysis are often industry- and company-specific; as a result the company has to select the most appropriate way to apply this concept in its particular situation.

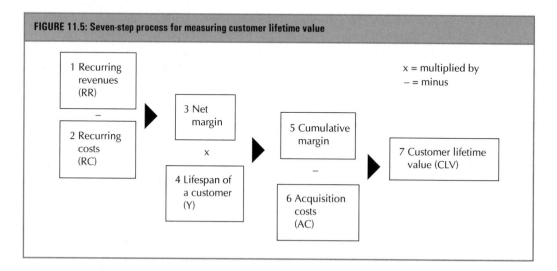

FIGURE 11.5: Seven-step process for measuring customer lifetime value

Note: Figure 11.5 as a mathematical formula:

$$CLV = (RR - RC) \times Y - AC \tag{1}$$

$$P = CLV \times C \tag{2}$$

$$P = [(RR - RC) \times Y - AC] \times C \tag{3}$$

Where CLV = customer lifetime value (accumulated profitability of a customer during lifetime)

RR = recurring revenues   Y = lifespan of a customer or number of transactions

RC = recurring costs   AC = acquisition costs

P = total profits   C = number of customers

11.8.2 Defining a customer

The first challenge is to define the customer unit. Is it an individual, an account, a household or a business address? A second challenge is linking customer information to a single customer record when they leave and return multiple times during their lifetime. The answer to these questions is industry-specific. The business organization has to identify the characteristics of its customer relationship and, on this basis, to define the customer unit and the customer lifetime cycle.

CLV for an organization is the net profit or loss to it from a customer over the entire life of transactions of that customer with the organization. Hence, the lifetime value of a customer for an organization is the net of the revenues obtained from that customer over the lifetime of transactions with that customer minus the cost of attracting, selling and servicing that customer, taking into account the time value of money (see Fig. 11.5).

In the context of new customers, it is important to consider acquisition costs when thinking about the CLV. For example, consider an organization that spends €1m to attract customers. If only a few customers actually make a purchase worth a few Euros each in the first period, then the costs incurred in the first period are acquisition costs, and ignoring this in the CLV models would give a positive lifetime value to each customer even though they may never make another purchase after their first purchase. Clearly, the lifetime value of such customers cannot be positive. In short, CLV is a concept that is forward-looking, and the right definition and modelling should consider the *essence* of the concepts as against rigid definitions.

In mathematical terms, CLV consists of taking into account the total financial contribution (i.e. revenues minus costs) over the entire life of a customer's business relationship with an organization. Despite its simplicity, the measurement of CLV requires great care. All cash flows involved in the process have to be identified and measured on a very detailed level, and allocated precisely to each customer or type of customer. Figure 11.5 represents a concise seven-step approach to measuring CLV.

11.8.3 Evaluating costs

The measurement of cost to the customer level poses the greatest challenge to CLV measurements. While revenue can usually be collected by the customer from the appropriate billing system, cost information is aggregated into general ledger departments and accounts, and requires a good deal of analysis and disaggregation before it can meaningfully be attached to individual customers or customer segments. The indirect costs are especially difficult to divide and allocate. In solving these problems, three key costing principles should be applied.

1   Customer costs must be related to the revenues they generate.
2   Not all costs within the organization should be attributed down to a customer level.
3   It should be made absolutely clear who can influence different types of cost and revenue.

11.8.4 Evaluating the duration of customer loyalty

The duration of customer business relationships is difficult to measure in the present economic environment, characterized as it is by unpredictability and rapid change. Many companies are using as their main predictive tool the analysis of historical data about the past behaviour of their customers, identifying specific segments and extrapolating the behaviour of these segments into the future. This method can be used successfully only in relatively stable market environments because it assumes that:

● customers will repeat their past behaviour in the future
● market conditions will not change significantly.

The method is, however, completely useless in dynamic, fast-changing environments, such as the high-technology industries. In such sectors, customers' needs and perceptions change fast, competition is intense and market conditions fluctuate widely. It is important therefore to connect these predictions with the external market environment. Many CLV/profitability models neglect the external environment of the company, and concentrate only on the relationship between the company and its customers. It is, however, dangerous to forget that this relationship does not take place in a marketing void. Market conditions might, and indeed do, change over time, impacting on organizations' policies and on customer needs and perceptions.

The duration and intensity of customers' loyalty is determined and influenced by customer satisfaction. It can be assumed that as long as a company's offer satisfies a customer's need, that customer will be loyal to the company. The measurement of customer satisfaction can therefore provide a platform for calculating, predicting and increasing customer profitability.

CLV is, therefore, much more than the simple forward projection of current spending levels. Ideally, we would like to be able to calculate the long-term profitability of a customer, but few companies capture the costs associated with serving a customer, and fewer still are able to associate specific costs with specific customers. In the absence of cost information, it makes sense to focus on the potential value of the customer in terms of the revenue that he or she can either generate directly or influence.

Summary

This chapter started by looking at the factors that determine the shape of the CRM strategy:

- customer loyalty
- customer satisfaction
- customer perception.

Customer loyalty is a subjective concept. Sometimes longevity of customer patronage and repeat buying are used as proxies for loyalty. Customer satisfaction is seen to be a function of the value created for the customer through the quality of service provided by the company and its employees. Satisfied employees are more likely to provide superior levels of service. When a company provides value for its employees, it improves the value that will ultimately be delivered to its customers.

Different segments of customers perceive value in different ways. Customers combine various elements of the company's value proposition in order to define the value from their own perspective.

CRM is a company-wide process that focuses on learning, managing customer knowledge and empowerment. It differs from one-to-one marketing in a very important way: one-to-one marketing is an individualized marketing method that utilizes customer information to build a long-term, personalized and profitable relationship with each customer. CRM is broad and systemic, whereas one-to-one marketing is focused and individualized.

As a relatively new marketing phenomenon for supplier companies, GAM is an organizational form employed by a multinational/global supplier company in order to co-ordinate and manage worldwide activities of servicing a customer centrally by a managed team.

CLV projects the future value of the customer over a period of years. One of the basic assumptions in any lifetime value calculation is that marketing to repeat customers is more profitable than marketing to first-time buyers. It costs more to find a new customer, in terms of promotion and gaining trust, than it does to sell more to a customer who is already loyal.

▶

CLV has a number of uses: (1) it shows marketers how much they can spend to acquire a new customer; (2) it provides a level of profitable spending to retain a customer; (3) it provides a basis for targeting new customers who look like a company's most profitable customers. Lifetime value analysis allows a marketer to identify its most valuable customers and profit from them over the long term by building relationships with them.

In mathematical terms, CLV consists of taking into account the total financial contribution (i.e. revenues minus costs) over the entire life of a customer's business relationship with a company. Despite its simplicity, the measurement of CLV requires great care. All cash flows involved in the process have to be identified and measured on a very detailed level, and allocated precisely to each customer or type of customer. Figure 11.5 represented a concise seven-step approach to measuring CLV.

Questions for discussion

1　Which factors would encourage long-term relationships with customers?
2　Is it possible to identify market factors that would suggest that a RM approach is not appropriate?
3　If a relationship requires investment and customers require added value from relationships, how is it that relationships are worth building?
4　What are the arguments for spending money to keep existing customers loyal (customer retention)?
5　Why is it important to consider CLV?
6　How can a company increase its CLV?
7　Argue for and against the statement – 'The customer is always right.'
8　What are the supplier's and buyer's motives for entering GAM?
9　Describe the different stages in GAM.
10　What are the most important factors for a supplier to consider in establishing and developing cross-cultural GAM relationships?
11　What do you consider the main requirements for ensuring longevity of alliances in international markets?

References

Arnold, D., Birkinshaw, J. and Toulan, O. (2001) Can selling be globalized? The pitfalls of global account management, *California Management Review,* 44(1): 8–20.

Harvey, M., Myers, M.B. and Novicevic, M.M. (2003) The managerial issues associated with global account management – a relational contract perspective, *Journal of Management Development,* 22(2): 103–29.

Prashantham, S. and Birkinshaw, J. (2008) Dancing with gorillas: how small companies can partner effectively with MNCs, *California Management Review*, 51(1): 6–23.

Wilson, K. and Millman, T. (2003) The global account manager as political entrepreneur, *Industrial Marketing Management*, 32(2): 151–8.

Zupancic, D. and Müllner, M. (2008) International key account management in manufacturing companies: an exploratory approach of situative differentiation, *Journal of Business to Business Marketing*, 15(4): 455–75.

CASE STUDY 11: EMBRAER

Are B2B buyer–seller relationships relevant in the business jet industry?

Embraer (Empresa Brasileira de Aeronáutica) is one of the world's largest aircraft manufacturers, along with Airbus, Boeing and Bombardier; Embraer (www.embraer.com) ranks behind only Bombardier in regional aircraft. Embraer's core competence is primarily the making of jets and turboprops that seat 21–116 passengers. The company also serves military markets – mainly the Brazilian Air Force – with transport, light attack and surveillance aircraft. Embraer makes more than half of its sales in the Americas, and it is rapidly increasing its customer base outside Europe and the Americas. Table 11.2 shows Embraer's financial development from 2005 to 2008.

(US $m)	2008	2007	2006
Revenue	6,335.2	5,245.2	3,807.4
Net income	388.7	489.3	390.1
Net profit	6.1%	9.3%	10.2%
Employees	23,509	23,734	19,265

TABLE 11.2 Embraer's financial development (2005–8)
Source: adapted from www.embraer.com

Hit hard by the global economic downturn, Embraer laid off about 20 per cent of its worldwide workforce in 2009.

Overall problem: currently the division with the 'business jets' only accounts for 14 per cent of the total turnover; commercial jets accounts for 67 per cent. In order to decrease Embraer's independence on commercial jets, the board directors have decided to focus more on the global sales and marketing of the Embraer Business Jets models (Lineage, Legacy and Phenom).

Company history and background

Embraer was founded in São José dos Campos, Brazil, in 1969 as a government company, with military leader Ozires Silva as its chairman. Embraer produced the country's first aircraft, the 19-seat Bandeirante, that year.

In 1973 Embraer delivered its first Bandeirante to the Brazilian Air Force. Its first pressurized aircraft (the Xingu) took flight in 1976, and Embraer made its debut at the Paris International Airshow in 1977.

Embraer opened a US office in 1980 and introduced the Tucano military training turboprop aircraft. The company developed AMX advanced pilot trainers in the early 1980s. In 1983 it rolled out its 30-seat Brasília jet. Business boomed in 1984, prompting the addition of 7,000 employees and production of 3,000 jets. In 1986 Embraer invested US$300 m (with Argentina and Brazil) to develop a Bandeirante replacement. The company began developing the ERJ 145, its first regional jet, in 1989. Military variants of the ERJ 145, including remote-sensing aircraft and maritime patrol/anti-submarine warfare aircraft, were also produced.

A global downturn in the air-transport industry forced Embraer to release 30 per cent of its workforce in 1990. Nearing bankruptcy, the company began privatization in 1991 and completed the process in 1994; key shareholders included Brazilian investment company Bozano, Simonsen and Brazilian pension funds PREVI and SISTEL.

In 1995 Ozires Silva left Embraer. In 1998 Embraer posted its first profit (US$109 m) since it was privatized.

Embraer signed a US$4.9 bn contract with Crossair (Switzerland) – its largest to date – for regional jetliners in 1999.

Also in 1999 the French aerospace consortium (Thomson-CSF – now called Thales – Aerospatiale-Matra, Dassault Aviation and Snecma) acquired 20 per cent of Embraer. Strong sales in the USA and Europe led the company to record earnings in 1999.

A year for firsts, 2000 saw Embraer's debut on the New York Stock Exchange.

In 2000 the company also entered the market for business jets with its Legacy jet.

Originally, Embraer was 51 per cent controlled by the Brazilian government; the remainder was held by private investors. With the privatization in 1994, control passed to three Brazilian investment groups (Previ and Sistel pension funds and Bozano Group), with each holding 20 per cent of the voting capital. Another 20 per cent was acquired in 1999 by a European consortium (EADS, Dassault Aviation and Thales Group hold 5.67 per cent each, and SNECMA holds 2.99 per cent), as part of a strategic partnership to develop advanced military aircraft. The remainder was publicly traded.

Segmentation of the business jet market

The business jet market can be segmented according to different criteria such as flight performance, range in kilometres, characteristics such as avionics, cabin size and equipment, fuel consumption and maintenance costs, noise level, and, of course, the price for the aircraft. In Table 11.3 the total market is divided into five categories:

Segment	Seats	Range km.	Price
			(million US$ – 2008)
Very Light Jet (VLJ)	4–7	2400–4000	3–5
Light	6–8	2600–4500	5–10
Light Medium	7–9	3500–5000	10–15
Medium	8–12	3700–6300	15–25
Long Range	5–19	5700–8300	25–35
Very Long Range	8–19	8000–13000	≥35

TABLE 11.3 Different business jet segments (2008 figures)
Source: adapted from HSH Nordbank: Sector Report – Business Jets, 2005

1   *The very light jet (VLJ) market*: this segment is emerging at the lower end of the market, that is, smaller planes and shorter range. This large market segment in terms of fleet numbers and number of units is comprised of affordable, tried-and-tested models, which offer a flexibility advantage over larger models as they are able to take off on short runways. The leading manufacturers in this segment are Cessna and Raytheon. However,

in market value, the VLJ market is only expected to be about US$250 m in 2008, less than 2 per cent of the total market size (in value) in Table 11.3. Embraer has no models in this segment.

2 *Light market segment*: the largest market segment in terms of fleet numbers is comprised of affordable, tried-and-tested models, which offer a flexibility advantage over larger models as they are able to take off on short runways. The leading manufacturers in this segment are Cessna, Bombardier and Raytheon.

3 *Light medium market segment*: the light medium segment is the second largest in terms of fleet numbers and will see the addition of new models in the coming years. Cessna plans to launch the Citation XLS and Sovereign, while Gulfstream will launch the G150. This segment is considered to have a big growth potential.

4 *Medium market segment*: this segment of relatively small intercontinental jets costing US$15–25 m is comparatively small. It is therefore surprising to see the host of new models that compete in this segment. If the market is weak, low sales figures represent a major risk for manufacturers in this segment. If the market develops positively, all models are expected to be produced in acceptable numbers, however.

5 *Long range market segment*: this segment is dominated by Dessault Falcon, Gulfstream, Bombardier and Embraer. Bombardier has launched its Challenger 800, and Gulfstream its G350, G450 and G550. Dessault Falcon has launched the 7X. This segment has good growth potential thanks to the new models and growing demand for larger jets.

Embraer business jets

Currently Embraer has the following product range of business jets:

- *Phenom 100:* capacity: 4–6 seats, range: 2,182 km, category: entry-level
- *Phenom 300:* capacity: 7–9 seats, range: 3,334 km, category: light
- *Legacy 450:* capacity: 8–10 seats, range: 4,260 km, category: light-medium
- *Legacy 500:* capacity: 8–12 seats, range: 5,556 km, category: midsize
- *Legacy 600:* capacity: 10–14 seats, range: 6,297 km, category: long range
- *Lineage 1000:* capacity: 13–19 seats, range: 8,334 km, category: very long range

Since the company entered this market in 2000 with the launch of the Legacy, this aircraft has met with increasing acceptance in the long range segment and achieved a 10 per cent market share in 2008, the largest market share in the category. By December 2008 the fleet of Legacy 600 jets had grown to 150 in 24 countries.

The global executive jet industry delivered approximately 900 executive aircraft in 2008 (see Table 11.4) – the largest volume ever and a 15 per cent increase over deliveries in the previous year. Embraer delivered 36 aircraft to this market in 2008, including 33 Legacy 600s, one executive version of the Embraer 175 and two Phenom 100s. This means that in 2008 Embraer had a 4 per cent market share in the worldwide business jet market (see Table 11.4).

The world market for business jets

The business jet fleet (in the world market) increased from approximately 5,000 aircraft in 1981 to approximately 14 000 (see also Table 11.4), corresponding with a compound annual growth rate (CAGR) of approximately 6 per cent.

The yearly deliveries (units sold) increased from 200 units in 1985 to approximately 900 in 2008 (see Table 11.4). Seventy per cent of the whole fleet is located in the USA.

The vast majority (95 per cent) of the business jet market is controlled by five competitors. These include Cessna (TXT), Dassault Falcon, Gulfstream (General Dynamics), Bombardier, and the former Raytheon aircraft (Hawker/Premier), which were acquired by Goldman Sachs Capital Partners and Onex in late 2006, both private equity firms. We restrict our analysis here to these five competitors. There are other manufacturers serving the high end including, for example, Boeing and Airbus.

Manufacturer	Current business jet fleet (Total number – 2008)	Unit sales 2008	Value sales 2008
Total	14,000	900	US$16 bn
	%	%	%
Cessna (Textron) (USA)	29	33	17
Bombardier (Canada)	15	15	27
Golfstream (General Dynamics) (USA)	15	23	25
Dassault Falcon (France)	10	10	15
Raytheon (USA)	30	15	10
Embraer	1	4	6
Total	100	100	100

TABLE 11.4 The world market for business jets
Source: different public sources

In 2009 several of the business jet manufacturers had problems, because of the financial crisis. For example, in April 2009, Bombardier had a 40 per cent drop in deliveries, compared to the same period in 2008.

According to *Aviation Week*, some 14 000 of business jets are in operation throughout the world. Twenty-five per cent of the total are more than 25 years old. Assuming that they have a useful life of 25–30 years, one can expect a substantial demand for replacements in the coming years. About one-third of yearly unit sales is attributable to replacements for business jets taken out of service and two-thirds to market growth.

The secondary market for used business jets is very well organized. If we regard the older jets as 'sediment', there is only a relatively limited number of young business jets for sale. These are marketed by a small number of dealers and brokers. Databases such as JetNet help bring buyers and sellers together and provide access to the specifications of nearly all jets available for sale worldwide such as flight hours of the individual turbines, location of the jet and maintenance information.

Nevertheless, the average number of years a used business jet stays in the market has reached a historical high.

Competition among manufacturers of business jets – Embraer's competitors

Cessna (Textron) is the clear leader on a unit basis followed by Bombardier and Raytheon. On a revenue basis, Bombardier and Gulfstream are the leaders.

Cessna (Textron) (USA)

Thanks to its ability to combine the fuselages, wings and engines in different ways, Cessna has traditionally had one of the largest product ranges behind Bombardier. Given that a large part of the range was launched in the past decade, Cessna is under no pressure to develop new models. Cessna's strengths also include a broad customer base and established service network. Cessna models account for about one-third of the global business jet fleet.

One of the company's weaknesses is the fact that it has no high-end model and therefore no presence in the upper market segment.

The key models in production are: CJ1, CJ2, CJ3, Citation Bravo, Encore, Excel, Citation X, Citation Mustang, Sovereign and XLS.

Bombardier (Canada)

Bombardier has the largest range of jets and mainly operates in the medium and upper market segment with the Learjet and Canadair (Challenger) series. According to industry experts, Bombardier will have difficulties in keeping its market share. This is primarily attributable to the strategy of the new chief executive officer (CEO), Paul Tellier, who attaches greater importance to profits than to market share. Accordingly, the main focus is no longer on the variety of models in the medium price segment.

The key models in production are: Learjet 31A, 40, 45/XR, 60, Challenger 300, 604, Global Express, Challenger 800 and Global 5000.

Gulfstream (General Dynamics) (USA)

General Dynamics' acquisition of Galaxy Aerospace helped Gulfstream more or less catch up with Bombardier. Gulfstream had a market share of approximately 25 per cent in the last decade and may even expand this share in the coming years. Good business jet sales are expected especially in the government and defence sectors.

Gulfstream's wide range of business jets are mainly positioned in the upper market segments. Besides the refinement of existing models, Gulfstream is also working on the design of a 'silent' supersonic jet.

The key models in production are: G100, G200, G300, G400, G500, G550, G150, G350 and G450.

Raytheon (USA)

The very small product range and a current market share of approximately 10 per cent makes Raytheon the smallest of the big five. While the Hawker Horizon was added to the product range in 2004, the company still lacks a business jet in the high-end segment. The company's future will largely depend on the success of the tried and tested models.

The key models in production are: Premier I, Hawker 400 XP, 800 XP and Hawker Horizon.

B2B customers and other intermediate players in the business jet industry

Who are the customers in this industry? Of course, business jets may be sold directly to big multinational companies with a large travelling need for their managers, or to super-rich people, for example, in the Middle East. But the main volume of business jets is sold to different kind of intermediates, as described below.

Figure 11.6 shows the structuring and explanation of the industry actors (commercial jet operators and intermediaries) in the business jet industry.

Commercial jet operators/intermediaries

As seen in Figure 11.6, the different operator models can generally be classified into four groups: charter/air taxi, fractional ownership (FO), full ownership and jet membership programme/private jet cards. The choice of a concept mainly depends on the estimated annual flight volume (in hours). Another aspect is whether the number of passengers is the same for each flight or whether it varies strongly. If transport requirements vary strongly (passenger numbers, distance between destinations), usage concepts with a free choice of the business jet type are preferable.

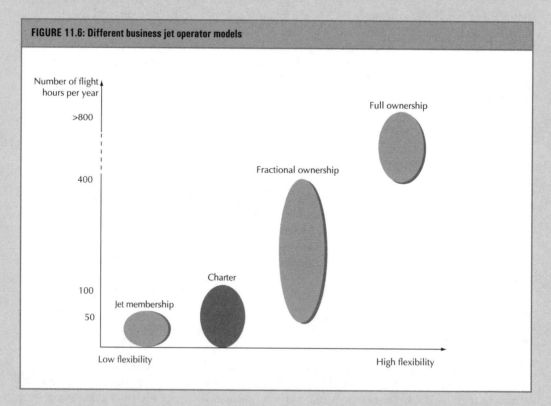

FIGURE 11.6: Different business jet operator models

Charter/air taxi

Charter/air taxi is recommended for companies travelling less than 100 flight hours per year. There should be at least four passengers per flight, however. This relatively low travelling volume would make (fractional) ownership of a jet uneconomical.

Charter concepts comprise on-demand charters and contract charters. In the case of on-demand (*ad hoc*) charters, availability of the jets is not guaranteed and prices are somewhat higher than for contract (block) charters. Contract charters are based on a longer-term contract stipulating a defined flight volume (in hours) for the term of the contract. Charter customers are charged for positioning costs and empty flights.

Corporate shuttles are a special form of contract chartering and allow a company's employees to travel between different production plants or branches. The time savings and the productivity of employees during the flights more than offsets the cost of a corporate shuttle, making them an attractive alternative to scheduled flights. To make a corporate shuttle profitable, some companies share the flight services, which would otherwise be too costly for a single company.

Private jet membership/jet cards

Jet membership models are derived from fractional ownership schemes and *ad hoc* charter programmes. Such models typically allow customers to use a defined number of flight hours in a certain jet type within a defined period of time. Unused hours usually lapse at the end of the agreed utilization period.

Jet membership cards enable customers to use several jets at the same time. Such systems are therefore recommended for travellers who have several destinations at the same time or overlapping flight schedules. The total flight volume should not exceed 50 hours per year as otherwise other usage concepts would be more favourable. Should the aircraft 'booked' by jet card not be available, another jet will be provided. If required, a larger jet or an aircraft with a larger range can be used – the costs will be charged in accordance with the exact number of hours travelled; if higher-quality models are used, the hours on the jet card will be used up more quickly (or more slowly if aircraft models of a smaller category are used). This is based on a defined translation factor. The flight hours must be paid in advance. Marquis Jet Europe's programme starts at 25 flight hours at €126 000. Private jet memberships avoid the disadvantages of other usage concepts such as capital requirements, non-availability of charter jets and additional costs for empty flights. The special aspect of private jet memberships is that the price is fixed in advance. Compared to charters, where the price for the same route may fluctuate over time, the price for jet memberships is always the same. Moreover, some jet membership programmes offer bonuses in the form of free flight hours for each return route. DeltaAirElite offers bonuses of up to 40 per cent (in flight hours). Nevertheless, jet membership cards have a relatively high fixed price and are recommendable for high net worth individuals rather than for corporations.

Fractional ownership (FO)

FOs are usually acquired by corporate customers who either wish to extend their own corporate flight service or who do not have the critical size to justify the use of their own corporate business jet. FO concepts are suitable for flight volumes of 50–400 hours per year. FO means that the user acquires a fraction of a certain jet. The minimum fraction to be acquired is one-sixteenth or 50 flight hours per year. Travellers with an annual volume of approximately 100 flight hours should acquire one-eighth. FO allows users to benefit from the advantages offered by a business jet without having to organize charter services on the one hand or having to perform the management tasks of a jet owner on the other hand. This task is performed by the operator of the FO programme.

Should a user's own jet (fraction) not be available at the desired time, another jet from the FO operator's fleet will be made available. This is made possible by exchange agreements with other FO owners, which aim to increase or guarantee jet availability. Most FO agreements have a term of five years. Some FO programmes require the FO to be repurchased by the FO operator every five years, while others merely require the operator's contract to be renewed to reflect current monthly and hourly rates. Unused flight hours can be carried forward to the following years and do not expire. However, the maximum total number of flight hours per five-year term is limited to 1,000. The number of flight hours acquired may be exceeded by a maximum of 50 per cent per year. In this case, users will however incur additional costs.

FO can be acquired by way of a one-time payment. NetJets offers a one-sixteenth fraction at a price starting at only US$200 000. Alternatively, this one-time payment can be refinanced via the FO company or the fraction can be leased. Monthly leasing fees are relatively high as they must compensate for the value impairment of the jet expected at the end of the term.

Different sizes of fractions available

In addition, the fractional owner pays a monthly fee to the FO operator, which covers all fixed costs such as pilot salaries and training, hangar fees and regular maintenance as well as administrative expenses and insurance costs. The fixed costs are spread over the different owners in accordance with their respective ownership fractions. The FO is capitalized as an asset by the owner's balance sheet, which means that it is subject to annual depreciation. In addition to the one-time payment and the monthly fees, users incur variable costs for the number of flight hours used. Variable costs include costs for fuel, maintenance costs and cabin crews and food as well as general tax on consumption and airport fees. Under applicable laws, fractional owners are responsible for the safety of the passengers and should therefore have sufficient insurance cover.

Should a user sell their FO, they will be charged a resale fee of 5–7 per cent of the current market value. Another disadvantage is the fact that in case the FO is returned or sold, the loss is higher than if the jet were fully owned due to the higher utilization rate.

The important aspect is that the buyer of an FO does not acquire the right to fly but also has actual fractional ownership of the jet. Nevertheless, fractional owners cannot use the whole jet as collateral. On the other hand, the rights of a fractional owner are not affected by the financial liabilities of other fractional owners. Fractional owners can pledge only their own share in the jet, and the continued operation of a partially pledged jet is guaranteed also in case of the realization of collateral by a creditor. At the bottom line, FO is almost always more expensive for the user than jet charters or full ownership and operation of a business jet. FO is an interesting option only for annual flight requirements of 50–400 hours.

NetJets Inc. (www.netjets.com), a Berkshire Hathaway company, is the worldwide leader in private aviation and provides the safest and most secure private aviation solutions. NetJets fractional aircraft ownership allows individuals and companies to buy a share of a private business jet at a fraction of the cost of whole aircraft ownership, and guarantees availability 365 days a year with just a few hours' notice. The NetJets programmes worldwide offer the largest and most diversified fleet in private aviation, which includes 15 of the most popular business jets in the world. Access to the NetJets fleet is also available in the form of a short-term lease, sold on an all-inclusive, pre-paid basis in 25-hour increments, through an exclusive alliance with Marquis Jet Partners. NetJets Inc. also offers aircraft management, charter management, and on-demand charter services through its subsidiary, Executive Jet Management.

The market for fractional aircraft ownership is growing quickly. Over the past decade, the total number of owner shares has grown from approximately 1,500 to over 7,000 expected this year. On average, the market has grown by 8.5 per cent annually. For the last two years, NetJets' market share has been in the region of 70 per cent based on the net value of aircraft sold and leased. NetJets has made more flights than all its competitors combined and manages more than 390 000 flights annually.

Flight Safety is a sister company of NetJets through Berkshire Hathaway and is the world's largest provider of aviation training, educating more than 75 000 pilots annually across 43 learning centres in the USA, Canada, France and the UK. FlightSafety will more than double the number of its existing simulators, creating its largest concentration of simulators in the country.

In 2007, NetJets worldwide flew over 390 000 flights, 237 000 000 miles to more than 173 countries, employing nearly 7,300 worldwide (3,957 pilots, 400 flight attendants). In the USA NetJets' fractional programme alone spent over US$34 m on catering; arranged more than 100 000 cars and limos; landed at over 1,500 airports; spent US$66 m on pilot training at FlightSafety International; and required over 1.8 million maintenance work hours.

Full ownership

FO is suitable for companies with more than 400 flight hours per year. The owner of the jet is also the operator and is therefore responsible for jet management; this task may also be assigned to an external service provider. Full ownership costs comprise the acquisition costs, annual depreciation and current operating expenses. When the jet is not needed, it may be chartered to other users, so that income is generated.

The end users

In terms of the number of business registered jets, North America leads the other continents by a wide margin. This means that North America is the world's most developed business jet market, with 70 per cent of all registrations. Canada only accounts for a small fraction (approximately 2 per cent) of the total number.

The share of business jets used for corporate purposes is relatively high, at approximately 90 per cent. The rest (approximately 10 per cent) is represented by the VIP segment (sports stars, rock stars, political leaders, etc.).

Reasons for using business jets

There are many reasons for companies, private individuals or the government to use business jets. Above all, there is the special flexibility offered by a business jet. These jets have a lower weight than scheduled aircraft and can therefore land on much shorter runways. This allows the user to choose a destination airport that is closer to the final destination than the usual major airports. This results in a shorter ground transfer to the final destination, which, together with the shorter airport check-in times in dedicated business jet terminals, leads to substantial cost savings compared to scheduled flights. The departure time is determined by the passenger and not by the airline, the passenger can fly straight to their desired destination, there is no need to change flights and no risk of missing connecting flights. Moreover, as a result of the stricter safety standards introduced after the 9/11 terrorist attacks, more time is needed for scheduled flights. General safety concerns regarding scheduled flights have also increased demand for business jet transport. For business travellers, the greater productivity during the flight is also an important argument in favour of business jets. Business travellers can talk to their employees or read files without being watched or disturbed by other passengers. Some models feature a conference room, Internet connection and other communications facilities. Business jets also offer much greater travelling comfort than regular flights. In some cases, passengers can drive straight to the aircraft in their private cars and board it without having to wait while their luggage is being safety checked. This way, they do not have to walk long distances as is the case in most major airports.

Time saving plays an important role

According to a Bombardier market study on European business jet customers, they attach importance to:

- time savings and convenience
- direct access even to remote destinations
- relatively new aircraft adapted to customers' personal tastes (colours, equipment)
- easy booking, payment and service provision
- safety of the jets and quality of the operators
- usage concepts that do not require users to own the jet
- avoiding public attention or criticism for using business jets.

Future perspectives

Going forward, we will see a growing number of partnerships between jet operators and other service providers for effective marketing support. American Express is a pioneer in this area. Together with Le Bas International (a charter company that co-operates with over 5,000 jet operators and airlines), American Express offers a bonus programme to its Platinum Card or Centurion Card customers. These customers can charter business jets using their credit card and benefit from special advantages such as high jet availability and more bonus points for their credit card turnover.

Marquis Jet's partnerships go even one step further. Marquis Jet customers who buy a yacht from Sea Ray get a certain number of flight hours as an incentive, depending on the yacht model chosen. Marquis Jet has also entered partnerships to offer services such as private jet plus rental car and private jet plus holiday club. This shows that private jets are well suited for being marketed in combination with other high-end products.

Questions

1 Please explain which relationships in the total value chain of business jets would be most important for Embraer to focus on.

2 Is GAM relevant to use for Embraer's Business Jet division? If yes, how?

Sources: www.embraer.com; HSH Nordbank (2005): Business jets – market, operator models, owners, market trends, secondary market; Datamonitor; Euromonitor

❖ LEARNING OBJECTIVES

After studying this chapter you should be able to do the following:

❖ Examine a typical conceptual framework for a marketing plan.
❖ Describe the structure of the marketing planning process.
❖ Explain the main contents of a marketing plan.
❖ Understand why the implementation part of the marketing plan is so important.

❖ Describe and evaluate the different ways of organizing the marketing department as part of the internationalization process of the company.
❖ Understand the important issues involved in implementing the marketing plan.

12.1 Introduction

We have now examined each of the components of a typical marketing mix. In developing a marketing plan, an organization will need to give careful consideration to each of these, while at the same time being careful not to fall into the trap of viewing each one in isolation. The mix should be viewed as a collective whole, and opportunities for synergy will only be exploited if it is regarded as such. Each element of the mix should consistently reinforce the 'message' being conveyed by the other elements. To ensure that the plan does represent a coherent whole, its author should ensure that the organization's approach to each of the marketing elements is presented therein in a clear and easy-to-read format. It should then become obvious whether ambiguities are present, then corrective action can be taken.

12.2 The process of developing the international marketing plan

The purpose of this section is to summarize earlier chapters. It is as well to remind ourselves at this point what the purpose of marketing planning is: to create sustainable competitive advantage. Basically, marketing planning is a logical sequence and a series of activities leading to the setting of marketing objectives and the formulation of plans for achieving them. Companies generally go through some kind of management process in developing marketing plans. In small to medium-sized enterprises (SMEs) this process is usually informal. In larger, more diversified organizations, the process is often systematized. Figure 12.1 offers one example of how to systematize the process of developing an international marketing plan.

12.3 E-marketing and its effect on the international marketing mix

The Internet has changed the way we do business. No longer is there a need always to have face-to-face contact with a supplier, sales person or customer service representative to purchase goods when this can be done with the click of a mouse. Evans and Wurster (1997, 1999, 2000) have argued that the Internet has given rise to a new economics of information, with the 'blowing up' of the trade-off between the richness of information involved in a transaction and the number of people that it can reach. The authors have argued that the Internet has made it possible for companies to reach a very wide audience, while at the same time doing so with richness of information through the enhanced volume, design and interactivity of content that is feasible on a website. Evans and Wurster identified three bases of competitive advantage: *reach* (referring to access and connection), *richness* (referring to detail and depth of information provided to customers) and *affiliation* (referring to whose interests the business represents).

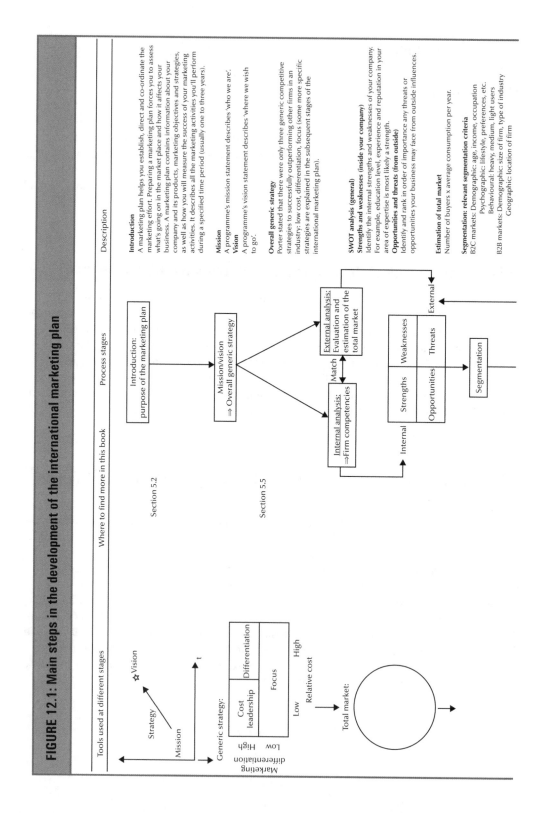

FIGURE 12.1: Main steps in the development of the international marketing plan

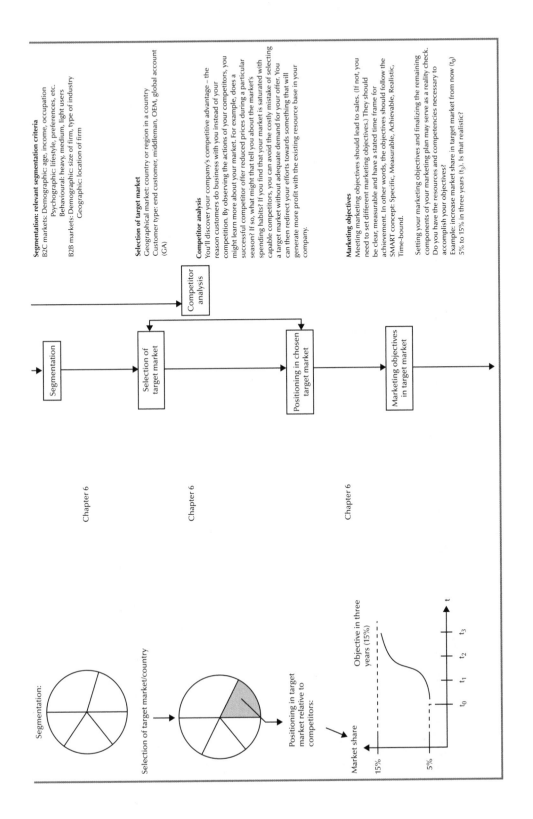

Segmentation: relevant segmentation criteria

B2C markets: Demographic: age, income, occupation
Psychographic: lifestyle, preferences, etc.
Behavioural: heavy, medium, light users
B2B markets: Demographic: size of firm, type of industry
Geographic: location of firm

Selection of target market

Geographical market: country or region in a country
Customer type: end customer, middleman, OEM, global account
(GA)

Competitor analysis

You'll discover your company's competitive advantage – the reason customers do business with you instead of your competition. By observing the actions of your competitors, you might learn more about your market. For example, does a successful competitor offer reduced prices during a particular season? If so, what might that tell you about the market's spending habits? If you find that your market is saturated with capable competitors, you can avoid the costly mistake of selecting a target market without adequate demand for your offer. You can then redirect your efforts towards something that will generate more profit with the existing resource base in your company.

Marketing objectives

Meeting marketing objectives should lead to sales. (If not, you need to set different marketing objectives.) They should be clear, measurable and have a stated time frame for achievement. In other words, the objectives should follow the SMART concept: Specific, Measurable, Achievable, Realistic, Time-bound.

Setting your marketing objectives and finalizing the remaining components of your marketing plan may serve as a reality check. Do you have the resources and competencies necessary to accomplish your objectives?
Example: increase market share in target market from now (t_0) 5% to 15% in three years (t_3). Is that realistic?

FIGURE 12.1: Main steps in the development of the international marketing plan – *continued*

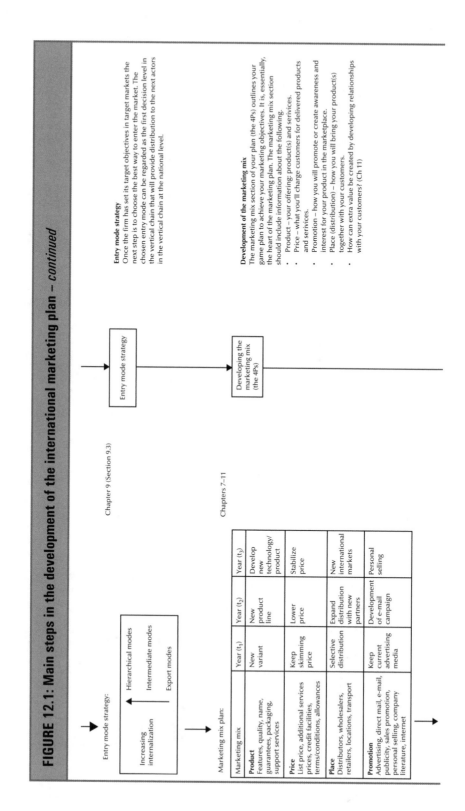

Entry mode strategy:

Chapter 9 (Section 9.3)

Entry mode strategy
Once the firm has set its target objectives in target markets the next step is to choose the best way to enter the market. The chosen entry mode can be regarded as the first decision level in the vertical chain that will provide distribution to the next actors in the vertical chain at the national level.

Hierarchical modes
Intermediate modes
Export modes

Increasing internalization

Developing the marketing mix (the 4Ps)

Chapters 7–11

Development of the marketing mix
The marketing mix section of your plan (the 4Ps) outlines your game plan to achieve your marketing objectives. It is, essentially, the heart of the marketing plan. The marketing mix section should include information about the following.

- Product – your offering; product(s) and services.
- Price – what you'll charge customers for delivered products and services.
- Promotion – how you will promote or create awareness and interest for your product in the marketplace.
- Place (distribution) – how you will bring your product(s) together with your customers.
- How can extra value be created by developing relationships with your customers? (Ch 11)

Marketing mix plan:

Marketing mix	Year (t$_1$)	Year (t$_2$)	Year (t$_3$)
Product Features, quality, name, guarantees, packaging, support services	New variant	New product line	Develop new technology/ product
Price List price, additional services prices, credit facilities, terms/conditions, allowances	Keep skimming price	Lower price	Stabilize price
Place Distributors, wholesalers, retailers, locations, transport	Selective distribution	Expand distribution with new partners	New international markets
Promotion Advertising, direct mail, e-mail, publicity, sales promotion, personal selling, company literature, internet	Keep current advertising media	Development of e-mail campaign	Personal selling

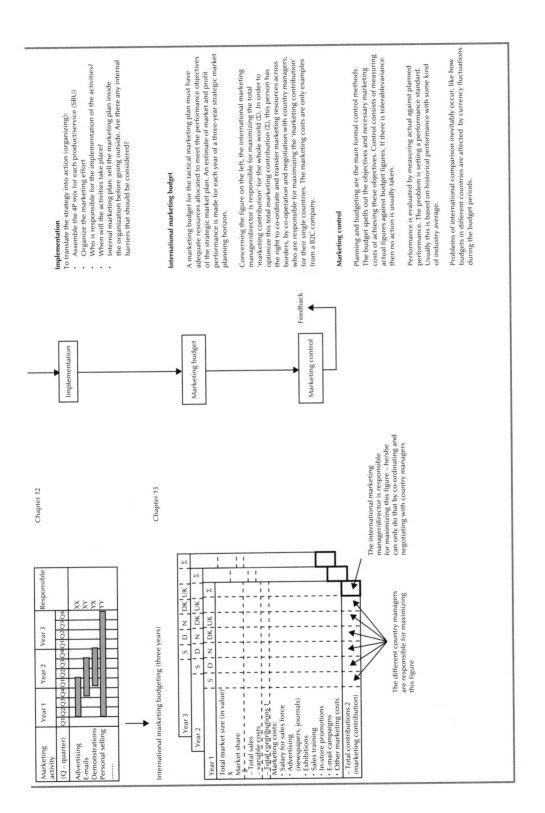

Implementation

To translate the strategy into action (organizing):

- Assemble the 4P mix for each product/service (SBU)
- Organize the marketing effort
- Who is responsible for the implementation of the activities?
- When will the activities take place?
- Internal marketing plan: sell the marketing plan inside the organization before going outside. Are there any internal barriers that should be considered?

International marketing budget

A marketing budget for the tactical marketing plan must have adequate resources allocated to meet the performance objectives of the strategic market plan. An estimate of market and profit performance is made for each year of a three-year strategic market planning horizon.

Concerning the figure on the left, the international marketing manager/director is responsible for maximizing the total 'marketing contribution' for the whole world (Σ). In order to optimize this total marketing contribution (Σ), this person has the right to co-ordinate and transfer marketing resources across borders, by co-operation and negotiation with country managers, who are responsible for maximizing the 'marketing contribution' for their single countries. The marketing costs are only examples from a B2C company.

Marketing control

Planning and budgeting are the main formal control methods. The budget spells out the objectives and necessary marketing costs of achieving these objectives. Control consists of measuring actual figures against budget figures. If there is tolerablevariance then no action is usually taken.

Performance is evaluated by measuring actual against planned performance. The problem is setting a performance standard. Usually this is based on historical performance with some kind of industry average.

Problems of international comparison inevitably occur, like how budgets in different countries are affected by currency fluctuations during the budget periods.

The Internet has made inroads into both the business to consumer (B2C) and business to business (B2B) segments, and online business is predicted to be the biggest growth area in the next decade or so. Traditional companies, the so-called 'brick and mortars' (*B&Ms*), are being pressured to respond to this competitive threat from new e-business upstarts. The so-called Internet 'pure plays' have been able to create strong online brand recognition, provide good customer service, and are open 24 hours a day, seven days a week, 365 days a year. Some of them even give customers the option of customization and allow them to communicate with other customers through communities or discussion forums. The ability to customize service allows customers to build a relationship with the company while also being able to purchase products that they like. Physical stores can provide customers with good service but they cannot provide customers with the convenience and easy accessibility of purchasing online. In order for B&Ms to remain competitive and regain market share in their industries, they have to make sense of how best to utilize the Internet.

12.3.1　The effect of the Internet on the international marketing mix

International Internet marketing has changed some elements of the marketing mix. Marketing on the Internet is a very different process from traditional marketing. The key to a more successful marketing effort on the Internet is an interactive strategy. However, this section focuses on the marketing mix dimensions that may be facilitated through use of the Internet.

Product

A product is anything that can be offered to a market for attention, acquisition, use or consumption, or that might satisfy a want or need. The management of the product mix refers to the development and commercialization of new products, as well as to decisions that determine the length of their cycles; namely, product rejuvenation and renewal or elimination decisions. The Internet leads to faster discovery of customer needs, greater customization of products to customer needs, faster product testing and shorter product life cycles. International marketers who use the Internet should have an in-depth understanding of the foreign marketing environment in order to be able to assess the relative advantages of their own products and services.

As part of a good marketing plan, a company must design new or improved products that meet the customer's current or latent needs, find an effective way to bring those products to the customer, and provide after-sales support. Delivering a great product is not, then, enough to gain customer loyalty. Manufacturers also need to provide online and offline after-sales service, which constitutes a new activity in the manufacturer's value chain. For this reason they need to employ and train customer service staff to service their customers on- and offline. Bulletin boards, user groups and virtual communities can also help customers to solve customer problems online, reducing the manufacturer's time and effort while strengthening its virtual community. In addition, remote service delivery plays a key role in shortening service delivery cycles.

The Internet can dramatically improve the entire product development process. This is especially true if the product being offered can be transformed into a digital product. For example, time zone differences provide a driver for software development. By using the Internet, development work on software or engineering prototypes can continue 24 hours a day through a relay of contractors working in different time zones. Microsoft, for instance, maintains a development centre in India for precisely this reason.

Price

The Internet has many influences on the price strategy; however, its use will lead to increasing standardization of prices across borders or to a narrowing of price differentials as customers become more aware of prices in different countries. For example, an international marketer's country-specific intermediates which advertise services locally (for the international marketer) have to recognize that there are international consequences to their promotions. For example, if an international publisher were to offer a 20 per cent discount on some products to its readers, readers all over the world can see this deal; but in some countries where the publisher already has distributors or does not need to discount in order to get business, the special offer is a problem. Furthermore, Smart agents (software programs that make meta-searches of the Internet for products meeting pre-specified criteria) may further combat attempts at price discrimination by uncovering different prices. Taken together, these factors suggest that use of the Internet will lead to increased standardization of prices across borders, or at least narrower price spreads across country markets.

In the B2B arena, it is expected that the bargaining power of customers is likely to be increased since they will become aware of alternative products and services. Besides, the ease of use of the Internet channel makes it easier for customers to swap between suppliers. It should be noted that there are still barriers to swapping: for instance, once a customer invests time in understanding how to use a website to select and purchase products, they may not want to learn how to use another service. It is for this reason that a company that offers a web-based service before its competitors has a competitive advantage.

The Internet has also made radically new pricing schemes possible, and these have encouraged start-ups to adopt pricing structures that depart a long way from traditional industry practice. The best-known example is the Priceline 'name-your-own-price' (C2B) model, which many people believed would become the dominant model for pricing, but is now seen as another variation on well-established pricing formulas. This approach works well with airline tickets because accurate, timely information about the best prices is hard to get and the seats must be sold before the flight. But customers must be willing to put up with the inconvenience of not being able to choose their airline or the time of day they will fly. Within this narrow niche, Priceline has a loyal and potentially profitable customer base. These conditions would not, however, apply to the long-distance telephone, automobile or mortgage markets, where prices are more transparent.

The final issue in the price dimension is currency rates. Shopping on the Internet needs to be convenient, which means trading in local currencies. Therefore, consumers are unlikely to search for information on currency conversion rates. Companies who wish to market their products internationally may consider adding a link from their web pages to a currency converter or providing an approximate conversion rate for each country to which they are prepared to make sales.

Distribution (place)

Physical distribution is the 'place' aspect of the marketing mix. The marketing channel can be defined as interdependent organizations involved in the process of making a product or service available for use or consumption. The Internet, by connecting end users and producers directly, will reduce the importance of traditional intermediaries (i.e. agents and distributors) in international marketing. To survive, such intermediaries may need to begin offering a different range of services. Their value added will no longer be principally in the physical distribution of goods but rather in the collection, collation, interpretation and dissemination of a vast amount of information. For example, a hospital in Egypt can put out a request for proposal (RFP) for equipment over the Internet, secure bids and select a supplier without going through local brokers and distributors, and have the products delivered directly by DHL or Federal Express, say. Few buffer inventories will be needed in the worldwide distribution system and less working capital.

However, if intermediaries can perform a different mix of services, made necessary by the Internet, they will continue to play critical roles and extract value. The distribution system of the organization must have some capabilities and competencies; for example, 24-hour order-taking and customer service response capability, and regulatory and customer-handling expertise to ship internationally. Companies should consider providing information on how the products are shipped and the precautions taken to ensure their quality on arrival. Quality guarantees and/or special consideration for international returns or refunds may also be necessary.

Undoubtedly, the Internet has reduced many distribution issues. It is borderless and the opportunity to sell over the net in a standardized way eliminates many natural barriers to entry. In addition, any business connected to the Internet can source other businesses' products by ordering them from their websites. Companies no longer have to put together long and expensive distribution channels to bring their products to the customer.

The early Internet literature indicated that it would eliminate the need for intermediaries. Early predictions called for *disintermediation;* that is, the disappearance of physical distribution chains as people moved from buying through distributors and resellers to buying directly from manufacturers. The reality is that the Internet may eliminate the traditional 'physical' distributors, but in the transformation process of the value chain new types of intermediaries may appear. So the disintermediation process has come to be balanced by a 're-intermediation' force – the evolution of new intermediaries (e.g. infomediaries – aggregators of information on the Internet) tailor-made for the online world.

Promotion

Promotion refers to all the various ways an organization undertakes to communicate its products' merits and to persuade target customers to buy from it. The use of the Internet allows sales departments to have interactive communications with their customers. Hard-selling and advertiser-push promotion strategies do not work well on the Internet. Global advertising costs, as a barrier to entry, will be significantly reduced as the Internet makes it possible to reach a global audience more cheaply. However, there are many online promotion techniques. Paying to place links on pages with audiences that mirror or include a company's target customers is less expensive than traditional media. In addition, 'free' advertising on other sites can often be exchanged for mutual links. Postings on Internet discussion groups, on topics relevant to specific products or markets, are another way for marketers to attract visitors to their sites. There are many offline promotion techniques that work to attract potential customers to websites, such as traditional forms of advertising (e.g. magazine advertising or word of mouth).

However, there is one critical issue for international marketers who use the Internet in their marketing: the new challenge facing companies is the management of a global brand and corporate logo. Consumers may become confused if an organization and its subsidiaries have different websites, each communicating a different format, image, message and content.

Therefore, an organization should clearly define its policies about branding on the Internet. Developing one site for each brand – while costly and limiting for cross-selling – is preferable when the brands have distinct markets and images. Finally, advertising on web pages other than the organization's own is possible (and increasingly common), but might not be well received. Customers merely wish to be presented with the hard facts about the subject matter on the pages they read. Note, moreover, that as more and more businesses establish an Internet presence, searching for potential suppliers will become impossible without the aid of high-quality directories to guide people towards relevant sites.

The 4Ps (product, price, place, promotion) model does not explicitly include any interactive elements; furthermore, it does not indicate the nature and scope of such interactions. However, earlier changes in the 4Ps have been the result of the interactive nature of the Internet, which requires a shift in the marketing paradigm, towards a more relationship-oriented approach, as discussed in Chapter 11.

12.4 Writing the international marketing plan document

Marketing planning is widely adopted by companies from all sectors. The process of marketing planning integrates all elements of marketing management: marketing analysis, development of strategy and the implementation of the marketing mix. Marketing planning can, therefore, be regarded as a systematic process for assessing marketing opportunities and matching them with a company's own resources and competencies. In this respect, the process helps businesses to effectively develop, co-ordinate and control marketing activities (Best, 2009).

Basically, the major functions of the marketing plan are to determine where the company is, where it wants to go and how it can get there. Marketing planning is able to fulfil these functions by driving the business through three kinds of activities: (1) analyses of the internal and external situations; (2) development of marketing strategy; and (3) design and implementation of marketing programmes.

The marketing planning process is linked to planning in other functional areas and to overall corporate strategy. It takes place within the larger strategic marketing management process of the corporation. To survive and prosper, the business marketer must properly balance the company's resources with the objectives and opportunities of the environment. Marketing planning is a continuous process that involves the active participation of other functional areas.

The *marketing plan* itself is the written document that businesses develop to record the output of the marketing planning process. This document provides details of the analysis and strategic thinking that have been undertaken, and outlines the marketing objectives, marketing mix and the plan for implementation and control. As such, it plays a key role in informing organizational members about the plan, and any roles and responsibilities they may have within it. The plan also provides details of required resources and should highlight potential obstacles to the planning process, so that steps can be taken to overcome them. In some respects the marketing plan is a kind of road map, providing direction to help the business implement its strategies and achieve its objectives: the plan guides senior management and all functional areas within the organization (Lehmann and Winer, 2008).

Once the core marketing analyses are complete, the strategy development process follows. The key during this phase of marketing planning is to base any decisions on a detailed and objective view from the analyses. In this part of the plan, the most appropriate target markets will be identified, the basis for competing and positioning strategies determined, and detailed marketing objectives presented. As these choices will affect how the business proceeds in relation to its customers and competitors, there must be consistency with the company's overall corporate strategy. The marketing strategy must also be realistic and sufficiently detailed to form the basis for the marketing programmes that follow. Some of the most effective marketing strategies combine a realism that is grounded in a systematic review of the company's existing position with foresight about possible longer-term competitive advantages.

The final stage of the marketing planning process involves the determination of marketing mix programmes and their implementation. A detailed explanation is needed of exactly what marketing tasks must be undertaken, how, by whom and when. There needs to be a clear rationale connecting these marketing mix recommendations with the analyses and strategy preceding them. A common marketing planning weakness occurs when businesses press ahead with detailed marketing programmes that are not well connected with the earlier stages in the planning process, or that simply replicate existing marketing mix tactics without making adjustments to reflect the topical issues identified in the analyses. The result can be misdirected marketing activities that are not closely aimed at the key target segments or that fail to take into account the competitive or wider trading environment.

Assuming that appropriate attention has been devoted to the marketing analyses and marketing strategy that guide the marketing programmes, managers must next ensure that sufficient detail is provided to make the marketing mix genuinely implementable. This means that each component of the marketing programme – product, price, promotion, distribution (place) and people – must be discussed separately and the tasks required to action it explored fully.

Those involved in planning will usually prepare some form of written marketing plan document in which to explain the outputs of the process. Table 12.1 illustrates the typical section headers used in this kind of document. The marketing plan provides a useful reference point for the analytical and strategic thinking undertaken, the detailed marketing objectives and marketing programmes, and their implementation and control. Managers are able to refer back to the document for guidance and should update it regularly to ensure that a full record of marketing planning activities is available. This document helps to focus the views of senior management, and explain the required marketing activities and target market strategy to other functional areas within the business, such as operations and finance (Dibb, 2002).

The key components of the final marketing plan are highlighted in Table 12.1 Note that the planning process format centres on clearly defined market segments, a thorough assessment of internal and external problems and opportunities, specific goals and courses of action. Business marketing intelligence, market potential and sales forecasting are fundamental in the planning process.

I	Title page
II	Table of contents
III	Executive summary
IV	Introduction and problem statement
V	Situational analysis
VI	Marketing objectives and goals
VII	Marketing strategies
VIII	Marketing programmes/action plans
IX	Budgets
X	Implementation and control
XI	Conclusion

TABLE 12.1 Framework for a marketing plan

Let us examine each section of the marketing plan structure in Table 12.1 in further detail.

12.4.1   I Title page

The title page is an identification document that provides the reader with the following essential information:

- legal name of business
- name of document ('Marketing Plan for …')
- date of preparation or modification of the document
- name, address, email and telephone number of the business or contact person
- name, address, email and telephone number of the individual or business who prepared the plan
- the planning period.

12.4.2   II Table of contents

This is the list of subjects covered in the marketing plan and where in the document to find them.

12.4.3   III Executive summary

This gives busy executives and managers a quick overview, in the form of a concise summary, of the key points in the marketing plan. This section encompasses a one-page (or thereabouts) summary of the basic factors involving the marketing of the product or service along with the results expected from implementing the plan.

12.4.4   IV Introduction and problem statement

The identification and clear presentation of the problem(s) or issue(s) facing the company is the most critical part of the introduction. Only a problem that has been properly defined can be addressed. You should move on to addressing the main problem fairly quickly. If there are sub-problems in the marketing plan that you feel you should identify, feel free to do so, but make sure you clearly identify the main problem. Be on the alert for symptoms posing as key issues and underlying problems – stick to the main issue as far as possible. Remember that strategic marketing problems are long term, involve large sums of money and affect multiple aspects of the organization.

12.4.5   V Situational analysis

Based on a comprehensive audit of the market environment, competitors, the market, products and the company itself, this section provides a condensed view of the market (size, structure and dynamics), prior to a detailed analysis of individual market segments, which form the heart of the marketing plan.

The process is based upon market segmentation; that is, homogeneous groups of customers with characteristics that can be exploited in marketing terms. This approach is taken because it is the one that is most useful for managers in developing their businesses. The alternative, product-oriented, approach is rarely appropriate, given the varying requirements of the different customer groups in the market in which most companies compete.

It is necessary to summarize the unit's present position in its major markets, in the form of a SWOT analysis for each major market segment, product or business group. The word SWOT derives from the initial letters of the words strengths, weaknesses, opportunities and threats. The analysis includes the following issues.

The company and its market

- Identification and evaluation of the competencies in the company (key personnel, experience, skills and capabilities and resources) in comparison with those of your competitors.
- The structure of your marketing organization (lines of authority, functions and responsibilities).
- Description of your total potential market (i.e. your potential customers).
- How does your product/service satisfy the needs of this market?
- Describe the particular customers that you will target.
- Size of (1) total potential market (number of potential customers), and (2) your target market. Support estimates with factual data.
- Growth potential of (1) total potential market, and (2) your target market. Look at local, national and international markets. Support estimates with factual data.
- Your current market share (company's sales divided by the total market sales in per cent).

Competitive environment

- Major competitors: name, location and market share.
- Compare your product/service with that of your major competitors (brand name, quality, image, price, etc.).
- Compare your company with that of your major competitors (reputation, size, distribution channels, location, etc.).
- How easy is it for new competition to enter this market?
- What have you learned from watching your competition?

- Are competitors' sales increasing, decreasing, steady? Why?

Technological environment

- How is technology affecting this product/service?
- How soon can it be expected to become obsolete?
- Is your company equipped to adapt quickly to changes?

Socio-political environment

- Describe changing attitudes and trends. How flexible and responsive is your company?
- New laws and regulations that may affect your business. What might be their financial impact?

Use SWOT analyses to assess the key issues that must be addressed. Summarize your internal and external assessment in the form of a SWOT matrix using the key points from the situation analysis.

12.4.6 VI Marketing objectives and goals

This states precisely the marketing objectives and goals in terms of sales volume, market share, return on investment, or other objectives or goals for your marketing plan. State these objectives in precise, quantifiable terms and give the time needed to achieve each of them (e.g. 'To obtain a sales volume of 3,000 units, equal to an increase in market share from 10 per cent to 12 per cent of total market, by the end of the next fiscal year').

What is the difference between a goal and an objective?

Goals are normally more general and may not be quantified. 'To establish our product as a market leader in the marketplace' is a goal. Objectives are normally quantified: 'To sell 50 000 units next year' is an objective. Objectives are also quantified in terms of sales, profits, market share, return on investment (ROI) or other measurements. Goals usually also have a longer time frame than objectives. Objectives are usually measurable targets set for a 'short' term, for example, a month or a year. Make sure that your goals and objectives fit together. For example, your ability to capture a stated market share may require lower prices and consequently a lower profit per sold unit.

12.4.7 VII Marketing strategies

How will you reach your objectives and goals (this is covered in Chapter 5). Which strategic models from Chapter 5 should be used (new market penetration, penetration, market development, etc.)?

12.4.8 VIII Marketing programmes/action plans

Marketing programmes are the actionable means of achieving desired ends. They outline *what* needs to be done, *how* it will be done, *when* it will be done and *who* will do it.

- How will you implement the above strategy?

- Product/service: quality, branding, packaging, modifications, location of service, and so on.
- Pricing: how will you price your product/service so that it will be competitive, yet profitable?
- Promotion/advertising: how, where, when, and so on.
- Selling methods: personal selling, mail order, and so on. Include number of sales people, training required, and so on.
- Distribution methods.
- Servicing of product.
- Necessary organizational development in the company.
- Other: add any other relevant information.

12.4.9   IX Budgets

Having detailed the steps that will be necessary to achieve the marketing objectives, the writer of the plan should then be in a position to cost the various proposals and to derive an overall marketing budget for the planning period. Of course, in reality, life is just not that easy. Cost will undoubtedly have been in the minds of marketing planners even before they commenced the marketing planning process. At the very least, the development of a suitable budget is likely in practice to have been an iterative process, with proposals being re-evaluated in the light of budgetary constraints.

There are a variety of ways of determining the marketing budget. The ideal would clearly be to specify the strategy and tactics that are felt necessary to achieve the marketing objectives, and then to cost these to arrive at an overall budget. This is usually referred to as the 'task method' of setting a marketing budget. Of course, in reality, this method is seldom employed since financial pressures from senior management, the budgeting/accounting practices of the organization, and uncertainty about resource attraction all hamper the derivation of an appropriate budget. In practice, therefore, budgets (concerning marketing costs) tend to be set using the following methods: percentage of sales, competitive parity or objective-task method (see Section 10.2).

- *Percentage of last year's sales*: there is a danger with this method in that if the company has been suffering from poor performance of late, reducing the marketing budget in line with sales could actually serve to worsen the situation. Clearly, when sales fall there is a strong case for enhancing, not reducing, the marketing budget.
- *Competitor matching*: using the amounts spent on marketing by the competition and matching their resource allocation.
- *What can be afforded*: perhaps the least rational of all the methods of budget calculation, this one involves the senior management of the company deciding what they believe they can afford to allocate to the marketing function in a particular year. Little or no reference is made to the marketing objectives, nor to the activities of competitors.

Irrespective of the method actually used, in practice it would be usual to specify how the eventual budget has been allocated and to include such a specification in the marketing plan itself. It would also be normal for an allowance to be made for contingencies in the event that monitoring by the company suggests that the objectives will not be met. Sufficient resources should then exist for some form of corrective action to be taken.

A *budget of cash flows* should also drawn up. This identifies whether a company will have enough money to meet its cash requirements on a monthly basis. Some sales will be made in cash while others may be made on credit. Because sales made on credit will not result in the receipt of cash until a later date, they must not be recorded until the month in which the cash will actually be received. Therefore, the percentage of sales to be made in cash and the percentage to be made on credit must be estimated. The percentage of credit sales should be further broken down according to the company's different collection periods (30 days, 60 days, etc.).

12.4.10   X Implementation and control

As soon as the plan has been implemented, the marketing management will then have to take responsibility for monitoring the progress of the company towards the goal specified. Managers will also need to concern themselves with the costs that have been incurred at each stage of implementation and monitor these against the budget. Thus, control mechanisms need to be put into place to monitor:

- the actual sales achieved against the budget
- the actual costs incurred against those budgeted
- the performance of individual services against budget
- the overall strategic direction that the organization is taking; that is, will the overall corporate objectives be achieved in a manner commensurate with the organization's mission?

If variances are detected in any of these areas, corrective action can then be initiated, if necessary by utilizing resources allocated in the budget for contingency.

12.4.11   XI Conclusion

This section briefly concludes the problems stated at the beginning of the report, based on the analysis in the marketing plan. The conclusion is not a summary. The executive summary will normally also include the key results of the market analysis.

Exhibit 12.1: *Seven steps to implementing personal selling and relationship building*

Although personal selling as a profession and function has evolved and changed dramatically over recent decades, one of the oldest and most widely accepted paradigms in the sales discipline is commonly referred to as the 'seven steps of selling' (Dubinsky, 1980/81; Manning and Reece, 2001; Weitz et al., 2001; Futrell, 2002). We now look at each of these steps in turn.

1   **Prospecting**: prospecting is the method by which sales people search for new customers and potential customers. One obvious reason for prospecting is to expand the customer base, which is important because most sales organizations lose customers every year. Many different methods of prospecting are available, such as referrals, networking, 'bird-dogging', cold

canvassing and numerous others. Prospecting usually includes a discussion of qualifying the prospect and thus developing some type of screening procedure.

Traditionally, sales people were expected to find their own prospects. However, many sales organizations today use telemarketers to perform the prospecting function. Once the prospect is found, the telemarketer may attempt a sale or may pass the lead to the appropriate sales person, depending on the structure of the organization. Use of the Internet now also allows potential prospects to approach the organization, and they are later contacted by a sales person. Technology has allowed the organization to become more cost efficient and effective in the prospecting step, freeing the sales person to focus on other sales functions. In particular, database marketing and customer relationship management (CRM) have enhanced marketing's ability to aid sales people in prospecting. As a result, the current evolution for prospecting means that sales people may no longer be performing the prospecting step as a systematic part of their job, but the step typically remains elsewhere within the organization.

2   *Preapproach*: the preapproach step includes all post-prospecting activities prior to the actual visit to a prospect or customer. The preapproach step occurs on virtually every sales call. Sellers do their research on the prospect or customer, familiarize themselves with the customer's needs, review previous correspondence, and pull together any other new and relevant material that might be appropriate to take along to the sales call itself. Preapproach activities also include talking with gatekeepers, doing homework on the customer (individual and organization), mentally preparing for the approach and presentation (rehearsal), and 'reading' the customer's office on entry. Today, a laptop computer loaded with customer data instantly makes a sales person highly customer knowledgeable. They have customer records at hand: their buying history and any personal information that might be useful. Well-executed CRM systems are excellent at providing the means to update any aspect of this customer information at any customer touchpoint (places where customers come in contact with the selling organization).

3   *Approach*: the approach usually takes the first minute or few minutes of a sale. It consists of the strategies and tactics employed by sales people when gaining an audience and establishing initial rapport with the customer. The approach includes opening 'small talk', the handshake, eye contact and generally making a good initial impression. A shift has occurred to a broader relationship approach where the sales person has probably already developed the foundation of an interpersonal network within the buying organization and the goal is to provide more information or solve some existing problem; that is, provide a solution. Because most sales do not occur on the first call but rather are a result of multiple calls and contacts with multiple people, establishing and building on this foundation is what eventually facilitates relationship selling.

4   *Presentation*: the presentation is the main body of the sales call and should occur after the sales person has predetermined the needs of the customer. This step can be one presentation or multiple presentations over a period of

▶

time. Goals for the sales presentation will vary. First-time buyers must get sufficient information to adequately understand the product's benefits, which may be facilitated by building the presentation around a product demonstration. Selling points and attributes are visualized and built around a call agenda or sales proposal. This step can be complex, and preparation is essential.

For many sales people, the presentation step has undergone a substantial transformation. Today's presentations are typically conducted over several meetings, with the sales person often doing more listening than talking.

The physical presentation has also undergone a transformation, spurred on by several factors. First, sales people can now use a PowerPoint-type presentation that can easily be adapted from call to call. Second, with the use of a laptop computer, a sales person can provide much greater depth of knowledge targeted to a specific customer. A third major transformative factor is the fact that today's presentations are often delivered by a team from the selling organization, rather than via the traditional approach of individual sales person presentations. Also more and more sales presentations are made to a buying centre, probably including an organization's executives, as opposed to a single purchaser. This change greatly affects the style and content of the presentation compared to the traditional way of presenting to a single purchaser.

5   *Overcoming objections*: objections can broadly be defined as customer questions and hesitancies about the product or organization. Sales people should expect that objections will be encountered in every sales presentation. A number of reasons exist for objections, and despite the fact that objections can delay the sales process, for the most part they should be perceived in a positive sense as useful. This is because, by revealing objections, true buyer needs can be uncovered. In the early days of selling, sales objections were viewed mostly as a hurdle that sales people had to overcome to get to the ultimate sale. More recently, a true objection might be viewed as a sign not to pursue the sale further because a need may not be met with a given product. Today's sales person, through either predetermined needs or multiple calls, is attempting to ascertain earlier and more precisely what the customer requires from the product. Listening and asking questions have become key elements of the transformation of the 'overcoming objections' step.

6   *Close*: the close is defined as the successful completion of the sales presentation, culminating in a commitment to buy the good or service. Once any objections have successfully been overcome, the sales person must actually ask for the order and thus begin the process of closing the sale. This step has traditionally been trumpeted as difficult for many sales people (especially new sales people) because many simply do not ask for the order. Many closing tactics are available.

The key goal of this step has moved beyond simply short-term physical closure to the successful realization of the mutual goals of both parties to the relationship, over the long run. Organizations today focus on the lifetime value of a customer. The goals to be achieved between seller and buyer must be mutually beneficial. Developing a long-term relationship with customers whose ROI is negative is bad business.

7   *Follow-up*: the traditional follow-up was typically done with a phone call or letter thanking the customer for the sale and determining if the product is meeting expectations. Frequently, the sales person would 'drop by' to see if any problems were occurring. The key transformative factor here is increased effectiveness of communication through technology. Today, email has become a dominant method of follow-up because of its ease of use and timeliness. In the era of relationship selling, the follow-up step has gained importance and is also now much quicker and more efficient to execute.

Customer relationship maintenance implies that the selling organization has assigned, on an ongoing basis, an individual or team to truly maintain all aspects of the business relationship. This may be the sales person themselves or it may be turned over to others. Sales organizations are currently altering their control and reward systems to account for this shift towards more ongoing relationship maintenance, often to customers with a large global organization, or multinational enterprises (MNEs): the so-called global accounts. This is also the basic idea behind the concept of global account management (GAM), which was discussed in Chapter 11.

Conclusion

The steps in the traditional seven-step selling process are sequential and cumulative in that a sales person starts with prospecting and works their way through to follow-up. The amount of time or effort in any one step may vary, but the traditional model requires that every step occur.

In contrast, the evolved selling process (Moncrief and Marshall, 2005) assumes that the sales person will typically perform the various steps of the process in some form, but that the steps do not necessarily occur for each sales call. Rather, they occur over time, accomplished by multiple people within the selling organization, and not necessarily in any given sequence. While the traditional seven steps reflect a selling orientation on the part of an organization, the evolved selling process reflects more of a customer orientation in that the focus is on *relationship selling;* that is, securing, building and maintaining long-term relationships with profitable customers.

Sources: adapted from Dubinsky, A.J. (1980/81) A factor analytic study of the personal selling process, *Journal of Personal Selling & Sales Management*, 1: 26–33; Futrell, C.M. (2002) *Fundamentals of Selling: Customers for Life*, 7th edn. Boston, MA: McGraw-Hill/Irwin; Manning, G.L. and Reece, B.L. (2001) *Selling Today: Building Quality Partnerships*, 8th edn. Upper Saddle River, NJ: Prentice Hall; Moncrief, W.C. and Marshall, G.W. (2005) The evolution of the seven steps of selling, *Industrial Marketing Management*, 34(1): 13–22; Weitz, B.A., Castleberry, S.B. and Tanner, J.F. (2001) *Selling: Building Partnerships*, 4th edn. Boston, MA: McGraw-Hill/Irwin

12.5 Barriers impeding the implementation of marketing plans, and what to do about them

Even though the benefits of adopting marketing planning are well established, the effectiveness of the process is not guaranteed. A range of barriers to effective marketing planning have been highlighted in the literature. Careful attention is, therefore, needed to ensure that marketing planning is implemented effectively. The starting point should be an appreciation of the likely barriers, so that preventative and remedial action can be taken. The following list is an amalgamation of the key issues raised by researchers in the marketing planning literature (Dibb, 2002; Simkin 2002).

- *Lack of marketing competency in the organization*: insufficient marketing knowledge or skills, poor grasp of the marketing concept in general, poor understanding of the distinction between the marketing planning process and its outputs, management's failure to see across individual market sectors or brands to grasp the 'whole picture'.
- *Isolation of marketing planning from other areas of the business*: poor involvement of functions, lack of enthusiasm for planning among non-marketers, no power for marketers to talk to other functions and the need to understand them better; these are all facets of one underlying problem in much marketing planning – non-marketers have a wealth of knowledge and insights to bring to marketing planning; research and development (R&D) personnel hear what is evolving elsewhere, technical managers understand what is feasible to produce/deliver, financial managers assist in bringing realism to the profitability debate.
- *Organizational barriers*: individual manager's 'empire-building' causes problems and detracts from the benefits to the company of structured planning. A lack of acknowledged corporate value given to planning, plus personal clashes, are facets of corporate life well known to most managers. The process of planning, however, requires sharing of information and ideas, effective communications, and a focus on the market rather than internal politics.
- *Too much short-term marketing planning*: too much emphasis on a one-year planning time frame, leading to plenty of short-term detail but little long-term vision.
- *Marketing plans developed in isolation rather than on marketing analyses*: inadequate marketing intelligence and/or lack of a marketing intelligence system (MIS), poor sharing of marketing intelligence, insufficient marketing analyses of customers, competitors and the wider trading environment, leading to a poor understanding of these areas.
- *Lack of managers' time resources for thorough marketing planning*: managers have difficulties balancing planning activities with the rest of their workload, so that the process is not fully implemented.

The need for a clearly defined process is fundamental to successful marketing planning. This process should incorporate the required analyses, strategic thinking and marketing programme development. However, if such a process is to be put into practice effectively and the barriers are to be avoided, businesses must also address certain infrastructure, processes and implementation requirements.

The recommendation is that marketers should use the following three solutions.

1 *Solution 1*: provide the necessary infrastructure and resources for marketing planning activities.

2   *Solution 2*: use a robust analytical process that is objective and complete in terms of the inclusion of the essential ingredients of marketing planning.
3   *Solution 3*: devote managerial time and attention to the ongoing management of the resulting plan's implementation.

We now look at each of these solutions in greater detail.

12.5.1   Solution 1: infrastructure requirements

The infrastructure requirements for marketing planning can be conceptualized as a series of prerequisites that organizations should address at the outset of the process.

The need to manage internal communication extends far beyond the marketing function. A well-orchestrated programme to manage interfunctional co-ordination is paramount. It is vital to ensure that communication of the planning exercise and its outcomes extends throughout organizational hierarchies and right down the distribution channels.

In addition, any marketing initiative requires purpose, process and robust propositions, whether it is an externally deployed marketing mix programme or an infrastructure requisite for successful marketing planning. Busy personnel cannot be expected to take time out from routine operations to undertake strategic thinking and develop marketing plans without being provided with the resources for tackling such tasks. Too often, senior managers expect a few line managers to undertake additional weighty tasks without being provided with the necessary extra resources.

12.5.2   Solution 2: robust processes

There is no point determining tactical marketing mix programmes if no analysis of the marketplace has been undertaken or if the target market strategy has not been updated accordingly to reflect these findings. An effective marketing planning process should include a coherent and integrated process of analysis, strategizing and tactical programme recommendation.

The skills to undertake marketing analyses, facilitate a strategic review and to modify often entrenched marketing tactics accordingly must be inherent or bought in from external agencies.

12.5.3   Solution 3: facilitation of implementation

Strategy and planning activities will not occur by chance and must be managed: schedules, reviews, performance assessments and remedial actions, with praise and criticism from senior management in the ongoing evaluation process. Without attention to these requirements, much good marketing thinking fails to result in actionable recommendations being implemented.

The output from planning is normally summarized in the form of a detailed marketing plan document. The robustness of this document is a key factor in determining the success of the planning process. To be effective, the marketing plan document must explain the background analyses undertaken during the planning process before specifying all aspects of the proposed marketing strategy and the marketing and sales programmes. The required marketing strategy elements should include details of target segments, an explanation of the basis for competing, and identification of product and brand positioning strategies. The marketing and sales programmes should encompass issues to do with product range, pricing terms, promotional tactics, methods and channels of distribution, and sales force planning. These recommendations must be seen to match the stated marketing objectives and arise out of the analyses of the market, customers, competitors and the wider trading environment that have been undertaken; that is, there must be a close connection between the desires, characteristics and buying behaviour of the company's target markets and the proposed marketing mix recommendations.

Three areas that are particularly vital to implementation, but that are sometimes overlooked in the marketing plan, warrant specific mention.

1   *Communicating planning outputs*: the importance of effective communication does not end once the marketing planning recommendations have been made. Instead, the emphasis shifts to ensuring clarity within and across functional areas, so that the newly designed marketing programmes can be consistently and thoroughly implemented. A detailed plan of communication activity is required that specifies how this can be achieved and who needs to be involved. This plan should extend beyond the organization itself to include all parts of the distribution structure.

2   *Specifying the required implementation resources*: an appropriate level of detail is needed to ensure sufficient finance, personnel and time are allocated to each of the marketing activities required. A weakness of many businesses' marketing plans is that they fail to provide these necessary implementation details, with the result that not all planned activities are put into practice. A key message is that marketing planning does not end when the marketing plan document has been prepared. At this stage, it is crucial that all aspects of the implementation details are attended to. Even once this part of the process is complete, the marketing plan document should continue to be updated on an ongoing basis.

3   *Handling changes in organizational structure, culture or distribution channels*: recognizing that planning may lead to organizational upheaval and change is an important infrastructure prerequisite. However, in order to ensure that such change happens in practice, part of the marketing plan must specifically consider required changes in organizational or distribution channel structure. The level of detail provided is especially critical. For modifications in company structure this should include physical changes to the organizational chart, alterations in reporting structures, managerial responsibilities and communication channels. Alterations to the channel structure must be accompanied by a detailed explanation of the required system for physical distribution, together with any repercussions for the activities of the sales force or those involved in distributing the organization's product base.

12.6 Organization structures for international marketing efforts

There are two main conditions to fulfil if a company is to succeed: to pursue a suitable marketing strategy and to have adopted an appropriate organizational structure. The company's organizational structure is a critical variable for the implementation of its international marketing plans. The following list highlights the main reasons for this:

- There may be difficulties in co-ordinating and controlling operating units (subsidiaries) of different sizes and levels of complexity.

- Personnel in different markets may have different objectives, abilities and expectations, and organizing such a heterogeneous group can be problematic.
- There may be excessive head office control that can be a barrier for the local implementation of marketing plans.

Effective marketing planning only comes about when the marketing strategy and organizational structure match.

The question 'Do we have the right organization for our strategy?' is something that all chief executive officers (CEOs) should be asking, and a failure to do so may bring with it the risk of failure. This question can be broken down into four 'basic' parts, the first two of which concern themselves with the division of responsibility among the labour force, while the remaining questions focus on co-ordination and control.

- What tasks are required to put the strategies into operation?
- To whom should these tasks be assigned?
- How interdependent are these tasks?
- How can the company be sure that the tasks assigned will be performed?

There are no right answers, and therefore right structures, for all companies, but successful companies are those that tend to have organizational structures that fit their specific needs in terms of their corporate objectives, strategies, corporate culture, and so on.

There are many ways in which a multinational company can be organized. These can be reduced to five organizational structure archetypes:

1 functional structure
2 international division structure
3 product-based structure
4 geographic structure
5 matrix structure.

We now look at each of these in turn.

12.6.1　Functional structure

At this early stage of internationalization, the company has no international marketing specialist and the domestic marketing department may have responsibility for global marketing activities.

The export department may be a sub-department of the sales and marketing department (see Fig. 12.2). The export department is the first real step in internationalizing the organizational structure. It is particularly suitable for SMEs, having low product and area diversities.

12.6.2　International division structure

As international sales grow, at some point an international division structure may emerge.

In Fig. 12.3, the company's activities are separated into domestic and international divisions, with a major objective being to develop its international business interests. This structure is most suited to firms that:

- wish to develop international business and greater international expertise
- do not have adequately trained executives to manage an international company.

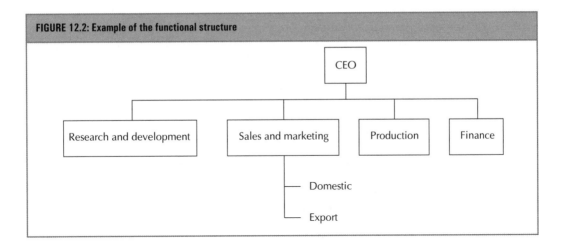

FIGURE 12.2: Example of the functional structure

However, there are drawbacks to this structure, which will be revealed as the company expands, bringing problems of co-ordination as the business becomes too diverse. In addition, as the domestic and international spheres develop, conflict may emerge in the areas of product development and R&D.

12.6.3   Product-based structure

The product-based structure is suitable for companies with more international business experience and with diversified product lines.

Under the product-based structure, the major focus is on product lines. The company is divided along product lines and each division becomes a cost centre, with the divisional head responsible for profit margins. A key feature is the decentralization of the structure, which allows local managers greater freedom in their decision-making (see Fig. 12.4).

This structure suits companies that have:

- a diversified product line
- products that have potential for worldwide standardization
- a wide variety of final customers
- production sites in many locations.

Major *advantages* of this structure are:

- decentralization
- a highly motivated group of divisional heads
- product development and elimination can be achieved relatively easily, without affecting the rest of the company's operations in any major way.

The *disadvantages* of this structure are:

- co-ordination problems could arise
- certain product areas may be overlooked, particularly minor ones
- when division heads move up the corporate ladder, there is a danger that they may bias policies in favour of their former product areas.

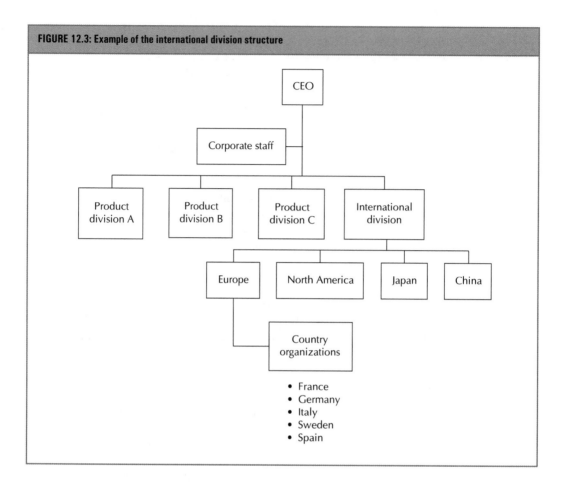

FIGURE 12.3: Example of the international division structure

12.6.4 Geographic structure

If product acceptance and operating conditions vary considerably across world markets, then the geographical structure is the one to choose. This structure is especially useful for companies that have a homogeneous range of products, but at the same time need fast and efficient adaptation to local market conditions. Typically, the world is divided into regions, as illustrated in Fig. 12.5.

There are two main reasons for dividing into different regions:

1   When sales volume in a particular region becomes substantial, there need to be some specialized staff to focus on that region, to realize more fully the potential of an already growing market.
2   Homogeneity within regions and heterogeneity between them necessitate treating each important region separately; therefore, a regional management centre becomes an appropriate organizational feature.

Parallel to a regional centre, each country has its own organizational unit. Country-based subsidiaries are characterized by a high degree of adaptation to local conditions. Since each

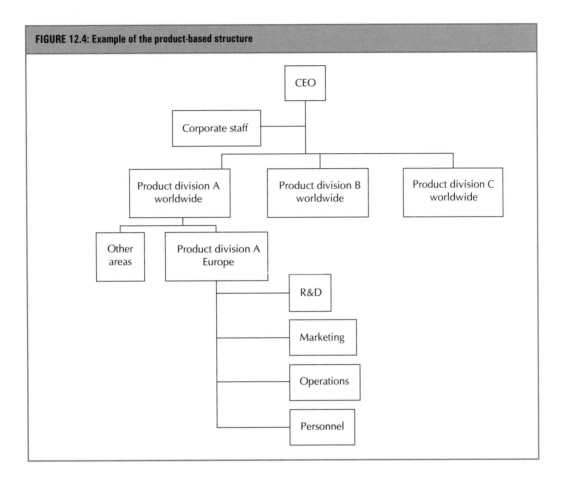

FIGURE 12.4: Example of the product-based structure

subsidiary develops its own unique activities and its own autonomy, it is sometimes relevant to combine local subsidiaries with a regional centre; for example, to utilize opportunities across European countries.

Firms may also organize their operations using a customer (key account or global account) structure, especially if the customer groups they serve are very different: for example, businesses and governments. Catering to these diverse groups may require the concentration of specialists in particular divisions. The product may be the same, but the buying processes of the various customer groups may differ.

The *advantages* of this type of structure are:

● there is a clear demonstration of authority
● the co-ordination of different functional areas of management is enhanced
● resources could be pooled.

The *disadvantages* of this type of structure are:

● for it to work efficiently, the structure depends on a small group of highly effective managers
● there is the likelihood that certain product lines will be ignored as there is no overall responsibility for a specific product.

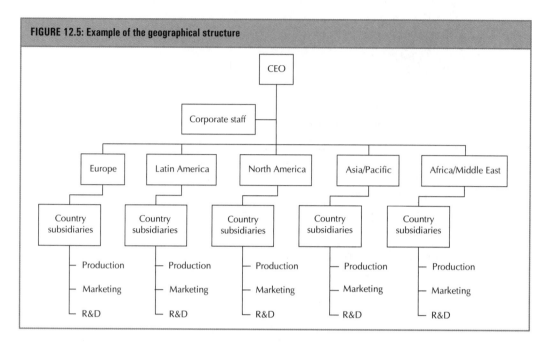

FIGURE 12.5: Example of the geographical structure

12.6.5 Matrix structure

The product-based structure tends to offer better opportunities to rationalize production across countries, thus gaining production cost efficiencies. On the other hand, the geographical structure is more responsive to local market trends and needs.

Some companies need both capabilities, so they have adopted a more complex structure: the matrix structure (see Fig. 12.6).

The strength of this structure is that it can respond to different political and economic environments because it incorporates the elements of product-based and geographic management. For example, the product manager would have worldwide responsibility for Product X, while geographic managers would be responsible for all product lines, including Product X, in the market. Thus, both managers would overlap and this is a good basis from which to make major decisions. Another feature of matrix structures is the duality that exists – in terms of dual budgeting, dual personnel evaluation systems, and so on. This could be seen as positive in that interdependence of opinion and contributions would be the outcome.

The major *disadvantages* of this structure are:

- the possibility of a power struggle as a result of the dual command structure – as illustrated in Fig. 12.6, the sales manager for Product Z in Brazil would have two superiors to refer to
- these structures tend to collapse in times of crisis
- communication becomes more complicated
- uncertainty exists in determining who decides what in certain circumstances.

12.6.6 Which organizational structure is best?

The structures adopted by organizations tend to reflect their management outlook, experience and history; they can even adapt the three basic types to produce hybrid models. The main

FIGURE 12.6: Example of the matrix structure

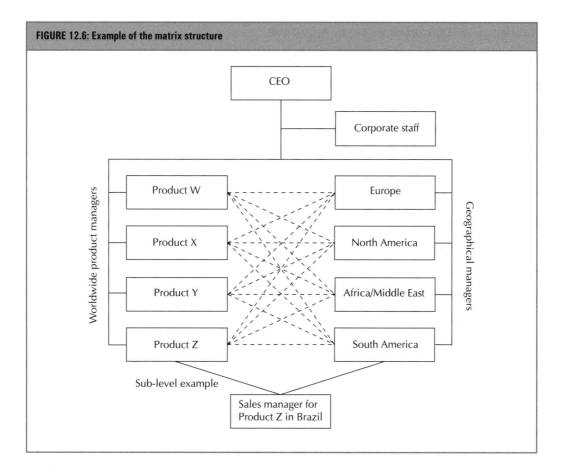

point to bear in mind, however, is that the best organizational structure is the one that fits the organization's environment and internal characteristics (the SWOT approach).

If the strategy changes or the organization makes further internationalization moves, this has to have some effect on the organization structure. Also, the organization structure might change if the management experiences problems with its existing structure.

12.7 The role of internal marketing

As more companies come to appreciate the importance of people in the implementation process, they are becoming disenchanted with traditional approaches to marketing implementation. These forces for change have been caused by several factors: high rates of employee turnover and the associated costs of this, and continuing problems in the implementation of marketing strategy. These problems have led many organizations to adopt alternative approaches to marketing implementation. One of these alternatives is internal marketing.

12.7.1 The internal marketing approach

The concept of internal marketing comes primarily from service organizations, where it was first practised as a tactic for making all employees aware of the need for customer satisfaction. Generally speaking, internal marketing refers to the managerial actions necessary to make all members of the organization understand and accept their respective roles in implementing marketing strategy. This means that all employees, from the chief executive officer to front-line marketing personnel, must realize how each individual job assists in implementing the marketing strategy.

Under the internal marketing approach, every employee has two sets of customers: *external* and *internal*. In the end, successful marketing implementation comes from an accumulation of individual actions where all employees are responsible for implementing the marketing strategy.

12.7.2 The internal marketing process

In the case of service organizations, the 4Ps marketing mix is felt to be inadequate. Some authors have suggested extending this to include people, process and physical evidence (the so-called 7Ps). To an organization providing a service to clients, the people element of the marketing mix is arguably the most important. After all, it may reasonably be argued that the people *are* the organization, so the internal marketing process is important.

Ensuring that all staff, whatever their status, deliver a service of the highest quality is a key issue for all organizations. The inseparability of services makes it impossible to distinguish between service production and service delivery, and it is the people of the organization who are, therefore, responsible for both. In this section of the marketing plan the organization must, therefore, give consideration to the people skills it will need in order to provide its service and, indeed, deliver every component of the marketing plan. This can then be matched against the profile of the existing human resource and appropriate gaps identified. The organization can then ensure that those 'gaps' are represented in the staff recruitment programme and that the appropriate person specifications are in place.

The interaction between the internal and external marketing programmes is illustrated in Fig. 12.7.

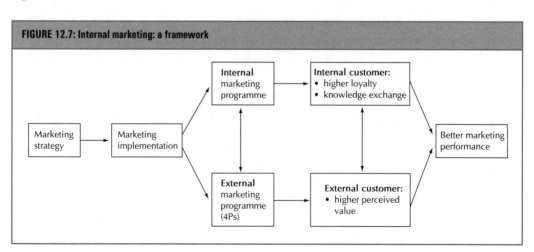

FIGURE 12.7: Internal marketing: a framework

It is, of course, usually much easier to develop and retain existing staff than it is to attain new ones. The second focus of this section of the plan is hence to identify what steps need to be taken in order to retain existing personnel. By far the easiest way of achieving this is probably to survey those who decide to leave and, having discovered their reasons for dissatisfaction, implement any changes that may be necessary to ensure that these problems are corrected. One can also ensure that an ongoing dialogue is maintained with existing staff so that they do not feel compelled to leave in the first place.

Summary

The success of a company depends mainly on its marketing activities and the effectiveness of these activities. In order to find out if the marketing function of the company is effective all aspects need to be analysed. With this information a strategic marketing plan can be created and applied in the years to come.

By analysing current marketing data, flaws in the planning and weaknesses in the company's (or the competitor's) products or strategies can be discovered. Appropriate action can then be taken to ensure a better functioning of the weak parts of the marketing engine or to make better use of the competition's weaknesses and flaws. This can best be done by performing a marketing analysis before writing a marketing plan. (If you have the marketing data readily available this is not necessary.)

The marketing plan has the following framework:

I   Title page
II   Table of contents
III   Executive summary
IV   Introduction and problem statement
V   Situational analysis
VI   Marketing objectives and goals
VII   Marketing strategies
VIII Marketing programmes/action plans
IX   Budgets
X   Implementation and control
XI   Conclusion

In the implementation of the international marketing plan one of the following organizational structures may be used:

- functional structure
- international division structure
- product-based structure
- geographic structure
- matrix structure.

The success of a marketing plan depends on three areas:

1   the process that is followed
2   the infrastructure that is established prior to and throughout the process

3 the implementation controls that are put in place; it is self-evident that effective marketing planning must be based on a clearly structured and well-articulated process; those involved in planning must understand the expectations that are being placed upon them and be provided with clear guidance as to what they must do; however, putting this process in place is not enough on its own to ensure success.

No matter how sound the analysis undertaken during the process, or the strategy and marketing programmes determined, insufficient attention at this final stage can lead to implementation breakdown. Care must also be taken to ensure that adequate implementation resources are made available and also to fully communicate the outcomes of the plan to all interested parties. Finally, the planning process and the resulting implementation of the plan's recommendations must be monitored closely so that remedial action may quickly be carried out in order to rectify any problems and remove obstacles to the successful implementation of the plan.

Questions for discussion

1. What kind of market information would be necessary for international marketing planning, and how might it be obtained?
2. What are the major challenges faced by marketers in developing and implementing international marketing plans?
3. Compare and contrast the marketing plan for an established product with that for a new product.
4. What are the practical internal issues to be addressed by marketers when developing an international marketing plan?
5. Comment on the view that companies will derive as much benefit from the planning exercise as from the marketing plan itself.
6. What are the main problems associated with the links between international marketing strategy and organizational structure?
7. What are the principal issues to be considered in organizational design?
8. How does a company's size at home and abroad influence the organizational structure?
9. Outline the main organizational structure types that are used by international organizations.
10. What are the advantages and disadvantages in adopting a matrix approach to organizational structure?

References

Best, R.J. (2009) *Market-Based Management: Strategies for Growing Customer Value and Profitability,* Pearson International Edition. Upple Saddle River, NJ: Pearson Prentice Hall.

Dibb, S. (2002) Marketing planning best practices, *Marketing Review,* 2: 441–59.

Evans, P.B. and Wurster, T.S. (1997) Strategy and the new economics of information, *Harvard Business Review,* 75(5); 70–82.

Evans, P.B. and Wurster, T.S. (1999) Getting real about virtual commerce, *Harvard Business Review,* 77(6): 85–94.

Evans, P.B. and Wurster, T.S. (2000) *Blown to Bits: How the New Economics of Information Transforms Strategy.* Boston, MA: Harvard Business School Press.

Lehmann, D.R. and Winer, R.S. (2008) *Analysis for Marketing Planning,* McGraw-Hill International Edition. New York: McGraw-Hill/Irwin.

Simkin, L. (2002) Tackling implementation impediments to marketing planning, *Marketing Intelligence & Planning,* 20(2): 120–6.

CASE STUDY 12: VICTORIA'S SECRET

Looking for new business opportunities in the European lingerie market

Victoria's Secret (owned by US Limited Brands, Inc.) sells women's intimate and other apparel, personal care and beauty products and accessories under the Victoria's Secret and La Senza brand names. Victoria's Secret merchandise is sold through retail stores, its website, *www.VictoriasSecret.com*, and through its catalogue. Through its website and catalogue, certain of Victoria's Secret's merchandise may be purchased worldwide. La Senza products may also be purchased through its website, *www.LaSenza.com*.

In January 2007, Victoria's Secret completed its acquisition of La Senza Corporation. La Senza is a Canadian speciality retailer offering lingerie and sleepwear as well as apparel for girls in the 7–14-year age group. In addition, La Senza licensees operate independently owned stores in 45 other countries. The results of La Senza are included in the Victoria's Secret segment.

The Victoria's Secret segment had net sales of US$5.604 bn in 2008 and operated 1,043 stores in the USA and 322 stores in Canada; in total 1365 stores.

At the moment it is not possible to buy Victoria's Secret in European stores, except in a London store and online. Top management has now decided that Victoria Secret's should expand to the European market. The next question is, which markets should be penetrated and how?

First, some information about the international underwear market.

General trends in the international underwear for women (lingerie) market

Generally, US women buy more lingerie than European women. One of the reasons is that Americans have a tendency to throw everything in the washing machine, so the wear out is quicker. Furthermore, lingerie in the USA is not sold through specialist shops (multi-brand shops) as in Europe, but through mass distribution channels such as Wal-Mart, which is estimated to have 20 per cent of the overall market. The US market is also much more price-driven, and lingerie (e.g. bras) cost a lot less.

In Europe there seems to be a difference between northern and southern countries. In southern Europe they buy more lingerie than in northern Europe. One of the reasons could be that women in southern Europe place more emphasis on feeling romantic and sexy. Also, the more intensive sweating in these countries may lead to more purchases of lingerie. Another explanation could be that the northern countries are colder and women wear thicker clothes, so they are not so worried about how their underwear looks.

In order to make the right approach to the lingerie market, it is vital to analyse and interpret attitudes around sex and body image correctly across international markets. In general the US lingerie market is very conservative compared to Europe, though brands like Victoria's Secret have moved the needle in the USA. While Scandinavia may have liberal attitudes to bodies and sexuality, other markets, such as India and Japan, are more demure.

As in other apparel designs, the trends in lingerie have been dictated by fabric developments. This has meant that glamour, the art of seduction and feminine charm are all ingredients in the current vogue. In addition, many bras are designed for women who partake in jogging, aerobics, tennis, and so on to gain maximum benefit from their active lifestyles.

Regarding the distribution of the lingerie, more and more of the textile turnover is now going to branches other than lingerie itself. For instance, Tesco in England is even offering fashion brands, mainly sourced from third countries, to its customers despite this practice being declared illegal by fashion brands. In Germany, for example, food retailers, drugstores and even coffee shops are also selling a significant amount of textile products. Thus, in the annual list of the largest textile retailers in Germany, the food discounter Aldi is ranked at number 9, and Tchibo – a chain of coffee shops – at number 13. In Germany, these non-textile retailers already have a market share of 12 per cent of the total textile market. They do not normally have a full assortment and only sell offers and special items, which they buy in huge quantities and sell at extremely low prices. Also, the idea of concept assortments is being used by some of them. Thus, the coffee chain Tchibo is selling every week, a completely different theme, wherein textile products are just a part of all on offer.

Only companies with a sharp profile are successful in the market. Here are some examples of successful specialty stores:

- French group Orsay is increasing its business with their specialty concept for girlies' fashion
- the German teeny specialist New Yorker
- Swedish H&M with its concept of top fashion products at discounted prices has been growing in almost all countries where it is present
- Spanish Zara has also been opening stores worldwide in a remarkably short time frame for a similar target group.

Other speciality stores are also registering remarkable successes. The best examples of this can be seen in sports and sports-fashion business, where speciality stores such as Runners Point (Germany), Karstadt Sport (Germany), Foot Locker (USA), Sports Expert (Austria), Decathlon (France), Sketcher (USA) and The Sports Authority (USA) are gathering more and more market share and expanding worldwide.

The lingerie segment, earlier a fixed part of normal textile and fashion stores, is also witnessing fast growth. For instance, Oysho (Zara, Spain), Women's Secret (Cortefield, Spain) and even Marks & Spencer (M&S) are starting their own chains of lingerie outside their traditional shops.

Generally, a polarization is taking place in the European lingerie market. The distribution of the lower-priced brands is being taken over by the huge retail chains, whereas the higher-priced brands are gaining market share by using their own concept shops, where the personal service plays a much higher role. At present, the losers in the industry are the 'in-between' brands, which are 'stuck in the middle'.

Vertical integration

More and more manufacturers are opening their own stores and more and more fashion retailers are selling their own retail brands.

The vertical integration is a result of increasing efficiency between production and distribution, given the assumption that organization of production is best made from the point of sale (POS). Middlemen and wholesalers, as well as middle activities like exhibitions, are cut out of the distribution channel to ensure that there are less costs and no losses of communication in the process. Success is more likely in cases where one company owns or controls the complete process from production to distribution. All fast-expanding fashion companies are working vertically. Wal-Mart, Zara, Uniglo, Mango, H&M, C&A and Esprit – all these successful international retailers fall into this category. Frequently, they work on a completely vertical system, while at other times they use a mixed system – selling own brands as well as manufacturer brands.

The world market for underwear

Over the last decades, there has been an increasing number of women worldwide participating in the workforce. Women's average disposable income is rising and the gender gap is closing, albeit at different rates in different parts of the world.

With their rising incomes, women are enjoying greater spending power and they now have the ability to decide (or co-decide) how resources will be distributed within the family. Higher levels of education for women and their higher salaries will ultimately increase their purchasing power. The traditional guilt that many women carried when spending on themselves is also expected to decline, leading to greater spending on women's products. This rising purchasing power and greater decision-making authority has made women, especially those in employment and aged 24–54, a large and powerful segment of the consumer market.

Price development

Average unit prices for clothing have declined worldwide over the last decades, as marketers sourced clothes from low-cost production locations. This situation gave customers more product choice at better prices, but the increased competition also forced manufacturers and retailers to keep their prices and margins down. The more intensive use of private label products is expected to drive average unit prices down even further, as retailers source products from low-cost locations to give themselves a competitive edge. To combat declining prices, manufacturers and retailers will seek new, more innovative products that are more insulated from price deflation.

Value of world market

In Table 12.2, the total world market for underwear (men and women) is estimated to €35.7 bn. The women's underwear (lingerie) market accounts for around 80 per cent of the total global underwear market, and the rest (20 per cent) is for the men's.

The biggest total market is still the USA, followed by Germany and the UK.

Country	Total market (€bn) in manufacturers' selling prices – 2008	Victoria's Secret – estimated market shares %
USA	11.0	5.0
Germany	4.2	0
UK	3.8	1.0
France	3.4	0.5
Italy	3.2	0
Russia	2.1	0
Other global markets (Australia, Japan, China, South America etc.)	10.0	0.5
Total world market	**37.7**	1.5

TABLE 12.2 The total market for underwear (men and women) in main international markets and estimate for total world market
Source: Hosea (2009); different public sources; own estimates

The underwear industry in North America continues to show a high level of mergers and acquisitions. In 2006, Sara Lee spun off Hanesbrands into its own publicly traded company and in January 2007, VF Corp. announced it would sell its intimate clothing brands to Fruit of the Loom. Also, in 2007, Victoria's Secret completed its acquisition of La Senza Corporation.

In the category 'other global markets', the underwear markets in the developing economies of Asia, eastern Europe and Latin America are characterized by extreme fragmentation, with countless independent private label products dominating the competitive landscape. These products have strong price advantages and are still preferred by consumers in the mass market. At the same time, they also copy the latest fashion trends and are thus able to keep their customers satisfied.

For example, in eastern Europe, the retail clothing market remains fragmented, lacking the presence of leading companies and brands. Open-air markets and family-owned clothing stores dominate the retail landscape. However, the distribution of underwear in the region is beginning to change as the share of specialist stores and retail chains is rising. The share of open-air markets is declining but it remains relatively high. Several retail chains, such as Peek & Cloppenburg, Stockmann, Debenhams, M&S, Top Shop and C&A, have all entered this region over the past two years.

The number of shopping malls in the region is growing, particularly in major central and regional cities, and this is increasing the penetration of organized retail, especially for chains. For example, in Poland, the Spanish company Inditex (Zara) is developing its brand portfolio, introducing new clothing brands such as Bershka, Pull and Bear, Oysho and Stradivarius. The British chain Next has just opened its first store in Poland while the Russian retailer Sela will be opening its first store in Warsaw.

In the future, the distribution share of big retailers will increase and the distribution share of less formal formats, such as open-air markets, will decrease, although open-air markets still maintain a share of about 35–45 per cent, depending on the specific clothing subsector being considered.

Furthermore, multinational underwear brands are not in the top 10 brands in countries like China, India and Russia, as domestic players are preferred for their price and style.

Retailing

The three biggest multinational clothing retailers in the world are GAP Inc., H&M and Inditex/Zara.

The US-based *Gap Inc.* is the largest clothing and underwear retailer, but with 90 per cent of its sales coming from the large US market. Gap brand stores are so popular in the USA that a shopping centre without a Gap or its subsidiaries, Banana Republic and Old Navy, is a rare sight. The retail chain offers own-brand men and women's underwear, women and children's clothing, and so on. The total GAP sales are US$17 bn, with 154 000 employees.

The largest European clothing retailers, Hennes & Mauritz (H&M), Inditex/Zara (Industria de Diseño Textil) and C&A Mode Brenninkmeijer & Co., enjoyed sales growth during the last decade.

H&M, the Swedish-based clothing retailer, followed a strategy of setting the pace of style and making couture affordable. The retailer saw its retail clothing sales grow, in the markets under study, from US$12.6 bn in 2004 to US$15 bn in 2008. The brand is the leader in the clothing markets in Sweden, Germany and the Netherlands.

Spanish company *Inditex/Zara* followed a strategy of selling multiple brands aimed at different target segments. The company has seven brands, the most popular being Zara, which is gaining market share all across Europe. In Poland, Zara is gaining market share despite being perceived as very expensive. Inditex reported retail sales of US$13 bn in 2008, up from US$8.8 bn in 2004.

C&A has a strong presence in several clothing subsectors in Europe. It leads the market in Belgium and is a close second in Germany, where it has gained brand salience through sustained underwear advertising on billboards, bus stops, and so on. The company has also enjoyed success in the Latin American markets of Brazil and Mexico, where it has experienced high sales growth. In 2008, C&A retail sales in the countries under study stood at US$11 bn.

In the following pages the three major European markets for women's underwear (lingerie) are described (UK, Germany and France) followed by one of the emerging markets (Russia), which is also characterized.

The UK market

Though more resilient than clothing, 2009 will be challenging for underwear retailers – for the first time since records began in 1988, underwear expenditure growth will be negative, as the recession forces consumers to be more frugal.

The underwear market is becoming more competitive than ever as non-specialists aim to supplement their clothing sales with underwear, giving consumers a wider choice of retailers to buy from. Moreover, value retailers are growing their share of the market, exerting downward pressure on prices and posing a greater threat to mid-market players.

Expanding into underwear provides an opportunity for clothing specialists to boost sales, and offers added convenience for the customers. Underwear sales through clothing specialists increased in the period 2003–2008. However, their proportion of the market declined during 2003–2008 due to M&S's loss of market share. But while the product is good at M&S, there is increasing price competition.

Key competitors including Next and Debenhams have been enhancing and expanding their ranges as well as sharpening price points.

The growth of grocery retailers looks to be as unstoppable in underwear as it does in outerwear – see below.

UK distribution – the threat of the grocery retailers

As grocers look to enhance their non-food offer through opening more space and the launch of new non-food-only fascias, clothing and lingerie are areas they are likely to expand in. This poses a series of threats to lingerie specialists. Range expansion and enhancement, product/own-brand innovation, department upgrades and strong advertising and marketing, as well as massive footfall, indicate that they will take an increasingly big share of the market.

A key development will be if these new players decide to stock name brands as well as their own labels, adding to competition for the mainstream retailers.

Grocers, in particular Asda and Tesco, pose a real threat to underwear specialists with their expanding ranges and growing store footprints. They continue to devote more space to clothing and underwear in-store as both retailers expand existing branches through extensions – including mezzanines that facilitate shop-in-shop departments. With more space added to stores, clothing departments have grown larger, giving more space to underwear and lingerie.

The development of non-food only stores under the Asda Living and Tesco Homeplus fascias has further expanded the retailers' clothing offers and, more importantly, given new growth opportunities as both chains find it increasingly tough to expand their grocery store footprints. These stores, still in their infancy, are set to pose a greater threat to underwear specialists going forward. However, located in retail parks they compete less directly with specialists and more with department stores and clothing specialists such as Next.

Sainsbury's

Sainsbury's is enjoying strong growth with its *TU collection* and is set to pose a greater threat going into 2009. From a smaller base than its two key rivals, with the range available in just 283 stores (in October 2008) and the full offer available in just 24 branches, TU has considerable expansion opportunity. With Sainsbury's set to increase its focus on non-food, TU is likely to form the cornerstone of its growth and with the brand reaching new heights of recognition as it expands into home wares, it is to become a more pronounced authority in the market. Sainsbury's aims to expand its clothing offer into 300 stores by 2010.

Asda

Besides just location and physical expansion, grocers have been enhancing their clothing offers with Asda, for example, relaunching the George label in late 2008. With the aim of appealing more directly to its core shopper through simplified ranges, improved quality and better in-store graphics, George has ambitious aims of regaining its position as the number one volume clothing brand from Primark by 2011.

Tesco

Tesco also has ambitious targets for its F&F and Cherokee brands.

Underwear specialists are insulated to an extent from the value-based offer of grocers because they are largely midmarket to high-end market. Specialists' higher positioning has more direct appeal to affluent customers and their competitive strengths lie in range, quality and service. However, mid-market players are arguably the most exposed to strained consumer finances and are at the greatest risk of losing shoppers seeking value-based alternatives.

In general, consumers, inspired by celebrity style, are buying more bras and pants and showing a tendency to trade up. The total underwear market in UK is estimated at €3.8 bn (2008) with sales of bras accounting for around a fourth of that value.

The sources of competition to traditional main street chains include supermarkets, mail order and online shopping. Because of this, retail prices have become aggressively competitive. The big corporate chains are claiming growing market share with fewer, but bigger, outlets. According to the Department for Business, Innovation and Skills (BIS), the largest shops and chains control about 75 per cent of the clothing market. The growing involvement of the grocery multiples is certainly adding low-price capacity.

Major retailers, especially M&S, have improved their segmentation of bras and pants with more premium ranges under sub-brands, adding to the overall choice for consumers. At the same time prices are dropping. This is due to cheaper imports, especially influenced by bras and pants coming in from eastern Europe and the Far East. This has helped the discounters to offer an even wider range of bras and pants at low prices. These two factors have both been influential in helping to stimulate demand.

Bras and pants have become a self-treat item for many women and are even a gift item at certain times of year. The branded houses have all worked hard at improving their styling, bringing in new fabrics, new construction techniques (especially for bras) and plenty of fashionable ideas.

Consumer research carried out by Mintel highlights just how an evolving interest in fashion is creating numerous opportunities for manufacturers and retailers. Women are more likely to have a 'wardrobe' of underwear, buying different styles and types for different occasions. Necessity may well drive the market but fashion influences are creating a 'must have culture' and stimulating demand. When Mintel asked UK consumers what made them buy a bra and pants in the last 12 months, 62 and 60 per cent, respectively, indicated replacement reasons. But 29 and 26 per cent of respondents indicated they bought bras and then pants 'to treat' themselves. This is an important factor that both suppliers and retailers can take into their marketing.

Table 12.3 shows the development in the lingerie (bra) market from 2000 to 2008.

Brand	2000 market share (%)	2008 market share (%)
Marks & Spencer	34	30
Triumph	7	6
Gossard	6	5
Playtex	5	5
Calvin Klein	2	5
Playtex	2	4
Grocery stores' brands (Asda, Sainsbury's, Tesco, etc.)	20	25
Others (Agent Provocateur, Primark, Debenhams, etc.)	24	20
Total	100	100

TABLE 12.3 Brand share in the UK bra market (2000–8)

Overall, the leading British high street chain M&S lost market share to the discounters (grocery retailers) and accounted for 30 per cent of UK bra sales, and similar market shares of briefs and hosiery. This has changed in downward direction since the consumers' appetite for all things branded has encouraged newcomers on to the lingerie scene. In the past, most female consumers have thought of lingerie as a necessity or a commodity, and not fashion-led. Even though much of the expensive and glamorous lingerie is imported from France and other European countries, US producers of upmarket and fashionable lingerie will most certainly also find a receptive audience in the UK. The likes of Gap, Benetton and Calvin Klein have already spotted a niche in this market, and are opening standalone lingerie formats. Figure 12.8 shows the brand positioning in the UK market (without Victoria's Secret). Figure 12.9 shows the positioning of Victoria's Secret compared to other lingerie brands in the brand pyramid.

German market

With a total market value of €4.2 bn (2002), Germany continues to be one of the largest European markets for underwear. Despite economic crises German women are spending more on lingerie than ever before. In addition to new fashion lingerie styles, individualism, decorative femininity and a new ethnic styling emphasize the new sleekness for the coming seasons. Fashion styles are rejuvenated by new colours and novel shapes. A surge in colour is found in the mixture of deep red with pink, green and intense yellow. Warm colours also add more life to the fashion. Manufacturers have recognized that their lingerie collections must include innovative colours and interesting shapes.

Successful penetration of the German market depends on a continuity of effort, regular participation in trade fairs, and the establishment of a sales office with warehousing, in either Germany or another European country. Appointment of sales agents is usually the first step.

The main countries of origin for imported lingerie to Germany in 2008 were: (1) China; (2) Turkey; (3) Poland; (4) India; (5) Romania; (6) Hong Kong; (7) Tunisia; (8) Italy; (9) Czech Republic; and (10) Hungary.

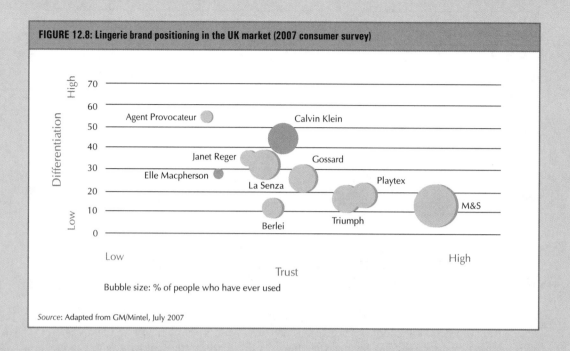

FIGURE 12.8: Lingerie brand positioning in the UK market (2007 consumer survey)

Source: Adapted from GM/Mintel, July 2007

The absolute brand market leader in the German lingerie market is Triumph, which has also got some German roots.

The big fashion chains worldwide are grabbing more and more market share in the lingerie market from the smaller traditional fashion retailers. For example, in Germany, a quarter of the market is covered by the four largest fashion retailers (Karstadt-Quelle, Metro-Group, C&A and Otto). The 84 large fashion retailers in Germany have over 60 per cent of the total market share. According to official numbers, in Germany, every fifth small- and medium-sized fashion retailer has been closing down in the past decade. This trend is also reflected in other countries. Even between the big ones, the competition is growing steadily and some of them, such as Gap, M&S and C&A, are facing problems. In the current scenario, if a retailer does not have a proper and tight concept, the market would react adversely very fast. It is only the big ones who have been able to defend themselves better with larger power and resources of their command.

French market

In 2008 French underwear sales were estimated at €3.4 bn. Although the economic recession of the past three years has been particularly difficult for the textile industry, the lingerie market segment has proven itself relatively impervious to the downward economic trends.

On average, a French woman purchases approximately five briefs and two bras per year. She renews her nightwear every year. Women aged 15–34 purchase more lingerie items than other age categories; however, they buy less expensive lingerie. The most important element for consumers is comfort.

The following lingerie trends were noted:

- *Romantic lingerie*: importance of second skin bras for an invisible look with more microfibres lace with tulle. This romantic lingerie is made with fabrics that are smooth and is often accentuated with little touches of sophistication (pearl and embroidery).
- *Beautiful lingerie*: sophisticated shapes with lace, floral embroidery and cut-away effects. Necklines are back, due to the cut-away effects, strappy looks and pretty, braided trim.
- *Sporty lingerie*: a ready-to-wear product with bright colours (red, blue, pink, yellow).

According to recent statistics, the average annual budget for lingerie per woman in France is €100.

Advertising

A key factor in establishing a brand in France is to have an adequate advertising budget. The foreign company should be able to promote its image and reinforce its position. New products should be aggressively marketed to appeal to French women's inherent 'passion for living' that influences their fashion preferences, expressing both their sensuality and feminity. For example, Calvin Klein recently did a large advertising campaign in the Parisian underground metro system.

Together with French companies US companies dominate the lingerie market. Market leaders in France are: Sara Lee (Dim, Cacharel, Playtex, Rosy); Warnaco (Warner's, Calvin Klein, Lejaby); Chantelle (Ava, Essensia Tulle, Mon Amour); and the Vanity Fair Corporation (Bolero, Variance, Carina, Siltex, Lou).

Russian market (including other CIS countries)

The potential number of lingerie customers in CIS (females aged 15 or more) is more than 100 million (see Table 12.4)

CIS area	Females (m)
Russia	65.7
Ukraine	21.7
Kazakhstan	6.3
Belarus	4.7
Baltics	3.3
Total CIS	101.7

TABLE 12.4 CIS female population 15+ years (2008)
Source: Silvano Fashion Group, 2008 Financial Report (www.silvanofashion.com)

The value of the Russian retail market (in manufacturers' selling prices) for lingerie is estimated to account for €2.1 bn in 2008.

The Russian distribution model is very much dependent on the traditional importers and distributors. The importers/distributors normally purchase merchandise from the manufacturer at their own risk, on the basis of an ex-works price to which they add 20–25 per cent for access costs (transportation, insurances, customs clearance), plus a subsequent 10–35 per cent mark-up. Most often these businesses do not use a purchasing office in the supplying country or countries, which explains why they may not necessarily be known by the same name everywhere. According to their size, importers/distributors ensure the presence of a running stock; ensure client services (product display, transfers, logistics, etc.); and ensure a minimum of marketing activity and media publicity. Among the advantages of this distribution model is the possibility for the supplier to rapidly access the market.

For manufacturers who do not wish to call on distributors, exclusive or not, there is another possibility: sales representation. According to Russian law, representation offices are not allowed to undertake sales activities. As such, the function of these structures is often to gather information on the market, identify potential clients, promote the brand/s by various means, even to ensure client follow-up and organize training sessions, as long as they do not proceed with invoicing. Orders are then placed on the overseas brand's letterhead and payments are addressed directly to the parent company, whereas transportation and customs formalities are at the client's discretion. The principal advantage of this system lies in the respect and application of the manufacturer's sales strategies in terms of recommended retail price, merchandising, display, product rotation and regional development.

Wholesalers represent another characteristic aspect of distribution in Russia and they must not be disregarded, mainly because of the 17 million sq km that make up the Republic of Russia: in the different more or less well-serviced regions, handover is assured by wholesalers who often also have a small direct sales activity on the side of their storage warehouses. For small retailers, this is the best supply solution because they are exempted from paying for merchandise in advance: settlement is done directly on the spot and in cash at the time of purchase.

The typical breakdown of the public retail price of lingerie in Moscow is as follows:

- factory price
- +transportation, insurance, customs 20 per cent
- +importer margin 20–30 per cent
- +wholesaler margin 18 per cent
- +boutique margin (St Petersburg, Moscow) 120–140 per cent

Source: ITMM

Consumer behaviour

In a survey made in 2004 in Moscow over half of the women interviewed confirm having bought underwear over the previous six months (see Table 12.5). These are mostly young women (age 16–29), or even women aged 30–39, who are the most fond of lingerie, but women in the 40–49 age group are still in the frequent purchasing considerations.

Women (16+, Russian cities 100,000+) in %	Total	16–29 years	30–39 years	40–49 years	50+ years	Moscow	St. Petersburg
% of women purchasing lingerie (in general) within last six months	62.8	74.5	72.5	68.4	48.5	68.1	60.3
% of women purchasing bras within last six months	28.3	39.0	35.4	32.4	16.6	31.1	27.7
% of women purchasing panties within last six months	38.4	49.6	45.7	41.2	27.1	39.6	35.3

TABLE 12.5 Survey among women in Moscow and St. Petersburg and other big cities
Source: adapted from R-TGI (Russian Target Group Index Survey), published in Intima France, Russia – Country of dolls, November 2005, Paris

In 2004 women aged 16 years or more from cities of over 100 000 inhabitants purchased over 88 million lingerie pieces (bras, panties and briefs) for a total amount of US$773 m. Over half the products were bought from open markets (52 per cent), then in boutiques (25.3 per cent), and lastly in department stores (10.2 per cent) or brand stores (7.5 per cent). As for the brands most purchased over the last six months of 2004, the brand Milavitsa (from Silvano Fashion Group) is ahead by far, followed by local or Italian brands.

As for the purchase price for a set (bra + panties), €30 seems to represent the psychological threshold for 40 per cent of the women interviewed. Sets in the €30–50 price range are still appealing to 35 per cent of women, whereas only 19 per cent are willing to spend €50–100, and 6 per cent over €150.

Retail distribution

Chain stores are the current trend. For example, there are currently no less than 10 lingerie chain stores in Moscow and, according to Russian professionals, they must reach a total turnover of €200 million. For the most part, they sell lingerie imported from western Europe, including those eastern countries that have recently joined the European Union (EU). Besides the widely advertised Tikka Orchidea (Wild Orchid), there is a growing number of multi-brand and mono-brand boutique networks, set up by importers/distributors, or even by regional retailers/wholesalers. Multi-brand chains are in the great majority and most of the time they belong to importers who fight for exclusivity of the most famous brands.

The leading multi-brand chain of luxury lingerie in Russia is the retail chain, *Wild Orchid*, with *Bustier* as number two in the retail market.

Among the single brand stores, *Milavitsa* is one of the best-known brands for medium-priced lingerie in Russia (located in Minsk, Belorussia). It builds on shop partnerships with Russian independents. *Triumph*, one of the leading western lingerie manufacturers, has its own representative office in Moscow and it is setting its marketing focus on creating store partnerships, with Russian independents entitling them to sell all brands of Triumph under one roof.

Global competitors in women's underwear (lingerie)

Triumph

Triumph International is one of the world's leading manufacturers of lingerie, sleepwear and swimwear and was founded as a family business in Germany in 1886. Still a family business (privately owned in its entirety by the family Spiesshofer & Braun), Triumph International has grown to 40 000 employees and an annual turnover of CHF2.5 bn (€1.7 bn).

Bad Zurzach in Switzerland has now become the headquarters of the parent company, Triumph International. Triumph enjoys a presence in over 120 countries encompassing the globe and is one of the leading underwear producers in the world. The company has 50 subsidiaries around the world. Its topselling markets are Germany, the UK and Japan.

In 2007 women's underwear accounted for approximately 80 per cent of the revenues. Its main brands are Triumph and Sloggi.

Triumph is estimated to have its best market share in Germany, followed by the UK and markets in the Far East. In China and India, Triumph has a relative good market position, though these markets are mainly dominated by domestic underwear manufacturers.

Hanesbrands, Inc., USA (Playtex)

The Group's principal activities are to design, manufacture, source and sell a range of apparel essentials such as T-shirts, bras, panties, men's underwear, kids' underwear, socks, hosiery, casual wear and active wear. It operates in four segments: Innerwear, Outerwear, International and Hosiery. The Group's brands include Hanes, Champion, C9 by Champion, Playtex, Bali, L Eggs, Just My Size and Wonderbra. The innerwear segment sells basic branded products such as women's intimate underwear, men's underwear, kids' underwear, sleepwear and socks. The outerwear segment sells products that are seasonal in nature such as casual and active wear. The international segment sells products in Asia, Canada and Latin America geographic locations. The hosiery segment sells leg wear products such as panty hose and knee highs.

In 2008 Hanesbrands' total net sales were down by 5 per cent to US$4.25 bn, compared with US$4.47 bn in 2007. Fifty-six per cent of total sales of Hanesbrands is innerwear. Their biggest customer is Walmart, which accounts for approximately 40 per cent of their total sales, while Target accounts for approximately 20 per cent. The biggest sales areas for Hannesbrands are North America, Latin America and Asia. Europe only accounts for approximately 20 per cent of their international sales

Two of Victoria's Secrets' more regional and European competitors are now described (see Fig. 12.9):

Marie Jo

Textile producer Van de Velde developed from a family enterprise in Belgium to become an important player in the European field of lingerie for women. Van de Velde SA designs and manufactures luxury lingerie items under three brand names: Marie Jo (feminine and fashionable lingerie), Marie Jo L'Aventure (individualistic lingerie) and Prima Donna (luxurious and comfortable lingerie for large sizes).

Van de Velde's most famous brand, Marie Jo, was introduced in 1981.

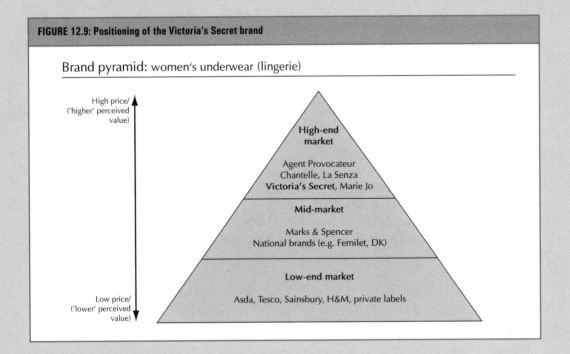

FIGURE 12.9: Positioning of the Victoria's Secret brand

Brand pyramid: women's underwear (lingerie)

High price/
('higher' perceived
value)

**High-end
market**

Agent Provocateur
Chantelle, La Senza
Victoria's Secret, Marie Jo

Mid-market

Marks & Spencer
National brands (e.g. Femilet, DK)

Low-end market

Asda, Tesco, Sainsbury, H&M, private labels

Low price/
('lower' perceived
value)

In the 1990s Van de Velde introduced two new, high-quality brands: Prima Donna and Marie Jo L'Aventure. Once again it was an overwhelming success. The Van de Velde image is currently one of a creative, fashionable and stylish design combined with good quality and major emotional value. Van de Velde has more than a thousand employees in five different countries.

In 2001 Van de Velde NV acquired a controlling share in the Hong Kong lingerie producer, Top Form. The strategic advantages of this move for the Belgians are easy to see – integrated management at lower costs, and an opening to the Chinese mainland market.

Van de Velde, whose turnover amounted to €80 m in 2008, has production operations in Belgium, Hungary and Tunisia. However, 51 per cent of all products designed and sold by Van de Velde were assembled by Top Form, out of Hong Kong and mainland China.

Chantelle

Chantelle lingerie has been a family-owned company for over 120 years. It has maintained its dedication to creating bras, panties, thongs and lingerie with the finest European laces and fabrics. Chantelle's commitment to fit, comfort, exquisite European styling and detail has allowed the company to establish itself in over 70 countries worldwide. Its sales in 2008 were €300 m.

The Chantelle brand is known throughout the world for its collections of fashionable and feminine lingerie. Delicate materials such as decorative lace and embroideries, high-end fabrics, support and comfortable cuts reflect the focus of Chantelle. Other brands of Le Groupe Chantelle include Latin-inspired Passionata and Darjeeling, for women who prefer the natural look.

Questions

1   Which geographical market in Europe would you recommend Victoria's Secret to focus on?
2   Please prepare a marketing plan for the chosen geographical market.

Sources: www.VictoriasSecret.com; www.limitedbrands.com; Hosea, M. (2009) Selling supportive strategies, *Brand Strategy*, December 2008/January 2009: 34–39; Parry, C. (2008) The boost it's been waiting for, *Marketing Week*, 6 March; G. Hanson (2006) Bustin out, *Scanorama – The SAS Group Magazine*, July/August: 39–45. Available online at www.infomat.com; Horne, J. (2003) *King of Bras*, Finance Asia.com Ltd, 26 May. Available online at www.financeasia.com/articles/e867a971–642e-11d7–81fa0090277e174b. cfm; Rehlin; Monget, K. (2004) Lingerie liaisons pick up steam, *Women's Wear Daily*, 188(7): 18–19; Anderson, I. (2004) Lingerie brand to follow Kylie work with digital blitz, *Marketing (UK)*, 22 February: 4–5; other public sources; Bainbridge, J. (2004) Women's underwear – beyond the basics, *Marketing Journal*, 8 December.

CHAPTER 13

Budgeting and control

❖ *LEARNING OBJECTIVES*

After studying this chapter you should be able to do the following:

❖ Understand why customer profitability is important.

❖ Define the concept of customer life time value (CLTV).

❖ Understand why CLTV is important.

❖ Describe the key elements of the marketing control system.

❖ List the most important measures for marketing performance.

❖ Understand the need for evaluation and control of marketing plans and their implementation.

❖ Explain how a marketing budget is established.

13.1   Introduction

An organization needs to budget in order to ensure that its expenditure does not exceed its planned revenue. This chapter discusses how to use a rational process for developing budgets and allocating resources. Furthermore, it outlines the need for a control system to oversee the marketing operations of the organization.

13.2   Marketing productivity and economic results

The productivity of an operation is related to how effectively the resources that are input in a process (manufacturing process, service process) are transformed into economic results for the service provider and value for its customers. The traditional productivity concept has been developed for manufacturers of physical goods as a production efficiency concept. Existing productivity models and productivity measurement instruments are also geared to the context of manufacturers. Moreover, they are based on assumptions that production and consumption are separate processes and that customers do not participate in the production process.

High productivity is generally assumed to be a 'good thing' as a productive operation is more likely to have lower costs. It is this close connection with the cost performance of an operation or process that accounts for the interest in understanding and measuring productivity. Although the definition of productivity appears straightforward, productivity can be difficult to deal with for several different reasons; first the outputs are usually expressed in different forms to the inputs. Outputs are often measured in physical terms such as units (e.g. cars produced), tonnes (of paper), kilowatts (of electricity) or value (Euros), for example. Second, the inputs are usually physically different and include measures of people (numbers, skills, hours worked or costs), and cost of input resources or marketing actions (Johnston and Jones, 2004) (see Fig. 13.1).

This complexity of relationships between inputs and outputs is affected by both the number of inputs and outputs as well as their measurement units, because different combinations of number and type of units can result in a huge number of productivity metrics, each having its own information value and reflecting different things.

In particular, the intangible nature of many services means that it is difficult to objectively define and measure the service outputs being provided. The measurement and management of inputs and outputs is also complicated because of the simultaneous production and consumption of many services, as well as their perishability and heterogeneity, as service encounters are experienced differently by different people or even by the same people in different circumstances.

Because the service (production) process and service consumption to a large extent are simultaneous processes, where customers participate actively, the resources or inputs used to produce services cannot be standardized more than to a certain degree. It is difficult to relate a given number of inputs, in volume or value terms, to a given amount of outputs. Frequently, it is even difficult to define 'one unit of service'. According to the traditional manufacturing-related productivity concept, productivity is defined as the ratio between outputs produced and inputs used, given that the quality of the outputs is kept constant (the constant quality assumption), or (according to Grönroos and Ojasalo, 2004):

$$\text{Productivity} = \frac{\text{Outputs produced}}{\text{Inputs used}} \mid \text{Constant quality of outputs}$$

Only if the quality of the production output is constant, and there is no significant variation in the ratio between inputs used and outputs produced with these inputs, can productivity be measured with traditional methods. The constant quality assumption is normally taken for granted and not expressed explicitly; therefore, the critical importance of this assumption is easily forgotten. However, in most service processes it does not apply. In services, it is not only the inputs that are difficult to calculate, it is also difficult to get a useful measurement of

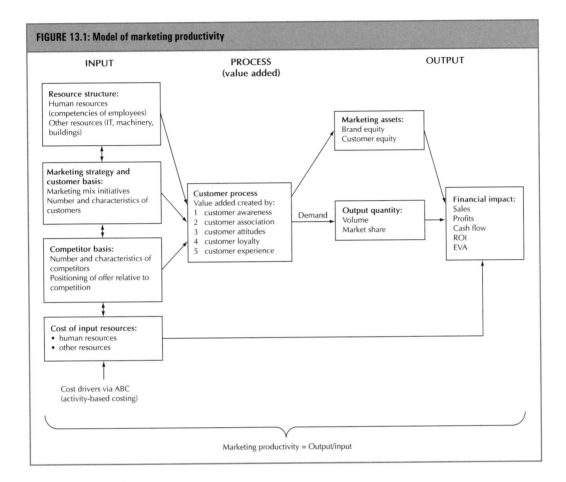

FIGURE 13.1: Model of marketing productivity

INPUT   PROCESS   OUTPUT
                      (value added)

Resource structure:
Human resources
(competencies of employees)
Other resources (IT, machinery,
buildings)

Marketing assets:
Brand equity
Customer equity

**Marketing strategy and
customer basis:**
Marketing mix initiatives
Number and characteristics of
customers

Customer process
Value added created by:
1 customer awareness
2 customer association
3 customer attitudes
4 customer loyalty
5 customer experience

Demand

Output quantity:
Volume
Market share

Financial impact:
Sales
Profits
Cash flow
ROI
EVA

Competitor basis:
Number and characteristics of
competitors
Positioning of offer relative to
competition

Cost of input resources:
• human resources
• other resources

Cost drivers via ABC
(activity-based costing)

Marketing productivity = Output/input

the outputs. Output measured as volume is useful only if customers are willing to buy this output. In manufacturing, where the constant quality assumption applies, customers can be expected to buy an output produced with an altered input or resource structure. However, in services we do not know whether customers will purchase the output produced with a different input structure. It depends on the effects of the new resources or inputs used on perceived process-related and outcome-related quality.

Hence, productivity cannot be understood without taking into account the interrelationship between the use of inputs or production resources and the perceived quality of the output produced with these resources. The interrelationship between internal efficiency and external efficiency is crucial for understanding and managing service productivity.

We first need to clarify the ways in which marketing activities build shareholder value. For example, when we talk of marketing 'investment', we must identify the marketing assets in which we invest and understand how the assets contribute to profits in the short run, and provide potential for growth and sustained profits in the long run. In this context, the spotlight is not on underlying products, pricing or customer relationships, but on marketing expenditures (e.g. marketing communications, promotions and other activities) and how these expenditures influence marketplace performance. The company should have a business model that tracks how marketing expenditures influence what customers know, believe and feel, and, ultimately, how they behave. These intermediate outcomes are usually measured by non-financial means such as attitudes and behavioural intentions. The central problem we address here is how non-financial measures of marketing effectiveness drive financial performance measures such as sales, profits and shareholder value in both the short and the long run (Rust et al., 2004).

It is important to understand that marketing actions, such as advertising, service improvements or new product launches, can help build long-term assets (e.g. brand equity, customer equity). These assets can be leveraged to deliver short-term profitability. Thus, marketing actions both create and leverage market-based assets. It is also important to distinguish between the 'effectiveness' and the 'efficiency' of marketing actions. For example, price promotions can be efficient in that they deliver short-term revenues and cash flows. However, to the extent that they invite competitive actions and destroy long-term profitability and brand equity, they may not be effective. Consequently, we examine both tactical and strategic marketing actions, and their implications.

13.2.1 Factors influencing 'marketing productivity'

You may find it useful to read this section in conjunction with Fig. 13.1.

Input variables

Resource structure

Resources are the basic input into the business processes; that is, technological, human, financial and organizational resources.

Marketing strategy

Marketing strategy and elements of it play a central role as input variables for winning and retaining customers, ensuring business growth and renewal, developing sustainable competitive advantages, and driving financial performance through business processes. A significant proportion of the market value of companies today lies in intangible off-balance-sheet assets, such as brands, market networks and intellectual property, rather than in tangible book assets. The leveraging of intangible assets to enhance corporate performance requires managers to move beyond the traditional inputs and outputs of marketing analysis and to incorporate an understanding of the financial consequences of marketing decisions, which include their impact on cash flows. On a more tactical level, managers implement marketing initiatives to increase short-term profitability. In most settings, this effort requires management of margins and turnover. Because better value to customers (or superior brands) can be tapped in terms of either price or volume, managers need to trade off prices (and therefore margins) against market share. Various programmes can be developed to enhance and sustain profitability (e.g. loyalty programmes, cross-selling, up-selling); how managers proceed is a matter of strategy. The question is, what type of expenditure has a greater influence on the value of a company's customer base: a new campaign for advertisements or improvements in the quality of service? How do elements of a co-ordinated marketing strategy influence the purchase behaviour of different marketing segments over time, and how does this affect the company's revenue streams? What are the disproportionate effects of changes in the structure of pricing on customer acquisition, retention and cross-buying? How do marketing and operations elements interact to grow or to diminish customer value?

Competitor basis

The competitive environment has a profound influence on the nature of marketing productivity. Marketing expenditure decisions, such as those about advertising, are often made with competitors in mind. Studies on advertising spending have identified two separate effects. On the one hand, competition can drive marketing spending higher, thus producing an escalation effect. Driven by a belief that gaining market share increases profit and enhances company value, companies increase marketing expenditures to gain market share, even as rivals do the same. Little evidence suggests that the expenditures have the anticipated results.

Cost of input resources

These input variables will mainly have an impact on the financial metrics, like return on investment (ROI).

Process variables

Value added is mainly created in the heads of the customers. It is only their evaluations that count in the end.

Customer process

To assess the impact of marketing expenditures on customers, it is important to understand the following five key dimensions, which can be considered particularly important measures of the customer mind-set.

1 *Customer awareness*: the extent to and ease with which customers recall and recognize the company, and the extent to which they can identify the products and services associated with it.
2 *Customer associations*: the strength, favourability and uniqueness of perceived attributes and benefits for the company and the brand.
3 *Customer attitudes*: the customer's overall evaluations of the company and the brand in terms of its quality and the satisfaction it generates.
4 *Customer experience*: the extent to which customers use the brand overall, talk to others about the brand, and seek out brand and information, promotions, events, and so on.
5 *Customer loyalty*: how loyal the customer is towards the company and the brand.

Because the strength and length of the customer or brand relationship matters, the company must consider multiple aspects of each customer's purchase behaviour, not just retention probabilities. Consequently, researchers have begun to model other purchase behaviours, such as cross-selling, word-of-mouth behaviour and profitable lifetime duration of customers. These behaviours, at the individual customer level, influence the aggregate level of the marketing assets of the company.

Output variables

Marketing assets

Marketing assets are customer-focused measures of the value of the company (and its offerings) that may enhance its long-term value. We focus on two approaches to assess marketing assets that have received considerable attention in the marketing literature: brand equity and customer equity.

The concept of *brand equity* has emerged in the past 20 years as a core concept of marketing. One view of brand equity suggests that its value arises from the incremental discounted cash flow from the sale of a set of products or services, as a result of the brand being associated with those products or services. Research on brand equity has sought to understand the conceptual basis for this remarkable value and its implications. The fruits of this research are changing how people think about brands and manage them. Managers have a deeper understanding of the elements of brand equity, of how brand equity affects buyer behaviour, of how to measure brand equity and of the influence of brand equity on corporate value. It is also important to note that brand equity leads to strength in the distribution channel. Thus, we assume that brand equity includes channel effects.

The concept of *customer equity* takes the company's customers' perspective. Building on previous definitions, we define customer equity as the sum of the lifetime values of all the company's current and future customers, where the lifetime value is the discounted profit stream obtained from the customer. The expansion of the service sector over time, combined with the resultant shift from transaction- to relationship-oriented marketing, has made the consideration of customer lifetime value (CLV) increasingly important. These events legitimate customer equity (i.e. the aggregation of CLV across customers) as a key metric of the company. CLV and customer equity are already in widespread use as marketing asset metrics in some industries, most notably in direct marketing and financial services. Customer equity measurement and monitoring is rapidly expanding in other industries too.

Output quantity

These are the traditional measures of marketing efficiency (sales volume and market share).

Financial impact

Financial benefits from a specific marketing action can be evaluated in several ways. ROI is a traditional approach to evaluate return relative to the expenditure required to obtain the return. It is calculated as the discounted return (net of the discounted expenditure), expressed as a percentage of the discounted expenditure. Commonly used retrospectively to measure short-term return, ROI is controversial in the context of marketing effectiveness. Because many marketing expenditures play out over the long run, short-term ROI is often prejudicial against marketing expenditures. The correct usage of ROI measures in marketing requires an analysis of future cash flows. It is also worth noting that the maximization of ROI as a management principle is not recommended (unless management's goal is efficiency rather than effectiveness), because it is inconsistent with profit maximization – a point that has long been noted in the marketing literature.

Other financial impact measures include the internal rate of return, which is the discount rate that would make the discounted return exactly equal to the discounted expenditure; the net present value, which is the discounted return minus the net present value of the expenditure; and the economic value added (EVA), which is the net operating profit minus the cost of capital.

In each case, the measures of financial impact weigh the return generated by the marketing action against the expenditure required to produce that return. The financial impact affects the financial position of the company, as measured by profits, cash flow and other measures of financial health.

If we take a look at the perceived service quality following from a given resource structure as inputs in a service process, it creates sales at a certain level. If the resource structure is changed, the cost level changes and so do perceived quality and the revenue-generating capability of the service provider. From this it follows that the productivity of service processes can be measured as the ratio between revenues and costs. This is a true measurement of service productivity. If revenues increase more than costs, productivity goes up. On the other hand, if a cost reduction leads to lost revenues, but the decline in revenues is less than the cost savings that have been achieved, productivity still improves. However, this may be a less recommendable strategy because in the long run it may lead to a negative image and unfavourable word of mouth, which can have a further negative effect on revenues.

Thus, cost reductions may lead to a bigger drop in revenues than the savings on the cost side. If this is the case, service productivity declines in the long run. Service-oriented productivity measures could be derived from the formulas above. However, we should keep in mind that there are problems with financial measures that have to be observed. Revenues are not always a good measure of output, since price does not always reflect perceived service quality. It may also be difficult to assign capital costs correctly to each type of revenue, respectively. Further, if businesses are subsidized by government, if prices are regulated or if competition is monopolistic, revenues may be a poor measure of quality. In addition, in all industries and competitive situations price may not reflect perceived quality very well. This is the case for many professional services, for example.

13.3 Marketing budgeting

The purpose of a marketing budget is to pull all the revenues and costs involved in marketing together into one comprehensive document. This is a managerial tool that balances what needs to be spent against what can be afforded, and helps its users make choices about priorities. It is then used in monitoring the performance in practice.

Budgeting is also an organization process that involves making forecasts based on the proposed marketing strategy and programmes. The forecasts are then used to construct a budgeted profit-and-loss statement (i.e. profitability). An important aspect of budgeting is deciding how to allocate the last available money across all the proposed programmes within the marketing plan.

The marketing plans and the annual budget are interlinked in many ways: the sales forecast, the pricing policy, the marketing expenditure budget and the allocation of resources. A budget is a detailed plan outlining the acquisition and use of financial and other resources over some given time period. The annual budget is commonly referred to as the 'master budget'. It has three principal parts: the operating budget, the cash budget and the capital expenditure budget. It is driven by the sales forecast. It has been noted that a sales budget for a company serves as a limit to be observed in establishing production budgets, selling and administrative budgets, cash budgets and budget plans. The budget plays a key role in an organization. It moves the organization from an informal reaction method of management to a formal controlled method of management. It can also act as a motivator and communicator, as well as assist in functional co-ordination and performance evaluation (McDonald, 2007).

There are four uses of a budget: first, to fine-tune the strategic plan; second, to help co-ordinate the activities of the several parts of the organization; third, to assign responsibilities to managers; and, fourth, to obtain a commitment that is the basis for evaluating a manager's actual performance.

Four major advantages of budgeting appear: first, it gives planning top priority; second, it provides managers with a way to finalize their planning efforts; third, it overcomes potential bottlenecks before they occur; and, fourth, it co-ordinates the activities of the entire company by integrating the plans and objectives of the various parts.

In summary, there are four main aspects to budgeting: the motivations aspect; the co-ordination of resources for their best use; setting benchmarks for performance; and as a cost control mechanism. The marketing plan is put together by members of the marketing team with input from the sales, finance and production departments. It is critical that senior executives accept the plan and lend their weight to it so that it is implemented. Both the annual budget as well as the marketing plan are used by companies as a short-term planning and control process. An integrated approach should enhance an organization's planning capabilities. The differences between the annual budget and the marketing plan are shown in Table 13.1.

Marketing plan	Annual budget
Short term, most often annual	Annual, short term
Compiled by marketing department with input from other areas	Compiled by finance with input from other areas
Integrated into the strategic plan	Integrated into the strategic plan
Used to implement and control a company's marketing activities	Used to co-ordinate functions and evaluate the performance of individuals
Concerns the use of company resources	Outlines the use of financial and other resources
Establishes benchmarks against which marketing accomplishments can be judged	Establishes benchmarks against which the company's performance can be measured
Has the sales budget as one of its outputs	Has the sales budget as its foundation

TABLE 13.1 Comparison between the marketing plan and the annual budget
Source: adapted from Abratt et al. (1994)

It is clear that the annual budget and the marketing plan are interwoven and should be part of the same process in organizations. The management implications are important. An organization works effectively when there is clear communication and co-ordination across functional lines. For effective implementation of an organization's strategy, the company must serve customers in the best manner possible. This will mean that all management policies and systems should be reviewed. An analysis of budgeting procedures, marketing planning processes and transaction flows will have to be undertaken. This analysis will have to be performed by both departments: whether it be a marketing audit, a budgeting process or a marketing planning exercise, personnel from both departments must be involved.

13.3.1 Profitability analysis

Regardless of the organizational level, control involves some form of profitability analysis. In brief, *profitability analysis* requires that analysts determine the costs associated with specific marketing activities to find out the profitability of such units as different market segments, products, customer accounts and distribution channels (intermediaries).

Profitability is probably the single most important measure of performance, but it has limitations. These are that (1) many objectives can best be measured in non-financial terms (maintaining market share); (2) profit is a short-term measure and can be manipulated by taking actions that may prove dysfunctional in the longer term (reducing research and development (R&D) expenses); and (3) profits can be affected by factors over which management has no control (e.g. the weather).

Contribution analysis is helpful in determining the yield derived from the application of additional resources (e.g. to certain sales territories). Contribution analysis attempts to determine the amount of output (revenues) that can be expected from a given set of inputs (costs). (You are probably familiar with break-even analysis, a type of contribution analysis used to determine the amount of revenue necessary to cover both variable and fixed costs.)

There are three ways to build a marketing budget that is based on a specific strategic market plan and the tactical marketing strategy designed to achieve the target level of performance.

1 *Top-down budget*: a new marketing budget based on projected sales objectives is determined, using past marketing expenses as a percentage of sales.
2 *Customer mix budget*: the cost of customer acquisition and retention, and the combination of new and retained customers, are used to derive a new marketing budget.
3 *Bottom-up budget*: each element of the marketing effort is budgeted for specific tasks identified in the marketing plan.

As this book has a customer-oriented approach, the customer mix budget will be discussed in the following section.

13.3.2 Customer mix budgets

Recognizing the customer as the primary unit of focus, a market-based business will expand its focus to customers and markets, not just products or units sold. This is an important strategic distinction because there are a finite number of potential customers, but a larger range of products and services can be sold to each customer. As shown in Fig. 13.2, a business's volume is its customer share in a market with a finite number of customers at any point in time, not the number of units sold.

Customer volume = Market demand (customers) = Market share (percentage)

Figure 13.2 presents an overall flowchart of how market-based net profits are derived. Customer volume, at the top of this diagram, is derived from a certain level of customer

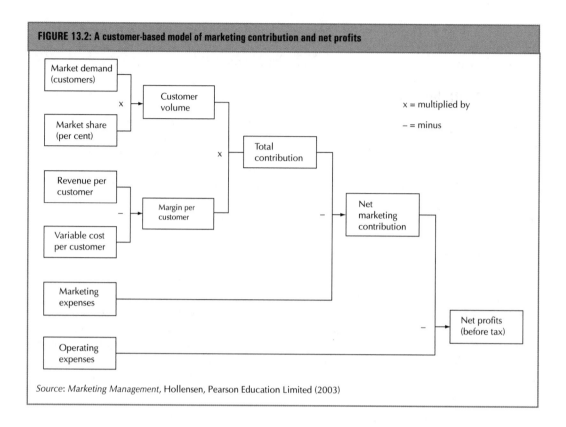

FIGURE 13.2: A customer-based model of marketing contribution and net profits

Source: *Marketing Management*, Hollensen, Pearson Education Limited (2003)

market demand and a business's share of that customer demand. Without a sufficient volume of customers, net profit will be impossible to obtain. Marketing strategies that affect customer volume include marketing strategies that:

- attract new customers to grow market share
- grow the market demand by bringing more customers into a market
- enter new markets to create new sources of customer volume.

Each of these customer-focused marketing strategies affects net profits, invested assets, cash flow and, as we see later, shareholder value. Thus, a key component of profitability and financial performance is customer purchases and the collective customer volume produced. Without customer purchases, there is no positive cash flow or potential for net profits or shareholder value (Gupta and Mela, 2008).

Figure 13.2 is a 'DuPont'-like illustration of the different budget element. Figure 13.3 is an illustration of the traditional marketing budget (per customer group or country) and its underlying determinants.

Customer-based budgeting recognizes that companies are increasingly turning away from traditional accounting methods, which identify costs according to various expense categories, and moving towards activity-based costing (ABC), which bases costs on the different tasks involved in performing a given activity.

The international marketing budget in Fig. 13.3 gives an indication of some of the underlying cost drivers in ABC.

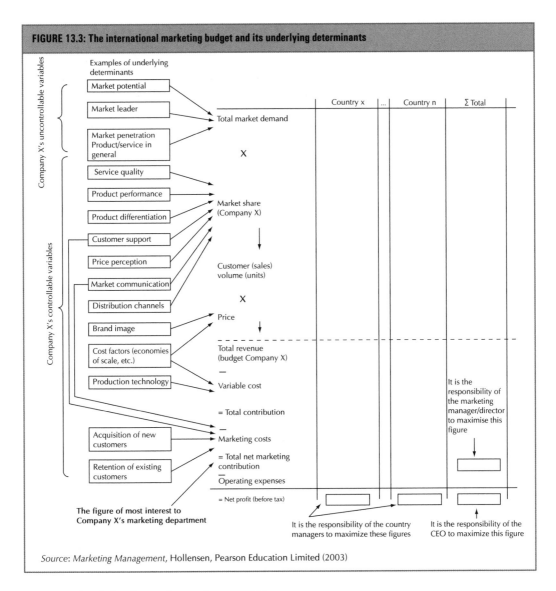

FIGURE 13.3: The international marketing budget and its underlying determinants

Source: *Marketing Management*, Hollensen, Pearson Education Limited (2003)

13.3.3 Activity-based costing (ABC)

To understand ABC systems, it is helpful to view the business as an entity that is engaged in performing a series of activities (e.g. R&D, product design, manufacturing, marketing, distribution and customer service) for the purpose of providing products (goods or services) to customers. In conducting these activities, the company incurs costs. To accurately attribute these costs to products, it is necessary to determine the consumption of activities by individual products. Accordingly, ABC involves the process of identifying the significant activities within the company, linking costs to these activities and measuring the consumption of the activities by the various products.

By using multiple cost drivers, ABC relates to cost with greater accuracy than traditional costing techniques. Traditional techniques typically rely on one to three volume-based cost drivers to trace overhead costs to products. ABC uses multiple cost drivers to reflect relationships existing between the activities and resources they consume.

An ABC analysis allows managers to pinpoint overhead resources to activities, products, services or customers with the objective of reducing or eliminating resource consumption. This technique can focus on improving the efficiency of an activity by reducing the number of times the activity must be performed, eliminating unnecessary or redundant activities, selecting a less costly alternative or using a single activity to accomplish multiple functions.

ABC implementation can provide greater visibility of how differently products, customers or supply channels impact profitability. The company can more accurately trace costs and determine the areas generating the greatest profit or loss. Product and customer profitability analyses performed by companies using ABC may significantly alter management perceptions of the status quo operation. Managers can target high cost products or services for reduction efforts. In conjunction with ABC, they can use other techniques such as repricing, minimum buy quantities or charging by service to improve profitability (Stapleton et al., 2004).

Looking at Fig. 13.3 the most important measures of marketing profitability may be defined as follows (Farris et al., 2006):

$$Contribution\ margin\ \% = \frac{Total\ contribution}{Total\ revenue} \times 100$$

$$Marketing\ contribution\ margin\ \% = \frac{Total\ marketing\ contribution}{Total\ revenue} \times 100$$

$$Profit\ margin\ \% = \frac{Net\ profit\ (before\ tax)}{Total\ revenue} \times 100$$

If we had information about the size of assets (accounts receivable + inventory + cash + plant + equipment) we could also define:

$$Return\ on\ assets\ (ROA) = \frac{Net\ profit\ (before\ tax)}{Assets}$$

(ROA is similar to the well-known measure ROI – return on investment.)

13.3.4 ROI and its applications

Customer profitability management requires a multi-level marketing ROI analysis covering a series of marketing activities that can be integrated and optimized for a customer or customer segment (Lenskold, 2004).

To apply marketing ROI at the customer level, it is necessary to have reasonable marketing ROI processes in place at the campaign level, including a corporate ROI threshold (or hurdle rate) at which the company will fund marketing programmes. There are three levels of marketing ROI analysis that should be applied where possible to guide marketing decisions: independent ROI, incremental ROI and aggregated ROI. Each of these can be effective at assessing and comparing marketing opportunities. When used together, the opportunity exists to truly optimize decisions that maximize customer profitability and total profits.

Independent ROI

The independent ROI analysis is completed for each decision that can stand alone. When managing marketing decisions at the customer level, this would involve assessing the independent campaigns directed at each customer. If the independent ROI exceeds the ROI threshold, that investment is generally justified unless the aggregated ROI analysis shows a higher-performing alternative. If the independent ROI does not meet the ROI threshold, this marketing activity may still be viable when assessed as part of a larger-scale customer-centric marketing programme.

Incremental ROI

When marketing activities are either dependent on or can be influenced by other marketing activities, an incremental ROI analysis should be completed. This ROI analysis isolates the incremental impact where interdependencies between campaigns exist. For example, an 'investment' in a cross-sell campaign on its own may generate a significant ROI but decrease the impact of an existing retention marketing campaign that follows. In such a case, the incremental ROI analysis would take into consideration both the additional profits from the cross-sell campaign and the lost profits from its impact on the subsequent retention campaign to determine if the investment into the cross-sell campaign should be made. Incremental ROI assessments help to protect against decisions based on ROI figures that represent the average of high-performing marketing efforts blended with low-performing marketing efforts.

The incremental ROI may be defined as:

$$\text{ROI} = \frac{\text{Incremental total contribution} - \text{Marketing 'investment'}}{\text{Marketing 'investment'}}$$

(Marketing 'investment' is a part of marketing costs in Figure 13.3.)

Aggregated ROI

The aggregated ROI analysis is based on the total returns relative to the total investment for a series of marketing activities directed to a specific customer or customer segment. This analysis works best when it aggregates only those marketing activities that can be decided upon collectively.

This could be a series of campaigns from a specific business unit within the company, all activity directed to the customer for a period of time or the entire lifetime of marketing activity, depending on the business model and management structure. Aggregated ROI analysis prioritizes total collective profitability ahead of independent campaign profitability, creating new opportunities to gain additional profits from existing marketing activities. This multi-level profitability analysis is beneficial to support customer-centric companies striving to integrate marketing activities across the customer relationship. For more product-oriented companies, it can also provide the financial insight necessary to motivate greater collaboration across the organization, eventually centring the planning and strategies on the customer.

Exhibit 13.1: *External and internal marketing metrics*

To ensure the marketing organization's continued existence and health, we must change senior executives' prevailing perception of marketing as an expense to one of marketing as an investment that enhances a company's overall profitability.

In today's competitive environment, many companies employ a balance-the-budget type of management. When revenue streams are good, these companies allow the marketing expense to flow. When profits decline, they employ quick-fix measures to address financial problems. To reduce expenditures, some companies cut marketing costs so that budgeted financial resources can flow directly to the bottom line. Others undertake strong marketing campaigns with the desired effect of immediately lifting revenue. Still others simply outsource their marketing functions to lower costs. The philosophy underlying these quick fixes is that marketing is an expense for which there is no appreciable or known return. At best, these approaches produce a short-term boost in profitability, but they produce little value in the longer term. Clearly, in these organizations the marketing investment is not appreciated. As marketers, we must turn around such myopic thinking. Our survival depends on it.

In order to change perceptions, we need to convince senior executives that a reduction in the amount of money budgeted to marketing activities prevents immediate and future returns on the corporate balance sheet. In this regard, perhaps the most significant activity marketers can engage in is to directly tie change (ROI) to specific marketing activities. The first step is to focus our marketing efforts and make causal connections between marketing activities and returns to the company. We can do this by establishing short- and long-term metrics, getting senior management's agreement on these metrics, setting performance goals based on these metrics and measuring our success against them.

A 'metric' is a performance measure that top management should review. It is a measure that matters to the whole business. The term comes from music and implies regularity: the reviews should typically take place yearly or half-yearly. A metric is not just another word for measure – while all metrics are measures, not all measures are metrics. Metrics should be necessary, precise, consistent and sufficient (i.e. comprehensive) for review purposes. Metrics may be financial (usually from the profit and loss account), from the marketplace or from non-financial internal sources (innovation and employees).

Metrics help the company achieve its specific goals. This puts pressure on the board to explain what 'success' will look like. Companies need multiple measures and these measures need to be relevant to the company's situation. It is important for each company to determine the relevant-to-them indicators of internal and external marketing 'health'.

External marketing metrics

Performance can be expressed as short-term (profit and loss account) financial measures 'adjusted' by the change in brand equity. Unfortunately, brand equity needs many non-financial measures, so the adjustment is conceptual, not in cash. It is this non-financial adjustment that distinguishes best practice metrics companies from the rest. Among the most important external marketing metrics are those shown in Table 13.2.

Customer metric	Measured by
Relative satisfaction	Consumer preference or satisfaction relative to average for market/competitor(s). The competitive benchmark should be stated.
Commitment	Index of switchability (or some similar measure of retention, loyalty, purchase intent or bonding).
Relative perceived quality	Perceived quality satisfaction relative to average for market/competitor(s). The competitive benchmark should be stated.
Relative price	Market share (value)/market share (volume).
Availability	Distribution, e.g. value-weighted per cent of retail outlets carrying the brand.

TABLE 13.2 External marketing metrics

The above-mentioned external metrics are calculated differently in different sectors. For example, loyalty may be the share of category requirements in packaged goods markets (e.g. the amount of Persil a user buys as a percentage of total laundry detergent purchases over a year), or the churn rate (percentage of customers lost over a given time period) in communications businesses such as mobile telephony.

So far we have focused on customers at various levels through to the ultimate users. For many metrics the question is not how satisfied the customer is, but how this compares with how satisfied the competitors' customers are. They may even be the same people. An 80 per cent satisfaction level is great if the rate for the competition is 70 per cent, but not so good if theirs is 90 per cent.

Internal marketing metrics

Monitoring the company's internal market takes two forms. We need to assess two things:

1 innovation health (i.e. how good your company is at achieving the kind of innovation you want)
2 how well attuned the staff are to understanding what the company is trying to achieve and how committed they are to doing it; in a sense, the company's employees are its first customers – if they do everything right, they will take care of external marketplace issues, including the end user.

3M very successfully uses just a few simple metrics, such as the proportion of sales attributable to recent innovations. Many other companies have copied these metrics, but few have succeeded because their leadership styles and cultures are different. The moral is that companies should get away from the detail and first measure these bigger picture variables. Thus, innovation is mostly a question of leadership, and then culture, rather than process. In large companies, much of the formal process gets in the way and should be dismantled.

Some companies, especially consumer service companies, see employees as their first customers. They believe that if management markets to employees correctly, then the front-line employees will take care of the external customers.

In this perception, internal marketing becomes, for the board, more important than external marketing and needs its own set of metrics. Some of the most important internal marketing metrics are shown in Table 13.3.

Employee metric	Measured by
Strategy	Awareness of goals (vision)
	Commitment to goals (vision)
	Active innovation support
	Resource adequacy
Culture	Appetite for learning
	Freedom to fail
	Relative employee satisfaction
	Aggregate customer brand empathy (composite index of how well employees see company brands as consumers do)
Outcomes	Number of initiatives in process
	Number of innovations launched
	% revenue due to launches during last three years

TABLE 13.3 Internal marketing metrics

Many companies now measure employee indicators but few cross-fertilize employee and customer survey techniques and measures. BP-Amoco is an exception in the way it does this. The oil giant found, unsurprisingly, a good correlation between employee and customer satisfaction.

Sources: adapted from Ambler, T. (2000) Marketing metrics, *Business Strategy Review*, 11(2): 59–66; Barwise, P. and Farley, J.U. (2004) Marketing metrics: status of six metrics in five countries, *European Management Journal*, 22(3): 257–62; Goodwin, K. (2004) Useful e-marketing metrics factor in outcomes, *Marketing News*, 38(10): 28–30; McCullough, W.R. (2000) Marketing metrics, *Marketing Management*, 9(1): 64–5

13.4 Controlling the marketing programme

At this point in the marketing planning process, the marketing plan is nearly complete. The final step is to plan how the organization will control the plan's implementation. Marketing control keeps both employees and activities on the proper track so the organization continues in the direction outlined in the marketing plan. However, employees in the organization often view 'control' as being negative. If individuals fear that the control process will be used not only to judge their performance but as a basis for punishing them, then it will be feared and reviled.

In preparing a marketing plan, marketers need to plan for three types of marketing control: annual control, profitability control and strategic control.

13.4.1 Annual control

Because marketers generally formulate new marketing plans every year, they need annual plan control to assess the progress of the current year's marketing plan. This covers broad performance measures (e.g. sales results, market share results) to evaluate the company's overall effectiveness. If a company fails to achieve this year's marketing plan objectives, it will have difficulty achieving its longer-term goals and mission. Although 'market share measures', for example, are driven by sales performance, they reflect relative competitive standing. These measures help senior managers gauge their company's competitive strength and situation over time.

13.4.2   Profitability control

This assesses the company's progress and performance based on key profitability measures. The exact measures differ from company to company, but they often include ROI, total marketing contribution, contribution margin and net profit margins. Many companies measure the monthly and yearly profit-and-loss results of each product, line and category, as well as each market or segment, and each channel. By comparing profitability results over time, marketers can spot significant strengths and weaknesses, and identify problems and opportunities early. Closely related to profitability control, productivity control measures the efficiency of, say, the sales force, promotions, channels and logistics, and product management. The purpose here is to measure profitability improvements through reduced costs or higher yield. Productivity is so important to the bottom line that some companies appoint marketing controllers to establish marketing productivity standards. Clearly, productivity control is connected not only with profitability but also with customer relationships.

13.4.3   Strategic control

This assesses the organization's effectiveness in managing the marketing function, in managing customer relationships, and in managing social responsibility and ethics issues – three areas of strategic importance. Whereas profitability controls are applied monthly or more often, strategic control may be applied once or twice a year, or as needed to give top management a clearer picture of the organization's performance in these strategic areas.

Summary

Marketing strategies in different international markets directly affect sales revenues per country. The marketing strategies also affect margins, total contribution and marketing costs. These effects, in turn, lead to the total net marketing contribution. Because operating (manufacturing) costs and overhead costs are beyond the control of marketing managers, net marketing contribution plays the most important role for the marketing department, to determine the profit impact of a marketing strategy.

As marketing plans are being implemented, they have to be monitored and controlled.

Control is the process of ensuring that global marketing activities are carried out as intended. It involves monitoring aspects of performance and taking corrective action where necessary. The global marketing control system consists of deciding marketing objectives, setting performance standards, locating responsibility, evaluating performance against standards, and taking corrective or supportive action in each single country and overall.

The most obvious areas of control relate to the control of the annual marketing plan, control of profitability and strategic control. The purpose of the global marketing budget is mainly to allocate marketing resources across countries to maximize worldwide total marketing contribution.

Questions for discussion

1 How would a non-profit organization apply financial budget control to its marketing plan implementation?
2 Given the dynamic and uncertain nature of the business environment, why would marketers bother drafting alternative marketing plans and budgets?
3 What are the main factors that affect marketing control systems?
4 Discuss the problems involved in setting up and implementing a marketing control system.
5 Why is the outcome of one year's marketing control an important input to next year's marketing plan?
6 Comment on the statement: 'Implementors are the most important country organizations in terms of buy-in for effective global marketing strategy implementation.'
7 Why is customer profitability sometimes a better unit of measurement than market profitability?
8 Assess the complexity of developing marketing metrics for a manufacturing organization and a financial services company.
9 Which factors can make the interpretation of performance difficult?
10 One of the most efficient means of control is self-control. What type of programme would you prepare for an incoming employee?

References

Abratt, R., Beffon, M. and Ford, J. (1994) Relationship between marketing planning and annual budgeting, *Marketing Intelligence & Planning*, 12(1): 22–8.

Farris, P.W., Bendle, N.T., Pfeifer, P.E. and Reibstein, D.J. (2006) *Marketing Metrics: 50+ Every Executive should Master*, 1st edn. Philadelphia, PA: Wharton School Publishing.

Grönroos, C. and Ojasalo K. (2004) Service productivity – towards a conceptualization of the transformation of inputs into economic results in services, *Journal of Business Research*, 57: 414–23.

Gupta, S. and Mela, C.F. (2008) What is a free customer worth?, *Harvard Business Review*, November: 102–9.

Hollensen, S. (2003) *Marketing Management*. London: Financial Times/Prentice Hall.

Johnston, R. and Jones, P. (2004) Service productivity – towards understanding the relationships between operational and customer productivity, *International Journal of Productivity and Performance Management*, 53(3): 201–13.

Lenskold, J.D. (2004) Customer-centric marketing ROI, *Havard Business Review*, January/February: 26–31.

McDonald, M. (2007) *Marketing Plans: How to Prepare them, How to use them*, 6th edn. Oxford/Burlington, MA: Butterworth-Heinemann.

Rust, T.M., Ambler, T., Carpenter, G.C., Kumar, V. and Srivastava, R.K. (2004) Measuring marketing productivity: current knowledge and future directions, *Journal of Marketing*, 68: 76–89.

Stapleton, D., Sanghamitra, P., Beach, E. and Julmanichoti, P. (2004) Activity-based costing for logistics and marketing, *Business Process Management Journal*, 10(5): 584–97.

CASE STUDY 13: MUSIC WORLD ENTERTAINMENT (MWE)

New worldwide organizational structure and the marketing planning and budgeting of Beyoncé's new album

On a sunny August day in 2010, the President and chief executive officer (CEO) of *Music World Entertainment* (*MWE*), Mathew Knowles, boards a plane from New York bound for London where, among other things, he is going to meet his daughter and megastar Beyoncé about the marketing campaign of her new CD release in Autumn 2010. In 2009 Beyoncé was one of MWE's best-selling artists, and Mathew is looking forward to meeting his daughter personally again.

Now in his job as President of MWE, Mathew uses the plane trip over the Atlantic to study the global music industry more thoroughly in order to get the best input for marketing of Beyoncé's coming CD in the UK market.

MWE

MWE was founded in 2003 by Mathew Knowles, who is also the father of one of MWE's artists, Grammy Award-winner Beyoncé. Today MWE (as part of Sony Music Entertainment) is one of the USA's leading entertainment and music conglomerates dedicated to bringing entertainment to the world. MWE's business includes record labels, artist and producer management, staff producers, artist development, Master Catalog series, investment and property holdings, including offices in Houston, Los Angeles, New York and London.

Under MWE, one of the record labels is Music World, which is the management and record company behind 200 million records sold to date, including releases by Destiny's Child, Beyoncé, Solange Knowles, Michelle Williams, Sunshine Anderson and the popular Music World Master Series releases, which include Chaka Kahn and The O'Jays.

Music World's list also includes artists signed to major label partners such as Columbia, Geffen Records and Interscope Records.

Mathew Knowles and his daughter Beyoncé

After completing his B.A. at Fisk University in 1975, Mathew Knowles worked for computing manufacturing company IBM. While his work was financially rewarding (he was earning a six-figure salary), he sought a greater challenge. He left his job at IBM to manage his eldest daughter's (Beyoncé's) singing career. Beyoncé started out in Girl's Tyme, which was the precursor to what was later to become Destiny's Child. Destiny's Child has since grown into one of the most successful 'girl group' in the history of pop music, selling millions of albums and earning multiple awards.

Mathew Knowles has been married to stylist and House of Dereon owner Tina Knowles since 1980. Together, they have two daughters, R&B singers Beyoncé and Solange Knowles, both of whom are managed by Mathew. Knowles and his family are members of St. John's Methodist Church. After almost 30 years of marriage, Beyoncé's mother has filed for divorce from her father. Tina Knowles filed for divorce in December 2009 after Mathew, 58, was named in a paternity suit by an actress.

MWE is a division of the major label Columbia Records, which again is a subsidiary of Sony Music Entertainment (SME).

In August 2008 the international media and entertainment companies Sony Corporation and Bertelsmann AG announced that Sony has agreed to acquire Bertelsmann's 50 per cent stake in Sony BMG. The new music company, to be called *Sony Music Entertainment Inc.* (*SME*), became a wholly owned subsidiary of Sony Corporation of America. SME's HQ is in New York.

SME operates music labels such as Arista Records, Upstate Records, Columbia Records (which MWE belongs to), Epic Records, J Records, Jive Records, RCA Records, LaFace Records and Zomba Records. The sale price was not disclosed when the deal was announced in August, but news reports valued it at US$1.5 bn.

The world music industry in 2009

A handful of music companies (operating through several hundred subsidiaries and over a thousand labels) account for most records sold in the advanced economies. Music publishing – production and licensing of intellectual property rights – is even more concentrated.

In 2009 the global recorded music industry was estimated to $30 bn. Total annual unit sales (CDs, music videos, MPs) in 2009 were approximately three billion. The approximate market shares on the world market are shown in Table 13.4.

Record company	Market shares (%) on the world market for recorded music (2009)
Universal Music Group	26
Sony Music Entertainment	20
EMI Group	13
Warner Music	11
Independent labels	28
Total	100 (= approximately US$30 bn)

TABLE 13.4   The global recorded music industry
Source: adapted from International Federation of the Phonographic Industry (IFPI), www.ifpi.com

Over the past 100 years we have seen the 'music industry' evolve through three basic stages, characterized by different technologies and different publishing organizations. Prior to the gramophone, when sheet music was the primary vehicle for disseminating popular music, the industry was dominated by music publishing houses. With the rise of recording (and subsequently broadcasting, which was driven by the availability of 'canned content'), those publishers were displaced by the record companies.

Today, increasingly the industry has involved entertainment groups that bring together a broad range of content distribution and repackaging activities – broadcast, film, video, booking and performance management agencies, records, music licensing and print publishing.

Beyoncé – one of the best selling R&B and pop artists

Beyoncé (whose real name is Beyoncé Giselle Knowles) is a US R&B singer, songwriter, record producer, actress and model. Born and raised in Houston, Texas, she enrolled in various performing arts schools and was first exposed to singing and dancing competitions as a child. Knowles rose to fame in the late 1990s as the lead singer of the R&B girl group Destiny's Child. According to Sony, Knowles' record sales, when combined with the group, have surpassed 100 million.

Beyoncé went to school at St. Mary's Elementary School in Texas, where she enrolled in dance classes, including ballet and jazz. Her talent in singing was discovered when her dance instructor began humming a song and she finished it, hitting the high-pitched notes. Although a shy girl, Beyoncé's interest in music and performing began unexpectedly after participating in a school talent show. Once she had a moment on the stage, she overcame her shyness and wanted to become a singer and performer. By age seven, Knowles had entered her first talent show, singing John Lennon's 'Imagine'. She won the contest and was honoured with a standing ovation.

In 1990, Beyoncé joined some auditions in a girl group, originally called Girl's Tyme. After a series of auditions Támar Davis (12 years), Beyoncé Knowles (10 years; managed by her father Mathew Knowles), Kelly Rowland (11; managed also by Mathew Knowles), and dancers/rappers LaTavia Roberson (10), Nikki Taylor (13), and her younger sister Nina Taylor (11) were chosen for the group. Girl's Tyme began rehearsing a variety of R&B, rap and pop songs.

Mathew and Tina Mathew were not satisfied with the group's name (Girl's Tyme). After long consideration of what the group's new name would be, nothing seemed right to Tina Knowles who became the group's stylist. She then came across a page in her bible. In the Book of Isaiah the word *Destiny* caught her eye; Mathew then added *Child*. Thus, the new name of the group was then changed to *Destiny's Child* in 1993.

Destiny's Child performed at local events and, after four years on the road, the group was signed to Columbia Records in late 1997. That same year, Destiny's Child recorded its major label debut song, 'Killing Time', for the soundtrack to the 1997 film, *Men in Black*. The following year, the group released its self-titled debut album, scoring their first major hit 'No, No, No'.

Destiny's Child's third album, *Survivor*, was released in May 2001, debuting at number one on the US *Billboard* 200 with 663 000 units sold. To date, *Survivor* has sold over 10 million copies worldwide, over 40 per cent of which were sold in the USA alone. The album created other number-one hits – 'Bootylicious' and the title track, 'Survivor'.

During the peak of Destiny's Child, Knowles released her debut solo album, *Dangerously in Love* (2003), which became one of the most successful albums of that year, and signalled her viability as a solo artist. The disbanding of Destiny's Child in 2005 facilitated her continued success: her solo album, *B'Day*, released in 2006, debuted at number one on the *Billboard* charts. Her third solo album, *I Am … Sasha Fierce*, was released in November 2008, and earned her 10 Grammy Award nominations. The album was preceded with the release of its two singles, 'If I Were a Boy' and 'Single Ladies (Put a Ring on It)'. While 'If I Were a Boy'' topped numerous charts worldwide, mostly in European countries, 'Single Ladies (Put a Ring on It)' went on to top the *Billboard* Hot 100 chart for four non-consecutive weeks, giving Beyoncé her fifth number one single in the USA.

'Halo', the fourth single off *I Am ... Sasha Fierce*, went on to peak at number five, becoming Knowles' twelfth Top 10 single on the Hot 100 as a solo artist.

Beyoncé has attained five Hot 100 number one singles, becoming one of the two female artists with the most number ones attained within the 2000s, excluding her three Hot 100 number one singles with Destiny's Child this decade. On 11 December 2009 Beyoncé was named Billboard's Top Female Artist of the Decade and fourth artist overall.

In late 2009, Knowles stated that she already begun work on her fourth studio album, aiming for it to be released in Autumn 2010. Beyoncé said that the album could take a more indie direction.

How to market in UK?

The typical value chain for a CD

The following shows how the 'value added' of a typical CD album is split among the various players in the value chain:

	£
Retail price to consumers	12
Price to retail	9
Price to distributor	6
Price to distributor (exclusive of artist royalty)	5

For a CD single the full retail price to consumers is about £2. But when a record is being pushed hard by the record label, retailers are offered big discounts in an attempt to shift units in the all-important first week. In such circumstances singles can retail for as little as 99p.

Development

In the music industry record labels will actively seek to sign up bands and artistes on long-term exclusive contracts. A key to success in development is to spot talent and to sign it up early.

Production

Production is relatively cheap in the music industry, and the cost of digital recording equipment and production of CDs is falling rapidly. Some consumers do not understand why the sale price of a CD is so much higher than the cost of producing the actual physical disc. But as described below there are many different activities and costs involved in creating songs and marketing the end result, the CD.

Distributors

Major distributors have a global network of branch offices to handle the sales, marketing and distribution process. Sometimes the distributors may outsource the physical distribution process.

Retail

Retailers put in orders to the wholesalers as and when albums and singles are required. In the UK the retail chains are dominated by HMV, Virgin/Our Price/Smiths, Tower, and so on. These chains account for about 80 per cent of the market.

The costs of a hit

Singles are released with the purpose of getting to the top of the charts. The financial risks involved in mounting an attack on the UK charts have never been greater. According to research carried out by BBC News Online, securing a Top 10 hit in the UK in the current climate is likely to cost a minimum of £125 000. Ever increasing amounts of financial resources are being thrown at marketing and promotion in the hope that a single will be picked up by MTV, radio and, perhaps most importantly, the major retailers, in order to secure the highest chart entry.

Biggest cost categories

Of course, the most important component of a CD is the artist's effort that goes into developing the music. Artists spend a large portion of their creative energy on writing song lyrics and composing music or working with producers and artists and repertoire (A&R) executives to find great songs from great writers. This task can take weeks, months, or even years. The creative ability of these artists to produce the music, combined with the time and energy they spend throughout that process, is in itself priceless. But while the creative process is priceless, it must be compensated. Artists receive royalties on each recording, which vary according to their contract, and the songwriter gets royalties too. In addition, the label incurs the costs of finding and signing new artists.

Once an artist or group has songs composed they then go into a studio and begin recording. The costs of recording, including studio fees, musicians, sound engineers, producers and others, must all be recovered by the price of the CD.

Then come marketing and promotion costs – perhaps the most expensive part of the music business today. They include increasingly expensive video clips, public relations, tour support, marketing campaigns and promotion to get the songs played. Labels make investments in artists by paying for both the production and the promotion of the album. New technology such as the Internet offers new ways for artists to reach music fans, but it still requires that some entity, whether a traditional label or another kind of company, market and promote the artist so that fans are aware of new releases.

For every album released in a given year, a marketing strategy is developed to make that album stand out from the others hitting the market. Artwork must be designed for the CD box, and promotional materials (posters, store displays and music videos) developed and produced. For many artists a costly concert tour is essential to promote their recordings.

Another factor commonly overlooked in assessing CD prices is to assume that all CDs are equally profitable. In fact, the vast majority are never profitable; for example, in the USA, 27 000 new releases hit the market every year. Most of these CDs never sell enough to recover costs. In the end, less than 10 per cent are profitable and, in effect, it is these recordings that finance the rest.

Marketing and promotion costs

Singles are essentially 3–4 minute advertisements for CD albums. Singles' sales guarantee chart places and, in turn, radio play – and that is why music label companies persist with them. They are a kind of loss-leader for albums, where the real money is made.

The biggest expense is normally the promotional video, which for a mainstream artist starts at about £40 000 and can cost anything up to £1 m (however, this is quite exceptional). If the music video is to be shown on, say, MTV, it has to comply with a number of requirements, which are set out by MTV (use of alcohol, sex, etc.).

It is common practice for the big retailers, HMV, Our Price and Virgin, to charge music label companies for promoting a single in their shops. This comes in the form of a 'singles pack', which guarantees a prominent position for the product in the shop. There are also bonuses to be paid to the sales force to check that the single is being properly promoted in-store.

The singles' chart – compiled each week by different organizations and TV stations – has always been the cornerstone of the UK music industry. More singles are sold in the UK than anywhere in the world – including the USA – where the album remains king. In 2000 it took an average of 118 700 sold singles to secure a number one spot in the UK chart. Since 2005 the UK singles' chart has combined actual release sales with legal online downloads. Initially, the proportion of digital sales to physical sales was relatively low, but now (2009) more than 80 per cent of single sales take place online. Sales via mobile telephones and video downloads are also now counted.

Here are some of the basic costs for a 'typical' UK top 10 single:

	£
Recording	3,500
Promotion video	100,000–150,000
Remixes (of the original single)	5,000–10,000
Merchandising	15,000
Posters	10,000
Stickers	5,000
PR (Press)	5,000
Promotion copies to radio stations, etc.	8,000
Website	20,000
Manufacturing costs (20p per CD)	10,000
Optional costs:	
Press advertisements	15,000
Billboard campaign	50,000
TV/radio/Internet advertising	200,000

Because of the high costs involved, combined with the general decline in the sales of CDs and singles (because of the trend towards online downloading of songs), many industry insiders think the singles' market cannot continue in its current form. One possible escape route is the radio-only release, where a track from an album is promoted to radio stations, but is not actually available to buy. This often happens in the USA, where there is less emphasis on singles' sales, and the singles' chart is largely based on radio play.

After landing in London, Mathew is well rested, but before his meeting with Beyoncé he has found out that you are a marketing specialist, and therefore he has the following questions for you.

Questions

1 How would you create a sales and marketing budget for Beyoncé's forthcoming single and album?

2 How would you control your budgets? What key figures would you monitor?

3 While he is in London, Mathew is also going to meet with his superiors in Sony Music Entertainment, and he would like to come up with some marketing recommendations for the UK market. Which marketing mix would you suggest to increase Sony Music Entertainment's share in the UK market, where the company has less than 20 per cent market share?

Sources: adapted from www.beyonceonline.com/us/home; www.musicworldent.com/; International Federation of the Phonographic Industry (IFPI). Available online at www.ifpi; www.sonymusic.com; www.columbiarecords.com/; www.sonybmg.com; RIAA, The costs of a CD. Available online at www.riaa.com/MD-US-7.cfm, 2003; BMG press release, New York, 23 January 2003; BBC News, Sony and BMG merger backed by EU, 19 July; BBC News, Sony BMG deal under new scrutiny, 13 July 2006.

CHAPTER

14

Ethical, social and environ- mental aspects of marketing planning

Chapter contents

❖ LEARNING OBJECTIVES

After studying this chapter you should be able to do the following:

❖ Understand why ethical issues are important for the company's marketing planning and marketing mix.
❖ Explain how ethical marketing is related to relationship building.

❖ Define 'social marketing'.
❖ Give examples of 'social marketing' campaigns.
❖ Explain the role of ethics in marketing planning.
❖ Differentiate among various levels of 'green' marketing.

14.1   Introduction

Until now we have examined the basic framework for marketing planning. In this last chapter of the book we turn our attention to some important issues that should be considered during the marketing planning process. The relevance of being ethical, social and environmentally responsible has grown considerably over the past few decades, in the light of public demands and changes in national laws. This chapter is divided into four parts:

1   Corporate social responsibility (CSR) (Section 14.2)
2   Ethical issues in marketing planning (Section 14.3)
3   'Social marketing' issues (Section 14.4)
4   Environmental/'green' issues (Section 14.5).

14.2 Corporate social responsibility (CSR)

In the 1960s 'marketing' was defined as a transaction between the provider and the receiver of the product, where the provider satisfies the goals of the receiver and obtains some type of compensation in return. The definition emphasizes the four components of the marketing mix (the 4Ps – product, price, place, promotion).

The notion of societal marketing introduced in the 1980s saw that marketing should incorporate society's interests into consideration as well.

Now the world has changed: *CSR* has become an important issue also among marketers in the corporate world.

The concept of CSR captures the dynamics of the relationship between business and society. According to Greenberg and Baron (2008: 25) CSR describes:

> **❝** business practices that adhere to ethical values that comply with legal requirements, that demonstrate respect for individuals, and that promote the betterment of the community at large and the environment. It involves operating a business in a manner that meets or exceeds those ethical, legal and public expectations that society has of business.   **❞**

Let us look into what the concept of CSR stands for. The core theme of CSR is to deal, interact and relate with stakeholders with an ethical approach that is not harming or hurting any stakeholder. CSR represents the voluntary (non-enforced) set of activities of a business organization. At the bare minimum CSR stands for being legally compliant to the rules of the land. But the dominant theme and directive of CSR is to better the condition of various stakeholders like the neighbouring local communalities, broader society and the natural environment. In the current debate, CSR has been seen as a continuous process of engagement with the stakeholders by a business organization (Rigby and Tager, 2008).

Porter and Kramer (2006) elaborated on an example of Nestlé's CSR initiatives, and concluded that CSR integrated to the value chain benefited Nestlé. Building on this example, it can be advocated that company CSR programmes should be so designed that the CSR activity forms part of the organization value chain by contributing either to the primary activities and/or the support activities. Such CSR initiatives help organizations to secure purchased inputs, reduce operational costs, smooth logistics and/or contribute to the marketing and sales function of the value chain. Similarly, CSR activities could also be intelligently planned to contribute to the support activities, like procurement, manpower development and so on, of the organization's value chain.

14.3 Ethics

Marketing ethics refers to morally right and wrong action in marketing. It can be defined in two ways. First, it is a discipline that involves the systematic study of the moral evaluation of marketing decisions, practices and institutions. Second, marketing ethics are the standards, or 'norms', applied in the judgement of marketing activities as morally right and wrong. More simply, marketing ethics is about the moral problems of marketing managers. It includes, for example, the ethical considerations associated with product safety, truth in advertising and fairness in pricing. It is an integral part of decisions regarding marketing planning.

Recent criticism of the ethics of marketing reflects increased societal concern about business practices, and has focused on specific issues, industries and organizations. However, there has been a long-standing suspicion of marketing. Many people associate marketing activities, especially selling and advertising, with dishonesty and 'tricks'.

Commentators who suggest that marketing heightens materialism, wastes scarce resources and makes consumption an end in itself, often ignore the role of the consumer in this process and the fact that marketing is a response to consumer preferences. Also frequently overlooked – particularly by critics of marketing's wastefulness – are the intangible benefits that products may provide, including the psychological and social benefits that often accompany marketing activities such as advertising and branding. Hence, an alternative view, often proclaimed by marketing practitioners, is that marketing actually serves society.

These arguments may be sufficient to counter the charge that marketing in general is unethical. However, they require assumptions that do not always hold. First, not all markets are competitive and not all consumers are well informed. Second, the law has limits and shortcomings. Third, marketing practices (such as advertising) are reflective of society.

14.3.1 Ethical issues in the marketing mix

The product

Ethical issues may arise in product policy throughout the product life cycle, from development to elimination. Product safety is often a significant ethical issue in product policy. There is a legal requirement in most countries to provide products worthy of sale and fit for their intended purpose. This requirement encompasses product safety. As well as this 'implied warranty', an absence of 'ordinary care' on the part of sellers (manufacturers, wholesalers and retailers) can give rise to charges of negligence under tort law, with the seller made liable for products proven defective that have caused injury. In addition, sellers must comply with safety regulations established by government agencies. Yet, there remain ethical considerations in product safety beyond those established by the law. Marketers have to ask: 'How safe should a product be?' It is not possible to create a risk-free environment, with products incapable of causing harm, largely because product safety is a function of the consumer as well as of the product's design and manufacture.

Pricing

Pricing is the most regulated area of marketing. There are legal prohibitions governing price-fixing, price discrimination, predatory pricing and transfer pricing. In some cases, unethical practices may be possible without actually being illegal.

Distribution

Ethical issues in distribution largely involve conflicts between channel intermediaries, typically reflecting a power imbalance in channel relationships. The size and market power of large retailers, wholesalers or manufacturers may often be open to abuse. The increasing power of the retailer has resulted in demands of suppliers that not all can meet; for instance, listing fees (fees required by retailers for listing a manufacturer's product) have escalated in the grocery trade, with some smaller suppliers crying foul when they are unable to match the fees paid by larger suppliers. Other channel-management issues include grey marketing, where some channel intermediaries have been criticized for free-riding on legitimate channel intermediaries who often face higher costs (e.g. because they have to provide higher levels of customer service).

Communication

The visibility of advertising, coupled with its role as persuasive communication, result in it being one of the most frequently criticized areas of marketing. Truth in advertising has been an ethical issue since the earliest use of advertising. In most countries, advertisers are subject to stringent self-regulation by industry bodies as well as government regulation. Advertisers must be able to substantiate claims about product performance, for example.

Abuses in advertising can range from exaggerated claims and concealed facts to outright lying. Such abuses range from the unethical, which they clearly are, to the illegal, which they may be. The US Federal Trade Commission (FTC) stepped in when KFC promoted the health benefits and low carbohydrate content of its chicken with the slogan, 'If you're watching carbs and going high-protein, go KFC'. Two pieces of fried chicken (skin removed) were being compared to the original Burger King Whopper. Small print at the bottom of the advertisement noted 'a balanced diet and exercise are necessary for good health' and that 'KFC chicken is not a low fat, low sodium, low cholesterol food'. The FTC required KFC to stop running the advertising, indicating the deceptive nature of the advertisement (Ferrell, 2004).

Sales people are not under direct continuous supervision; rather, they are under constant pressure to produce sales and are faced with additional temptations offered by the myriad of opportunities for unethical behaviour that the position invites. Some of the more common areas of sales-related misconduct are as follows:

- overselling
- promising more than can be delivered
- lying or making exaggerated claims
- failing to keep customer confidences by divulging information to competitors
- offering inappropriate or illegal entertainment.

So, the persuasive purpose of the sales task often creates conflicts for the sales person. These conflicts arise largely within three interfaces: the sales person–customer, the sales person–company and the sales person–competitor.

In the sales person–customer relationship, the best opportunity to maintain ethical standards is through: competent buying and selling, supported by training; insistence on purchase contract performance; acceptance testing; and so on. Most sellers respect the buyer who is thorough and honest in the conduct of the buying office or buying centre, and will usually respond in kind.

The major ethical issues listed under the sales person–competitor interface are largely illegal under laws prohibiting misrepresentation and unfair competition and anti-trust legislation.

14.3.2 Ethics in 'global marketing'

More generally, a serious and unresolved situational ethics problem often occurs in global marketing. No international code of business ethics exists because each society's ethics vary – some slightly and others greatly. Fortunately, most of the world's major religions and cultures share common norms and ethics, and would answer the questions in an 'ethical checklist' in a similar way. But in some countries bribes, kickbacks, and dishonesty in advertising, selling and dealing are much more acceptable than in others. How should foreign companies behave in such markets? If they do not tolerate such standard practices, they risk not doing business and may be further hated for arrogantly imposing their values where they are not wanted. For example, should European garment manufacturers be concerned about working conditions in the offshore factories that produce many of their clothing lines?

Bribery

Commercial bribery is ordinarily illegal, but the potential gains from this generally unethical practice are often so great that it can be found in many markets and in all countries. Bribery is defined as 'the offering, promising or giving [of] something in order to influence a public official in the execution of his/her official duties' (Sanyal and Samanta, 2004). Bribes can take the form of money, other pecuniary advantages (e.g. a scholarship for a child's college education) or non-pecuniary benefits (e.g. favourable publicity). In the international context, bribery involves a company from country A offering financial or non-financial inducements to officials of country B in order to obtain a commercial benefit.

Bribery tends to occur more often in less-developed countries, especially those with a recent colonial past. In these countries the full bureaucratic apparatus of the modern state has been introduced with little regard for the limited capacity of the economy to sustain it. Government officials have heavy responsibilities and much social status but their salaries are often very low in comparison to their social and familial obligations. The need to maintain status, and the heavy burden of traditional obligations encourages corrupt behaviour. Thus, corruption is the result of a combination of opportunity (which comes from the office held) and personal/familial obligations. In addition, the high cost of enforcing rules relative to the available resources, as well as the reluctance of people in power to prosecute corrupt acts (being corrupt themselves), allows such behaviour to persist.

Often it is difficult to distinguish between a bribe, a gift to show appreciation and a reasonable commission for services rendered. Accepting or giving gifts may or may not be ethical, but the practice of gift-giving comes under close scrutiny at many B2B companies. If the giving of a gift is done as a condition of doing business (subtle or otherwise), then clearly the act is immoral and unethical; further, it causes prejudice against those who fail to give a gift. Many companies have stopped the practice of giving holiday gifts to customers, offering instead to contribute to a customer's favourite charity. The problem with this approach, however, is that even those gratuities given to create legitimate goodwill may influence the purchasing decision in some way. Common sense and social intelligence should be good guides in keeping the selling company within ethical boundaries.

The ethical standards of morality that constrain marketing decision-making should be a product of the combination of personal conscience and the morality of the company as stated in its code of ethics. Ethical behaviour is required to make the market work efficiently and to keep it free and open. Marketing planners must therefore respond to the almost universal ethical codes involved in trading – to be honest and not conspire to cheat and steal – but their decisions as to what to offer the marketplace and how to offer it also have an impact on the prevailing values and ethics of a society. Some products and marketing practices are ethically questionable. This heavy responsibility cannot simply be shrugged off. The enlightened leadership that marketing planners are expected to display is most put to the test when they are faced with ethical dilemmas created by conflicts of interest among customers, employees and owners.

14.4 Social marketing

Social marketing can be understood as the application of commercial marketing technologies to the analysis, planning, execution and evaluation of programmes designed to influence the voluntary behaviour of target audiences in order to improve their personal welfare and that of their society.

Social marketing has a clear relationship to commercial marketing. Still, social marketing is distinct from commercial marketing in that it focuses on resolving social problems, whereas commercial marketing focuses on producing various goods or services for a profit. The 'customer' of social marketing is normally not expected 'to pay a price equal to the cost of providing the service', whereas the customer of commercial marketing is expected to do so. Furthermore, social marketing should not be confused with socially responsible marketing, something in which all marketers should be engaged. Socially responsible marketing is commercial marketing that appropriately takes into account its social responsibilities in marketing ordinary products and services.

As such, social marketing focuses on influencing people's behaviour away from ways of acting or lifestyles that are designated as leading or contributing to a social problem, and towards other ways of acting and lifestyles that will improve these people's well-being (or the well-being of others). This attempt to change people's behaviour may also involve modifications in their attitudes, values, norms and ideas. Indeed, it may also require behavioural and value changes in the communities or groups of people with whom they live and/or associate.

The well-being of individuals and/or society is not simply subjectively identified by the individuals involved but is subject to determination through processes of social argumentation and justification. This does not mean that everyone will agree with these processes.

Social marketers target people who may not believe, at least at the outset, that they suffer from a problem or any deficiency in their welfare. As such, social problems are identified independently of what any particular person or people may or may not believe. It is compatible with social marketing that the people social marketers address strongly believe that they do not have a problem. These might include teenagers who abuse alcohol or drugs, fathers of Muslim girls in Bangladesh who do not believe their daughters should receive an education, or men in parts of Africa who wish to have their future wives undergo female circumcision.

Exhibit 14.1: *The social marketing of Population Services International (PSI)*

PSI has become the leading social marketing organization in the world, specializing in HIV/AIDS prevention, family planning, and maternal and child health. PSI has almost 65 000 employees in the 70 countries where it operates, of which 98 per cent are citizens of the countries they serve. PSI programmes are funded by foundations and other private donors, and by governmental development assistance and multilateral agencies.

Social marketing, as practised by PSI, combines education to motivate healthy behaviour with the provision of required health products and services to lower-income people. PSI motivates a wide variety of healthy behaviours, including use of products and services. PSI procures products, establishes an office and distribution system, and sells the products through the wholesale and retail network, primarily to lower-income persons. Products and services are branded, attractively packaged, widely marketed, effectively promoted to the poor and selected target groups, and sold at low prices that are affordable to the poor. Since this retail price is often even lower than the manufacturing cost (so the poor can afford the price), donor contributions are a vital element of the social marketing process.

A key ingredient of successful social marketing is effective communications to encourage the adoption of appropriate health practices (including proper use of the products and services). This is done by brand-specific advertising as well as by generic educational campaigns, using a mix of strategies and channels, including mass media and interpersonal communications, to reach the target audience(s).

PSI markets condoms for AIDS prevention, a wide range of contraceptives for family planning, and a number of health products aimed especially at women and children, such as oral rehydration solutions, mosquito nets, clean water kits, vitamins, antibiotics and iodized salt. Many of these products are donated to PSI by foundations, multilateral international organizations or the overseas development agencies of donor governments. In other instances, donors provide funds to PSI, which procures products at favourable rates on the international market. PSI has also started to socially market health services such as voluntary HIV counselling and testing, and reproductive health services.

14.4.1 Social marketing and relationship building

Social marketing is about changing behaviour: encouraging people to give up smoking, take exercise or visit a sexual health clinic (Andreasen, 1994; Hastings, 2003).

These changes do not, for the most part, occur overnight. They involve a series of steps from initial contemplation through to reinforcement after the fact, a process that is both dynamic and precarious: the individual can regress or have a change of heart at any point.

Social marketing is founded on trust, and therefore it is necessary to start thinking in terms of long-term relationship building. Transactions are shallow and inadequate by comparison. If someone is trying to give up smoking, how much better to interact with them regularly and customize the offering to their needs at any particular stage in the process, rather than fire off *ad hoc* messages. Add to this the opportunity for cross-selling and up-selling, and the case becomes compelling. A telephone helpline that provides support for those quitting smoking can easily be used to encourage other lifestyle decisions, say about diet or physical activity.

As in commercial marketing, relationship building on this scale will be information technology-dependent. Progress down this path has already begun. Database-mining techniques have been used to improve targeting in dietary and mammography interventions.

Databases used to generate bills could be adapted and customized to deliver positive health messages or products. Association with such messages and the health organizations that generate them could help make billing a less negative process and improve the company's corporate image. Moving from transactions to relationships adds the vital dimension of time to the social marketing exchange, which turns trust into commitment and enables long-term, strategic planning.

Figure 14.1 shows that social marketers need to think about building relationships in the same four domains as commercial companies. These are described in more detail below.

1 *Buyer partnerships*: a distinction is made between the ultimate customer (the beneficiary of the social marketer's endeavours), such as the smoker, and the funder of their activities, such as the government health department (Bagozzi, 1974). With the latter, good relationships can ensure that projects are set realistic objectives and that evaluation feedback will be in a form that helps policy decision-making. The resulting trust and commitment also reduces the tendency to determine renewed funding purely on the basis of bottom-line results. More fundamentally, building relationships with funders enables the social marketer to influence the setting, as well as the implementation, of the policy agenda, which strengthens not just the discipline's effectiveness but also its ethical foundation. Without it, social marketers run the risk of becoming political pawns, who might deliver micro effectiveness but ignore macro issues.

2 *Supplier partnerships*: in the case of suppliers, such as advertising agencies or market research providers, long-term relationships help bridge cultural differences between the private and public sector, and ensure that progress is built on consensus, matched agendas and clearly agreed long-term goals.

3 *Lateral partnerships*: the benefits of working with governments and other controllers of the social context have already been discussed. Strategic alliances with competing social marketers can facilitate efficiency savings and improve competitiveness, just as in commerce. They can also help prioritize issues. This is vital given the current fragmented social marketplace where organizations compete for public attention by highlighting the particular danger of their choosing. At any given moment, the public has to choose between the varying threats of speeding drivers, environmental tobacco smoke and

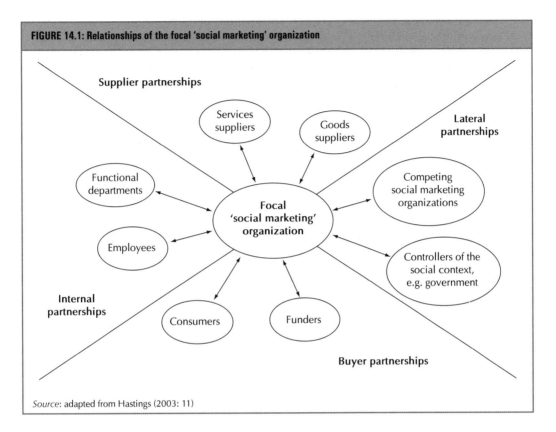

FIGURE 14.1: Relationships of the focal 'social marketing' organization

Supplier partnerships

Lateral partnerships

Services suppliers

Goods suppliers

Functional departments

Competing social marketing organizations

Focal 'social marketing' organization

Employees

Controllers of the social context, e.g. government

Internal partnerships

Consumers

Funders

Buyer partnerships

Source: adapted from Hastings (2003: 11)

alcohol abuse (none of which is completely within their control). A combined approach, based on long-term alliances, could transform threats into a multifaceted opportunity to improve health and well-being.

4   *Internal partnerships*: as in commerce, fulfilling relationships with external stakeholders depends on the whole organization pulling together. Great data mining and strong interactive communications will be undermined if the dispatch office is unresponsive or the receptionist is obstructive. This multiplicity of potential relationships presents challenges as well as opportunities. Decisions have to be made about which stakeholders to prioritize and how to handle them.

14.5   Environmental/green issues

Responsible green marketing has evolved into a complex, integrated, strategic and tactical process. As such, it is a holistic approach rather than the simple 'marketing hype' or tactical opportunism practised by some. It expands on the basic transaction concept by minimizing a transaction's negative impact on the natural environment. Understanding corporate motivations and pressures for 'greening' is essential, because it shapes how green marketing is implemented throughout all organizational activities.

Green, or environmental, marketing is expected to change customers' outlook, provide a new direction for competition and gain market acceptance for innovative environmental solutions. Within the framework of environment-conscious management, green marketing has a duty to ensure that environmental pollution is avoided or reduced at every stage of market-oriented activity (planning, co-ordination, implementation and inspection). The aim is to achieve corporate objectives by permanently satisfying the needs of current or potential clients while exploiting competitive advantages and safeguarding social legitimacy (Meffert and Kirchgeorg, 1998).

In the long run, ecologically and economically ineffective partial solutions could jeopardize the credibility and legitimacy of the enterprise in the market as well as in the community at large. To avoid this, it is essential that marketing management should develop a specific conception of green marketing.

14.5.1 Levels of 'green' marketing

Green marketing activities can occur at three levels in the company (Polonsky, 2001): strategic, quasi-strategic and tactical.

1 In *strategic greening*, there is a substantial fundamental change in corporate philosophy, such as the Australian company CarLovers designing its entire carwash process as a closed-loop, recycled-water system (Hollensen, 2004).
2 *Quasi-strategic greening* entails a substantial change in business practices. To reduce water consumption, for example, some hotel chains have begun asking guests to indicate when they want their towels washed by leaving them on the bathroom floor or in the bath.
3 With *tactical greening*, there is a shift in functional activities, such as promotion. For instance, in times of drought water authorities might use promotional campaigns to encourage consumers to behave in a more responsible, water-conserving manner.

These three levels can be used to identify the amount of change a company requires and may reflect the degree of commitment to various environmental objectives. Take the example of a jeans manufacturer who, in the early 1990s, promoted the fact that it would donate a proportion of each sale to be used for planting trees. Such a tactical activity might have been viewed with intense scepticism because there is no apparent logical link between making jeans and planting trees.

14.5.2 Environmental issues in relation to the marketing mix

Product

A product life cycle analysis can provide a sound basis for more eco-friendly solutions to the problems associated with product and packaging policies. In order to resolve product-related environmental problems, it is necessary to analyse the various spheres of responsibility of the supplier, manufacturer, distributor and consumer. From now on, marketing specialists will have to analyse the organization of closed-loop value chains with all the consequences of this for product design (long-life products, the growing importance of after-sales service, the sale of utility instead of products). Instruments of product policy include product innovation, product variation and product elimination designed to bring programmes into line with ecological requirements. While product variations involve modifying existing products in accordance with ecologically oriented demands, ecologically oriented product innovations entail launching entirely new product concepts on the market.

The introduction of 'take-back' regulations in most European countries obliges both producers and retailers to develop eco-friendly products, packaging and logistic alternatives as part of their product policy. The new regulations are based on the principle of sustainable development and aim to ensure that producers will be forced to play an active part in implementing a circular economy. This new definition of product responsibility can be regarded as a further step in the implementation of the prevention and 'polluter pays' principle, which has guided environmental policy in European countries.

Eco-friendly solutions often require a modification of the logistics and goods representation at the point of sale. The preparation of an ecological balance sheet for packaging materials and packaging systems (e.g. non-returnable and multi-way packaging) will ultimately be the only means of finding out which form of packaging can be considered the most environmentally friendly.

Distribution (place)

Just as producers have traditionally had to choose between various kinds of distribution channel, so they now have to concern themselves increasingly with the task of choosing an appropriate 'retro distribution' channel. The implementation of the closed-loop value chain in green marketing forces us to rethink the distribution mix.

Closed-loop supply chains consist of a *forward supply chain* and a *reverse supply chain*. Loops can be closed in several ways: reusing the product as a whole, reusing the components or reusing the materials. Most closed-loop supply chains will involve a mix of reuse options, where the various returns are processed through the most profitable alternative.

There are five key business processes involved in the reverse chain (Krikke et al., 2004). The importance and sequence of these processes may differ from chain to chain.

1   *Product acquisition*: this concerns retrieving the product from the market (sometimes by active buy-back) as well as physically collecting it. The timing of quality, quantity and composition needs to be managed in close co-operation with the supply chain parties close to the final customer.
2   *Reverse logistics*: this involves the transportation to the location of recovery. An intermediate step for testing and inspection may be needed.
3   *Sorting and disposition*: returns need to be sorted by quality and composition in order to determine the remaining route in the reverse chain. This sorting may depend on the outcome of the testing and inspection process. However, the disposition decision depends not only on product characteristics, but also on market demand.
4   *Recovery*: this is the process of retrieving, reconditioning and regaining products, components and materials. In principle, all recovery options may be applied either in the original supply chain or in some alternative supply chain. As a rule of thumb, the high-level options are mostly applied in the original supply chain and the lower-level options in alternative supply chains. In some areas, the reuse in alternative supply chains is referred to as 'open-loop' applications.
5   *Redistribution and sales*: this process largely coincides with the distribution and sales processed in the forward chain. Additional marketing efforts may be needed to convince the customer of the quality of the product. In alternative chains, separate channels need to be set up and new markets may need to be developed.

The objectives of European Union (EU) eco regulation are to promote products with a reduced environmental impact throughout their entire life cycle and to provide better information to consumers on the environmental impacts of products. The EU eco-labelling scheme, issued as a regulation, applies directly to all member states and is EU-wide. It is a voluntary scheme and should be self-financing.

Pricing

While green products are often 'priced higher' than traditional goods, this does not always mean they cost more, especially when one considers all associated costs. Often, green goods have higher initial out-of-pocket expenses but lower long-term costs.

Decisions relating to pricing are mainly determined by the consumer's sensitivity to price, but the need to integrate the cost of legally stimulated pollution control now plays an increasingly important role in this domain.

Pricing strategies should be based on a segmentation of actual and potential target groups classified with the aid of three criteria:

1　ecological awareness
2　personal affectedness
3　willingness to pay a price for pollution control.

Segments displaying varying degrees of price sensitivity constitute the basis for price differentiation strategies.

As a matter of principle, lower introductory prices for eco-friendly products help customers to reorientate their buyer behaviour, thereby facilitating a more rapid diffusion of eco-friendly products. Combined costing at the expense of non-eco-friendly products can ensure a necessary balance here. The return of used packaging and products raises the question of pricing incentives for retro distribution.

Exhibit 14.2: *Marketing planning from an Islamic ethical perspective*

Islam provides a framework that shapes the moral and ethical behaviour of a growing number of Muslim consumers around the globe. These consumers constitute about one-quarter of the total world population and represent a majority in more than 50 countries. In addition, an increasing number of Muslim countries represent some of the most affluent consumers in the world.

There is a growing momentum towards the formation of a Muslim trading bloc. Also the current political mood indicates that there appears to be a definitive push towards greater 'Islamization' of countries where Muslims are in the majority (e.g. Egypt, Algeria, Pakistan, Sudan and Afghanistan to name but a few) in the form of a return to the application of Islamic law (Shari'ah) to all facets of life and thought.

Islamic teachings and religious beliefs are completely incorporated in all economic activities in Muslim countries. It follows that a person's entire life represents a series of activities for which they are responsible and will be accountable for to God. Given that commercial transactions are part and parcel of people's daily lives, in Islam undertaking of each and every transaction represents a task that must be executed in accordance with Islamic law and teachings. It is not surprising to learn, therefore, that marketing ethics merit special attention in Islam and constitute a separate discipline underpinned by the documented practices of the Prophet himself.

It follows from the above that any commercial activity, from an Islamic perspective, is governed by two principles: first, submission to the moral order of God and, second, empathy and mercy to God's creations, which implies refraining from doing harm to others and thus preventing the spread of unethical practices.

Islam does not recognize any division between the temporal and the spiritual dimensions. It can appear, at times, to be in conflict with contemporary western marketing practices based primarily on profit maximization. According to the Islamic perspective, such pursuits, based on satisfying material objectives alone, will impede the rational thinking of people and will make them the slaves of marketing companies.

Sources: adapted from Al-Buraey, M.A. (2004) Marketing mix management from an Islamic perspective: some insights, *Journal of International Marketing & Marketing Research*, 29(3): 139–53; Saeed, M., Ahmed, Z.U. and Mukhtar, S.-M. (2001) International marketing ethics from an Islamic perspective: a value-maximization approach, *Journal of Business Ethics*, 32(2): 127–42; Zainul, N., Osman, F. and Mazlan, S.H. (2004) E-commerce from an Islamic perspective, *Electronic Commerce Research & Applications*, 3(3): 280–94

14.5.3 Communication

One of the most difficult questions to address is 'What environmental information should be communicated and how should it be communicated?' A primary issue is that there must be something worthwhile to talk about. A good deal of environmental promotion has been labelled 'greenwash' – that is, having little, if any, real ecological meaning. This type of superficial tactical greening is no longer appropriate, and both consumers and regulators are unwilling to accept it. Communicating substantive environmental information is a more appropriate approach to take, but requires real activity changes in order to be meaningful.

Many organizations realize that green promotion alone is becoming less effective, so they are shifting to promoting ecological attributes in addition to more traditional ones. It is questionable, for example, whether environmental sponsorships and cause-related marketing programmes will be effective, especially if they are seen as unrelated to an organization's core marketing activities or products. Thus, all green promotional activities need to be evaluated carefully to ensure that the organization is not criticized for greenwashing.

Green promotion needs to communicate substantive environmental information to consumers that has meaningful links to corporate activities. Thus, promoting some real environmental attribute of a product or organization requires a change in the product, process or corporate focus (integration with other activities). Organizations should work out holistic, environmentally friendly solutions to their problems before offering information to the public. Yet, even when this necessary condition is fulfilled, problems can arise when organizations attempt to apply classical advertising techniques (e.g. emotional and empirically oriented sales messages) to the organization of the credible, environmentally oriented marketing messages that can, must or ought to be transmitted. They must also determine to what extent communication in the relevant sector is dominated by environmental arguments.

Summary

CSR is the continuing commitment by organizations to behave ethically and contribute to worldwide economic development while improving the quality of life of the workforce and their families as well as of the local community and international society at large.

Ethics means the standards by which behaviour is judged. Why, though, do we need ethics when we already have the law, which tells us what we can and cannot do? One answer is that the letter of the law is generally considered to be only a minimum ethical standard.

Standards and beliefs about what is right and proper change over time. Thus the question of ethics is becoming more important as our economy becomes more competitive and global, and our technology more complex. Marketing ethics involves moral judgements, standards and rules of conduct relating to marketing decisions and situations.

Bribery distorts the operation of fair bargaining, and sales people should resist any temptation to bribe or accept bribes from those decision-makers who might want to engage in such activity. The use of bribes, although widespread and considered acceptable behaviour within some cultures, should be refused tactfully, allowing sales people to act in the best interests of their employers and in fairness to all customers. Bribery is not only unethical, it can also be illegal.

Social marketing can be defined as the planning and implementation of programmes designed to generate social change (e.g. stop smoking by lifestyle change). Social marketing is a system that can be used to change the way people think or behave. It is still based on concepts of commercial marketing, though. Social marketing, like commercial marketing, utilizes research to tailor messages to a particular target audience. For example, if an organization is promoting an issue of major importance to encourage women to take part in annual mammogram testing, the target audience would obviously be women. Consequently, a social marketing campaign would concentrate on adapting commercial techniques to attract and persuade women as necessary.

The goal of social marketing is to get people to think differently about old ideas, and to focus on new concepts that will add values to their lives. Social marketing is especially prevalent among non-profit organizations, government agencies, community-based organizations, private foundations, social/health/issue coalitions, and indeed any entity that wants to effect social change.

The last decade has seen a paradigm shift in commercial marketing, from transactional to relational thinking, and social marketers need to grasp the opportunity this presents. This has dramatic implications for the discipline, changing it from a branch line of public health to a whole new way of thinking about social problems.

Although environmental issues influence all human activities, few academic disciplines have integrated green issues into their literature. This is especially true of marketing. As society becomes more concerned with the natural environment,

▶

businesses have begun to modify their behaviour in an attempt to address society's 'new' concerns. Some organizations have been quick to accept concepts like environmental-management systems and waste minimization, and have integrated environmental issues into all organizational activities.

Green marketing incorporates a broad range of activities, including product modification, changes to the production process and packaging changes, as well as modifying advertising. Yet, defining green marketing is not a simple task. Indeed, the terminology used in this area has varied and includes: green marketing, environmental marketing and ecological marketing.

No matter why an organization uses green marketing there are a number of potential problems that must be overcome. One of the main ones is that organizations using green marketing must ensure that their activities are not misleading to consumers or industry, and do not breach any of the regulations or laws dealing with environmental marketing.

Another problem organizations face is that those who modify their products due to increased consumer concern must contend with the fact that consumers' perceptions are sometimes incorrect. One example of this is that McDonald's is often blamed for polluting the environment because much of its packaging ends up as roadside waste. It must be remembered, however, that it is the uncaring consumer that chooses to dispose of their waste in this inappropriate fashion.

Questions for discussion

1 What conflicts of ethical issues and acceptable corporate behaviour might face a company operating across a spread of international markets?
2 What are the major competing views of corporate responsibility?
3 Why should marketers be concerned with using environmental (green) metrics of performance?
4 How important is the question of bribery in international marketing? What can be done on an international basis to counter it?
5 What role do you think cultural differences play in ethical standards?
6 What are the key elements of a successful corporate ethics programme?

References

Andreasen, A.R. (1994) Social marketing: its definition and domain, *Journal of Public Policy and Marketing*, 13(1): 108–14.

Bagozzi, R.P. (1974) Marketing as an organized behavioral system of exchange, *Journal of Marketing*, 38: 77–81.

Ferrell, O.C. (2004) Business ethics and customer stakeholders, *Academy of Management Executive*, 18(2): 126–9.

Greenberg, J. and Baron, R.A. (2008), *Behavior in Organizations.* Englewood Cliffs, NJ: Pearson Prentice Hall.

Hastings, G. (2003) Relational paradigms in social marketing, *Journal of Macromarketing*, 23(1): 6–15.

Hollensen, S. (2004) *Global Marketing: A Decision-oriented Approach.* London: Financial Times/Prentice Hall.

Krikke, H., Blanc, I.L. and Vedde, S. (2004) Product modularity and the design of closed-loop supply chains, *California Management Review*, 46(2): 23–39.

Meffert, H. and Kirchgeorg, M. (1998) *Marktorientiertes Umweltmanagement*, 3rd edn. Stuttgart: Schäffer-Poeschel.

Polonsky, M.J. (2001) Revaluating green marketing: a strategic approach, *Business Horizons* 44(5): 21–31.

Porter, M.E. and Kramer, M.R. (2006), Strategy and Society: the link between competitive advantage and corporated social responsibility, *Harvard Business Review*, 84(12): 56–68.

Rigby, D. and Tager, S. (2008) Learning the advantages of sustainable growth, *Strategy & Leadership*, 36(4): 24–8.

Sanyal, R.N. and Samanta, S.K. (2004) Determinants of bribery in international business, *Thunderbird International Business Review*, 46: 133–48.

CASE STUDY 14: (RED)

Fighting AIDS in Africa through alliances

(RED)'s primary objective (www.joinred.com) is to engage the private sector in raising awareness and funds for the Global Fund to help eliminate AIDS in Africa.

(RED) is a business model created to raise awareness and money for the Global Fund by teaming up with the world's most iconic brands to produce (PRODUCT) RED branded products. A portion of profits from each (PRODUCT) RED product sold goes directly to the Global Fund to invest in African AIDS programmes, with a focus on women and children.

Bono and Bobby Shriver created (RED) in 2006 to engage the private sector in the fight against AIDS in Africa. After they set up DATA (Debt, AIDS, Trade, Africa) together in 2002, it became apparent that while DATA leveraged investment from the public sector to the Global Fund, a need remained for greater private sector funding.

Since its launch in the Spring of 2006 until the end of 2009, more than US$150 m has been generated by (RED) for the Global Fund. (RED) money is at work in Swaziland, Rwanda, Ghana and Lesotho.

Bobby Shriver has been announced as the chief executive officer (CEO) of Product Red, and Bono is an active public spokesperson for the brand.

The AIDS problem in Africa plus some facts about HIV/AIDS

HIV: the human immunodeficiency virus is a retrovirus that attacks the cells of the immune system. HIV is transmitted through an exchange of bodily fluids (e.g. exposure to infected blood, during sexual activity with an infected individual, by sharing needles). It can also pass from an infected mother to her child. HIV is the virus that eventually causes AIDS.

AIDS: an acquired immune deficiency syndrome diagnosis is made when symptoms that indicate the disease (primarily a decrease in the number of immune system cells in a person's bloodstream) are identified by a doctor in a HIV-positive person.

About 33 million people worldwide are living with HIV/AIDS. In 2008, approximately 2.5 million people were infected with HIV. Approximately 2 million people died from AIDS in 2008. In India about 2.4 million people have HIV/AIDS, while in South Africa 5.7 million are infected. Most victims are infected through heterosexual sex, and women are at particular risk, because they have been raped, because they are sex workers or have multiple partners and/or because they have no power to demand that the men in their lives wear a condom. The women account for an increasing percentage of the HIV/AIDS victims – now they constitute 50 per cent of all HIV/AIDS victims.

- Every minute five people around the world between the ages of 10 and 24 are infected with HIV.
- There are 2 million children under the age of 15 living with the disease worldwide.
- Most children under the age of 15 who have HIV/AIDS are infected through their infected mothers; that is, through mother–child transmission.
- Sexual activity (the main route of disease transmission) starts in adolescence for most people worldwide.
- Poverty, lack of education, lack of medical resources, and the commercial sexual exploitation of children also help to spread HIV/AIDS among children worldwide.

- Children with HIV/AIDS may be stigmatized and/or rejected by their families and communities. This discrimination fosters ignorance about HIV/AIDS and stigma against testing for treating the disease, in turn making it difficult to halt the spread of HIV/AIDS.
- Children are orphaned when their parents die from HIV/AIDS.

Progress has been made in the drive to reduce HIV infections in Africa, with 14 countries reporting a decline in the prevalence of the disease. This is great news and proves the fight can be won. But AIDS remains one of the greatest challenges facing the world today. An estimated 3,800 men, women and children die in sub-Saharan Africa every day, in addition to 6,000 new infections every day among 15–24-year-old men and women.

All funds generated by sales of (PRODUCT) RED products will support Global Fund-financed programmes that positively impact the lives of people affected by HIV and AIDS in Africa. (RED) money provides access to education, nutrition, counselling, medical services, and the two pills a day individuals need to stay alive. This includes programmes in countries such as Rwanda, which has a proven track record and ambitious targets. For example, in the past two years, Rwanda has increased the number of people receiving treatments for HIV and AIDS ten-fold.

(RED) states that its main principles are:

- to expand opportunities for the people in the continent of Africa
- to respect its employees and ask its partners to do the same with their employees and the people who help make their products or deliver their services
- to promote HIV/AIDS awareness policies and practices in the workplace
- to see the power of a community mobilized for hope, health and progress
- to ask its partners to uphold the same principles.

About the Global Fund

The Global Fund is a unique global public/private partnership dedicated to attracting and disbursing additional resources to prevent and treat HIV/AIDS, tuberculosis and malaria. It was established in 2002 with the support of then UN Secretary General Kofi Annan and the world's leaders to dramatically increase resources to fight three of the world's most devastating diseases. This partnership between governments, civil society, the private sector and affected communities represents a new approach to international health financing. The Global Fund works in close collaboration with other bilateral and multilateral organizations to supplement existing efforts dealing with the three diseases. Since its creation in 2002, the Global Fund has become the dominant financier of programmes to fight AIDS, tuberculosis and malaria, with approved funding of US$18.4 bn for more than 600 programmes in 144 countries. Until 2009, programmes supported by the Global Fund have saved 4.5 million lives through providing AIDS treatment for 2.3 million people, anti-tuberculosis treatment for 5.4 million people and the distribution of 88 million insecticide-treated bed nets for the prevention of malaria.

Global Fund financing has also:

- reached 62 million people with HIV counselling and testing
- provided 3.2 million AIDS orphans with basic care and support
- reached 91 million people with community outreach services for one or several of the three diseases
- trained 7.6 million health or community workers to deliver services.

(RED) is the Global Fund's largest private sector contributor

The Global Fund, working together with (RED) and the countries in question, has selected established grants with sound performance to receive money raised through (RED). To 1 January 2010, (RED) partners have generated US$150 m for the Global Fund. No overhead is taken out of these funds – 100 per cent of this money flows to the Global Fund-financed AIDS grants in Ghana, Lesotho, Rwanda and Swaziland.

In these countries this money is helping to finance comprehensive national HIV and AIDS programmes led by the ministries of health to provide antiretroviral treatment for children and adults, assist in the prevention of mother-to-child transmission of HIV, and support essential counselling and testing activities to reduce the overall risk of HIV transmission.

Additional contributions of funds will continue to be made to these programmes as they achieve tangible, measurable results in their lifesaving work. Additional amounts of money are sent by the Global Fund to (RED) grants according to the grants' own requests to the Global Fund – usually every 3–6 months. As with all Global Fund grants, additional funds are sent only once results in-country have been reported and verified.

The business model – about (RED) and (PRODUCT) RED

(RED) is *not* a charity. It is a business model designed to create awareness and a sustainable flow of money from the private sector into the Global Fund, to help eliminate AIDS in Africa. Consumers buy (PRODUCT) RED, and at no cost to them, money is sent directly to the Global Fund.

(RED)'s primary objective is to engage the private sector in raising awareness and funds for the Global Fund to help eliminate AIDS in Africa. Companies whose products take on the (PRODUCT) RED mark contribute a significant percentage of the sales or portion of the profits from that product to the Global Fund to finance AIDS programmes in Africa, with an emphasis on the health of women and children. Current partners are: American Express (UK only), Apple, Bugaboo, Converse, Gap, Emporio Armani, Hallmark, Dell, Nike and Starbucks. Since its launch in the Spring of 2006 until 1 January 2010, US$150 m has been generated by (RED) for the Global Fund.

One example of co-operation between (RED) and a private company is the RED–Nike partnership.

The Nike–RED partnership

Nike, Inc. based near Beaverton, Oregon, is the world's leading designer, marketer and distributor of authentic athletic footwear, apparel, equipment and accessories for a wide variety of sports and fitness activities. Wholly owned Nike subsidiaries include Converse Inc., which designs, markets and distributes athletic footwear, apparel and accessories; Cole Haan, which designs markets and distributes luxury shoes, handbags, accessories and coats; Umbro Ltd., a leading UK-based global football (soccer) brand; and Hurley International LLC, which designs, markets and distributes action sports and youth lifestyle footwear, apparel and accessories.

On 30 November 2009 (the day before World Aids day) some of the world's best footballers joined Bono at the announcement of the partnership between Nike, Inc. and (RED).

Didier Drogba (Chelsea), Joe Cole (Chelsea), Andrei Arshavin (Arsenal), Marco Materazzi (Inter Milan), Denilson (Arsenal), Lucas Neill (Everton), Clint Dempsey (Fulham) and Seol Ki-Hyeon (Fulham), came together in London to announce a partnership between Nike, Inc. and (RED).

This unique partnership delivers a two-pronged approach to fight HIV/AIDS in Africa by delivering funds to support programmes that offer education and medication on the ground and will harness the power of sport to engage youth around the world in the fight against AIDS in Africa.

Nike has a proven history of elevating global causes to create consumer awareness and participation. As a global brand and creative company, Nike can play a role in amplifying this important issue. With Africa's World Championship in football in June/July 2010 as the catalyst, Nike is joining the (RED) movement to fight HIV/AIDS in Africa.

The Nike and (RED) concept is a simple one that invites people to 'Lace Up. Save Lives' by purchasing a pair of (NIKE) RED™ laces. One hundred per cent of the profits from (NIKE) RED laces will be split equally between the Global Fund to fight AIDS, tuberculosis and malaria.

The (RED) Nike laces can tie athletes around the world together with people living under threat from HIV in Africa in a beautiful way. Among end-consumers wearing these (RED) Nike laces is a sign that you care about others, so this product is giving the buyer of the shoes a certain image.

In this way (RED) has created a sustainable way to engage business in funding the fight against AIDS in Africa on a grand scale. Its partnerships not only deliver funds to buy medicine to keep people alive but also provide the leverage needed for to demonstrate to the public sector that private partnership works to garner additional support. The addition of Nike to the (RED) initiative will only strengthen this impact, with the message to millions of football fans around the world about engaging them in this issue through their passion for sport.

(NIKE) RED laces were available on 1 December 2009 at Nike store locations and key retailers worldwide. In addition, (NIKE) RED laces were available at nike.com for purchase. And additional (NIKE) RED products were introduced in the coming months.

Criticism of (*RED*)

PRODUCT (RED) has been criticized for not having an impact proportional to the advertising investment, for being much less efficient than direct charitable contribution, and for having a lack of transparency with regard to the amount of money going to charity as a percentage of every purchase. Some critics argue that a retail middleman between donor and charity is unnecessary; donors should just give. One spoof campaign known as BUY (LESS) mocks the consumerist bent of (RED) with its own call to 'BUY (LESS) CRAP!'. The BUY (LESS) campaign encourages people to forgo the premium-level products and donate directly to charities. The BUY (LESS) campaign carries the slogan, 'Shopping is not a solution. Buy (Less). Give More.'

Another critique is that (RED)'s expansion into traditional fund-raising techniques, such as art auctions, undermines its claim to be a different and more sustainable approach to raising money for AIDS. Other critics have pointed out that its emphasis on funding treatment for AIDS sufferers meant that large amounts of the money will ultimately end up with

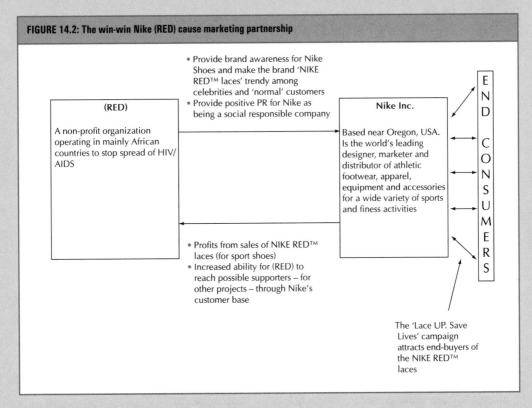

FIGURE 14.2: The win-win Nike (RED) cause marketing partnership

(RED)

A non-profit organization operating in mainly African countries to stop spread of HIV/AIDS

- Provide brand awareness for Nike Shoes and make the brand 'NIKE RED™ laces' trendy among celebrities and 'normal' customers
- Provide positive PR for Nike as being a social responsible company

Nike Inc.

Based near Oregon, USA. Is the world's leading designer, marketer and distributor of athletic footwear, apparel, equipment and accessories for a wide variety of sports and finess activities

- Profits from sales of NIKE RED™ laces (for sport shoes)
- Increased ability for (RED) to reach possible supporters – for other projects – through Nike's customer base

E N D   C O N S U M E R S

The 'Lace UP. Save Lives' campaign attracts end-buyers of the NIKE RED™ laces

pharmaceutical companies 'unwilling to distribute their drugs for free'. Many accuse the campaign of profiting by using diseases as a marketing vehicle.

Questions

1 What have been the key competences of (RED) since it started in 2006?
2 How are these competences utilized in (RED) alliances?
3 What do you think about the critics about (RED) – discuss pros and cons.
4 Which future alliance partners would it be relevant for (RED) to cooperate with?

Sources: www.nike.com/nikefootball/red/home?locale=en_US; www.joinred.com/Home

INDEX